Democratisation in the 21st Century

The 2010s has been a critical period in the continuing trend of the spread of democracy worldwide. From the Arab Spring countries of Tunisia, Libya, Egypt and Yemen to the unfolding turmoil in Myanmar and Ukraine, by way of the upheavals in Burkina Faso, Senegal and Ivory Coast, social mobilisation against autocratic, corrupt or military regimes has precipitated political transitions that are characteristic of 'democratisation'.

Democratisation in the 21st Century examines the state of democratisation theory and practice and reopens and revives the democratic transition debate, exploring the factors that lead to the demise of autocracy, the pathways and processes of change and the choices for an eventual consolidation of democracy. For all its insights and shortcomings, the framework of transitology – a body of literature that has comparatively and through case study analysis examined common patterns, sequences, crises and outcomes of transitional periods – has been largely eschewed. The essays, written by international democratisation specialists, tackle the series of questions raised by a body of literature that remains highly useful to gaining an understanding of contemporary political turbulence and transformation.

This book will be of key interest to scholars, students and practitioners of governance, democratisation, comparative politics, international relations, political science and, more broadly, history.

Mohammad-Mahmoud Ould Mohamedou is Deputy Director and Academic Dean at the Geneva Centre for Security Policy and Adjunct Professor in the International History Department at the Graduate Institute of International and Development Studies in Geneva. He is also Visiting Professor in the doctoral school at Sciences Po Paris.

Timothy D. Sisk is Professor and Associate Dean for Research at the Josef Korbel School of International Studies and steering faculty of the Sié Chéou Kang Center for International Security and Diplomacy, University of Denver, USA.

Democratization Studies
(Formerly Democratization Studies, Frank Cass)

Democratization Studies combines theoretical and comparative studies with detailed analyses of issues central to democratic progress and its performance, all over the world.

The books in this series aim to encourage debate on the many aspects of democratization that are of interest to policy-makers, administrators and journalists, aid and development personnel, as well as to all those involved in education.

25 **Democratic Transitions**
Modes and outcomes
Sujian Guo and Gary A Stradiotto

26 **Political Leadership, Nascent Statehood and Democracy**
A comparative study
Ulrika Möller and Isabell Schierenbeck

27 **Democracy, Participation and Contestation**
Civil society, governance and the future of liberal democracy
Edited by Emmanuelle Avril and Johann Neem

28 **Democratic Transformation and Obstruction**
EU, US and Russia in the South Caucasus
Nelli Babayan

29 **Politics and Democracy in Microstates**
Wouter Veenendaal

30 **Democratizing Central and Eastern Europe**
Successes and failures of the European Union
Luca Tomini

31 **Causes and Consequences of Democratization**
The regions of Russia
Anastassia V. Obydenkova and Alexander Libman

32 **Democratization in EU Foreign Policy**
New member states as drivers of democracy promotion
Edited by Benedetta Berti, Kristina Mikulova and Nicu Popescu

33 **Democratisation in the 21st Century**
Reviving transitology
Edited by Mohammad-Mahmoud Ould Mohamedou and Timothy D. Sisk

Democratisation in the 21st Century
Reviving transitology

Edited by
Mohammad-Mahmoud Ould Mohamedou
and Timothy D. Sisk

LONDON AND NEW YORK

First published 2017 by Routledge

2 Park Square, Milton Park, Abingdon, Oxfordshire OX14 4RN
711 Third Avenue, New York, NY 10017

Routledge is an imprint of the Taylor & Francis Group, an informa business

First issued in paperback 2018

Copyright © 2017 Selection and editorial matter: Mohammad-Mahmoud Ould Mohamedou and Timothy D. Sisk; individual chapters: the contributors

The right of the editors to be identified as the authors of the editorial mater, and of the authors for their individual chapters, has been asserted in accordance with sections 77 and 78 of the Copyright, Designs and Patents Act 1988.

All rights reserved. No part of this book may be reprinted or reproduced or utilised in any form or by any electronic, mechanical, or other means, now known or hereafter invented, including photocopying and recording, or in any information storage or retrieval system, without permission in writing from the publishers.

Notice:
Product or corporate names may be trademarks or registered trademarks, and are used only for identification and explanation without intent to infringe.

British Library Cataloguing in Publication Data
A catalogue record for this book is available from the British Library

Library of Congress Cataloging in Publication Data
Names: Mohamedou, Mohammad-Mahmoud, 1968– editor, author. | Sisk, Timothy D., 1960– editor, author.
Title: Democratization in the 21st century : reviving transitology / edited by Mohammad-Mahmoud Ould Mohamedou and Timothy D. Sisk.
Description: Abingdon, Oxon ; New York, NY : Routledge, 2016. | Series: Democratization studies ; 33 | Includes bibliographical references and index.
Identifiers: LCCN 2016013478| ISBN 9781138673823 (hardback) | ISBN 9781315561677 (ebook)
Subjects: LCSH: Democratization. | World politics–21st century.
Classification: LCC JC423 .D47834 2016 | DDC 320.9–dc23LC record available at http://lccn.loc.gov/2016013478

ISBN: 978-1-138-67382-3 (hbk)
ISBN: 978-1-138-32642-2 (pbk)

Typeset in Times New Roman
by Wearset Ltd, Boldon, Tyne and Wear

Contents

List of figures	vii
List of tables	viii
Notes on contributors	ix
Foreword	xii
Acknowledgements	xviii

1 **Introduction: turbulent transitions into the 21st century**   1
   MOHAMMAD-MAHMOUD OULD MOHAMEDOU AND
   TIMOTHY D. SISK

2 **Reviving transitology: democratisation then and now**   12
   MOHAMMAD-MAHMOUD OULD MOHAMEDOU AND
   TIMOTHY D. SISK

3 **Divergent and partial transitions: lessons from Ukraine and Egypt**   29
   KATERYNA PISHCHIKOVA AND RICHARD YOUNGS

4 **Electoral transitions: stumbling out of the gate**   49
   PIPPA NORRIS

5 **Democratisation in the Asia-Pacific: two steps forward?**   75
   BENJAMIN REILLY

6 **The transition in East-Central Europe**   93
   ANDRÉ LIEBICH

7 **Successes and breakdowns: democratisation in Sub-Saharan Africa**   113
   JULIEN MORENCY-LAFLAMME

8	**Thirty years past: transitology in the Southern Cone** DIEGO ABENTE-BRUN AND IGNACIO GONZÁLEZ-BOZZOLASCO	135
9	**Transitology *à l'Arabe*: confirmation and challenge** BAHGAT KORANY	144
10	**From transitology to consolidology** PHILIPPE C. SCHMITTER	167

References	185
Index	205

Figures

2.1	The global rise of democracies and 'partial' democracies	12
4.1	Electoral integrity and wealth	57
4.2	Electoral integrity and human development	58
4.3	Electoral integrity and natural resources	61
4.4	Electoral integrity and perceptions of corruption	63
5.1	Freedom House 'electoral democracies' 2015	89

Tables

4.1	The PEI Index and its components correlated with economic indices	60
4.2	Structural conditions and electoral integrity	64
7.1	Regime status in Sub-Saharan Africa	114
9.1	The Human Development Index	148
9.2	The Fragile/Failed State Index	148
9.3	The Global Peace Index	148
9.4	The Governance Index	150

Contributors

Mohammad-Mahmoud Ould Mohamedou is Deputy Director and Academic Dean of the Geneva Centre for Security Policy and Adjunct Professor at the Graduate Institute of International and Development Studies in Geneva, as well as Lecturer in the doctoral school at Sciences Po Paris. He was previously Associate Director of the Harvard University Programme on Humanitarian Policy and Conflict Research in Cambridge, Director of Research of the International Council on Human Rights Policy, and Research Associate at the Ralph Bunche Institute on the United Nations at the City University of New York Graduate Center. His published works include *Understanding Al Qaeda – Changing War and Global Politics* (Pluto, 2011), *Contre-Croisade – Le 11 Septembre et le Retournement du Monde* (L'Harmattan, 2011) and *Iraq and the Second Gulf War – State-Building and Regime Security* (Austin and Winfield, 2002).

Timothy D. Sisk is Professor and Associate Dean for Research at the Josef Korbel School of International Studies, University of Denver and steering faculty of the Sié Chéou Kang Center for International Security and Diplomacy at the School. He is also an Associate Fellow of the Geneva Centre for Security Policy. Prior to joining the University of Denver in 1998, Sisk was a Program Officer and Research Scholar in the Grant Programme of the United States Institute of Peace in Washington. He is the author or editor of a dozen books, scholarly articles and research reports, including *State-Building – Consolidating Peace after Civil War* (Polity, 2013), *From War to Democracy – Dilemmas of Peacebuilding* (with Anna Jarstad, Cambridge University Press, 2008) and *The Dilemmas of State-Building – Confronting the Contradictions of Postwar Peace Operations* (with Roland Paris, Routledge 2009).

Diego Abente-Brun is Senior Associate Researcher at the *Centro de Investigación y Difusión de la Economía Paraguaya* and a senior researcher at CONACYT-Paraguay. He is the author or co-editor of several books, including *El Régimen Stronista – Naturaleza, Sustento y Longevidad* (El Lector, 2014), *Clientelism, Social Policy and the Quality of Democracy* (ed. with Larry Diamond, John Hopkins 2014) and *Latin America's Struggle for Democracy* (with Marc Plattner and Larry Diamond, John Hopkins, 2009).

x   Contributors

Ignacio González-Bozzolasco teaches Comparative Politics at the Catholic University of Asunción in Paraguay. He is the author of *La Encrucijada del Cambio – Análisis sobre la Realidad Social y Política del Paraguay Contemporáneo* (Asunción, 2013), *El Nuevo Despertar – Breve Historia del Movimiento Intersindical de Trabajadores del Paraguay* (Asunción, 2013) and *Represión, Cooptación y Resistencia – El Movimiento Sindical Paraguayo* (Asunción, 2014).

Bahgat Korany is Professor of International Relations and Political Economy at the American University in Cairo (AUC) and Director of the AUC Forum. He is an honorary professor at the University of Montréal and has been an elected member of Canada's Royal Society since 1994. He has also been a visiting professor at various universities including Sciences Po Paris, Oxford University and Harvard University. He has published nearly one hundred book chapters/articles in specialised periodicals and twelve books. His first book, *Social Change, Charisma and International Behaviour* was awarded the Hauchman Prize in Switzerland. In 2010–2013, he was the lead author of the tenth anniversary special volume of the United Nations Development Programme's *Arab Human Development Report*. In 2014 he was chosen by the International Studies Association to receive the award 'Global South Scholar' for life-achievement, succeeding the late Ali Mazrui.

André Liebich is Honorary Professor of International Politics and History at the Graduate Institute for International and Development Studies, Geneva. A faculty member from 1989 to 2013, he was previously Professor of Political Science at the University of Québec in Montréal. His interests lie in Central and East European history and politics, modern political thought and ideology, and international history and theory. His current research deals with nationhood and statehood, and minority and diaspora politics. His published works include *From the Other Shore – Russian Social Democracy After 1921* (Fraenkel Prize, 1995) and *Les Minorités Nationales en Europe Centrale et Orientale* (Geneva: Georg, 1997).

Julien Morency-Laflamme is Lecturer and doctoral candidate at the University of Montréal. He is a specialist in democratic transitions and civil–military relations in Africa with extensive research in Benin and Togo, as well as more broadly across the continent. His research focuses on military responses during regime crises and on the consequences of military factionalism in African states.

Pippa Norris is the McGuire Lecturer in Comparative Politics at the John F. Kennedy School of Government at Harvard University and ARC Laureate Fellow and Professor of Government and International Relations at the University of Sydney, as well as Director of the Electoral Integrity Project. A political scientist and public speaker, her research compares election and public opinion, political communications, and gender politics. She also served as Director of the Democratic Governance Group in the United Nations

Development Programme, New York and as an expert consultant to many international organisations such as the World Bank, the Council of Europe, and the Organization for Security and Co-operation in Europe (OSCE).

Kateryna Pishchikova is Associate Professor of Political Science at the eCampus University in Italy, and Associate Researcher at the Madrid- and Brussels-based think tank FRIDE. Previously, she spent a year at the Transatlantic Academy in Washington, D.C., working on a collaborative project that dealt with the state of Western democracy and liberal world order. She was also Visiting Scholar at Cornell University, Research Fellow at the *Scuola Superiore Sant'Anna* in Pisa, Italy and Visiting Scholar at the Kennan Institute of the Woodrow Wilson Centre for International Scholars in Washington, D.C. She is the author of *Promoting Democracy in Postcommunist Ukraine – The Contradictory Outcomes of US Aid to Women's NGOs* (Lynne Rienner, 2011).

Benjamin Reilly is Dean of the Sir Walter Murdoch School of Public Policy and International Affairs in Perth. He is a political scientist specialising in democratisation, comparative politics and political development. He was formerly Professor of Political Science, Head of the Policy and Governance program and Director of the Centre for Democratic Institutions in the Crawford School of Public Policy at the Australian National University (ANU). He has worked with the Australian government, the United Nations and other international organisations, and held visiting appointments at Harvard, Oxford and Johns Hopkins universities. Reilly has authored or edited several books, and received financial support from the Carnegie Corporation of New York, the United States Institute of Peace, the East–West Centre, the National Endowment for Democracy and the Australian Research Council.

Philippe C. Schmitter was Professor of Political Science in the Department of Political and Social Sciences at the European University Institute in Florence. He was nominated Professorial Fellow at the same institution. He is now Emeritus Professor of the Department of Political and Social Sciences at the European University Institute. He is a graduate of the Graduate Institute of International Studies in Geneva, and earned his doctorate at the University of California at Berkeley. He has published books and articles on comparative politics, regional integration in western Europe and Latin America, on the transition from authoritarian rule in southern Europe and Latin America, and on the intermediation of class, sectoral and professional interests.

Richard Youngs is Lecturer at Warwick University. He obtained his BA (Hons) at Cambridge University, and his MA and PhD at Warwick University. He has held positions as Analyst at the Foreign and Commonwealth Office, Research Fellow to the European University project on democracy promotion, and from 2001–2004 was European Union Marie Curie Fellow based at the Norwegian Institute for International Relations in Oslo.

Foreword

What is the status of democracy around the world? There appears to be a widely expressed view, particularly evident in mainstream media, that democracy is in decline. Many academics, politicians and media commentators consider that the 'third wave of democratisation' has come to an end. Others deem that what was labelled as a possible fourth wave, linked to the so-called 'Arab Spring', has shown all the contradictions of ambiguous, unfinished and unaccomplished democratic transitions. The post-Arab uprisings period appears to have added weight to this assessment. Hopes from the start for a period of democratic progress or breakthrough quickly fell into growing disillusionment with political processes throughout the region as the uprisings gave way to a wave of reaction and violent chaos.

As noted by the editors of this book, Mohammad-Mahmoud Ould Mohamedou and Timothy D. Sisk, some analysts[1] have described a democratic recession as having taken place since 2006, referring to the decline in aggregate Freedom House scores every year since then.[2] I am aware of legitimate concerns about democracy's capacity to effectively deal with such developments and potential shocks, and I have no intention of minimising the concerns expressed by many analysts and practitioners. However, I would first of all like to stress that there appears to be considerable evidence supporting the notion that 'global democracy' has remained stable over the last decade and, relative to the 1980s, has in fact improved markedly. When reviewed from a medium-term perspective, the overall trend of democratisation processes shows evidence of remarkable worldwide progress over a period of almost forty-five years notwithstanding the current severe political and economic stresses confronting existing democracies. In spite of such challenges, the number of electoral democracies has increased from about thirty-five in 1970 to sixty-nine in 1989–1990 and 125 in 2015.[3] However, democracy is much more than holding periodic elections. The quality of democratic institutions and processes, as well as what they deliver to citizens, are at the core of building sustainable democracies worldwide.

This book shows that learning from the successes as well as the failures of past experiences is a critical factor for deepening knowledge on democratic transitions. Although any transition process is unique, each provides learning points for others, as shown by the demand for comparative experience generated in-country in all contexts that have been defined as 'transitional' over the last decade, from the Arab region to Myanmar, from the Middle East and North Africa to the Caucasus. *Democratisation in the 21st Century* argues that the body of knowledge on democratic transitions, revived by solid comparative research on political regime transformations, may contribute policy-relevant recommendations and help us understand 'turbulent transitions in countries seeking to emerge from autocracy'.

How relevant is this conversation to democracy assistance? Its importance cannot be underestimated. In Chapter 1, Mohamedou and Sisk make a convincing argument about reclaiming the concept and the field of analysis of 'transitology' in the light of the findings of comparative analyses of recent transitions whose unfolding is still underway. Such analyses seem – despite notable contextual differences – to corroborate the validity of some generalisations about sequencing, common patterns, crises and related challenges.

Over the past fifteen years, transitology has grown as a contested field among both scholars and practitioners. In 2002, Thomas Carothers famously criticised an oversimplification of transitions – then prevalent in the field of democracy assistance – grounded in modernisation theories and in the analysis of the experience of southern European and Latin American democratisation processes. This approach, which he labelled a 'transition paradigm', was based on an understanding of democratic transitions as linear and incremental paths from autocracy to democracy. According to Carothers,[4] by emphasising the expected patterns of continuity and discontinuity in political change processes, many democracy promoters attributed excessive importance to the design of formal democratic institutions and reforms, thus failing to take account of the grey zone in which many transitions got stuck before reaching a consolidation stage. By questioning the assumptions of democracy promoters who uncritically adopted transitology as a paradigm for action, he observed that political change towards democracy is never linear and often faces reversals.

In 2014, a reconsideration of the 'transition paradigm' highlighted that the most recent processes, such as the aftermath of the Arab uprisings, led practitioners to critically reconsider the simplistic renderings of the findings from the literature on democratic consolidation. For example, the important role of political parties as a means of electoral mobilisation was stressed vis-à-vis the conventional priority assigned to civil society support in transitional settings.[5] This book contributes to deepening the analysis of democratic transitions by focusing on many interrelated issues: the hybrid nature of political transformations (Kateryna Pishchikova and Richard Youngs), the quality and integrity of elections (Pippa Norris), as well as a number of global trends and regional variations. These include the disjuncture between comparative generalisations and regional experience in Asia that highlights the respective spheres of influence of China and the United States in the region (Benjamin Reilly); the role of political culture in transitions in East-Central Europe (André Liebich); the impact of actors' actions on outcomes in transitions in Africa (Julien Morency-Laflamme); the nature of the socio-economic and political cleavages that led to authoritarian regimes and their influence during and after transitions to democracy in Latin America (Diego Abente-Brun and Ignacio González-Bozzolasco); and the fragility of authoritarian regimes and the role of social movements in transitions in the Arab region (Bahgat Korany).

An important chapter written by one of the leading theorists of democratic consolidation, Philippe C. Schmitter, concludes the book. This is a particularly insightful reflection on the shift in 'transitology' from the analysis of 'political causality' to the consideration of 'bounded rationality' in assessing transitions to and consolidation of democracy or, better said, 'democracies'.

How relevant is the proposed analysis to the current policy debates at the United Nations? Although the word 'democracy' is not mentioned in the United Nations (UN) Charter, most of the UN peace operations since the end of the Cold War have supported key dimensions of democracy as part of their mandates. Some issues addressed in this book, such as the holding of elections, especially in post-conflict situations, constitute standard components of the mandates of such missions. Other issues – for example, the trade-off between stability and political and institutional reforms – are at the core of the painfully difficult negotiations that result in political settlements negotiated under the aegis of the UN, often in the context of complex political transitions. Member states pay greater attention to how the degree of internal democracy and regime 'legitimacy' may affect the way they are perceived by the broader UN membership. This may explain the growing – although not yet overwhelming – consensus on new international norms and standards, such as those related to international election observation as a factor motivating governments in 'grey zone transitions' to accept election observers in order to balance the maintenance of power through managed elections.

Democracy-building actors, including those from within the UN system, are working both in and on transitional settings. A revival of policy papers on democratic transitions has marked the aftermath of the Arab uprisings. In 2012, the United Nations Development Programme (UNDP) published a paper entitled 'The Political Economy of Transitions – Analysis for Change' that stressed, among other elements, the need for a political economy approach. Such approaches should take a long-term perspective by looking at the interaction between political and economic processes in society and by providing insights into how the social contract between individuals, communities and the state has come into question within political transitions.

This book is highly relevant to UN policy debates in many other ways. First, with regard to peace and security, all major crises addressed by the UN Security Council imply a combination of political, economic and/or social transitions. Cases like the 2013 crisis in the Central African Republic show that even in the most tragic of contexts the international community often seeks to legitimise the government and to foster a transitional process. The recent reviews of the UN peace operations[6] and peacebuilding architecture,[7] as well as the review on women, peace and security held fifteen years after the adoption of Security Council Resolution 1325,[8] have all underscored the importance of a comprehensive approach to the management of international crises. They stressed the need for an in-depth understanding of the political landscape within each context, a better consideration of the interests of local and international political actors and an assessment of their impact on peace and conflict dynamics.

Second, in the field of human rights, both the 2015 International Democracy Day and the recent tenth anniversary of the establishment of the Human Rights Council were celebrated by focusing on an issue that falls squarely in the grey zone of political transitions. This is the shrinking democratic space for civil society, an especially acute challenge in countries that undertook complex transitions from autocracies, or where authoritarian regimes limit or deny freedom of association, speech and expression to opposition movements.

Third, in the area of development, the 2030 Agenda for Sustainable Development has significantly advanced the understanding of the political implications of development beyond the traditional dimensions of economic, social and environmental sustainability. The quality of accountable institutions matters for the achievement of an ambitious transformative agenda, especially in countries marked by political, as well as social and economic, transitions.

Fourth, new challenges are emerging, like the inadequate efforts at countering violent extremism, or addressing large movements of refugees and migrants. This book is useful as it highlights some of the contradictions brought about by political transitions, where transnational impacts go well beyond the borders of the specific countries and regions addressed. Ambiguous international responses to such challenges, including military interventions or restrictive policies vis-à-vis refugees and asylum-seekers, raise issues of coherence as they may question the very foundations and principles of democratic ideals.

Fifth, the importance of the quality of leadership in democratic transitions should also be taken into account. A recent publication sponsored by the International Institute for Democracy and Electoral Assistance (International IDEA), based on interviews with thirteen leaders who played a key role in countries such as Brazil, Chile, Ghana, Indonesia, Mexico, the Philippines, Poland, South Africa and Spain,[9] has shed some light on the important issue of the role of leaders in democratic transitions. The interviews do not call for 'one-size-fits-all' approaches or simplistic toolboxes of 'best practices' for democratic change. While each transition differed in inception, trajectories and outcomes, their experiences pointed at four broad clusters of recurrent challenges: preparing for the transition; ending the authoritarian regime; making and managing the transfer of power; and stabilising and institutionalising the emerging democracy. Although these challenges did not necessarily occur in linear fashion, they were common to each democratic transition process.

Sixth, international actors can support electoral reform and strengthen participation, but they should stop believing that technical fixes exist to what are fundamentally political issues. International actors have been providing so-called democracy assistance at the technical level in the Arab region for many years – but within the context of a geopolitical framework which supported autocracy against the wishes of the citizens of the region. This needs to change. Democracy support will go nowhere unless it is a fundamental part of a coherent approach by international actors including foreign, security and economic development policies. International actors also need to have patience and take a long-term perspective – elections or constitution-building processes should not be rushed or conducted according to an external timetable, but should be nationally-driven processes. International actors should also adopt a 'peer approach' to democracy cooperation, in which the old donor–beneficiary relationship is consigned to the scrap heap and there is genuine partnership, mutual learning and sharing of experience.

One issue to which international actors need to pay particular heed is economic inequality. This has been identified as one of the major global risks in the coming years. In seeking to support the emergence of sustainable democracy in transitional settings, international actors therefore need to take into account economic and trade issues – rather than having a purely technical focus on democracy assistance.

Lastly, the analysis proposed in this volume is important to the advocacy of a democracy perspective throughout the UN system, on the basis of a nuanced understanding of processes of democratic transition. Policy advocacy needs solid policy-oriented research. This need has emerged, for example, during the intergovernmental negotiations on the Sustainable Development Goals (SDGs) framework, included in the 2030 Agenda for Sustainable Development. The process highlighted political sensitivities around concepts that only fifteen years ago had been at the core of the Millennium Declaration, such as the interlinkages between human rights, democracy, good governance and development. Reluctance by some member states to even mention the concept of accountability, on the grounds that it would have opened the door for political conditionalities on aid, widened the political divide along old fault lines reminiscent of Cold War blocs. Allegations of double standards while dealing with transitional processes also played a role in crystallising and entrenching such positions. In this context, together with other strategic partners I engaged in consultations on behalf of International IDEA within the Open Working Group on the SDGs for the inclusion, among other goals, of what eventually would become SDG#16 on peaceful and inclusive societies, access to justice and effective, inclusive and accountable institutions. Its adoption, and related accountability mechanisms for monitoring progress on the implementation of the 2030 Agenda, countered the conventional view that development primarily depends on the implementation of macro-economic policies accompanied by adequate infrastructures and technology transfers: it should also take into account the delicate relationships between peace, justice and the quality of institutions. Evidence-based analysis like the one proposed in this book constitutes a powerful resource for advocacy efforts of this kind.

Massimo Tommasoli
Permanent Observer for the Institute for Democracy and Electoral Assistance to the United Nations, New York, May 2016

Notes

1 For example, Diamond and Plattner, *Democracy in Decline?*
2 Diamond, 'Facing Up to the Democratic Recession'.
3 Freedom House, *Freedom in the World 2016*.
4 Carothers, 'End of the Transition Paradigm'.
5 Diamond *et al.*, 'Reconsidering the "Transition Paradigm"'.
6 United Nations, 'Uniting our Strengths'.
7 United Nations, 'Challenge of Sustaining Peace'.
8 Coomaraswamy, 'Preventing Conflict, Transforming Justice, Securing the Peace'.
9 Lowenthal and Bitar, *Democratic Transitions*.

Acknowledgements

Our own journey back into the world of transitology began in 2012 with a conversation at a conference in which we were both taking part in New York. As fast-paced events had recently dramatically engulfed the Middle East and North Africa and as unsatisfactory analyses proliferated with all manner of hasty scenarios elaborated, we began thinking that a longer-term and more theoretically grounded perspective was necessary to put the social revolts in that region in context. One meaningful way to do that was to dust off, or revive, long-standing democratisation theory. We decided to research and write a monograph that would help 'reboot' what we regarded as a particularly important and fertile academic tool developed in the late 1960s and early 1970s to understand the complex process of political transition.

We had both engaged with transitology in our earlier respective work but had moved away from it to explore issues related to political violence, state-building and war. That monograph was published in November 2013 as a *Geneva Paper* under the auspices of the Geneva Centre for Security Policy (GCSP). We wish to thank the GCSP for giving us an opportunity to reflect on those issues, and we extend our thanks to then director Ambassador Fred Tanner and to Centre director Ambassador Christian Dussey and all our colleagues there.

Thanks also to our respective colleagues at the Graduate Institute of International and Development Studies in Geneva, in particular Phillipe Burrin, Davide Rodogno, Riccardo Bocco, Gopalan Balachandran and Jussi Hanhimaki, as well as the Institute's students who engaged on these issues, and the Josef Korbel School of International Studies at the University of Denver, particularly students in the Korbel core seminar in comparative politics who ably critiqued the GCSP paper's ideas and furthered understanding of the democratisation conundra through their research and writing on these themes. Discussions with other colleagues helped us refine our thinking, and we notably thank in that regard Karim Émile Bitar and Nadia Marzouki.

Our editor at Routledge, Andrew Taylor, deserves special thanks for his role in bringing this book to fruition. His enthusiasm and support was, from the outset, key in helping us forge ahead.

Our most heartfelt thanks go to the contributors Diego Abente-Brun, Ignacio González-Bozzolasco, Bahgat Korany, André Liebich, Julien Morency-Laflamme,

Pippa Norris, Kateryna Pishchikova, Benjamin Reilly, Philippe C. Schmitter and Richard Youngs who all did a superb job in helping us take this debate to the next phase while connecting it to our earlier work.

Lastly and most importantly, we owe a debt of gratitude to our respective families for their support. We dedicate this book to them, respectively, Shainese, Bahiya, Kemal and Zaynab; and Andrea and Victoria.

Mohammad-Mahmoud Ould Mohamedou and Timothy D. Sisk
Geneva and Denver, June 2016

1 Introduction
Turbulent transitions into the 21st century

Mohammad-Mahmoud Ould Mohamedou and Timothy D. Sisk

The early decades of the twenty-first century will be remembered as a critical period in the long-term trend, characteristic of the twentieth century, towards the increasing spread of democracy worldwide. From the Arab Spring countries of Tunisia, Egypt, Libya and Yemen to the turbulent yet progressing transition from military rule in Myanmar, social mobilisation against autocratic, corrupt or military regimes has precipitated political transitions that are characteristic of transitions from authoritarian rule, or 'democratisation'.[1] As in the previous century's experiences of countries transitioning from authoritarian rule toward presumably more inclusive democracy, the 2000s' sweeping political and social change is turbulent, unpredictable, fraught with violence and rife with crises, reversals and halting change as old orders are resistant and new social contracts between citizen and state often remain elusive. Not all transitions away from authoritarian rule lead automatically, or quickly, to democracy.

Like earlier 'waves' and country-specific processes of democratisation, such as the short-lived but critical Prague Spring in Czechoslovakia in 1968, the Revolution of the Carnations in Portugal in 1974, or the now celebrated (yet quite violent) transition from apartheid to democracy in South Africa in 1994, today's transitions are perplexing. Are early twenty-first century countries-in-turmoil in a long and difficult but inexorable transition toward democracy, or are today's experiences somehow unique and different and requiring of new explanations and theories?

A body of scholarly literature and practitioner reflection known as 'transitology' – a literature that explores the factors that lead to *the demise of autocracy, the turbulent pathways of change* and *the choice for an eventual consolidation of democracy* – explores precisely these processes. However, its application to current cases seems at best uneasy.[2] Some have argued that the contemporary transitions are not moving in the direction of democracy and that civil war or reversion to authoritarianism is likely across the board, that the 'door is closing'[3] on even the latest moment of democratisation. In our view, in examining political liberalisation attempts that have been taking place in recent years – notably those leading up to and in the wake of the Arab Spring –dominant perspectives have exhibited a conspicuous absence of the literature on transitions to democracy over the past forty or so years. The combined effect of the emphasis on narrow regional narratives and immediate political dynamics has stripped the understanding of a new generation of political transitions of a deeper background of transitology which carries much relevance, albeit one in need of updating in the light of recent cases.

This book features contributions by scholars of democracy and democratisation processes from around the world that reopen, and revive, transitology theory and its related debates. The chapters in these pages, written by political liberalisation specialists, tackle the series of questions raised by a body of literature that remains highly useful to understanding contemporary political turbulence and transformation. Together, they seek to take the debate on transition into the next generation by establishing a link with past experiences and analyses.

Against the background of the first phase of transitology, a number of interrogations arise today. Can democratisation processes be studied regardless of whether they actually arrive at a consolidated democracy as an outcome? Can political and socio-economic transitions be systematised beyond their own contexts and specificities? What are the implications for international democracy-building assistance? Are transitions universal or area specific? Where do transitions fit in the overall picture of political transformation?

The turbulence that followed the Arab Spring of late 2010 and early 2011 marked a new phase of socio-economic and political transformation in the Middle East and North Africa. The notion of an 'Arab Spring'[4] harkened back both to the 1848 People's Spring and to the Prague Spring reform movement of 1968 – the latter an ultimately ill-fated attempt to use social movement protests to topple an authoritarian regime. The Prague Spring, it should be recalled, was indeed a period of short-lived liberalisation and not full democratisation. Soviet forces invaded to halt the reforms in August 1968 and democracy, now seemingly consolidated, did not fully come to the Czech and Slovak republics until the early 1990s.[5]

The collapse in 2011 of long-standing authoritarian regimes in Tunisia, Egypt and Libya, together with social movements, protest and rebellion in Yemen, Bahrain and Syria, further reflected a *zeitgeist* of actual or prospective transitions to democracy in the region. These rapid and largely unanticipated transitions reflected a 'punctuated equilibrium' from the decades of 'neo-patrimonial authoritarianism' that had long characterised regimes in the Middle East and North Africa region. Further from the epicentre of the new transitions in the area, countries such as Guinea, Maldives, Nepal and Zimbabwe have all seen troubled transitions in recent years as autocracies collapse, teeter or endure in the face of uprisings aimed at ending decades of military, traditional and repressive rule.

Reviving transitology

The collective argument of this book is that it is time to bring 'transitology' back in; that is, to reassert, review and revise, and develop further theories, concepts and approaches to understanding turbulent transitions in countries seeking to emerge from autocracy. The Arab Spring cases are of course each unique, as are the pathways countries such as Tunisia, Morocco, Egypt, Yemen, Libya or Syria followed in the last few years. This was true of earlier waves of democratisation as well; each pathway is unique while at the same time generalisable patterns can be seen. These and other contemporary transitions nonetheless reflect four enduring aspects of *transitology*, or the study of transitions from one regime to the next, and in particular from authoritarian rule to inclusive democracy. Transitology focuses on the common or generalisable attributes of the democratisation process across a wide variety of experiences, including insights about the conditions under which authoritarian regimes are vulnerable to popular challenge, patterns of mass mobilisation and elite pact-making, pivotal or choice moments often stimulated by crises, electoral processes and experiences of rewriting the rules of the political game through constitution-making. Further, generalisations can be found about understandings around the uncertainty, turbulence and volatility of regime-to-regime transitions, which often bring trade-offs between conflict management, transitional justice and democratisation as such. There is also a set of findings that grapple with the centrality of the transnational aspects of these changes, or the strong effects of international–domestic interactions in which outsiders have strong, internal influences in what are mostly endogenous or domestic processes. Finally, there are new dimensions of the transitology debates, particularly the changing role of political communication and participation, largely through social media.

Our objectives in reviving transitology in this book are multiple: we seek to reintroduce and restate findings from comparative politics on political regime transformation, relate this prior work to the contemporary cases, describe how today's transitions differ from or resemble previous experiences and how they present new challenges. Ultimately, the chapters in this book – and particularly the final chapter by esteemed transitology scholar Philippe Schmitter – offer some initial policy-related recommendations and new directions for the study of transitions across regime types.

Policy analysis to assess the nature and lasting consequences of several current waves of social and political upheaval is, in particular, lacking a firm framework of guidance. As a result, the understanding of momentous transformations is impressionistic, formulaic, short-term and unscientific. Moreover, there are – in our view – premature claims that, for instance, the Arab Spring has 'failed'. While area studies scholars have provided insights into the dynamics of these cases, such analysis has been typically devoid of efforts to build broader generalisations that are useful to policymakers seeking to see beyond the day-to-day headlines. Often, improvised analogies or culturalised ('Arabellions'[6]) political jargon categories, such as 'regime change', are resorted to unhelpfully to analyse complex, multifaceted and usually long-term exit strategies from authoritarianism.

Analyses of the Arab Spring have tended to be minimally historical and have often lacked a comparative dimension. In examining political liberalisation attempts taking place in the early twenty-first century, notably those leading up to and in the wake of the Arab Spring, dominant perspectives have exhibited a conspicuous absence of the literature on transitions to democracy over the past forty or so years. For all its insights and shortcomings, the language of transitology – our term for a body of literature that has comparatively and through case-study analysis examined common patterns, sequences, crises and outcomes of transitional periods – has been largely eschewed.[7] Accordingly, the uprisings, revolts and revolutions that emanate from the Middle East and North Africa region now seem in some ways unrelated to initial efforts aimed at bringing to an end an authoritarian system of rule and renegotiating a new, democratic social contract. Perhaps only Tunisia, where four civil society groups were collectively awarded the Nobel Peace Prize in 2015, has been recognised as having clearly progressed through the various stages of transition and is now possibly embarking on a path to a process of 'consolidology', to use Schmitter's term.

Similarly, when explicitly referred to in this current debate, the notion of 'transition' has been used in relation to short-term political developments, often ongoing,[8] or collapsed into larger development-oriented roadmaps.[9] The wider public and external policy-makers, fearing instability and uncertainty, seek quick solutions and simple outcomes – what some have termed 'instant democracy'.[10] Whereas the process of transition is a lengthy one, in contemporary policy parlance 'transition' is, in effect, being increasingly misleadingly equated with a different sequence, namely that shorter period between the fall of the dictator and a free (or merely trouble-free) election. For example, in seeking to reformulate US policy in the wake of the Egyptian (mostly endogenous) social uprising against the longstanding US-allied regime of President Hosni Mubarak, US President Barack Obama acknowledged it with a rather shorted-sighted perspective on the transition: 'It is my belief that an orderly transition must be meaningful, it must be peaceful, and it must begin now'.[11] Similarly, in May 2013 French President François Hollande demanded ('I insist ... these elections must take place')[12] that elections be held in Mali by July of that year following France's military intervention in that country. The combined effect of the emphasis on regional narratives, external interference and immediate political dynamics has stripped the understanding of a new generation of political transitions of a deeper background of transitology which carries much relevance for the contemporary cases.

The neglect of, or resistance to embrace, the transition paradigm in the context of the Arab Spring debate is arresting. Above and beyond the question of whether there exists a universal or even common pattern to the process of transition to democracy, the challenges facing societies undergoing transition have undeniably some commonalities – across time, space and cultures. To be certain, the *process to* (the transition) must be distinguished from the *pursued aim*, namely democracy, which is a value that can everywhere be desired, pursued, resisted, contested, redefined, possibly achieved and then secured, consolidated, hijacked, broken down or reconstructed. Democracy is ultimately elusive and subject to various definitions (and assessments of its 'quality'[13]), a debate which this book will not be concerned with. Democratisation processes can be studied regardless of whether they actually arrive at a consolidated democracy as an outcome, especially given the difficulty of the consolidation concept in terms of its empirical validity and the reality that 'consolidation' itself is more of a spectrum than a condition as such.[14] Indeed, much can be learned about the conditions for successful transitions from those that are aborted or hijacked.

Notably absent in the analysis of these new transitions has been a close and systematic look at whether the concepts and findings from earlier studies of regime-type transition, ostensibly in the direction of democracy as today's dominant regime-type, can be usefully applied to understanding the often wrenching, convoluted and in some instances violent dynamics of the Middle Eastern and North African early twenty-first century transitions. Can political and socio-economic transitions be systematised beyond their own contexts and specificities?

About this book

The literature on previous waves of democratisation can indeed shed light on contemporary contexts; thus, a close look at how prior research has addressed key questions is essential. This is particularly the case since significant amounts of political change continue to occur around the world but the ongoing era of political change has no dominant directionality.[15] This book explores these questions. Under what conditions do long-standing autocracies collapse, and survive, when there are massive social movements aimed at toppling their rule? What are the conditions under which transitions may be 'hijacked' by capable and wily incumbent elites through the suppression of social movements and the stifling of political opposition? When and why do incumbent and opposition elites agree to a 'pacted transition', by which the vital interests of these regimes and their challengers are addressed in tacit or explicit negotiations of the new rules of the political road? What do we know of the efficacy, and weaknesses, of interim governments and transitional power-sharing outcomes in smoothing the turbulence of transitions? Do transitions stimulate, enable or exacerbate ethnic and religious mobilisation and conflict? What role do various turning points play on the transition road, such as electoral moments, constitutional crises and violent incidents? When, if ever, can new democracies be said to be 'consolidated'?

In answering these questions, the authors in this book present three principal, integrated arguments. First, *there is arguably a common and now increasingly recognisable pattern of democratic transition*, i.e. a sequence that transcends the local set of values beyond cultural idiosyncrasies, contrary to the arguments of some that have portended the 'end' of the transition paradigm. Second, *common patterns, crises and sequences across cases are identifiable but are in need of updating* as recent waves of transitions are expanding the field of study and policy practice. Finally, *the challenges facing the societies, institutions and individuals during these phases can be addressed successfully* as the difficulties of a transition process rest to a large extent on internal leadership, coalition-making and negotiation and external assistance. Such support can be effective through advocacy of global norms, technical assistance and by way of broader capacity-development engagements in countries experiencing transition. In many cases, there is also a role for much greater involvement by international actors (to both progressive and ill effect), which then must engage in constructive dialogue with national actors about the nature, sequencing, timing and process of decision-making related to the management of transitions.

In Chapter 2, we argue in greater depth that it is time to 'bring transitology back'. That is, we contend that in the present context it is important to restate, re-examine and enrich further theories, concepts and approaches to understanding turbulent transitions in countries seeking to emerge from autocracy. Focusing on the common attributes of the democratisation process across a wide variety of experiences, the transitology perspective emerged from analysis of the transitions that have occurred since 1974 and broadened more extensively in the post-Cold War period. The literature addresses the pathways of transition, including likely triggering events, collective action in social movements and patterns of revolt, regime repression and escalating political violence.

Democratisation theory emphasises the importance of strategic interactions between elites and citizens in complex processes that involve revisiting the basic rules of the political game. The current 2010s post-globalisation wave of transition has introduced new and important qualitative aspects to the transition cycle, in particular the transnational dimension, which must be accounted for more fully in the next phase of conceptual development in transitology studies. Bringing transitology back in to the debates on the Arab Spring, and more broadly in other contexts, focuses attention on fostering more peaceful and enduring transitions to democracy and it offers the possibility of articulating more historically-informed analyses of socio-political and security change.

In Chapter 3, Kateryna Pishchikova and Richard Youngs find that recent years have seen a growing number of partial transitions, in which moments of apparent democratic breakthrough lead not to full consolidation but to hybrid regimes. Many scholars argue that hybrid regimes are a fairly stable regime type in their own right. They are not regimes halfway towards democracy but regimes that have found a way to maintain stability through only a partial degree of political liberalisation. This chapter investigates whether recent evidence from Ukraine and Egypt reinforces or questions this well-established position. Ukraine squandered the potential of the 2004 Orange Revolution and apparently settled into a hybrid status. It may next be on the verge of reinitiating reforms towards better quality democratic transition. Egypt made an apparent breakthrough in 2011, but its putative transition was subsequently aborted. It remains unclear whether the country is en route to wholesale autocracy or to being a more stable hybrid regime. In the light of these events, this chapter asks whether the Ukrainian and Egyptian cases in fact demonstrate that hybrid transitions may not be so enduring – or whether, more subtly, they tell us that hybrid regimes may indeed be both enduring *and* unstable at the same time. In short, by drawing on the two cases of Ukraine and Egypt, Pishchikova and Youngs show how improving our understanding of the hybrid nature of political transformations can provide a valuable addition to democratic transition theory.

Chapter 4 focuses on the electoral moment, a key turning point in all transitions. Pippa Norris argues that contemporary interest in the issue of elections as a mode of transition has been revived during the post-Cold War era by the expansion in the use of elections as a standard part of peace-building and state-building initiatives by the international community, as well as by the contention that, at least in Africa, repeated experience of successive elections (irrespective of their quality) has played an important role in strengthening processes of democratisation, civil liberties and political rights. The applicability of this mix to other world regions, such as Latin America, has been strongly critiqued. Scholars have suggested that what matters in this process are the timing and sequencing of elections, and the design of electoral systems. The debate about the role of elections in achieving stable states and democratic transitions continues within the international community. The core aspect of the debate examined by this chapter is whether it is the *repeated experience* of electoral contests which is critical in processes of transition from absolute autocracy and processes of democratisation, or whether what matters is the *quality of elections* and, in particular, levels of 'contentious' elections. The chapter concludes that the problems of contentious elections can be observed to rise with the transition from absolute autocracy, peaking in hybrid regimes, before falling again in mature democracies.

In Chapter 5, Benjamin Reilly evaluates three distinctive dimensions of East Asia's democratic experience that stand out when analysed from a comparative viewpoint. The first is its mode of democratic transitions, particularly the contrast between the 'pacted' regime transitions advocated in the scholarly literature and the mostly 'people power' revolutions that have prevailed in Southeast Asia in particular. Second is the way in which institutional reforms have played a key part in Asia's democratic evolution experience – leading to a distinctive 'Asian model' which privileges some dimensions of democracy (e.g. concentrated power and majority rule) over others (e.g. broader representation and minority rights). The third touches on issues of geopolitics: the region's genuine democratic transitions have all been concentrated in maritime rather than mainland Asia – the result, it is argued, of a range of international factors centred on the competing spheres of influence of the US and China in the Asia-Pacific region.

When do 'transitions' end and normal democratic politics begin? In Chapter 6 André Liebich finds that the fall of Communist regimes in Central and Eastern Europe was so unexpected and so sudden that little thought was given, there or elsewhere, to what would follow. As the only default option, former Communist states eagerly adopted capitalist economic models, Western security structures and, superficially, universal values. A quarter of a century later, however, these countries display striking divergences from the norms to which they appeared to adhere thus raising the question of whether the ills they suffer can really be attributed to the discomforts of transition. To move from totalitarianism to democracy one has to change both the grammar and the vocabulary but to move from totalitarianism to nationalism one only has to change the vocabulary. This has proved to be the easy way out of Communism, with repercussions even in the domain of privatisation and, of course, electoral politics. As the former communist countries have gradually been admitted into the European Union (EU), their political culture has affected that of the EU more than the EU has succeeded in transforming the political culture of its new members.

Since 1989, the political landscape of Sub-Saharan Africa has shifted radically. While multi-party regimes were the exception during the Cold War, few closed authoritarian regimes survived the turn of the twenty-first century. Julien Morency-Laflamme observes in Chapter 7 that a number of electoral democracies in Africa were born before the turn of the century. All transition processes on the continent highlight certain dynamics which allow reconsideration of 'transitology' in regard to the African cases – namely, the extensive impact of the actors' actions on outcomes. Successful democratisation stories in the subcontinent all share a number of characteristics associated with formal and informal pacts, namely restraint in the demands and actions of the main political forces. Inversely, failed transition processes and regressions to authoritarianism were regularly the result of particular actors' attempts to monopolise state resources. Reviewing the 'democratic wave' of the 1990s in order to pinpoint the factors behind the 'success stories' and cases of authoritarian reversals, the chapter analyses contemporary examples of democratic improvements and breakdowns in the light of these older undercurrents.

It has been thirty years since the critical wave of democratisation and 're-democratisation' in the Americas. Diego Abente-Brun and Ignacio González-Bozzolasco start, in Chapter 8, from the premise that the 'Southern Cone' cases in Latin America proffer lessons learned in a historical-structural framework. Their analysis focuses on three distinct stages or *moments*, each with its own logic: the nature of the authoritarian regimes that preceded the transition process; the transitions processes *stricto sensu* and the characteristics of the democratic regimes engendered by them. Transitions from what? The first moment has to do with the nature of the authoritarian regimes but also with the nature of the socio-economic and political cleavages they sought to suppress or overcome. Transitions why? Hence, the second moment, the transitions per se, must be looked at not only in terms of forms, tactics or paths but also of how the democratising forces sought to overcome the very same cleavages that led to the emergence of the authoritarian regimes in the first place. Transitions to what? Finally, the third moment leads us to analyse both the type of democratic regimes that the transitions led to and the new challenges that they generated.

The 'Arab Spring' took many by surprise even as some observers had long contended that there was a gap between the aspirations of an educated, mostly middle-class citizenry and old-style autocratic, Arab nationalist regimes. The United Nations Development Programme (UNDP) had pointed out in a series of *Arab Human Development* reports beginning in 2002 that there were structural imbalances between society and its needs and political orders in the region.[16] Is this another example of the difficulty of forecasting in social analysis, or does it rather reflect deeper problems about the conceptual geography of Middle East and North African (MENA) studies? In Chapter 9, Bahgat Korany assesses the question of whether the Arab Spring does in fact constitute a regional wave of transitions to democracy, or are the conditions so unusual that there are no historical or regional comparisons to be made? He argues that Middle East and North Africa scholarly studies specifically need to rethink their unit/level of analysis and analytical lenses. Rather than singularising authoritarian durability, MENA experts need to look also at authoritarian fragility. Similarly, instead of over-emphasising 'politics from above', 'politics from below' and street parliaments have to be brought in. Bahgat Korany notes that an emerging polarisation between *deep state* and *deep society* may deviate democratic transition from its objectives of an inclusionary process and coalition-building. The time for a paradigm shift has therefore come. Such a shift not only needs to account for the decline of 'Arab exceptionalism', but also has to address the challenges of transition and the continuing revolutionary process. What are the dynamics of the different groups, their assets and liabilities? How far are issues of religion/identity impacting on the character and evolution of the transition process? To answer these questions and others, conceptual and empirical challenges have to be addressed. Conceptually, though social movement theory is now presented as a relevant alternative lens, its applicability has to be assessed critically and supplemented (rather than supplanted). Empirically, countries of the 'Arab Spring' have also to be classified so that it no longer continues to be perceived as one uniform pattern, a monolithic transition.

The book concludes with a forward-looking chapter from one of the founding scholars of transitology. Philippe Schmitter – a scion of earlier transition work – contends in Chapter 10 that, at least since Plato and Aristotle, political theorists have sought to explain why, under the kaleidoscopic surface of events, stable patterns of authority and privilege manage to survive. While they have rarely devoted much explicit attention to the choices and processes that brought about such institutions in the first place – this would be, strictly speaking, the substantive domain of what we have called *consolidology* – they have accumulated veritable libraries of data and findings about how regimes, especially democratic ones, manage to 'change and yet remain the same'. The apprentice 'consolidologist', therefore, has a lot of 'orthodox' theoretical assumptions and widely accepted empirical material to draw upon when studying the likelihood of the success or failure of 'newly-existing democracies'. On the one hand, the likelihood that practitioners of this embryonic (and possibly pseudo) science can draw more confidently from previous scholarly work should be comforting. On the other hand, there still remains a great deal of work to do before we can understand how the behaviour of political actors can become more predictable: how the rules of democracy can be made more mutually acceptable and how the interactions of power and influence can settle into more stable patterns. This closing chapter explores what might be the fundamental assumptions of this new science. On the basis of what has happened so far in more than sixty countries since April 1974, it advances a number of reflections on this tortuous process of regime transformation with the hope that such a foray will be useful in orienting future research – and equally in guiding the practice of policy-makers.

In sum, transitology has long contended with the fact that democracy as such is a highly contingent outcome in such processes – as the Prague Spring metaphor evidences – and that there may well be contextualised transition outcomes without significant or lasting democratic advances. Contemporary research also sees this as essentially a separate, yet equally engaging, problem.[17] In sum, the authors in this book argue that bringing transitology back in to the debates on fostering more peaceful and enduring transitions to democracy militates against the exceptionalism erroneously associated with the new transformations, and that such a perspective offers the possibility of articulating more historically-informed analyses of socio-political and security change. In turn, this may offer some insights into formulating improved policy at international, regional and local levels.

Notes

1 For the latest data analysis of long-term trends in governance and regime type, including forecasting models and projects to 2050, see Hughes *et al.*, *Strengthening Governance Globally*, p. 8. Forecasts based on futures modelling of core indicators of security, capacity and inclusion in governance lead to estimates of more countries experiencing transitions away from partial regimes (anocracy) and autocracy as putative underlying causal drivers of democratisation, particularly education and incomes, rise around the world.
2 See, for example, the debate in the January 2014 edition of the *Journal of Democracy* (Volume 25, 1), Diamond *et al.*, 'Reconsidering the "Transition Paradigm"', and that in the January 2015 edition of the same journal (Volume 26, 1), Plattner, 'Is Democracy in Decline?', as examples of the issues ('decline', 'recession', 'poor performance', 'splintering', 'waning', 'decay') in the current debate.
3 Masoud, 'Has the Door Closed on Arab Democracy?'.
4 Several terms have been used to refer to the series of regional uprisings in the Middle East and North Africa that followed the popular movement initiated against President Zine Abidine Ben Ali in Tunisia in December 2010 in the wake of the self-immolation of street vendor Mohamed Bouazizi: i.e. 'Arab Spring', 'Arab Awakening', 'Arab Uprisings', 'Arab Renaissance' and 'Arab Revolutions'. Each term is imperfect and carries limits in its analogy or imagery. Avoiding this semantic discussion, this book will use the common term 'Arab Spring' while taking note of important reservations concerning its use.
5 Olson, 'Democratisation and Political Participation'.
6 Börzel *et al.*, 'Responses to the "Arabellions"'.
7 Exceptions include Brookings Doha Centre, *The Beginnings of Transition*; Liu, *Transition Challenges in the Arab World*; Aly and Elkady, *The Good, the Bad and the Ugly*; Hachemaoui, *La Tunisie à la Croisée des Chemins*; Najšlová, *Foreign Democracy Assistance in the Czech and Slovak Transitions*; and Foran, 'Beyond Insurgency to Radical Social Change'.
8 See, for instance, United Nations Development Programme (UNDP), 'Arab States Transitions Must be Locally Led and Driven, Says UNDP Chief', 22 June 2011.
9 For example, United Nations Education, Scientific and Cultural Organisation (UNESCO), '*Feuille de Route: Démocratie et Renouveau dans le Monde Arabe – L'UNESCO accompagne les Transitions vers la Démocratie*', report on a roundtable, 21 June 2011.

10 See W. Pal Sidhu, 'The Perils of Instant Democracy', *Mint* (Delhi), 30 July 2013.
11 Barack H. Obama, 'Remarks by the President on the Situation in Egypt', White House, Office of the Press Secretary, 1 February 2011.
12 François Hollande, 'Point de Presse Conjoint du Président de la République et de Mahamadou Issoufou, Président de la République du Niger', Élysée Présidence de la République, 10 May 2013.
13 See Diamond and Morlino, *Assessing the Quality of Democracy* and the 'State of Democracy' approach employed by the International Institute for Democracy and Electoral Assistance (IDEA), www.idea.int/sod.
14 Schedler, 'What is Democratic Consolidation?'.
15 Carothers and Samet-Marram, 'The New Global Marketplace', p. 6. See also Carothers and Youngs, 'The Complexities of Global Protest'.
16 See the summary of the evolution of these reports, and links to them, at www.arab-hdr.org/about/intro.aspx.
17 In their analysis of international–domestic transitions to democracy Stoner *et al.* also argue that 'the domestic and international causes of successful [democracy] ... are often different than those of the initial time of transition'. See Kathryn Stoner, Larry Diamond, Desha Girod and Michael McFaul, 'Transitional Successes and Failures: The International-Domestic Nexus', in Stoner and McFaul, eds., *Transitions to Democracy*, p. 5.

2 Reviving transitology

Democratisation then and now

Mohammad-Mahmoud Ould Mohamedou and Timothy D. Sisk

Since the Revolution of the Carnations in Portugal in 1974 which overthrew the Second Republic *Estado Novo* regime (1933–1974) – much despised for its internal 'dirty war' and violations in colonial contexts abroad (notably in Angola and Mozambique) – a pattern of generally increasing democratisation globally seems well-supported in comparative analysis. The Polity regime type data project, managed at the Centre for Systemic Peace, has become the most consistent dataset for comparative, quantitative analysis of regime types since the mid-1970s. The project scores regimes over time on a 21-point scale that ranges from 'fully-institutionalised' autocracies through to 'fully-institutionalised' democracies. The long-term results are informative, and they have a direct bearing on our argument that the transitions literature has high salience to contemporary cases. Figure 2.1

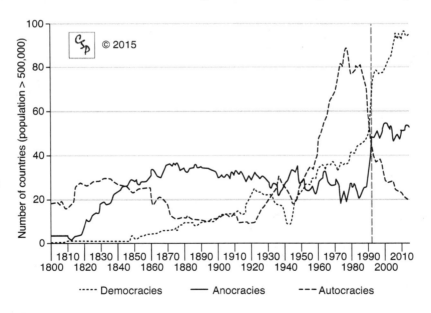

Figure 2.1 The global rise of democracies and 'partial' democracies (source: Centre for Systemic Peace, www.systemicpeace.org).

shows the long-term trajectories dramatically: over time, the number of democracies in the international system has grown considerably, especially since the end of the Cold War in 1989 following already steady growth in democratisation since the Portuguese transition kicked off the present trend in the mid-1970s. The number of partial 'semi-democratic' or 'semi-authoritarian regimes' – 'anocracies' in the Polity nomenclature – has also risen as the number of fully autocratic regimes has declined.

It is in the nature of periods of transition in the international system to be defined by what came before and after them: bipolarity and unipolarity for the Cold War, nonchalance and insecurity for 9/11 and order (albeit authoritarian) and disorder (albeit democratising) for the Arab Spring. The coincidence of these three successive moments is also, importantly, taking place at the same time as the information and technology revolution. This transition and globalisation context has resulted in a number of fluid[1] and on-going global turbulences in the grammar of international relations, which, it is submitted, can be charted through a framework that deciphers the process that underwrites the passage from one condition to another.

Origins of the transitology concepts

Earlier contemporary eras were dominated by colonialism (the late nineteenth and early twentieth centuries), wars (the two world wars and the decolonisation wars for most of the first half of the twentieth century) or ideological competition (the second half of the twentieth century with the Cold War). Whether democratisation evolves in waves or causally-related sets of transitions is debatable, primarily because it is difficult to discern one wave from the next. Is there a contagion effect that spreads ideas across borders? For example, the Arab Spring had been preceded regionally by the collapse of the regime of Saddam Hussein in Iraq by force in 2003 (again, to better or ill effect[2]), and major countries such as Indonesia witnessed transitions from authoritarian to democratic regime type in the late 1990s following the collapse of the Suharto 'New Order' regime in 1998.

Since 1989, the world has arguably been experiencing one large and extended moment of global transition unpacked in three different, yet equally consequential, moments generating transitions: post-Cold War in the 1990s, post 11 September in the 2000s and post-Arab Spring in the 2010s. Indeed, these three phases were preceded by 're-democratisation' in the Americas, notably Argentina, Brazil, Chile and Peru. It was in these cases that now common concerns with issues of transitional justice (which in turn had precedence in early cases, notably in post-World War II Germany and Japan) in particular emerged together with mechanisms that proliferated globally such as truth and reconciliation commissions. It was also in the study of these phases that crucial insights were gained into the role of social movements in toppling control by military-led 'bureaucratic–authoritarian' regimes, and aspects of the transition such as the role that pacts between the military and the opposition played in the course of transition.

Moreover, one of the most engaging elements of these early transitions was the strong role played by 'founding' elections – those first held in the course of democratisation (or in some cases, re-democratisation, as there had been earlier, failed attempts at democracy in Argentina and Brazil especially). Finally, the celebrated case of 'people power' in the Philippines, which saw the ousting of General Ferdinand Marcos in 1996, was a touchstone in the literature on regime change and democratisation; so, too, was the counterpoint of Tiananmen Square in 1989 and the failure of a student-led, putatively democratic movement against the Communist Party of China in Beijing.

In the immediate post-Cold war period, democratisation was aided by a 'unipolar' moment globally and 'turbulence' in the international system more broadly, which rearranged the nature of external (i.e. Cold War-focused) global alliances. At the same time, in 1989 the focus shifted away from Communist or capitalist global alliances to 'good governance' and the emergence of other norms such as 'humanitarian intervention' (which would evolve into the global Responsibility to Protect by 2005) that further chipped away state sovereignty, much as the Universal Declaration of Human Rights and agreements such as the Helsinki Charter had done during the Cold War. The transitions of the late 1980s and early 1990s were dramatic: countries such as Poland saw non-violent social movements topple Communist party dictatorships; South Africa came through from apartheid as a stable, non-racial democracy by 1996; and other countries such as El Salvador and Nicaragua also emerged from conflict to witness progress in democratisation.

Research on the causes, pathways and outcomes of democratic transition also surged during this period, from large-N quantitative studies of transitional processes to deeply described analytical case studies.[3] In such analyses, there is support for the original thesis of Seymour Martin Lipset in 1960 that modernisation, or increasing incomes, education and diversity of economies is closely associated with popular demands for democracy.[4] In some ways, the modernisation thesis was seen in the most recent cases of the Arab Spring, as the *Arab Human Development Report* of the United Nations Development Programme (UNDP) had long noted that the Middle East and North Africa region had lower levels of inclusivity and democracy (particularly for women) than its overall level of socio-economic development – especially levels of education – would predict.[5] The advent of the middle class in developing countries has also arguably been an underlying driver of many transitions in the contemporary period.

In summary, the transitology perspective emerged from analysis of the transitions since 1974 and broadened more extensively in the post-Cold War period. In it, one finds a focus first on the *causes of collapse* of the authoritarian region. In the long view, modernisation does matter – it is much harder to coerce a more wealthy, educated and informed society – and thus human development is critical to setting the conditions for popular challenges to authoritarian regimes.[6] At the same time, countries that have natural resource rents, such as Libya, have seen more enduring authoritarian regimes that have ruled mostly through patronage and clientelistic networks, which in effect offset the broader development of middle-class, democracy-seeking spectrums of society.

The literature also addresses the *pathways of transition*, including likely triggering events, collective action in social movements, patterns of revolt, regime repression and escalating political violence. Studies on South Africa's transition, for example, showed that over time the regime was unable to repress a massive and internationally supported social movement. Instead, the apartheid regime gradually negotiated its way out of power in a series of pacts or elite agreements, followed by a more fully inclusive constitutional assembly to draft a new social contract.[7]

Thus, democratisation theory emphasises the importance of strategic interactions between elites and citizens in complex processes that involve revisiting the basic rules of the political game. Such processes are fraught with uncertainty, and are often accompanied by violent conflict as the old order collapses and the new order has not yet fully emerged.[8] However, given the right conditions the period of transition is a strategic moment for substantial gains in, e.g. women's rights and representation, particularly when conditions are favourable for women to organise in civil society associations across lines of contention, whether these are in terms of supporters of the former or new regime, class or identity.[9] Moreover, when new institutions are chosen there may be the opportunity, often through a combination of external and internal pressures, to create institutions that include women's quotas in electoral processes and within political parties. In Latin America, representation quotas for women have become a strategically gender-sensitive way to institutionalise norms of more equal gender participation in political parties and governance, even if they are differentially effective in implementation.[10]

In the late 1990s and into the early 2000s, Ukraine, Georgia, Kyrgyzstan and Serbia (among others) experienced the so-called 'colour revolutions' in which large social movements led by civil society organisations and students sought to bring democracy drawing on the principles and tactics of nonviolent civil resistance. Yet, in these varied cases, the revolutions themselves were followed by disputed elections, reversals or democratic decline. However, these cases suggest that democracy does come in waves and that there are 'diffusion' or transnational effects. The often ambiguous outcome of so many colour-revolution transitions has led critics to suggest that the transition paradigm is too teleological and that it is unable to effectively account for countries that start celebrated transitions, but end up in a political limbo – much like the cases of the contemporary Arab Spring.

Critiques of transitology

The lapse in visibility of transitology is a result of the mid-to-late 1990s and 2000s transition fatigue whereby the 'end of the transition paradigm' had, for instance, been forcefully and capably argued.[11] That many of the prior celebrated efforts at regime change had ended up with anocratic or 'grey zone' regimes, and that there were so many concerns about the inability of democracy building aid – often channelled to nascent civil society – to tip the balance in such contexts, soured many analysts to the democratisation perspective. Moreover, the misuse of democratisation as a justification for regime change by force by the neo-conservatives in the United States, in the early years of the George W. Bush administration, led to the ill-considered invasion and occupation of Iraq in 2003. This further raised concerns that democratisation was a code word for a realist pursuit of regional power by an ideologically driven unipolar global hegemon, the United States.

The main critique levelled against transitology is that it is excessively teleological. Thomas Carothers argued: 'the transition paradigm has been somewhat useful during a time of momentous and often surprising political upheaval in the world. But it is increasingly clear that reality is no longer conforming to the model'.[12] It is also argued that the paradigm is geographically narrow in scope and that it is inapplicable to specific (new) situations, whose alleged exceptionalism escapes the boundaries (whatever these may be) of transitology. Yet at the very time that the obsolescence argument was put forward, rebellion was brewing in the Middle East and North Africa leading a few years later to the 2011 uprisings which immediately raised precisely the issue of... transitions.

Another limitation is that there has not been enough demarcation in the study of the establishment of democracy *ex nihilo*, i.e. where it was altogether absent as distinguished from a situation where some attempts have been made and where the norm needs to be more formally adopted. Admittedly, part of the problem is the vagueness that can be attributed to all three dimensions: 'transition', 'process' and 'democracy'. In particular, the consolidation phase was too often addressed together with the transition phase (and indeed the term 'consolidology'[13] at times used interchangeably with 'transitology'). Experiences in the 2010s have indicated that the *rupture* moment – the momentous events associated with a break from the past – can be extended, substantially highlighting the need to devote more attention to the break moment rather than the more elusive phase of consolidation (see, for example, Putnam *et al. Making Democracy Work* and Linz and Stepan *Problems of Democratic Transition and Consolidation*). What is then needed is more nuance and complexity in the charting of variegated trajectories away from the rupture moment. The conflation of experiences can be reductionist if the points of departure and arrival are not precisely circumscribed.

Yet another limitation is that transitology has also, to some extent, taken for granted the inevitability of transitions. Yet it may well be that some post-revolutionary situations do not actually initiate, however haphazardly, a transition process, ever lingering for an extended period in the (active or frozen) conflict-ridden aftermath of the uprising. Such a non-transition state may well be what Libya is in today in the aftermath of the NATO intervention and the fall of Muammar Gaddafi, or what Algeria experienced in most of the 2010s in terms of socio-political stasis running parallel to the Arab Spring. Witnessing the debate on the uprisings that have shaken the Arab world since 2011, one is struck by the minimal comparative attention given by analysts and actors alike to the experience of other democratisation processes.

The scant concern with what took place *earlier* and *elsewhere* in terms of attempts at introducing or reintroducing democratic dynamics partakes of a practice that both questions the universality of these challenges and which proceeds with a region's political culture as the main explanatory starting point.[14] Yet the experiences of Western Europe from the post-Medieval state formation period to World War II,[15] of Latin America's social movements and 'pacted rupture' (*ruptura pactada*), of Eastern Europe's civil society activism and of Sub-Saharan Africa's national conferences[16] are all directly related to the efforts underway in the Middle East and North Africa. Indeed, the strife which, for instance, rapidly overtook Yugoslavia after the optimism of 1990 helps put in perspective the post-Arab Spring evolution of Libya or Syria. The latter-day transformations do not take place in a vacuum, and comparative thinking and practice that learns from other settings has value and merit in that regard. Indeed, research has shown that demands for democracy through mass social mobilisation are often driven by 'pocketbook protests', in which everyday quotidian life is inhibited by poor governance of autocratic, often deeply corrupt, regimes.[17]

As noted, up until now few Arab Spring studies have been concerned with transition per se. Some attempts have been made to go beyond the specifics of the region, but they remain concerned with the revolutionary phase[18] or with rear-view approaches on the impact of authoritarianism.[19] The minimising of the relevance of earlier transitions betrays, however, a certain self-centeredness, if not a type of neo-Orientalism, on the part of Arabists and other Middle East and North Africa ('MENA') experts.[20] Arguably, close examination would reveal that all the related developments so far in the Middle East and North Africa since the self-immolation of Mohamed Bouazizi in Tunisia in December 2010 can be accounted for under the transition paradigm (political and constitutional reform, power competition, disorder and strife, ethnic and religious mobilisation and polarisation, power vacuum, disenchantment, old order nostalgia, military takeover and international influence or a lack thereof).

Finally, transition has brought together political scientists, sociologists and anthropologists but not security experts. Yet, if anything, the post-Arab Spring debate reveals the need to factor in the security dimension in transitions beyond existing general consideration of whether democratisation leads to disorder, strife or civil war. What kind of transition can there be if a prolonged period materialises – years in post-Ba'athi Hussein Iraq, for instance – where violence dominates the daily lives of citizens? The contemporary resistance within the Arab World to analogies with previous transitions is reminiscent of the earlier similar rejection of parallels between Eastern Europe and Latin America, or from Latin America to African contexts. In the same manner that transitologists were shunned away from post-Communism studies, today's students of transitions are kept at bay by Arabists. Yet what might matter more in the next phase of understanding the 'MENA' is not necessarily so much familiarity with the Sykes-Picot treaty but rather with pact-making, constitution-drafting and institution-building.

Investigating comparatively[21] corporatist arrangements, state retreat from its functions, societal alternatives for political expression, and exclusionary politics enables the sharpening of analytical tools to understand contemporary transformation in that part of the world.

Such invalidating of transitology – as well as the complex empirical challenges its introduction or reactivation has been generating in large parts of the South[22] – was also a sign of the times with the combined post-9/11 neo-authoritarian dynamics in many parts round the world[23] merging with an excessive association of the transition framework with the recent experiences of post-Soviet Union countries.[24] With good reason, the hybridity that came to materialise at that juncture gave pause to some, generating the coinage of new terms such as 'uncertain regimes', 'semi-democratic regimes', 'competitive authoritarianism', 'facade democracy' or 'illiberal democracies'.[25] Moreover, it is clear from research that countries with mixed or semi-authoritarian regime types may be particularly vulnerable to debilitating social violence: autocracies tend to be stable through effective repression, and democracies through participation and compromise, while semi-democratic or semi-authoritarian regimes tend to generate their own violent challengers to the state.

In such contexts, electoral moments in particular are windows of vulnerability to violence as a pattern of opposition mobilisation and repression by the regime threatens to escalate. To be sure, doubts had been expressed earlier as to whether 'democracy was just a moment'[26] and such 'pessimism'[27] was largely the result of admittedly excessive optimism in the wake of the end of the Cold War (a revealing fact is that the *Journal of Democracy* was founded in 1990). In point of fact, the issue of transition to democracy is at once a constant twofold question (how to get there and which means to use?) – made up of cumulative attempts at approximating to a universal process of transition whose components would be identified clinically – and the sum total of different and specific experiences in Western Europe, Latin America, Asia, Sub-Saharan Africa and, more recently, the Middle East and North Africa. In such a context, it is then particularly important to revisit democratic transition theory and uncover what it has to offer to the understanding and management of contemporary transitions. In so doing, it is here understood that:

1 What is imperfectly referred to for shorthand purposes as 'transitology', and which can also be termed 'democratisation literature', is a young, vast and still tentative work in progress.
2 Democracy is a complex concept with no consensus on any particular set of institutional manifestations.
3 The multiplicity of experiences of seeking to break away from authoritarianism render the attempt at systematising those journeys arduous but not altogether impossible.

Many critics of transitology have focused on the problem of electoral processes in societies emerging from autocracy or from civil war. Some scholars such as

Jack Snyder, for example, have highlighted the motivation of political elites in electoral processes in societies divided along ethnic, sectarian or religious lines to 'play the ethnic card' as a way to induce fear among the population and to manipulate a fearful population into supporting more extreme positions on issues such as territorial autonomy or secession. This in turn generates a 'security dilemma' among other groups, who counter such mobilisation with their own claims, thereby generating a centrifugal or outward spin to the political system. Under such conditions of deep social division elections become nothing more than an 'ethnic census'.[28]

The problem of elections as conflict-inducing is directly related to three additional factors. The first of these is the incredibly high stakes of winning and losing in a context in which losing the election may jeopardize personal or group security (there is no sense that one could live to fight a future election). This problem seems particularly acute in presidential elections (as in Côte d'Ivoire in 2010) when the election is perceived by the protagonists as a zero-sum game with a winner-takes-all outcome. Similarly, in Iraq, insurgents who expected – with good reason in this context – to be systematically excluded from power mobilised to disrupt governorate or provincial elections in 2013. Indeed, sectarian violence increased in Iraq as the process of democratisation has not been sufficiently inclusive of elements of the *ancien régime*, and in 2014 pushed some Sunni segments into the hands of the organisation of the Islamic State (IS).

The second additional factor is the allure to some parties of using strategic violence as a way to influence either the process or the outcome (or both) of the balloting. In parliamentary elections in Afghanistan in 2005, and again in 2010, insurgents targeted election workers (both international and Afghan) and sought to disrupt balloting as a way of undermining the legitimacy of the process and of the regime of President Hamid Karzai. The third factor is that when the capture of state power leads to access to natural resource export derived rents or revenue, there may well be an incentive to use violence, intimidation and electoral fraud as a route to enrichment. Sudan's elections in 2010 are a case in point: the Khartoum regime used a wide array of tactics to ensure beyond doubt that the ruling National Congress Party (NCP) would stay in power and indeed retain access to the revenue derived from exports of crude oil from South Sudan that is pumped northward through to the oil tanker terminal at Port Sudan.

Finally, the detractors of elections in democratising contexts also see them as sometimes serving to legitimise governments that have won militarily on the battlefield and are able to use the position of state incumbency as a way to cloak the regime in legitimacy while not allowing for open opposition. This is the case with those who view parliamentary elections in Rwanda in 2013 as legitimising the rule of the Rwandan Patriotic Front and President Paul Kagamé in a poll in which opposition forces had been imprisoned or otherwise suppressed for fostering ethnic 'divisionism'.[29] The 2015 extension of a 'third term' for the Rwandan president demonstrates that institutions alone do not make for sustainability of the democratic 'rules of the game'; in this instance, internal norms of what constitutes legitimacy and democratic popular support appear to trump global norms. Thus, much of the recent scholarship on transitology has focused on the question of electoral processes and the problem of managing election-related violence in contexts where democracy is not yet fully institutionalised, or where the necessary conditions for a sustainable democracy appear to be absent.[30]

With these important caveats – and noting that the question of the pertinence or the lack thereof of the transition paradigm has been asked before[31] – it can be said that transitology is not therefore a body of research limited to the historically confined study of 1970s, 1980s and 1990s transitions to democracy in Southern Europe, Latin America, Eastern Europe or Africa. Such forays marked the inception of a crucial field of study concerned with the processes of democratisation that is highly relevant to a new generation of transitions now unfolding, notably in the Middle East and North Africa and in globally significant cases such as Myanmar, raising both conceptual and practical issues.

We argue in this book, first, that the literature already features a measure of consensus on some key elements of the method of transitioning as it relates in particular to the sequence of the transition and its requirements; second, that the current post-globalisation wave of transition has introduced new and important qualitative aspects to the transition cycle, in particular the transnational dimension which was present in prior contexts but must be accounted for more fully in the next phase.

Democratic transition: founding moment and forward movement

What, ultimately, is 'transition'? The shift from a system built on coercion, fear and imposition (and conflict) to one based on consent, compromise and coalition-building (and peace) is no easy task. Nor is it a quick or linear process. In effect, such a transition in the underlying rules of politics implies a set of transformative tasks towards a form of government where leaders are selected through competitive elections. This has been described as a process of 'transforming the accidental arrangements, prudential norms and contingent solutions that have emerged (during transitions) into structures, i.e. into relationships that are reliably known, regularly practiced and habitually accepted'.[32] Democratic transition is, then, centrally about political *transformation* and re-negotiating the underlying rules of the political game. The nature of the transformation is at the heart of this exercise; not solely the replacement of political regimes, but the creation of a new order aimed at democratisation that gives representation and political voice. As Klaus Müller and Andreas Pickel note when commenting on the different dimensions of a paradigm: '*it informs social scientific work* by demarcating fundamental problems ... *it informs policy-making*, especially in terms of fundamental reform approaches [and] ... *it informs ideology and political action* by embodying fundamental values and visions of social order'.[33]

Transformation towards what? Democracy is the end result of a process of democratisation and political liberalisation. Specifically, transitions are an open-ended attempt at the realisation of democracy. To the extent that, as noted, the *process to* is qualitatively different from the *aimed at* goal, an important dimension arises as it relates to transitions, namely the centrality of performance. Although, 'transition' or 'political transition' can be found to refer to the passage towards modernity, development, economic viability or democracy, the term and phrase are commonly used to refer to the latter. Democratisation can therefore be defined as (i) a political and socio-economic process characterised by (ii) the gradual evolution/movement/progress/march towards (iii) a system of government anchored in democratic principles, namely and chiefly representation, inclusivity, accountability and civil and political rights. In particular, this implies a process away from an earlier system – an *ancien régime* – which generally took the form of authoritarianism or dictatorship. In turn, it implies a key moment in that sequence of rupture, i.e. a break from the old (non-democratic order) to the new (rights-accommodating) political environment.

Against that background, transitology is not transition. One is the science, the other the object of study. It is important to note that not all insights gathered in the study of the political transformation of a given country away from authoritarianism will apply elsewhere, including in the same region. However, transitology is by nature an eminently comparative exercise, aimed at producing contingent generalisations about the nature and process of political change. Transitology is therefore a specialisation in social sciences continuously concerned with transformation. Though open-ended in the manner in which the sequence comes into play and is unpacked, change is not altogether value free. It is teleological in the sense that the norm pursued is the one of democracy. Even when the phrase is limited to 'political transition', the assumption is that such transition is towards democracy.

The literature on transitions to democracy is varied and rich. It is composed of several important contributions[34] which do not represent a single, overarching body but rather several strands that meet at key points constitutive of the markers of transition theory. Dankwart Rustow's April 1970 'Transitions to Democracy'[35] article is arguably the founding text of democratic transition theory. Writing in *Comparative Politics*, Rustow insightfully argued that transitions do not usually emerge from high levels of modernisation and development but more often from contingent choices and specific local factors. That said, there are typical background conditions for successful transitions, first among which is a shared understanding of national unity: if some sense of who constitutes 'the people' is absent, transitions can devolve into competing claims for separate projects and sovereignty. Rustow also argued that transition can be conceptualised as two distinct phases: the 'preparatory phase' which involves a long struggle between political factions over the state, and a 'decision phase' after the outcome of such a struggle in which political factions (led mostly by elites) agree to democratise in a mutual security pact. The Rustow perspective is echoed in the work of political sociologists John Higley and Michael Burton who, in evaluating cases such as Sweden's transition to democracy in the 1920s, also argued for a close focus on the contingent choices of elites within democratisation processes.[36]

Importantly, Rustow argued that the development of democracy depends on the presence of one key requirement, namely national unity. This dimension was then the inevitable basis for the institutionalisation of rule-based political contest. In other words, Rustow proposed a theory revolving around the process and the actor wherein the actors come in equally as regards the struggle, leadership and choice. Following this pioneering work, subsequent authors also explored the essential notion that democratisation is the outcome of contingency and choice, based on actor decisions as they seek to navigate the uncertainty between the old regime and the newly-negotiated order.

Perhaps the most influential of these is the work of Guillermo O'Donnell, Philippe Schmitter and Laurence Whitehead who together produced a four-volume work on *Transitions from Authoritarian Rule: Tentative Conclusions about Uncertain Democracies* in 1986. They, too, emphasised the key role of elite contingency and choice within transition processes as the critical factor in democratisation, arguing that it becomes possible when there are splits within the dominant regime over how to handle protests and, when faced with the inevitability of change, the military switches allegiance from the old governing elites to the newly-legitimated elites. Engagingly, this volume closes with Schmitter's lifelong reflections on observing what appears as a trend line in Figure 2.1 (see Chapter 10).

A final aspect of transitology is the importance of understanding that transitions involve renegotiation of the basic rules of the game of politics. Many of the issues that arise are on the sequencing of such processes of institutional change, particularly in electoral processes that lead to the election of constitution-making bodies, as has been the case in Tunisia and Libya with the constituent assemblies in 2011 and 2012 respectively. Central among the questions that are left open are the territorial bases of the state and the degree of federal or decentralised rule (a key question in Nepal, for example, which has transitioned from Hindu monarchy into a new constitution that federalises, and secularises, the state) and the basis or political economy of wealth sharing in cases where natural resources are coincident with claims for autonomy (as in the Kurdish region of Iraq). In societies divided by deep ethnic, sectarian or religious social cleavages – many of which are emerging from civil war or widespread political violence such as in Nepal – much of the debate over institutional choice involves a delicate balance among institutions designed to share power and lead to inclusive, yet capable, ruling coalitions.[37]

What summary lessons does transitology give us? We suggest the following twelve key insights from the transitology literature are most pertinent to today's cases of democratic transitions.

1 *Transitions can occur in any structural context.* They represent an explicit choice by a community to try and proceed towards democracy. Mechanisms are necessary to flesh out democracy while institutional controls can vary. The issue of transition raises the question of what specific means are selected to achieve the democratic goal.

2 *Transitions tend to congregate in waves.* Materialising sporadically, such cycles are an indication of moments whereby conditions conducive to a demand for democratisation reach a fulcrum point initiating a visible phase. The 'wave' analogy was put forward by Samuel Huntington in his 1993 book, *The Third Wave*. This construct implies that democracy follows a 'global advance'[38] logic.

3 *Transitions take time,* and there is no uniformly similar end result. Transitions have an unpredictable end result, an 'uncertain "something else" … which can be the instauration of a political democracy'.[39] The rule-bounded nature of democracy is tested by the open-ended nature of democratisation. Transitions are uncertain because they seek to introduce predictability (of rule, political behaviour, institutional structures and commitment to outcomes). The common project is from a disorderly (violent) system to one that is rule-bounded (peaceful).

4 *There is no single path to democracy* but there are requirements and there are necessary dynamics, notably inclusion and redistribution. The values of democracy are similar but their expression can differ in specific contexts. Some struggles to achieve democracy have been motivated by the pursuit of 'justice', others have occurred in the name of '*égalité*' (equality) or '*libertad*' (freedom) and yet again others with a view to securing '*utumwa*' (liberation) or '*karama*' (dignity).

5 *Transitions represent a founding moment and a forward movement.* This interlinked two-part process is anchored in a rupture from or abandonment of earlier ways of doing politics and the gradual adoption of new ones. If democracy rests on the practice of its components (respect of freedoms, enactment of civic responsibility, tolerance of difference and sharing of communal burden), then similarly democratisation rests on the ideally conscientious acting out of its multiple commitments.

6 *Transitions are reversible.* Democratic legitimation is a complex process and authoritarian regression can occur. Regimes can aim to pre-empt crises by appearing to democratise or can seek to maintain a system through a controlled transition that gives the appearance of opening up. Cosmetic, façade or virtual processes that are meant to give an appearance of democracy are particularly detrimental to the securing of democracy in a context where it needs to advance tangibly. Similarly, an increase in undemocratic behaviour in an already democratic setting can lead to a retreat of democracy.[40]

7 *Transitions are almost invariably conflictual* and can often lead to violence. While some analysts have perhaps oversold this point, there is good reason to suggest that in the course of transition there is a mobilisation – often along identity lines – that can induce a 'security dilemma' and which can lead to transition-related violence. Pre-existing conflicts are collapsed into a new structure which at once inherits them and seeks to solve them in novel ways. In particular, previously repressed voices can find space for expression and empowerment. The challenge of addressing violence is therefore

present before, during and after a political transition. It is both an incipient and a continuing problem.

8 *Transitions can unleash new vulnerabilities to social conflict*, particularly in cases of ethnic or narrow minority regimes. Violence can emerge because transitions are inherently uncertain, crisis prone and are typically periods of deep economic and social turbulence. Specifically, this issue comes to the fore because during transitions, the state (*primus inter pares* and holder of the official monopoly of violence) suffers a loss of legitimacy which it has to re-establish on new, representative grounds; regaining the legitimacy of the state to rule is essential if violence is to be managed – as the war riven post-2011 pathway to transition in Libya attests.

9 *The economy occupies a central place during transitions*. Economic malaise and popular frustration often precede the collapse of autocratic regimes. Yet the pursuit of political change concomitantly with economic reform creates the reality of a dual process which can yield 'transitional incompatibility',[41] bringing the crucial question of sequencing back to the fore.

10 *Transitions are a comprehensive process* with ramifications for most dimensions of the social, economic and political environment. In time, a successful transition widens to generate a 'democratic culture' and, over time, to 'habituation' to the new rules of the political game. Constitutional processes are central to this activity with a constitution representing more than just a text or a narrative; it is the expression of a new social contract.

11 *Transition occurs in a sequence of stages*. There exists much 'uncertainty'[42] as to the temporal delimitation of the phases, notably as regards the consolidation phase. Sequencing is crucial, particularly with regard to elections. The choice of sequence involves a trade-off between the stability offered by early elections on the one hand, and the political and legal vacuum caused by establishing a new political order without a basic legal consensus on the other. Early elections legitimise the transitional regime, but disadvantage new political parties by depriving them of the necessary time to organise.[43]

12 *Actors are key to the process of transition*. Among these, the leadership piloting the transition and civil society are eminently central to the process. The strategic capacity of these groups is fundamental, as is the dynamic of appearance of new actors. The opening of the system featuring demanding actors (often previously repressed) is a difficult and contentious exercise. Hence, agency is particularly central to the process of transition. It is no surprise that efforts to mediate the Libya transition, following the then successful but ultimately ill-fated transitional elections of 2012, has been a repeated strategic objective of the United Nations' effort to restore a unified pathway of transition toward stability for Libyan elites.

Conclusions: promises and limits of transitology

The conceptual foundations of this book offer an approach to reviving an important perspective for understanding dramatic political changes in a manner better informed by experiences of the past. We do assert that even though there is imprecision in the transitology concept – as many of the contributors to this volume note – the notion offers a compelling framework for evaluating in a more contingent and systematic way the opportunity to see both progress and regression in contemporary transitions. The principal utility of the construct is that it illuminates well the vulnerability of the phase(s) during which the development of a democratic ethos and the establishment of democratic institutions are pursued.

Hence, the stripped-down statement of transitology is fourfold:

(i) an aim to create a generalisable theory of democratisation and the ability to explain processes of democratisation in different social contexts; (ii) the conviction that democratisation is a one-way and gradual process of several phases; (iii) an emphasis that the single crucial factor for democratic transition is a decision by the political elite and not structural features; and (iv) the normative belief of neoliberal nature, that the consolidation of the institution of democratic elections and other reforms of its own accord establish effectively functioning states.[44]

Against this, the primary usefulness of transitology is that it points to a process which carries a measure of universality. In spite of the diversity of authoritarian situations – which include dynamic reconfigurations such as those of the so-called 'deep state'[45] – with each new wave, analysts insisted on the novelty or uniqueness of the new situations only to wake up a few years later to realise how little had changed in the basic requirements of the steps needed to generate or regenerate[46] democracy.

Among the promises of transitology, the following dimensions can be further identified:

- understanding better the conditions under which autocratic regimes are vulnerable to challenge and collapse;
- deciphering the context in which elites choose to negotiate rather than fight;
- contributing to assessment instruments that seek to discern vulnerability to election-related violence and associated conflict-prevention activities;
- identifying the most vexatious choices and sequencing problems on which to focus facilitative international assistance;
- determining which specific institutional manifestations of democracy are appropriate for any given context, consistent with a consensus that arises from internal bargaining and not international imposition;
- seeing contexts in a long-term, appreciative perspective on the nature, pace, scope and end-state of change.

The contributions that follow in this volume achieve these aims in their analysis of contemporary regions, contexts and cases. While we have reserved the final words for an esteemed colleague, Philippe Schmitter, we conclude the conceptual chapter of this volume with some additional findings on both the promises and weaknesses of the transitology lens. It is clear, by way of immediate admission, that the absence of any single 'ideal type' transition process is not in and of itself a weakness. What may be more important is the indication of progress. The overarching value of transitology is, therefore, that it introduces universal categories in order to understand layered developments and the rebuilding of politics. It seeks to understand systematically the journey about societal maturation beyond community defiance and the limitations of the 'place' moment (Tahrir Square, Pearl Square, Plaza de Mayo, Puerta del Sol, La Bastille, Umbrella Square, Taksim Square, Euromaidan and so forth) towards the institutionalisation of systemic processes.

In the wake of the Arab Spring, three aspects are emerging as key dimensions of latter-day transitions: the role of *social media*, the question of *transnationalism* and the *security* dimension. First, the long-term impact of the widely acclaimed social media that contributed to the downfall of the autocratic Middle East and North African regimes must be examined further. To be sure, the role of technology will remain intrinsically ambivalent. Social networks may contribute to empowering citizens, but the same technology may also be used against them for control and repression.[47] Whether virtual groups can ensure democratic or civic compliance is among the questions that need to be explored further as the new transition processes mature. Similarly, the current sociopolitical transformations are being altered by transnational dynamics which were previously less important or altogether absent. Here again, the transnational dimension of transitions has been noted before.[48]

Second, in the early twenty-first century the transnationalism dimension has overtaken the grammar of international relations. The post-Arab Spring has illustrated the dynamic further taking it into new uncharted territories both of transition and of conflict. The overflowing of the impact of the Libyan revolution onto the Sahel and the engulfing of the Syrian civil war by regional actors – notably from the Levant, the Gulf and the Maghreb as well as foreign fighters coming from the Americas, Europe and Asia, and proxy support for the different protagonists from global powers such as Russia and the United States – indicate how important this new dimension has become.

Finally, developments around the Arab Spring are also shedding light on the importance of successful breakthroughs as preconditions for additional democratic development. A contribution in relation to this question was made by Ray Salvatore Jennings in a 2012 report issued by the United States Institute of Peace (USIP). Calling for 'the need to identify a breakthrough paradigm', Jennings identified an important dimension of the gathering discontent storm before the rupture: 'As revolutionary potential builds in breakthrough venues, "irregular" communities of dissent increasingly test the political waters, some for the first time'.[49]

Transitology is especially useful in looking beyond the immediacy and intricacy of the moment towards a longer-term view that identifies the markers of progress on the road map of democratisation. The road to democracy is indeed arduous. Change is engineered with difficulty beyond the battle cries (*ruptura, solidarność, perestroika, irhal, dégage*) and political transformation generates uncertainty. Transitions involve struggles for power and the pacification of the political process is no easy task. Transitology's task is then undeniably ambitious and at the same time elegantly simple. It seeks to elucidate the spatio–temporal logic of *a path which is also a moment*. Societies in flux and states in mutation awaken from 'the fairest dawn' to try and morph into a new, more legitimate and responsive political system. Transitions are indeed about a founding moment and a forward movement. Yet the mainstay of the exercise is the explication, which is still an investigation, of the resulting passage. Ultimately, transitology offers the promise of a general theory of political transformation and it appears to stand the test of time in looking forward to perhaps further such moments well into the twenty-first century.

Notes

1 On the value of 'fluidity' as a focus for understanding the 'how' of transitions, see Banegas, 'Les Transitions Démocratiques'.
2 See Claire Spencer *et al.*, *Iraq*.
3 For an overview of this literature, see Geddes, 'What Causes Democratization?'.
4 Lipset, *Political Man*.
5 See Kuhn, 'On the Role of Human Development'.
6 Geddes, 'What Causes Democratization?'.
7 Sisk, *Democratization in South Africa*.
8 For an examination of this aspect building on Samuel Huntington's 1968 inaugural *Political Order in Changing Societies*, see Francis Fukuyama, *Political Order and Political Decay*.
9 Baldez, 'Women's Movements and Democratic Transitions'.
10 Jones, 'Gender Quotas, Electoral Laws and the Election of Women'.
11 Carothers, 'End of Transition Paradigm'. See, similarly, the special issue of *Esprit*: 'Transition Démocratique: La Fin d'un Modèle', *Esprit*, January 2008.
12 Carothers, 'End of Transition Paradigm', p. 6.
13 See the analysis of Philippe C. Schmitter in Chapter 10.
14 Barrington Moore notes that 'to explain behaviour in terms of cultural values is to engage in circular reasoning' (Moore, *Social Origins of Dictatorship and Democracy*, p. 486). He adds: 'The assumption of inertia, that cultural and social continuity do not require explanation, obliterates the fact that both have to be recreated anew in each generation, often with great pain and suffering'.
15 See Lowe, *Savage Continent*.
16 See, for instance, Daloz, *Transitions Démocratiques Africaines*.
17 Bracati, 'Pocketbook Protests'.
18 See, notably, Bennani-Chraïbi and Fillieule, 'Pour Une Sociologie des Situations Révolutionnaires'.
19 See, for instance, Nayed, 'Beyond Fascism'.
20 See Mohamedou, 'Neo-Orientalism and the e-Revolutionary'.
21 Kamrava and Mora, 'Civil Society and Democratisation in Comparative Perspective'.
22 Among these challenges, Jochen Hippler notes: 'Weak and poorly functioning state apparatuses are not made more efficient but are in fact made devoid of any function whatsoever ... A 'democratisation' of these structures is then purely a matter of form ... One result is that the citizens in the South become disillusioned with their democracy'. See Hippler, *The Democratisation of Disempowerment*, pp. 24–25.

23 Notably in the Middle East and North Africa. See, for instance, Schlumberger, *Debating Arab Authoritarianism* and King, *The New Authoritarianism*.
24 See, for example, Gans-Morse, 'Searching for Transitologists' and Holzer, 'The End of the Transitological Paradigm?'.
25 See Diamond, 'Elections Without Democracy'; Levitsky and Way, *Competitive Authoritarianism*; and Zakaria, 'The Rise of Illiberal Democracy'.
26 Kaplan, 'Was Democracy Just a Moment?'. Kaplan writes: 'I submit that the democracy we are encouraging in many poor parts of the world is an integral part of a transformation towards new forms of authoritarianism'.
27 Carothers, 'Stepping Back from Democratic Pessimism'; and Gilley, 'Democratic Triumph, Scholarly Pessimism'.
28 Snyder, *From Voting to Violence*.
29 'Rwandan Elections: Safe and Sorry', *The Economist*, 21 September 2013.
30 See, for example, Bekoe, *Voting in Fear*.
31 See, notably, Karl, 'From Democracy to Democratization and Back'; and Jankauskas and Gudžinskas, 'Reconceptualising Transitology'.
32 Schmitter, 'Some Propositions about Civil Society', p. 4.
33 Müller and Pickel, 'Transition, Transformation and the Social Sciences', p. 29, emphasis added.
34 Of particular note, among numerous others, is the work of Lisa Anderson, Richard Banegas, Sheri Berman, Carles Boix, Valerie Bunce, Thomas Carothers, Ruth Berins Collier, Robert Dahl, Larry Diamond, Giuseppe Di Palma, John Entelis, Steven M. Fish, Barbara Geddes, Stephen Haggard, David Held, Guy Hermet, Samuel P. Huntington, Ken Jowitt, Robert Kaufman, Bahgat Korany, Steven Levitsky, Juan J. Linz, Arend Lijphart, Seymour Martin Lipset, Cynthia McClintock, Michael McFaul, Barrington Moore Jr., John Mueller, Guillermo O'Donnell, Marina Ottaway, Robert D. Putnam, Lucian W. Pye, Geoffrey Pridham, Adam Przeworski, Benjamin Reilly, Dankwart A. Rustow, Ghassan Salamé, Andreas Schedler, Philippe C. Schmitter, Amartya Sen, Alfred Stepan, Susan Stokes, Crawford Young, Richard Youngs, Lucan A. Way, Laurence Whitehead and Howard J. Wiarda.
35 Rustow, 'Transitions to Democracy'.
36 Higley and Burton, 'The Elite Variable in Democratic Transitions and Breakdowns'.
37 Roeder and Rothchild, *Sustainable Peace*.
38 Liu, *Transition Challenges in the Arab World*, p. 2.
39 O'Donnell et al., *Transitions from Authoritarian Rule*, p. 3.
40 See Todorov, *Les Ennemis Intimes de la Démocratie*.
41 Armijo et al., 'The Problems of Simultaneous Transitions'. See also Haggard and Kaufman, *The Political Economy of Democratic Transitions*.
42 Schedler, 'Taking Uncertainty Seriously'.
43 Liu, *Transition Challenges in the Arab World*, p. 2.
44 Jankauskas and Gudžinskas, 'Reconceptualising Transitology', p. 181.
45 For an insightful attempt at conceptualising the deep state, see O'Neil, 'The Deep State'.
46 Slater, 'The Architecture of Authoritarianism'.
47 Benkirane, 'The Alchemy of Revolution'.
48 See, for instance, Cichok, 'Transitionalism vs. Transnationalism'.
49 Jennings, 'Democratic Breakthroughs', p. 34. Examples of novel 'irregular community' are the civil society movement known as *le balai citoyen* (citizen's broom or civic broom) which led the campaign to unseat Burkina Faso's president, Blaise Compaoré, in October 2014, or the *ça suffit* (enough) campaign launched in February 2016 by Chadian organisations against President Idriss Déby.

3 Divergent and partial transitions
Lessons from Ukraine and Egypt

Kateryna Pishchikova and Richard Youngs

A core challenge to the study of democratic transitions is that countries increasingly follow very different paths of political reform. It is now a well-established observation that there is no standard or uniform template of democratisation. In recent years, the variation in reform experiences has become even more marked and self-evident. Revisiting transitions theory must involve a close look at this question of democratisation's contrasting fates. As noted throughout this book, the analytical debate has shifted in the direction of questioning the significance of overarching patterns and of emphasising how states are subject to their own unique set of contingent political trends.

The comparison between events in the 2010s in Ukraine and Egypt demonstrates in dramatic form such variation in transitions experiences; it also shows that divergent outcomes depend on a combination of mutually constitutive structural and agency factors. Since the popular protests that overthrew the regime of President Viktor Yanukovych early in 2014, Ukraine has begun implementing many democratic reforms. It is far from being a democracy of good quality and many vestiges of predatory and autocratic power dynamics remain within the country's political system. Yet, Ukraine is more democratic than it was a few years ago and a freely elected coalition government came to power and committed formally to extending the reach of democratic norms. This stands in sharp contrast to the situation in Egypt. Egypt made a dramatic breakthrough in 2011 when a popular uprising removed President Hosni Mubarak from power. After many twists and turns, the country's putative transition stands aborted. In many respects, Egypt has become more authoritarian than it was before 2011.

How is it that two of the most inspiring and often cited democratic uprisings of recent years have ended up taking such different paths? At first sight, the overthrow of largely authoritarian regimes in Egypt and Ukraine appeared to be similar phenomena. Popular uprisings triggered brutal regime crackdowns before disgraced leaders ignominiously fled the scene. In both countries, largely free and fair democratic elections followed, in each case bringing key sectors of the erstwhile opposition to power. In each case, the newly-enfranchised administrations committed to democratic reforms and launched processes to reform the constitution. Yet, beyond these similarities the two experiences diverged. In Egypt, popular frustration with the democratically elected Muslim Brotherhood government grew to the point that the military intervened to take back power, with the support of a large part of the population. The military's promise to follow a road map back to democracy was soon jettisoned and its authoritarian grip on power incrementally tightened. In Ukraine, powerful vested interests, political rivalries and conflict in the Donbas region combined to slow down promised reforms, but for now the country remains on a track of meaningful 'transition'.

In this chapter, we examine what broader lessons can be gleaned from comparing the cases of Ukraine and Egypt, and in particular their divergent paths after apparently promising regime removal in 2014 and 2011, respectively. We make this comparison here partly in an attempt to go beyond regionalist perspectives on political change that have dominated the study of transitions over the past two decades; by comparing these two cases we can ask whether there are patterns that extend beyond regional specificities.[1] We focus on several factors that are pertinent to accounting for the two countries' divergent reform paths. These include: the possibility or absence of lesson-learning from previous reform experiences; the different roles played by the army and security forces; the potential for consensus-building; the different ways in which incipient democratisation related to embedded liberal or illiberal social identities; differences in the post-revolution evolution of civic mobilisation; variations in political economy structures; and the contrasting influence of external factors.

In tune with this book's overarching theme, the chapter concludes that Ukraine and Egypt are two of the most high-profile cases calling for a reopening of transitions debates; we point to the need to conceptualise more deeply the variability of transition outcomes across geographic regions and moments of transition.

Variety of transition outcomes

The literature on the so-called 'Third Wave' of democratisation[2] defines transition as a period between the fall of the old autocratic regime and the installing of a new one, whatever that might be. The focus of the literature on transitions in Latin America and Southern Europe was mostly on the actions of key actors that come together to manage transition, for example through elite pacts. As transitions took place in other parts of the world and at different historical moments, the scenarios of transition changed and so did the crucial variables: the fall of the Soviet Union[3] was very different from the subsequent colour revolutions[4] and from the uprisings in the Arab world.[5] Criticism focused[6] on the fact that both in scholarly work and policy practice, the term 'transition' became a short hand for democratisation – an outcome that the original analyses of transitions in fact never took for granted. Indeed, the seminal work on transitions talks about four possible outcomes of transition: democracy, authoritarianism, unstable shifts between regime types and violent revolution.[7] Recognising and focusing on the multiplicity of transition scenarios and outcomes is one area in which this field of inquiry needs to develop, both in terms of empirical knowledge and theory building.

One stream of literature that tried to address the varied and uncertain nature of transition outcomes is the one that focuses on so-called hybrid regimes.[8] This conceptually blurred and broad category comprises otherwise very different countries that are neither fully democratic nor completely authoritarian.[9] Within democratisation literature, a hybrid regime is a regime that lacks crucial institutional components – e.g. a multi-party system where elections are not free or fair, protection of some civil liberties but not others or deficient rule of law. For example, Larry Diamond's typology of hybrid regimes focuses on election abuse.[10] He defines four types of hybrid regime, according to the criterion of electoral competitiveness: competitive or 'electoral' authoritarian, uncompetitive 'hegemonic' authoritarian, electoral (illiberal or minimal) democracy and 'ambiguous' regimes on the border between electoral authoritarian and electoral democratic. Following a similar rationale, Guillermo O'Donnell argued that what is missing from non-consolidated democracies is the rule of law, including public accountability and control of corruption.[11]

The hybrid regime literature helps underscore the idea that transition outcomes that may seem indeterminate and incomplete are in fact very common and persistent. It points us to the likelihood of varied outcomes resulting from what in their early stages may appear to be very similar transition experiences. Once we acknowledge that the most common result of transition is not a permanent end state of perfect liberal democracy but one of many possible varieties of hybridity, then explaining variation in political outcomes becomes more pertinent. How variation in outcomes relates to underlying structural conditions is also a question that requires greater investigation. This linkage refers to the question of what factors or pre-existing structural features set transitions on a particular course and of the ingredients for success or failure. Systematically linking these factors to particular transition outcomes remains an underexplored area of research, even though each has received a degree of attention in the literature.

The socio-economic 'preconditions' argument goes back as far as the 1960s with works by Seymour Martin Lipset and W.W. Rostow that see democracy as a by-product of industrialisation and economic growth.[12] The central idea is that citizens in wealthier countries are more likely to demand democracy, both because they see it as conducive to better economics[13] and because affluence brings a shift to post-materialist values.[14] The 'third wave' literature, with its focus on agency, paid limited attention to cultural, historical and socio-economic legacies that shape the process of regime change as well as subsequent developments in each country.[15] After the end of the Cold War, when transitions seemed to be happening anywhere and everywhere, the 'preconditions' school seemed to have fallen into oblivion. Yet, as some transitions have evidently failed while others have succeeded, the question of whether deep political reform requires certain preconditions once again seems relevant. Recent trends suggest that this remains an important component of what enables democratisation to dig deep roots: though hardly a guarantee of success, certain socio-economic structures are more conducive to democratic consolidation than others. These include a sizeable middle class and dispersed ownership of key economic assets. Indeed, more recent research redeems the importance of underlying structural factors as it shows that some democratic institutions, such as elections, come about quicker and with more ease than others, such as the rule of law.[16] Such hierarchy, according to the authors of that research, explains the most common sequencing of democratisation in which competitive elections come before other democratic components. Aiming at 'thicker' definitions of democracy, scholars working in this tradition argue that structural factors pertaining to political culture rooted in the legacies of the past represent the most influential factor in explaining long-term success or failure of democratisation.[17]

The importance of elite pacts during the transitions in Latin America and Southern Europe[18] produced a certain blindness towards the role of mass mobilisations during the transition. Although there was rich research on civic action in authoritarian regimes,[19] these were often seen as cultural–historical accounts and overlooked by comparative political science and international relations literature. Conceptually, links between civil society and political change run through a number of influential studies in social sciences.[20] Several works have argued in favour of a greater focus on contentious action in the studies of democratisation.[21] Making a more systematic link between democratisation theory and social movement studies can help account for different kinds of outcomes. Different forms and degrees of social mobilisation have become an important variable in explaining different forms and degrees of political transition.[22]

In addition, there has been insufficient attention to the role of social, religious and cultural identities in transitions. It is often assumed that those who oppose an autocrat are democrats by default, when the reality of political alliances that emerge is often more complex. Civil society is often seen as an unequivocally benign force. Although the dominant vision of mass protests tends to be skewed towards beautiful images of squares lit by hundreds of thousands of flashlights or coloured by a sea of open umbrellas, the empirical reality of mass mobilisation is complex and diverse. Protests tend to be heterogeneous in terms of their ideologies and the degree of institutionalisation of their different elements. They can include the 'bad' elements of civil society, radical groups or paramilitary organisations. Their civility, legitimacy and accountability cannot be taken for granted.[23] While there may be unity of cause among the protesters before the ousting of an autocrat, clashing identities and illiberal agendas are a hindrance to the ensuing democratisation.

By comparing two landmark cases – Ukraine and Egypt – that belong to two different geographic regions and moments of transition, we highlight here how a number of structural factors pertaining to political institutions, social and cultural identities and political economy interact in complex ways with the agency of key elites as well as that of street protesters and civic actors, leading to highly divergent transition outcomes.

Democratisation in Ukraine: fits and starts

Post-Soviet Ukraine, unlike some of its neighbours, has never fully consolidated into an authoritarian regime, yet its democratisation over the last quarter of a century has been half-hearted, democratic breakthroughs alternating with authoritarian turns. Observing some of the key elements of this process is useful for gaining an understanding of the factors that foster or hinder democratisation. The dramatic EuroMaidan protests and the transition that followed bring to light some of these elements.

Ukraine has a number of democratic institutions in place; however, their quality remains low. A number of reforms were planned in the mid-2010s, yet by most accounts the process has remained slow and superficial.[24] The country has a multi-party system and regular elections, yet political parties remain underdeveloped and serve most often as a front for personal politics. There have been several attempts to implement a constitutional reform that would establish a mixed presidential–parliamentary system to decentralise power. Yet, constitution-making in Ukraine since its independence in 1991 is more illustrative of elite struggles to (re)distribute political power than of a genuine reform process. Ukraine went from a powerful 'super-presidential' system in the 1990s to an imperfect attempt to introduce a presidential–parliamentary system in 2005 that was repealed in 2010 by President Yanukovych but reinstated in 2014 following the EuroMaidan revolution.[25] This process remains incomplete.

The so-called EuroMaidan protests, which lasted for three months in late 2013–early 2014, were initially provoked by the government's decision not to sign the Association Agreement with the European Union. Yet the uprisings quickly developed into a large-scale movement against the authoritarian and corrupt politics of President Yanukovych. Elected in a clean but tight election in 2010, Yanukovych quickly moved to centralise his power. In addition to repealing the constitutional amendments and bringing back the presidential system, he passed a number of by-laws that gave him wide unilateral powers to hire and fire executive branch officials, as well as appoint to law enforcement posts without the parliament's approval and indirectly influence judicial appointments. He strengthened his Party of Regions that came to dominate the majority of central and regional posts and the executive agencies. In fact, he became the first Ukrainian president to be backed by a strong political party: his control over the legislature – unlike that of his predecessors – was not based on bargaining and coalition-building but on his party's outright dominance.[26] Yanukovych's grip on the parliament was indeed remarkable. During the 3 months of the Euro-Maidan protests, attempts at reaching a compromise through parliamentary voting were consistently blocked by the pro-President's majority. Moreover, a series of undemocratic laws that were to criminalise the ongoing protests were voted for despite the opposition's attempts at blocking them. The President retained control over his MPs until only a few hours before his hasty departure late on 21 February 2014.

Here lies an important difference between the Orange Revolution of 2004 and the EuroMaidan revolution. While the former produced a political bargain that was agreed by all key players under pressure from the protesters, the latter escalated into a violent stand-off that came to an abrupt end when the President secretly fled the country – reportedly after realising that the police were no longer going to protect him from the protesters' rage. This meant that no political force, in or outside of the parliament, could claim to have contributed to resolving the crisis. While the pro-Presidential forces – despite jumping ship the morning after and putting the blame for the violence squarely on the fugitive President's shoulders – were fully implicated in the crisis, the opposition parties were discredited for not having been able to effectively represent the protesters in the parliament and to bring about change through political means. The parliament was delegitimised and needed a fresh start, something that the parliamentary election in October 2014 delivered only in part.

Paradoxically, Yanukovych's departure gave a boost to the country's oligarchs who could re-engage with the well-tried strategy of safeguarding their economic interests through the corrupt allocation of administrative posts in exchange for political support.[27] Political parties in Ukraine remain relatively underdeveloped and highly personalised. While electoral politics may be polarised, the behind-the-scenes alliances are not. Although electoral turnover is common in Ukraine, the personalities and interests represented in parliament have remained the same over the past two decades.[28] Indeed, the majority in the post-EuroMaidan parliament are veterans of post-Soviet politics and there are only a few new faces.[29] The reform-minded 'fresh blood' MPs report feeling a besieged minority and frustrations over not being able to deliver significant change.

After the EuroMaidan, there was a partial leadership change with the new president and a number of new appointments to top positions. None of these figures were new to politics, however. The subsequent president Petro Poroshenko had been in politics since the late 1990s, and was in fact one of the co-founders of the Party of Regions (the party of the ousted president Yanukovych). Other younger faces, like the head of the National Defence and Security Council Oleksandr Turchynov or Prime Minister Arseniy Yatsenyuk, arguably represented a different generation but were nonetheless well-embedded in the old party structures. It remains to be seen whether in the medium- to long-term the pressure for change from society will be strong enough to push the political elite towards different ways of conducting politics. The governing coalition in the post-EuroMaidan parliament remained fragile. It comprised several competing parties and voting was often an occasion for intra-faction bargaining, the outcome of which seemed to be the continued impunity promised in exchange for political loyalty.[30] Anti-corruption cases continued to be used for elite infighting and not for an impartial cleansing of politics. In the context of secret pacts and impunity concessions, no leader had the credibility or the freedom to pursue genuine reform. In this sense, pluralism and competition become a hindrance rather than an enabling factor, a curse not a blessing.[31]

What was new according to some accounts, however, was the nature of citizen mobilisation, both during and after the EuroMaidan.[32] Civil society in Ukraine has come a long way since the early 1990s, and especially in the aftermath of the EuroMaidan. Although both the Orange Revolution of 2004 and the EuroMaidan of 2014 have been central to ousting corrupt and increasingly authoritarian leaders, there are crucial differences between these two mobilisation cycles. The so-called EuroMaidan followed a different pattern of mobilisation, had much larger numbers of protesters and lasted longer. It was characterised by an unprecedented persistence and remarkable self-organisation, quite uncommon for a post-Soviet mass mobilisation. Subsequently a lively volunteer movement has emerged throughout the country that is active in dealing with the consequences of state violence during the Euromaidan, and in providing assistance to the military and civilians engaged in and affected by the ongoing conflict in Donbas.

Opposition parties were following the protesters rather than leading them; in fact, the protests came at a time when opposition parties were failing to mobilise the electorate. During the parliamentary election in 2012, opposition organised protests did not attract a large following. Indeed, as many as ninety-two per cent of the EuroMaidan protesters were not affiliated to or mobilised by any political organisation.[33] This is in stark contrast to the Orange Revolution that was planned well ahead of time and with the close involvement of the opposition candidate Victor Yushchenko.

A single, most reported sentiment after the EuroMaidan was the fear that the mistakes of the Orange Revolution would be repeated.[34] This awareness in civil society of the need to invest in the post-revolutionary phase meant that civic initiatives have had much more follow through than during the previous protests. By way of comparison, the much-heralded *Pora* youth movement that had done the bulk of the mobilisation and organisation during the Orange Revolution split up not long after the events and has played no significant role either as a movement or as a political force in the past decade. The EuroMaidan, on the other hand, produced or helped consolidate a number of initiatives that have become even more active since, from independent media projects, to volunteer initiatives and pro-reform civic platforms. It is too early to tell whether any of these will have a tangible impact on Ukraine's politics but it is already clear that civil society actors are working harder than ever to institutionalise their activities and make them sustainable over time. Civil society organisations have certainly received a boost from the EuroMaidan experience and their learning curve has been impressive.

New coalitions for reform emerged in the aftermath of the protests and there were experiments in new mechanisms for cooperation between civil and political society. The protest mood remained high in the country. Again, this is different from the Orange Revolution, which produced no substantive follow-up either by civil society or by political groups. In addition, unlike the Orange Revolution, EuroMaidan was not confined to the capital but spread to become a nationwide phenomenon. In mid-January 2014, after another round of police violence and the failure of the opposition to pass an amnesty law for those detained during earlier clashes with the police, the protests spread to the regions. A number of smaller 'Maidans' sprang up. The buildings of regional authorities were occupied throughout the country.[35] Disillusionment with Yanukovych's rule, his refusal to open a real dialogue with society and the violence against the protesters all contributed to the spread of protests. The scale of violence and intimidation and the number of victims were unprecedented in Ukraine's recent history. The high human cost put an end to any remaining apathy and cynicism on the part of Ukrainian citizens, forging an understanding that things could not go back to 'business as usual'.

The EuroMaidan agenda evolved during the three months of protests from being a narrow foreign policy issue (Association Agreement with the European Union) to include domestic grievances, most importantly discontent with corruption and the lack of the rule of law. Although President Yanukovych's departure became one of the key demands after he went too far in trying to quash the protests, the overall EuroMaidan agenda was about deep systemic transformation rather than simply a change of leadership. This was a precious development given the risk of cultural and regional identities and agendas hijacking the scene. It emerged as a basis for coalition-building and reconciliation politics but it also remains very fragile. The subsequent socio-economic crisis[36] and the ongoing armed conflict in parts of Donbas gave a boost to identity politics and sidelined the debates on structural reform. This raises concerns about further radicalisation of society and heightens the risk of people taking to the streets again but in a more confrontational fashion this time. It also privileges more radical and populist parties.

Violence during the revolutionary phase coupled with armed conflict gave space and purpose to civic groups that are neither civil nor liberal. The results of both the presidential election in May 2014 and the parliamentary vote in October of the same year show that radical parties do not have a large following. The poster child of the anti-Kyiv propaganda, the ultra-right wing Right Sector, never made the threshold for entering parliament, taking less than one per cent of the votes. The more moderate nationalist *Svoboda* party, despite its high visibility during the EuroMaidan, got fewer votes (below 5 per cent) than it had done during the previous election in 2012. These are good counter-arguments to rebut those who portray the 2014–2016 years of Ukraine's politics as a 'fascist' or 'radical nationalist' coup. They are no guarantee, however, against centrifugal forces taking over Ukraine's politics in the future.

An important element that may help load the dice in favour of further democratisation is the cumulative effect of external democracy support activities in Ukraine that have been generous[37] and continuous, as they have never faced any political resistance from the country's power holders. Numerous criticisms of these efforts notwithstanding,[38] they helped create a constituency and a set of policy frameworks that are important to further democratisation. At the same time, however, the growing 'Ukraine fatigue' within United States' policy circles and disagreements within the European Union over an appropriate Ukraine policy risk undermining these modest achievements. Ironically, while the change in the region's geopolitics requires an upgraded and clear strategy on the part of Western countries, they seem to be moving towards a less ambitious low-common-denominator approach. Therefore, while a number of domestic features may be favourable to further democratisation, international factors may be producing the opposite effect.

It is too early to say whether post-EuroMaidan Ukraine will make any progress in strengthening and democratising its institutions, improving their accountability and establishing the rule of law. What is important for our discussion here is the evolutionary component and the mutually constitutive relationship between state and society, between political elites and civic activists. The early lesson from Euromaidan is that Ukrainian society may be becoming a force and an actor in its own right. This will certainly lead to further transformations in the underlying 'hybrid' political structure. Whether these will come about in response to more protest events or through gradual reform, or both, remains to be seen.

Egypt: back to square one?

Egypt's 2011 revolution has not led to democratisation. For the moment, it is clear that powerful dynamics of authoritarianism have reasserted themselves. Transition appears to have been aborted. Egypt provides a sobering lesson in how precipitously an apparent democratic breakthrough can be squandered. It requires updated analytical explanations for failed transition. Yet, many observers insist that today's Egypt is not the same as it was pre-2011. Politics, social demands, civic organisation and identities have all shifted. Consequently, Egypt's future trajectory remains difficult to predict. Popular pressure for democratisation has not completely abated, even if a climate of fear and intimidation currently discourages civic activism. The military backed regime that took power in July 2013 has taken Egypt back to a more absolute form of authoritarianism than existed under Hosni Mubarak's final years.

In the years before the 2011 revolution, the Mubarak regime had allowed a degree of political space to emerge. Semi-competitive elections were held. The Muslim Brotherhood became more prominent and embedded sociologically at community level. Civil society organisations mushroomed. A number of governance and economic reforms were tentatively implemented. Egypt was not on its way to democratic transition, but it was seen as fitting the mould of a new Arab 'liberalised autocracy'. Analysts argued that, like other Arab governments, the Mubarak regime had opened up sufficiently to depressurise social discontent without fundamentally compromising its own grip on power or dominance over decision-making. This appeared to constitute a sophisticated 'upgrading' of authoritarianism.[39] The popular revolution that ousted Mubarak in January 2011 demonstrated that this partial liberalisation had not found the key to stability and regime durability. The story of the hugely impressive social mobilisation of early 2011 is well known. What interests us here is why this failed to produce democratisation in line with so much of the transition literature.

It soon became apparent that, from Cairo, the Supreme Council of the Armed Forces (SCAF) was able to control and shape the terms of its own retreat after the ousting of Hosni Mubarak. Throughout 2011, the army enhanced its own executive powers. While it formally retained a commitment to democratisation, the military piloted the transition in an increasingly opaque fashion. Many concluded that Egypt had suffered a soft coup, the army gaining power in return for pushing Mubarak out. They feared an encroaching 'Mubarakism without Mubarak'. Over 10,000 people were sent to military tribunals in the months following Mubarak's toppling. Extra-judicial killings dramatically increased in number. The SCAF seemed keen to extract itself from everyday politics but would not fully subordinate itself to a civilian administration. In a complex, three-player game between the army, the Islamists and the liberals, no single player was able to visibly advance the agenda in their desired direction against the combination of the other two.

Mounting frustration with SCAF restrictions and reform delays led to street protests and violent reprisals. As the dust cleared from these, the Muslim Brotherhood's political party, Freedom and Justice (FJP), gained a clear victory in the first round of parliamentary elections. It was followed by the Salafi al-Nour party in a strong second position. As a result of another bout of protests, presidential elections were brought forward to May 2012. The SCAF had opted for the route of completing a constitution before elections, but now the poll was held prior to the constitution being finished, leaving it uncertain what people were actually voting for. However, the elections produced a major breakthrough. After days of high drama, during which the SCAF withheld election results in an effort to shoehorn in its own candidate, the Brotherhood's Mohamed Morsi was declared victor. The SCAF handed power to the country's first freely elected civilian leader. Morsi sacked the senior SCAF leadership and reduced the army's powers over parliament and the executive.

While transition was back on track, divisions ran deep. The SCAF had suspended parliament before the elections; now there was the question of when new parliamentary polls would be held and whether the Muslim Brotherhood would regain its majority. Former regime personnel of the 'deep state' remained in place, deliberating on how far to accept the remit of the new president. Morsi appointed a largely technocratic government, with few party militants. One expert has labelled the new Egypt an 'officers' republic' as senior army officials in practice retained the 'guardianship' over the deep state and economy that they had enjoyed under Mubarak.[40]

In a battle with these forces, Morsi availed himself of draconian, centralised powers. Liberals walked out of constitutional talks as religious clauses were discussed. Ironically, it was now the liberals who were not fully engaged in the democratic process. Morsi gave himself sweeping new powers over judicial review at the end of 2012. The constitution was then finalised in a matter of days and put quickly to the vote. The document centralised presidential powers and protected the army's position. Liberals opposed the document, and polarisation deepened after its approval. The Muslim Brotherhood insisted it would accept the full range of citizenship and minority rights; doubts remained among liberals as to whether it would indeed do so in practice. The National Salvation Front formed in November 2012 to coalesce opposition forces; it decided to boycott parliamentary elections. Morsi initiated a national dialogue to bring the constitution's opponents back on board through concessions. However, after further lethal protests in early 2013 Morsi moved closer to the army, to the chagrin of protestors, who were now even less willing to accept the new constitution. Notable experts saw Egypt's danger not so much in Islamist illiberalism as a familiar 'dominant party over-reach' that had blighted transitions around the world.[41]

Indeed, in a dramatic turnaround of alliances, it was popular outrage at Morsi's appropriation of new powers that pushed the army to oust the president and reassume control of the government in July 2013 – a move that provided the most potent symbol of how far the Arab spring had struggled to meet initial expectations. Liberals were now strikingly supportive of the military intervention. The coup was the result of strong democratic checks and balances not having been created prior to elections and the adoption of a new constitution. Salafists emerged as key players as they distanced themselves from the Muslim Brotherhood and engaged with the army.

During the autumn of 2013, the army-controlled interim government gained in popularity, gradually tightened political space and pushed the Brotherhood once more to the margins, using even more repressive violence than during the Mubarak years. Liberals in the interim cabinet began to criticise more strongly draconian security provisions and new laws restricting both the right of assembly and civil society support. The United States and European governments criticised these measures yet also intensified their security cooperation with Egypt, signed new investment and energy contracts, released economic and military aid to the regime and pulled back from their engagement with the Muslim Brotherhood. Western governments had over-indulged Morsi, and were now over-indulging the new ruler, General Abdelfattah al Sisi. Western powers insisted their engagement was aimed at building bridges in order to keep the transition on track; but by now any meaningful democracy support had dried up. Saudi Arabia pumped in over twenty billion dollars, with other Gulf nations also supporting al Sisi generously.

The new constitution that was adopted by way of a referendum held in January 2014 gave increased powers to the army and elements of the judiciary that supported the coup, but reduced the role of parliament. Conversely, the document removed restrictions on personal status rights introduced by the Muslim Brotherhood in the 2012 constitution and enhanced human and especially gender rights protection. It also banned religion-based political activity, to the detriment even of the Salafists who supported the military's removal of President Morsi.

In May 2014, General al Sisi was elected with ninety-six per cent of the vote in a virtually uncontested presidential election. After he assumed the presidency, the new regime clamped down brutally with tragic loss of life against opposition protests and then moved to outlaw more comprehensively the Muslim Brotherhood. While the new constitution contained formal advances in rights, critics noted that in practice the state was by now using less restrained repression. Prominent human rights activists were arrested in December 2014. There was an increase in violent attacks, attributed to jihadists. For a while it remained uncertain whether Egypt was witnessing a reconstitution of the old authoritarianism or the painful embedding of a semi-competitive polity. The army and al Sisi talked of a 'road map' back to democracy and insisted they had intervened to safeguard the spirit of the 2011 revolution from the Muslim Brotherhood's usurping of liberalism. However, during 2014 and 2015 al Sisi incrementally narrowed the political space through draconian new laws restricting protests and civil society activities. The regime imprisoned thousands of Muslim Brotherhood members. Over 10,000 people were arrested on terrorism charges as the regime reverted to increasingly brutal tactics in a vain effort to contain a jihadist uprising. The government attempted harsh security clampdowns against radical groups in the Sinai, with heavy loss of life and little strategic effectiveness. Parliamentary elections were pushed back into 2015 and, when they were held, were a highly controlled farce that garnered an extremely low turnout.

Notwithstanding the return of authoritarianism, Egypt has undoubtedly changed in ways that mean it has not reverted to pre-2011 conditions. Society is patently less deferential. Religious identity is itself defined and framed in less hierarchical terms.[42] Economic actors are more acutely aware of how urgently Egypt needs dispersed market power to create wealth, and that unreconstituted statist dirigisme has failed to foster balanced economic development. The international community has been weak but it was not as willing to overlook the most serious and egregious human rights abuses as it was before 2011.

Ukraine and Egypt: explaining the differences

Although Ukraine and Egypt exhibit self-evident differences, there are valuable lessons that can be drawn from their contrasting experiences of transition. There are a number of factors that help explain the two countries' different transition outcomes.

The value of second attempts

Ukraine's 2004 Orange revolution was squandered. It failed to generate sustained democratic reform, producing instead endless bickering by the warring factions in power and paving the way for the electoral comeback of Victor Yanukovych. This has taught a powerful lesson to the reform-minded politicians, civic activists and the general public about the need for deep institutional change. Although most analysis has concentrated on the failures of the Orange Revolution, it also provided civic activists and society at large with important lessons about the need to consolidate the protest's gains and to keep up the pressure for reform, transparency and accountability. One could speak of a learning curve that was absent in Egypt as its civic actors had no experience of managing a political transition of any kind.

Egypt had no such recent experience to draw from: civic activists were not able to see how quickly the spirit of the revolution could subside; reformers from different factions could not see how their failure to compromise with each other would allow the forces of autocracy to regain the ascendancy; and liberals were too easily fooled into thinking that the army intervened in 2013 to protect liberalism from the Islamists rather than to quash all forms of open debate per se. Egyptian protesters did not invest enough into channelling the protest energy into institutionalised politics: their role in elections, in building political parties and in constitution-writing could have been greater. They failed to engage with the political process from within, sticking to street protests as a strategy instead.[43] The pre-2011 mass mobilisation experience in Egypt, although substantive, was limited to 'street politics' with protests being an outlet for citizen anger without further occasion to engage with political institutions.[44]

Political competition and alliance-building

In Ukraine, more than two decades of competitive politics seem to have produced a relatively resilient dynamic: the authoritarian turn by President Yanukovych had only lasted 3 years before the EuroMaidan took place. Yanukovych's departure was as abrupt as his rule seemed solid just days before that. His miscalculations were as much the reason for this as a number of structural features of the Ukrainian polity whose geography, economy and regional identities all preclude a stable centralisation of power. The immediate consensus by all political players after the removal of Yanukovych – not necessarily out of a genuine commitment to democracy – was that power centralisation was not acceptable. Ironically, this was in many ways a reinstatement of the post-Soviet status quo, whereby political competition is instrumental to protecting vested interests. Complex power distribution promotes power-sharing arrangements. Such political pluralism is both a safeguard against authoritarian backsliding and a major obstacle to genuine reform.

In Egypt, polarisation between Islamists and secularists militated against classical patterns of alliance-building and pacts. Failed democratisation became an almost self-fulfilling prophecy. President Morsi insisted he needed to force through constitutional changes and other reforms because the 'deep state' was aligned against him and determined to thwart his democratic intentions. Yet the more he sidelined inclusive processes, the stronger that opposition to him became. Real power-sharing was not accepted by any of the key actors – the military, Islamists or liberals – for different reasons but with the same tragic outcome. Because each key actor was highly suspicious of the others, Egyptian politics quickly became a zero-sum game, wherein whoever gets a chance engages in a fierce (and often illiberal) fight with the opponents, who are expected to do the same, if given a chance.

Economic structures

In Egypt, previous economic liberalisation under the Mubarak regime had empowered state cronies and vested interests rather than a genuinely independent and pro-democratic private sector. The army retained control of large sectors of the economy. There was no strong pressure for democratic reforms from the business sector. In Ukraine, a key factor was that powerful economic interests – the country's infamous oligarchs, in particular – withdrew support from the Yanukovych regime and believed some form of transition would help them protect their interests more effectively. Ukraine's oligarchs may not be democrats, but they compete against each other and require some form of open market structure. This is very different to the way that Egypt's far more paternalistic power dynamics pervade economic activity.

Liberal versus illiberal identities

While civic protestors in both Ukraine and Egypt agitated for democracy, the two uprisings were underlain by very different debates about identities. For Ukrainian protestors, democratic transition was an integral part of forging a more European and liberal identity for the country. This was not the case in Egypt. The Muslim Brotherhood adhered to a very partial or illiberal vision of democracy and fell into the temptation of trying to colonise rather than democratise the state.[45] While the Muslim Brotherhood moved towards more a moderate position in order to protect itself during Mubarak's rule, after 2011 it adopted an increasingly illiberal position in order to satisfy its conservative electorate. It did not make the switch from social movement to fully recognised, professional political party well. As it now suffers acute repression, the movement faces a crucial test. Egypt is unlikely to retain any degree of hybrid political openness without moderate Islamists having some form of political presence or representation.

In Egypt, liberalism and democracy increasingly collided in a way that was not the case in Ukraine. This explains why most self-defined liberals supported the army's coup in 2013: they believed democracy needed to be sacrificed in order to rescue liberalism. Egypt's 'deep state' was anxious and non-committal, weighing the shifting alliances and power re-alignments until it felt that decisive steps needed to be taken against the Morsi administration. The international community was equivocal in its reaction to the 2013 coup. The illiberal forces in Ukraine, on the other hand, despite retaining high visibility, did not manage to secure a decisive presence in the country's power structures. Although they remain a polarising element and may certainly perform better in future elections (indeed, the local elections in October 2015 sounded some alarm bells), they do not pose a direct threat to the country's democratisation at the time of writing.

The experience of violence by the protesters is crucial in both cases. A direct experience with violence raises the stakes, making protesters much less tolerant or open to compromise. It creates the space and a sense of purpose for more radical groups that would otherwise remain on the margins. It also 'normalises' moments of incivility as a necessary evil. Although inevitable in a violent revolutionary scenario, all these tendencies are inimical to democracy in the long run. This is the reason why reconciliation is extremely important in the post-revolutionary phase – something both countries failed to deliver. Although the situation in Ukraine is no doubt more democratic than in Egypt, an almost deliberate failure to promote reconciliatory politics coupled with the loss of territorial integrity and an ongoing armed conflict have planted time bombs that may blow the country's tentative achievements to pieces, should the overall economic, social or geopolitical situation take a turn for the worse.

Strong versus weak armed forces

The unique history, embedded power and prestige of the Egyptian military gave authoritarian forces significant leeway. In the 2011 revolution, the role of senior army figures was instrumental in convincing president Mubarak to step down. Thereafter they exerted significant control over the incipient transition. The army was willing to allow genuine political competition to the extent of allowing the Muslim Brotherhood to take power. In all this, it never lost its power, its alliance-building influence or its legitimacy with a large part of the Egyptian population. This gave al Sisi a huge margin for manoeuvre when the army intervened in 2013, allowing him sufficient support to re-establish strong autocratic structures before any unease among the wider population was stirred. In Ukraine, the armed forces were weak and did not play any significant political role. The military did not intervene during the EuroMaidan. The President's coercive power relied on small but cohesive special forces, such as the riot police. They were an effective instrument of protest oppression during the stand-off with protesters but never amounted to an autonomous political force. If anything, because of the violence, the Ministry of Interior was largely discredited after the events.

International factors

While international factors may not have been primary variables in explaining transition outcomes in Ukraine and Egypt, they were relevant. The policies of external actors reinforced transition dynamics at some moments, while sapping such momentum at others. Western governments were less cautious about supporting transition in Ukraine than in Egypt. Even in Ukraine, their support for transition was held back by geostrategic and domestic concerns, and this ambivalence played into the persistent features of hybridity in the country. Since 2013, the European Union and the United States have offered a wide range of support to Ukraine's democratic transition, and of greater depth than they provided after the 2004 Orange Revolution. Some have judged a democratic Ukraine to be essential to limiting Russia's geopolitical influence, while others felt that a proactive stance in Ukraine may create additional tensions in the region, and unnecessarily so. Russia's increasingly assertive policies are explicitly aimed at manipulating the political process in Ukraine through a range of tactics that go beyond the conflict in Donbas. Unlike during the first two decades after the end of the Cold War, international influences in Ukraine today push the country in two opposite directions. For some reformers in Ukraine this is reason to intensify the pace of democratic transition; for others, it is a scenario that encourages reforms to be frustrated and diluted.

In Egypt, geopolitical calculations have been different. Western governments supported the 2011 revolution, but only in reactive mode. Ironically, they were so keen to see an Islamist government succeed in leading a democratic transition that they were insufficiently alert to how president Morsi's centralising control was paving the way to a military coup. Even democratic reformers in Egypt did not seek the kind of close alignment with European Union rules and policies that Ukrainian reformers did. Since the 2013 coup, the United States and European Union have struggled for leverage in Egypt. They have criticised the return to autocracy, but have also increased security cooperation with the regime. And the external influences coming from Saudi Arabia and the United Arab Emirates have eased authoritarianism's return, as these countries have provided al Sisi with billions of dollars in support and active encouragement in weakening the Muslim Brotherhood. While a detailed study of international policies is beyond the scope of this chapter, it suffices to observe that contrasting external influences are another factor that help explain the variation on transition outcomes between Egypt and Ukraine.

Implications for transitology

The cases of Ukraine and Egypt have produced some of the most dramatic political events of recent years. The two countries experienced stirring democratic breakthroughs, in which social protests drove out corrupt and authoritarian regimes. 'Tahrir' and 'Maidan' have become perhaps the two most globally resonant emblems of a new type of democratic activism that flows from broad-based social movements. The two countries' trajectories are of particular significance to transitions analysis. This is because these two cases of dramatic breakthrough happened despite widespread predictions that such change was highly unlikely. They took place against an analytical background of work that focused more on explaining the apparent resilience of liberalised authoritarianism or unconsolidated democracy. Hence, in the aftermath of such dramatic, unexpected movements, broader analytical reflections come into view.

Events in Ukraine and Egypt are far from having run their course and outcomes are still highly uncertain. Ukraine is making tentative steps down the path of transition, albeit with significant resistance and limitations to deep structural change, while Egypt appears to be heading towards more repressive autocracy. In the next phase, it is possible that the situations could reverse. Ukraine may slip backwards, as conflict simmers and the opponents of reform regain firmer footing; and in Egypt, civil society may reawaken and begin to push back against the brutality of the regime. Even if such a dramatic reversal were to occur, it would in a sense validate our central point: namely, that the courses taken by transitions are highly *varied* and *changeable*, rather than unfolding in accordance with any expected, uniform and linear script. With that caveat, we offer the following tentative thoughts on how our comparison relates to this book's overarching themes.

First, *authoritarian regimes are stable until they are not*. It is striking that so few people predicted the sudden emergence of social revolts – either in Ukraine during the period in which Viktor Yanukovych was incrementally tightening non-democratic levers of control, or in Egypt from 2005. This should caution us in future to take greater care in making sweeping assumptions that political change is unlikely, based on surface features of regime stability.

Second, *transitions are characterised by a high degree of changeability*. Both cases discussed in this chapter clearly put political agency back at the centre of analytical explanation. Social mobilisation drove forward political opening in very different structural contexts. In the initial moments of dramatic change, in 2011 in Egypt and 2013 in Ukraine, agency seemed to outweigh structural variation as a variable. Compared to the classics of transitology,[46] recent revolutions demand an opening up of the empirical and analytical focus from elites to other societal actors. While the focus on contentious action per se is not new, the linkages between different types of actors have been explored insufficiently.[47] Our comparison between Ukraine and Egypt shows how potent social movements and protests were relative to elite pacts, but it also suggests that the ultimate impact of such social and political agency can be very different. Recent evidence from these two countries reinforces the observation that incipient transitions are eminently reversible. This chapter has unpacked how in each of our two cases a combination of structural and agency impediments continues to militate against fully successful democratisation. In explaining the divergence of outcomes in what started out as two similar citizen-led democratic breakthroughs, our two cases suggest the need for more focus on the mutually constitutive relationship between the state and society, between elites and civic activists.

A generalisable lesson might be that the changeability in transitions is greater today than in previous periods – in both 'forward' and 'reverse' directions. Also, where liberalism precedes democratisation, the outcome of transition is likely to be different from cases where it does not. Here, our case studies give empirical backing to some of Philippe Schmitter's observations in Chapter 10: that compared to the periods of previous waves of transition, there is today a greater multiplicity of actors to be taken into account, a wider range and shifting patterns of identities, broader sets of international linkages and more uncertainty and volatility which diminishes actors' chances of finding expression through political party systems. Together, these elements of fluidity offer potential for change and a challenge to predictability, while also cutting across familiar patterns of consolidation. Our two case studies suggest that there are both more potent enabling factors but also more confining variables militating against significant movement towards consolidation.

Third, *transitions can move in different directions.* At present it seems that the direction of change in Ukraine is towards deeper democratisation while the dominant dynamic in Egypt is one of deeper authoritarian control. Ukraine's degree of pluralism before the EuroMaidan revolution was greater than Egypt's before the 2011 revolution – even though both qualified as 'hybrid' or 'weak authoritarian' regimes. In Egypt, the Mubarak regime allowed a degree of opening before nervously seeking to reverse such modest liberalisation; this raised and then crushed citizen's expectations – the explosive combination that triggered mass protests. Both countries have fluctuated in 'forward' and 'reverse' directions for a decade now. The balance of political forces in Ukraine is likely to ensure that this changeability continues there. While authoritarianism currently appears to have firmly re-established itself in Egypt, some civic legacy of the 2011 revolution remains, suggesting that this country's political structures may also not be entirely set in stone.

Finally, *structural changes are relevant to explaining contrasting degrees of democratisation.* The two cases shed light on the limits of political competition and pluralism in a system where the political rules are not taken for granted and serve as instruments of power. Despite all the dramatic social mobilisation and upheavals and, in response, the violent attempts to reassert autocratic control, both countries have retained key features of an autocratic regime and predatory politics, although to a very different degree. In Ukraine, revolutionary, bottom-up pressure has led to political dynamics based more on elite trade-offs and negotiated concessions. These dynamics continue to forestall far-reaching change to the 'rules of the game', even as they also serve to keep some elements of pluralism and prospects for reform alive. In Egypt, on the other hand, the promptness with which authoritarianism has reasserted itself in a new guise shows how such deep structures are difficult to dislodge.

In summary, in examining transitions we should be alert to combinations of change and continuity: political events may take very different turns across different countries, and move back and forwards in moments of high drama, while underlying structures endure and some of the challenges related to hybrid regimes present common concerns across countries whose superficial politics take very different courses.

Notes

1. Mohammad-Mahmoud Ould Mohamedou and Timothy Sisk, Chapter 2 of this book.
2. Huntington, *The Third Wave*.
3. Beissinger, *Nationalist Mobilisation and the Collapse of the Soviet State*.
4. Kalandadze and Orenstein, 'Electoral Protests and Democratisation'.
5. Stepan and Linz, 'Democratisation Theory and the "Arab Spring"'.
6. Carothers, 'End of the Transition Paradigm'.
7. O'Donnell *et al.*, *Transitions from Authoritarian Rule*, p. 3.
8. Levitsky and Way, *Competitive Authoritarianism*; Mikael Wigell, 'Mapping "Hybrid Regimes"'.
9. Morlino, *Changes for Democracy*.
10. Diamond, 'Elections Without Democracy'.

11 O'Donnell, 'Why the Rule-of-Law Matters' in Diamond and Morlino, *Assessing the Quality of Democracy*, pp. 3–17.
12 Lipset, *Political Man*; Rostow, *The Stages of Economic Growth*.
13 Rueschemeyer et al., *Capitalist Development and Democracy*.
14 Inglehart and Welzel, *Modernisation, Cultural Change and Democracy*.
15 Grugel and Bishop, *Democratisation*.
16 Møller and Skaaning, 'Regime Types and Democratic Sequencing'.
17 Ekiert et al., 'Democracy in the Post-Communist World'.
18 O'Donnell et al., *Transitions from Authoritarian Rule*; Karl, 'Dilemmas of Democratization in Latin America'.
19 See for example, Beissinger, *Nationalist Mobilisation and the Collapse of the Soviet State,* on the former Soviet Union; on Asia, Boudreau, *Resisting Dictatorship*; and on the Middle East, Bayat, *Life as Politics*.
20 Keane, *The Power of the Powerless*; Keane, *Civil Society and the State*; and Tilly, *Social Movements*.
21 McAdam et al., *Dynamics of Contention*.
22 Della Porta, *Mobilising for Democracy*.
23 Chambers and Kopstein, 'Bad Civil Society'; Kaldor and Muro-Ruiz, 'Religious and Nationalist Militant Groups'.
24 Razumkov Centre, *Ukraine 2015–2016*; regular reform updates are available on the website of the National Reform Council, www.reforms.in.ua.
25 Kudelia, 'If Tomorrow Comes'.
26 Kudelia, 'The House that Yanukovych Built'.
27 On the distribution of key economic assets and competing business interests in Ukraine, see Åslund, *How Ukraine became a Market Economy and Democracy*; Kudelia, 'The Sources of Continuity and Change of Ukraine's Incomplete State'.
28 Hale, *Patronal Politics*.
29 By some counts we are talking about approximately 300 'old guard' MPs and only thirty EuroMaidan activists in the 450-seat parliament.
30 Oleksandr Holubov, 'Poroshenko's Catch-22', Carnegie Moscow Centre, 23 November 2015, available at http://carnegie.ru/commentary/2015/11/23/poroshenko-s-catch-22/im7n#.Vld3GqUjwrQ.twitter.
31 Way, *Pluralism by Default*.
32 Pishchikova and Ogryzko, 'Civic Awakening'.
33 Kyiv International Institute of Sociology, 'Maidan-2013: Who Protests, Why and For What?', poll conducted among the Maidan participants on 7–8 December 2013; and N. Shapovalova, 'Ukraine's Prodemocracy Movement', *FRIDE Commentary*, 3 February 2014, Madrid: Fride.
34 Authors' interviews.
35 Although these protests were taking place predominantly in the west and centre of the country, they spilled over into a number of provinces in the east and south, including those that had given considerable support to Yanukovych in 2010 and to his Party of Regions in 2012 (for example, the cities of Kyrovohrad, Dnipropetrovsk, Mykolaiyv and Zaporizhzhya).
36 The economy shrunk by seven per cent in 2014 and by twelve per cent in 2015 according to World Bank Updates, available at www.worldbank.org/content/dam/Worldbank/document/eca/ukraine/ua-macro-april-2015-en.pdf; UN estimates for 2015 are that eighty per cent of Ukrainians live on less than five dollars a day.
37 In the 1990s, Ukraine was the third largest recipient of bilateral aid by the United States, after Egypt and Israel. During the first two post-Soviet decades the United States government gave almost US$4 billion in technical assistance to Ukraine; democracy support programmes were a prominent, if small, part of it. The European Union, through its European Neighbourhood Policy, offered a comprehensive partnership that encompassed fostering of democratic norms and gradual reform. The European

Union assistance was more focused on government and state institutions; its distinctive approach centred on norms and standards approximation.
38 Mendelson and Glenn, *Power and Limits of NGOs*; Pishchikova, *Promoting Democracy in Postcommunist Ukraine*.
39 Two of the most cited assessments during this period were Brumberg, 'The Trap of Liberalised Autocracy' and Heydemann, 'Upgrading Authoritarianism in the Arab World'.
40 Sayigh, 'Above the State'.
41 Carothers and Brown, 'The Real Danger for Egyptian Democracy'.
42 Roy, 'There Will Be No Islamist Revolution'.
43 Brown, 'Egypt's Failed Transition'.
44 Bayat, *Life as Politics*.
45 Hamid, *The Temptations of Power*.
46 O'Donnell et al., *Transitions from Authoritarian Rule*.
47 Della Porta, *Mobilising for Democracy*.

4 Electoral transitions
Stumbling out of the gate

Pippa Norris

One of the first steps in most regime transitions following the downfall of an autocrat is to hold direct multi-party elections. It is hoped that this process will endow the new regime with legitimacy at home and abroad, strengthening its authority to rebuild fragile states and unify deeply divided societies. Elections are now a universal practice in peace-building and state-building missions, as the international community seeks to channel aid and assistance through a legitimate government. Nevertheless, electoral transitions remain fraught with danger. Some contests succeed by producing popular regimes which gradually strengthen human rights and democratic institutions, including inclusive parliaments, independent courts and stable states. Yet contentious elections can also feed social conflict and breed discontent. Moreover, many autocracies have learnt to use a series of manipulated and fraudulent elections to maintain their grip on power, containing and suppressing popular discontent behind a veneer of legitimate contests.

The most severe risks of contests failing to transition towards democracy are commonly thought to arise when attempting to organise elections under a wide range of challenging conditions, including in poor and illiterate societies with scattered rural populations that lack access to modern communications and transportation, in deeply divided states emerging from years of conflict and in countries with a long legacy of authoritarian rule and little, if any, experience of democratic practices. If transitional elections succeed, they do not, by themselves, guarantee further progress towards developing stable democratic states. Nevertheless, if elections fail, for whatever reason, then prospects for a sustainable process of democratisation fade. In this regard, they are an essential first step in any transition towards democracy despite the fact that some contests stumble and fall coming out of the gate.

The challenges associated with attempting to hold popular contests under very difficult circumstances are perhaps best illustrated by contemporary events in Afghanistan. Successive elections for the presidency, *Wolesi Jirga*, and provincial councils have been held in this country since 2004. This is despite a traditional political culture with tribal allegiances and rival forms of regional authority and elite patronage rooted in semi-feudalism; poor communications and transportation infrastructure over a vast territory; low levels of literacy and schooling (the 2013 UNDP Human Development Index ranked Afghanistan 175th out of 186 countries worldwide, and second from the bottom in terms of the Gender Inequality Index); a murky politics characterised by endemic corruption and violence; and weakly institutionalised political parties, among peoples who have lived under violent conflict for decades. In 2009, widespread complaints about ballot stuffing led the Independent Election Commission to organise a complete recount.

The second round of the 2014 presidential elections saw more than 150 reported incidents of violence on polling day. In the aftermath, the leading presidential contender, Abdullah Abdullah, demanded that the Commission cease the count mid-way through due to alleged irregularities – an event followed by mass protests, the resignation of the chief commissioner and delays in announcing the results. The results of the audit suggest that perhaps as many as two million fraudulent votes were cast out of eight million in total. In the end, a brokered power-sharing agreement resolved the outcome but this also violated the spirit of the election. A detailed study of the Afghan experience over successive elections since 2004 concluded that the process strengthened the power of ruling elites but did little to develop representative democracy.[1]

To help gain an understanding of these types of problems, and the role of elections in transitions, the first part of this chapter describes modernisation theories of democratisation that are rooted in the classic accounts of Seymour Martin Lipset. The second part considers which structural factors from the previous research literature are plausible candidates to explain why elections succeed or fail, and also how the quality of elections can best be conceptualised and operationalised. The chapter then examines the cross-national evidence to analyse the process. The conclusion summarises the main findings and considers their implications for electoral transitions from autocracy.

Modernisation and mass politics

As Mohammad-Mahmoud Ould Mohamedou and Timothy Sisk discuss in Chapter 1, the earliest approach to understanding successful transitions from autocracy and subsequent processes of democratisation is rooted in theories of developmental studies, political economy and political sociology, exemplified by the long tradition established by Seymour Martin Lipset in the mid-twentieth century.[2] The so-called 'Lipset thesis' argues that democracies (and, by extension, levels of electoral integrity) flourish best in industrialised and post-industrial societies characterised by conditions of widespread literacy and education, with a substantial affluent, professional middle class and a pluralistic range of civic associations serving as a buffer between citizens and the state.[3] The original claim by Lipset specified most simply that: 'The more well-to-do a nation, the greater the chances that it will sustain democracy'.[4]

Development consolidates democracy, Lipset theorised, by expanding access to information derived from literacy, schooling and the mass media; broadening the size of the middle classes; reducing the extremes of rural poverty; facilitating intermediary organisations such as labour unions, professional associations and voluntary organisations; and promoting the cultural values of legitimacy, moderation and social tolerance. The shift from agrarian to industrial capitalist production weakened the feudal grip of the traditional landed estates. Newly-unionised urban workers and middle class professional groups demanded access to the voting franchise and mobilised around rival parties that reflected their interests. Lipset emphasised that extreme social inequality maintained oligarchy or tyranny, while more egalitarian conditions, and in particular the swollen ranks of the middle classes, facilitated mass political participation and moderate political parties:

> Only in a wealthy society in which relatively few citizens lived in real poverty could a situation exist in which the mass of the population could intelligently participate in politics and could develop the self-restraint necessary to avoid succumbing to the appeals of irresponsible demagogues.[5]

During the 1970s, Dankwart Rustow reinforced the Lipset argument by claiming that the transition to democracy could be attributed to a predictable series of social changes accompanying economic development and societal modernisation – as predicted by indicators such as per capita energy consumption, literacy, school enrolment, urbanisation, life expectancy, infant mortality, the size of the industrial workforce, newspaper circulation and radio and television ownership.[6] The social determinism implicit in the more mechanical versions of modernisation theories has been subject to considerable criticism, especially the neglect of the role of actors, institutions, social movements and key historical events that contribute to overturning dictatorships and founding democracies. After all, middle-income nations such as Russia, Venezuela and Malaysia have experienced major problems with democracy and elections, which are not confined by any means to the world's poorest societies.

Nevertheless, following in Lipset's footsteps the relationship between wealth and democracy has, in subsequent decades, been subject to rigorous empirical inquiry. For more than half a century the association has withstood repeated empirical tests under a variety of different conditions, using cross-sectional and time-series data with a large sample of countries and years, and with increasingly sophisticated econometric models, as well as in many historical accounts of political developments occurring within particular nation states. Many studies have reported that wealth is associated with the standard indicators of democratisation, although the precise estimates of effects are sensitive to each study's choice of time period, the selection of control variables specified in causal models and the basic measurement of both democracy and economic growth.[7] Thus, the Lipset hypothesis has been confirmed by successive studies as well as in more recent work where Lipset revisited the original thesis.[8] The major challenge to the conventional wisdom has arisen from the work of Adam Przeworski, Michael Alvarez, José Antonio Cheibub and Fernando Limongi, who argue that greater economic development does not *cause* the downfall of autocracies and the initial steps towards democratisation (which arise from multiple unknown causes, such as the death of a dictator, splits in the ruling party or external invasion). However, after passing a certain threshold level, a comfortable level of economic development does *consolidate* democratic institutions and thereby serves as a buffer preventing reversions to autocracy.[9]

In a previous work, I used time-series cross-national data during the 'third wave' era since the early-1970s and compared the impact of wealth (log GDP per capita) on four alternative measures of democratisation (by Freedom House, Polity IV, Vanhanen and Przeworski *et al.*/Cheibub and Gandhi), to double-check the robustness of the relationship in well-specified models incorporating many structural controls.[10] The evidence confirmed that wealth was significantly positively associated with each measure of democracy, showing a robust relationship, as many previous studies have reported. The underlying reasons for this relationship continue to be debated but separate models testing the effects of education and literacy on democratisation displayed a particularly strong link, as Barro earlier highlighted, suggesting that societies which invest in human capital are more likely to sustain democratic regimes.[11]

Social structure and electoral integrity

Besides development, my earlier study concluded that many additional structural fixed conditions proved significant:

> Democracy was usually more probable in countries which shared an ex-British colonial legacy, in regions which had seen the spread of democracy, in states outside the Middle East, in ethnically homogeneous societies and in countries with smaller populations ...; the models explained between half and two-thirds of the variance across the comparison, suggesting a relatively good fit, although ... many outlier cases can be found among both rich autocracies and poor democracies.[12]

Do similar structural conditions determine where elections succeed and fail? Since elections are a necessary – although far from a sufficient – condition for democratisation, similar patterns can be expected to be observed. The modernisation thesis can therefore plausibly be extended for our purposes to generate a series of testable propositions about the socio-economic conditions thought to be most favourable to strengthening elections as a mode of transition. Studies of fixed constraints typically focus on wealth and income (and thus indicators of economic growth, human development and social inequality), as well as the role of physical geography (the size and location of a state), inherited colonial legacies, patterns of ethnic heterogeneity, deep-seated cultural attitudes and values and the distribution of natural resources. Conditions in each society are regarded from the modernisation perspective as largely static, or else like phenomena such as human development and political culture which are believed to evolve at a glacial pace over successive decades or even centuries.

Contemporary multi-party elections, once largely the preserve of industrialised Western nations, have spread worldwide. They are attempted today under many challenging social conditions. These include extremely poor and divided developing societies, fragile states and transitional or hybrid regimes that lack both the military control used to maintain order in fully authoritarian states on the one hand, and the shared cultural values and accumulated experience of elections found in consolidated democracies, on the other. Since 2000, all but eleven countries worldwide have held national elections, and only a handful of states such as Saudi Arabia, Qatar and Oman have never held direct parliamentary elections.[13] Popular referendums to determine constitutional issues and state secession have also become more common, such as in Montenegro (2006), South Sudan (2011) and Crimea (2014). The growth of decentralised governance has led to more contests for state and local office, and the number of contests has multiplied within the twenty-eight European Union (EU) member states due to direct elections to the European Parliament since 1979.

Therefore, one plausible theory seeking to explain the distribution of flawed and failed elections around the globe lies in structural or fixed conditions which make contests inherently risky enterprises. Sceptics highlighting the perils of elections can point to an earlier wave of institution-building, when European-style parliaments were transplanted to many African societies during the winds of change era of decolonisation, only to collapse as the military or big men usurped power.[14] As Robert Dahl noted, where the underlying conditions are highly unfavourable, it is improbable that democracy could flourish under any institutional design. By contrast, if the underlying conditions reduce the risks, then democracy is likely to take root under almost any type of constitution.[15]

Despite the plausibility of structural explanations, and the extensive body of political economy and sociological literature testing the effects of wealth and security on democratisation, surprisingly little systematic research has, by contrast, analysed the impact of structural conditions on the quality of elections. One notable exception is work by Sarah Birch which examined whether a range of socio-political conditions heightened the risks of electoral malpractice, including cross-national levels of economic development, trade dependence, foreign direct investment, corruption, social inequality and urbanisation.[16] Each of these factors can be regarded as 'structural' constraints on elections, since it is difficult to alter many of these conditions in the medium- to short-term, if at all. For example, countries cannot reinvent their histories, or easily avoid conflict and refugees flowing across their borders from neighbouring states, although obviously states attempt to accelerate economic growth and human development, with greater or lesser degrees of success. Fully specified models should therefore control for a range of structural conditions. Such accounts are most powerful in explaining long-term trajectories of political development and the general probabilities of democratisation worldwide. They are less helpful in accounting for the specific timing and particular type of short- or medium-term fluctuations in electoral integrity.

The policy implications of fixed conditions for the international community are largely the need to be strategic in prioritising the choice of country interventions, since high risks are associated with attempts to strengthen electoral integrity in the most challenging environments. A wide range of indicators have been developed by scholars and these are consolidated for analysis in the cross-national and cross-national time-series datasets assembled and distributed by the Quality of Government Institute based at the University of Gothenburg in Sweden.[17]

When analysing the cross-national evidence, it is important to consider conventional assumptions about the direction of causality in complex interactive processes. Ethnic heterogeneity and population divisions by religious, linguistic, racial and nationalist identities, for instance, are conventionally treated by researchers as enduring or 'fixed' characteristics of societies. Yet constructivist accounts emphasise that the political salience and meaning of latent ethnic identities can be either heightened or moderated by the rhetorical appeals of party leaders – and thus by the institutional incentives to mobilise either ethnic or inter-communal appeals arising from the electoral rules.[18] The physical boundaries of the nation state are regarded from the structural perspective as largely stable, even though geographic distances for trade and access to Western markets are shrunk by developments in transportation, communications and modern technologies. Similarly the mapped boundary lines of the nation state are occasionally reshaped by secession and conquest, as in Eastern Ukraine, as well as by enlargement of regional associations, such as Romania (2007) and Croatia (2013) joining the EU, and by broader processes of globalisation and cosmopolitan communications.[19] Similarly access to the production of natural resources like oil and natural gas have been transformed by technological developments, such as hydraulic fracking that has facilitated the exploitation of new areas of hydrocarbons, while regulatory policies can either mitigate or exacerbate the impact of state capture of natural resources. Factors such as a culture of corruption can also be regarded as the effect of lack of electoral accountability, as much as a cause of why contests fail.

Despite these complex issues of interpretation and the limits of the available longitudinal evidence, the effect of several long-term conditions which are genuinely independent of electoral integrity within the time-span of a specific contest – including the impact of physical geography, colonial legacies and population size – are examined using cross-national data in this study. These conditions are properly specified as fixed in the models: holding elections in some of the world's largest countries, such as India, Nigeria or Indonesia, for example, may plausibly provide more serious logistical and organisational challenges compared with contests in, say, Guatemala or Jamaica. Nevertheless, national elections per se cannot effect a country's physical geography or population size in the short-term (although even here a few notable exceptions exist, since previous secession referendums, such as in Bangladesh, Sudan and Crimea, can determine a country's contemporary national borders and electorate in subsequent contests).

Measuring perceptions of electoral integrity

For the dependent variable, this study draws primarily upon evidence of whether elections meet international standards derived from the techniques of expert surveys. These methods have been widely used in political science including in Transparency International's expert survey of perceptions of corruption,[20] the Varieties of Democracy project under development by the Institute for Good Government[21] and several expert surveys of political party ideologies and policy positions.[22] To provide comprehensive evaluations of each stage of the electoral cycle, this study utilises data from the Electoral Integrity Project expert survey on Perceptions of Electoral Integrity (PEI-2.5) covering all national elections around the globe during a twenty-four month period from mid-2012 to mid-2014, excluding micro-states (with populations below 100,000). The study selects a cross-section of electoral experts to participate in the survey, including both domestic and international respondents. The survey interviews around forty electoral experts from each country, generating a mean response rate of around twenty-eight per cent across the survey. *Electoral experts* are defined in the PEI study as political scientists (or scholars in related social science disciplines such as law, history, political economy or political sociology) who are knowledgeable on one or more of the following topics: elections, electoral systems, electoral administration, voting behaviour, public opinion, campaigns, political communications, mass media, democracy and democratisation, political parties and party systems, human rights and national politics. All these topics touch on different dimensions of the underlying concept of electoral integrity. '*Expertise*' is defined by publication of scholarly articles, books and conference papers or teaching at university level on these topics, and/or by membership and participation in professional research groups, disciplinary networks and organised sections on the above topics with organisations such as the International Political Science Association.

The instrument used for the expert survey relies upon multiple questions, not simply an overall 'pass/fail' summary judgement. Social psychological research suggests that breaking estimates into their components parts, or greater granularity, usually generates more accurate answers.[23] The forty-nine items about electoral integrity contained in the questionnaire are designed to capture expert judgments about whether specific national elections meet internationally-recognised principles and standards of elections.[24]

Economic and human development

The core Lipset thesis concerns the role of economic development (conventionally monitored by each society's per capita GDP) which is closely associated with notions of societal modernisation, including the spread of industrialisation, urbanisation and education, as well as the related role of the broader notion of human development – as measured by the United Nations Development Programme (UNDP) where longevity and education are added to the measure of per capita GDP. While it is commonly assumed that higher quality elections occur in richer nations, the empirical evidence supporting this claim is not in fact well-established. In one of the most systematic comparative analyses, Birch used multivariate models to test the impact of a series of structural variables on electoral malpractices. The study found that GDP growth was not significantly correlated with many measures of election quality (by Freedom House, the Economist Intelligence Unit and Kelley's Quality of Elections Dataset). Moreover, she also reported that growth was significantly related to her Index of Electoral Malpractices, but in a *positive* direction (suggesting that higher growth led to lower quality elections), for reasons which remain unclear.[25] Birch's study did not test the direct effects of levels of economic development on malpractices, however, to avoid problems of multi-collinearity in the models.[26] Any interpretation of the relationship also needs to consider using time-lags to partially overcome possible issues of endogeneity. Lisa Chauvet and Paul Collier reversed the relationship to test the impact of the frequency of holding elections (of any quality) on economic policies in developing countries. They reasoned that regular contests strengthened the incentive for governing parties to improve their economic performance in order to win votes and retain office. The study reported that the more frequently elections are held, the better the policies, as measured by the World Bank Country Policy and Institutional Assessments.[27]

To start to describe the comparative evidence without any controls, Figure 4.1 shows the observed correlation between contemporary levels of electoral integrity measured by the summary PEI-2.5 Index and levels of economic development lagged by 5 years (to reduce the danger of endogeneity, since the quality of elections could affect income), measured by per capita GDP (in purchasing power parity) in 2009 from the World Development Indicators. The bivariate correlation without controls displays a significant and strong relationship ($R = 0.583$, $P = 0.00$); as expected affluent post-industrial societies such as Norway, the Netherlands and Austria also have the highest quality elections according to the overall PEI-2.5 Index. By contrast, some of the poorest societies under comparison had the worst electoral performance, including Cambodia, Djibouti and the Democratic Republic of Congo. Moreover, the results proved consistent when the sub-components of the PEI survey were broken down further, revealing that wealth was significantly correlated (at the conventional 0.05 level) with all the indicators, with the exception of district boundaries (see Table 4.1).

Nevertheless, the best fit line displayed in Figure 4.1 is not linear but quadratic, *suggesting that a stepped shift occurs in the integrity of elections once a certain minimum level of moderate economic development is reached.* The estimate suggests that integrity is most likely once countries achieve a per capita income of roughly $15,000 or more (in constant 2005 dollars). Thus, it can also be observed that many contests which experts rated positively as 'high integrity' (ranked in the top thirds of the PEI index) showed a wide scatter across the top oval. Therefore, contests in many middle-income nations scored well, such as Chile, Argentina and Lithuania, all rated by experts as similar or better than the quality of elections in the United States. At the same time another cluster of

Electoral transitions 57

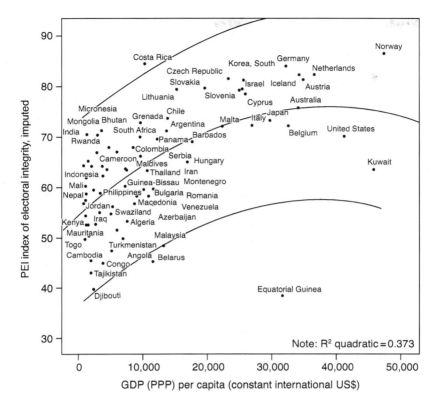

Figure 4.1 Electoral integrity and wealth (sources: PEI Electoral Integrity Index, Electoral Integrity Project 2014 – expert survey of Perceptions of Electoral Integrity, (PEI-2.5); per capita GDP in purchasing power parity (PPP) in 2009 from the World Development Indicators included in the Quality of Government Cross-national Dataset www.qog.pol.gu.se/data/).

poorer countries can be observed with per capita income below $15,000 (in the bottom oval) and in this category societies varied sharply in the quality of their elections, ranging from low income Tajikistan and Djibouti with flawed contests, to poor countries such as Mali, Bhutan and Nepal, which had elections rated more highly by experts. The observational pattern suggests there is a link – as expected, richer nations tend to have better quality elections – but the relationship is both a stepped shift once a minimal level of wealth is reached in a society and several exceptions such as Equatorial Guinea and Kuwait show that the links are far from deterministic. In this regard, the observed relationship is closer to the Alvarez *et al.*, version of modernisation theory rather than the classic Lipset thesis.[28] In subsequent ordinary least squares (OLS) multivariate regression analysis, per capita GDP is transformed by estimating the square root in order to model the stepped shift more accurately.

58 P. Norris

To test the Lipset thesis further, the UNDP's Human Development Index arguably provides a superior measure of societal modernisation, by combining wealth, longevity and education. Reflecting Amartya Sen's notion of human development, this index monitors the quality of people's lives, not simply the success of the economy.[29] The series of annual UNDP Human Development Reports have convincingly demonstrated that many societies, such as Equatorial Guinea and Iraq, with moderate levels of median income at national level (derived from natural resources) lag behind in relative levels of schooling, longevity and living conditions.[30] Education, in particular, provides cognitive skills, knowledge and cultural attitudes which are widely regarded as vital for citizen's informed choices and active participation in civic affairs. The comparison observed in Figure 4.2, without controls, confirms that the Human Development Index is more strongly correlated with the quality of elections than GDP alone,

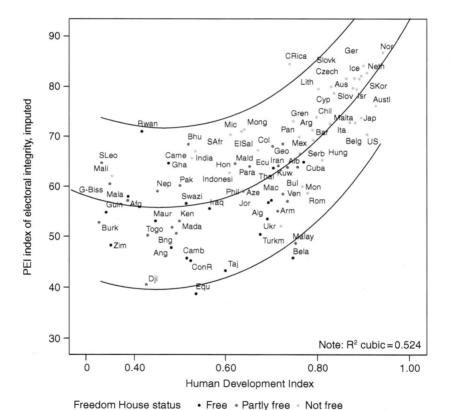

Figure 4.2 Electoral integrity and human development (sources: PEI Electoral Integrity Index, Electoral Integrity Project 2014 – expert survey of Perceptions of Electoral Integrity, (PEI-2.5); Human Development Index 2009 (combining income, longevity and education) from UNDP included in the Quality of Government Cross-national Dataset www.qog.pol.gu.se/data/).

although again contrasts can be observed between low development societies such as Rwanda and Bhutan, with relatively positive scores in the quality of elections, and Djibouti and Angola, which perform poorly. The cubic line rather than a linear relationship provides the best overall fit, suggesting a far from straightforward progressive shift. Table 4.1 displays strong and significant correlations across all eleven sub-components of the electoral cycle.

Natural resources and corruption

There are a few cases which can be observed as clear outliers in the relationship between wealth and electoral integrity – most notably oil-rich (but human development poor) Equatorial Guinea. The well-known 'resource curse' is another related structural explanation: countries with GDP highly dependent upon abundant reserves of non-renewable mineral resources, such as Kuwaiti oil, Democratic Republic of Congo gold or Sierra Leone diamonds, usually produce less diversified and less competitive economies, more income inequality with less investment in social policies that build human capital and a heightened danger of state capture and rent-seeking by ruling elites.[31] Lootable natural resources which can be smuggled across borders, such as diamonds, rare minerals, ivory, cocaine and heroin, are making countries particularly vulnerable to criminal cartels, civil war, insurgency and rebellion.[32] Assessing the degree to which an economy is dependent upon natural resources is not easy, however, especially given the black market trade in illicit goods. To measure the distribution of natural resources, this study draws upon the World Bank's measure of total natural resources rents for 2012 (percentage of GDP), where these rents are the sum of oil, natural gas, coal, minerals and forest. Given the unequal distribution of resources across countries, the measure is logged for a better linear fit. 'Rents' are estimated as the difference between the value of production of these resources at world prices and the total costs of production. 'Rentier states' are those like Saudi Arabia which derive all or a substantial portion of their national revenues from the rent of indigenous resources to external clients.

Figure 4.3 shows that, without any prior controls for the wealth of a country, there is only a strong negative correlation ($R=-0.450$, $P=0.000$) between the distribution of natural resources and the PEI Index of electoral integrity. Further analysis in Table 4.1 confirms significant correlations linking resource rents with all of the PEI sub-indices from stages in the electoral cycle. Nevertheless, there is a substantial dispersion of observations across the regression line in Figure 4.3; for example, countries with higher per capita revenues derived from resources include Equatorial Guinea (ranked worst in integrity), Kuwait (ranked moderate) and Norway (ranked extremely highly). Natural resources usually appear to function in many rentier states as a curse for many dimensions of democratic governance, but reservoirs of natural resources in mature democracies do not inevitably depress the quality of elections.

What of related direct measures of corruption? The resource curse can be expected to heighten the risks of electoral malpractices, since ruling elites in

Table 4.1 The PEI Index and its components correlated with economic indices

	GDP per capita, PPP (constant international US$)	Human Development Index	Total natural resources rents (% of GDP)	Corruption Perceptions Index (CPI)
PEI index of electoral integrity	0.583**	0.645**	−0.450**	0.726**
Electoral laws index	0.225*	0.239*	−0.391**	0.444**
Electoral procedures index	0.529**	0.625**	−0.390**	0.653**
Voting district boundaries index	0.191	0.385**	−0.294**	0.241**
Voter registration index	0.585**	0.638**	−0.351**	0.561**
Party and candidate registration	0.458**	0.515**	−0.431**	0.590**
Media coverage index	0.271*	0.248*	−0.371**	0.416**
Campaign finance index	0.516**	0.556**	−0.388**	0.527**
Voting process index	0.521**	0.653**	−0.321**	0.592**
Vote count index	0.481**	0.623**	−0.504**	0.622**
Results index	0.533**	0.594**	−0.294**	0.579**
Electoral authorities index	0.473**	0.526**	−0.441**	0.673**

Sources: PEI Electoral Integrity Index and its sub-components, Electoral Integrity Project 2014 – expert survey of Perceptions of Electoral Integrity, (PEI-2.5); CPI from the Quality of Government Cross-national Dataset www.qog.pol.gu.se/data/; Total natural resources rents as % of GDP (2012) from the World Bank, World Development Indicators.

Notes
* Correlation is significant at the 0.05 level (2-tailed).
** Correlation is significant at the 0.01 level (2-tailed). N = 85 countries.

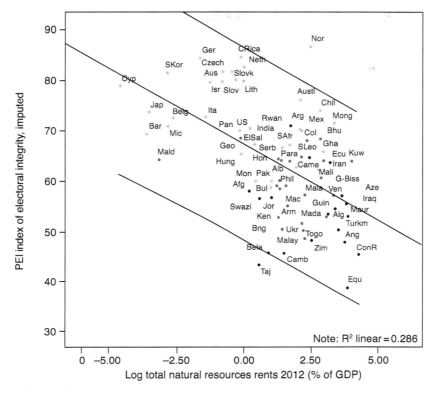

Figure 4.3 Electoral integrity and natural resources (sources: PEI Electoral Integrity Index, Electoral Integrity Project 2014 – expert survey of Perceptions of Electoral Integrity, (PEI-2.5); log total natural resources rents 2012 (% of GDP), World Bank World Development Indicators. http://data.worldbank.org/indicator/NY.GDP.TOTL.RT.ZS).

rentier states control assets which can be deployed to gain support and maintain their grip on power, particularly through clientelism, patronage and corruption. For example, when faced with continuing anti-government protests, riots and social unrest following uprisings elsewhere in the region, Bahrain, which obtains ninety per cent of its state revenues from oil, substantially boosted state subsidies discounting the price of petrol, utilities and food, in an attempt to maintain support for the regime. There is also some empirical support for the proposition that patronage politics is linked with poor quality elections: Birch analysed cross-national data and reported that Transparency International's Corruption Perception Index was associated with incidence of electoral malpractices.[33]

However, care is needed when interpreting the direction of causality in this relationship. Acts such as the abuse of state employees, patronage politics and vote-buying can clearly serve to undermine electoral integrity, especially where a pervasive culture of kleptocracy undermines public trust and confidence in electoral procedures and authorities. Yet it could also be argued that by breaking the chain of electoral accountability, so that crooked leaders can no longer be thrown out of office through the ballot box, corruption should be understood as primarily the product, rather than the cause, of poor quality contests. Thus, again, it is important to lag the independent measure of corruption as a partial control for problems of endogeneity in cross-national analysis.

Comparative evidence of the frequency of actual corrupt behaviour is notoriously difficult to gather with any reliability, not least because these acts are often illicit and hidden. To monitor perceived corruption, as a close proxy, this study draws upon Transparency International's Corruption Perceptions Index (CPI), based on compiling many expert sources, first launched in 1995. There are questions about whether reported corruption perceptions reflect the lived experience and underlying reality of corruption, and whether such perceptions are uniform across cultures.[34] Nevertheless, the CPI is widely used by scholars and by the international community, including being incorporated into the World Bank Institute's Good Governance indices.[35] One note of caution is in order. It would be expected that the expert perceptions of electoral integrity would probably closely reflect broader perceptions of corruption – not least because the composite PEI Index includes some related questions on political finance, although the term 'corruption' was not used explicitly in the design of the PEI questionnaire. As a partial control for endogeneity, the CPI was measured in 2007–2011, lagged before the year of the election. Figure 4.4 shows the correlation between the lagged CPI and the PEI Index, without controls. The observed results confirm the existence of a strong and significant bivariate relationship (R=0.726, P=0.000). Moreover, the CPI was strongly and significantly linked with all the sub-components of the PEI with one exception (voting boundaries). Like wealth, the quadratic line provided the best fit, suggesting a stepped shift or 'plateau' effect. The simple correlations therefore suggest that perceptions of corruption (which are also strongly linked with the macro-level distribution of resource rents) are associated with perceptions of electoral integrity.

Several of the observed relationships of the key economic factors can be tested more systematically by examining the multivariate analysis presented in the first model in Table 4.2. The four successive models add additional blocks of factors, removing any which caused problems of multi-collinearity. Thus, the models did not include the UNDP's Human Development Index since, not surprisingly, this index is strongly inter-correlated with wealth, by definition and construction. The models also excluded the Transparency International subjective measure of Perceptions of Corruption, since this was so strongly correlated with per capita GDP and the objective measure of resource rents, generating similar problems of multi-collinearity.[36]

The first model tests the effects of wealth (transformed by the square root of GDP per capita in purchasing power parity) and the measure of natural resource

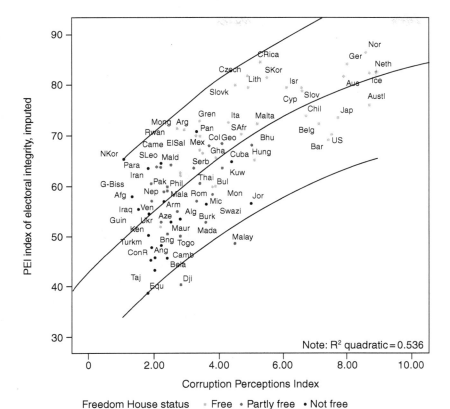

Figure 4.4 Electoral integrity and perceptions of corruption (sources: PEI Electoral Integrity Index, Electoral Integrity Project 2014 – expert survey of Perceptions of Electoral Integrity, (PEI-2.5); Corruption Perceptions Index 2009 included in the Quality of Government Cross-national Dataset www.qog.pol.gu.se/data/).

rents on the PEI Index. The results in Table 4.2 confirm that both wealth and natural resources were strongly and significantly related to the PEI Index; not surprisingly, most richer countries had better quality elections, while at the same time resource-rich states usually tended to suffer worse malpractices. These two factors alone explained considerable variance in the PEI Index (Adjusted $R^2 = 0.426$).

Geography

Were other structural conditions also important? The physical geography of a country can be expected to matter for processes of democratisation and development in several ways, including a state's location close to the equator (and thus

Table 4.2 Structural conditions and electoral integrity

| | Model 1 | | Model 2 | | Model 3 | | Model 4 | | Model 5 | |
| | Economy | | And geography | | And ethnicity | | And colonial legacy | | And state history | |
	B	S.E.	B	S.E.	B	S.E.	B	S.E.	B	S.E.
Economy										
Wealth (Sqrt per capita GDP PPP)	0.102***	0.020	0.090***	0.026	0.050*	0.032	0.047	0.026	0.025	0.033
Natural resources (% GDP)	−1.92***	0.527	−1.91***	0.553	−1.77***	0.001	−1.73**	0.546	−0.997	0.001
Geography										
Population size (000s)	—	—	0.001	0.000	0.001	0.000	0.001	0.001	0.001	0.000
Latitude	—	—	5.66	6.01	14.71*	6.097	14.56*	6.42	11.46	6.83
Area size (sq. km)	—	—	0.001	0.000	0.001	0.000	0.001	0.000	0.001	0.000
Ethnicity										
Linguistic fractionalisation	—	—	—	—	1.11	4.034	0.937	4.07	0.649	3.95
Religious fractionalisation	—	—	—	—	2.23	4.490	2.15	4.84	2.61	4.68
Predominant Muslim society (0/1)	—	—	—	—	−5.20*	2.65	−5.08	2.68	−4.15	2.55
Predominant Catholic society (0/1)	—	—	—	—	4.67	3.06	4.14	2.56	2.38	2.83
Predominant Orthodox society (0/1)	—	—	—	—	−7.52*	3.66	−6.99*	3.33	−7.87**	3.22
Middle East region (0/1)	—	—	—	—	2.85	3.88	2.54	4.42	5.71	4.55

Colonial legacy								
Previous British colony (0/1)	—	—	—	—	0.575	2.67	0.148	2.81
Year of independence	—	—	—	—	-0.009	0.009	-0.004	0.008
State history								
History of democracy 1972–2010 (FH)	—	—	—	—	—	—	1.49***	0.474
History of conflict 1972–2004 (UCDP)	—	—	—	—	—	—	-0.041	0.087
Constant	56.4		55.5		55.3		73.4	58.3
Adjusted R^2	0.426		0.415		0.499		0.493	0.544

Sources: PEI Electoral Integrity Index Electoral Integrity Project 2014 – expert survey of Perceptions of Electoral Integrity, Release 3 (PEI-3); all other indices from the Quality of Government Cross-national Dataset www.qog.pol.gu.se/data/.

Notes

1 B – Beta Coefficient, S.E. – standard error.
2 *, **, *** – degree of statistical significance.
3 OLS (ordinary least squares) Regression analysis where the PEI Perceptions of Electoral Integrity Index is the dependent variable in eighty-five countries. All models used tolerance tests to check that they were free from problems of multi-collinearity.

vulnerability to tropical diseases and distance from access to global markets), the physical size and terrain of a state (and thus types of agricultural production and distances from the federal government) and population size.[37] By extension, geographic factors are also plausible underlying conditions which could affect the quality of elections. At the simplest level, immense logistical challenges are posed when organising elections in large and populous countries. In India, for example, over 814 million citizens were entitled to vote in 930,000 polling stations during the 2014 general elections, involving five million polling personnel and civil police forces with nine staged phases of voting from 7 April to 12 May, with ballot boxes carried to from remote communities in deserts and far-flung mountainous villages. The estimated total cost of the general election campaign was US$5 billion, of which around US$577 million for running expenses came from the public purse.[38] The logistical, financial and technical challenges shrink to more manageable proportions in smaller states. Nevertheless, the importance of the size of nations on electoral integrity needs to be tested empirically, not least because the role of physical geography as a deep driver of economic growth and development has been strongly debated among political economists with some rival schools arguing that 'institutions rule' in determining economic growth, especially the colonial legacy concerning the institutions of rule of law and private property.[39] Other aspects of physical geography, including the location of a country in relation to neighbouring states (and thus patterns of regional diffusion, the influence of hegemonic states, the spillover effects of conflict and the permeability of cross-border communications) are treated in this study more properly as international influences upon elections.

The results of the empirical analysis presented in Model 2 in Table 4.2 show that despite the assumed importance of physical geography, once models control for wealth and natural resources, population size and area size of a country are *not* significant predictors of electoral integrity. After all, despite the immense logistical hurdles which Indian elections encounter, according to PEI more severe problems occur with contests in the smaller states of neighbouring Bangladesh and Pakistan. The latitude of a state (i.e. its distance from the equator) approaches the conventional cut-off point for statistical significance, however, and it crosses this threshold in subsequent models. A heated debate continues to rage in political economy, following William Easterly and Ross Levine, as several scholars have emphasised that geographic latitude is critical for development as it serves as a proxy for many other factors, including the type of agricultural crop production, distance to global trade markets, ecological threats, vulnerability to tropical diseases and the existence of deep-rooted poverty.[40] The results of the analysis in Models 2–4 in Table 4.2 suggest that for all these reasons, the latitude of a state's location also plays a role in increasing the dangers of electoral malpractices occurring in states close to the equator.

Ethnic heterogeneity and religious cultures

Ethnic heterogeneity is widely regarded as another condition which heightens the risks of failed elections – and indeed failed states and failed economies.[41] Deeply divided societies with a high level of ethnic fractionalisation among distinct religious, linguistic, nationalistic or racial communities are also believed to be most vulnerable to armed internal conflict.[42] Multi-ethnic societies are widely assumed to face particularly serious challenges in holding democratic elections, maintaining political stability and accommodating rival communities. Hence, Edward Mansfield and Jack Snyder argue that holding early elections as part of any peace-settlement in poor and conflict ridden states can exacerbate tensions, by producing populist leaders who seek to heighten latent ethnic identities to maximise their popular support.[43] In this view, it is important in this context to follow a sequential process, first reconstructing the core functions of the state to maintain security and manage the delivery of basic public services before subsequently moving towards elections.

Tensions among different ethnic communities are generally thought to undermine government legitimacy, social tolerance and inter-personal trust, all of which are believed to lubricate the give-and-take of political bargaining and compromise which characterise democratic processes. In the worst cases, ethnic conflict may lead to deep-rooted and prolonged civil wars and occasional cases of outright state failure, as exemplified by developments in Bosnia-Herzegovina, Rwanda, Sudan, Azerbaijan, Chechnya and Sri Lanka.[44] Ethnic heterogeneity is monitored in Model 3 in Table 4.2 using Alberto Alesina *et al.*'s estimate of linguistic and religious fractionalisation, as these types of social cleavages differ across world regions.[45] It should be noted that although this data source provides comprehensive estimates for all countries worldwide, it only gives an indication of the homogeneity or heterogeneity of a society using relatively crude measures, without attempting to assess the political salience and cultural meaning of these cleavages. The cross-national measurement of ethnic divisions remains a tricky and complex issue. For example, in the United Kingdom, Welsh nationalism is strongly tied to linguistic cultural identities, with roughly one-fifth of the population able to speak Welsh, whereas north of the border, the issue of Gaelic is less salient for feelings of Scottish nationalism, except on the islands. By contrast, Northern Ireland is divided between Protestant and Catholics, and by social class and income, not by language. Thus, the Alesina *et al.* measures, drawn from incomplete sources, capture only a very imperfect and limited dimension of all these types of identity politics in the British Isles.

In addition, debate continues about the importance of the predominant religious culture in a society. In particular, it is questioned whether the robustness of the authoritarianism (and thus the failure of electoral integrity) that has taken root throughout most states in the Middle East and North Africa, despite the Arab Uprising, can be attributed primarily to the rentier states and sharp social inequalities generated by oil dependent economies in this region; or is this a broader phenomenon which can be attributed to deep-rooted cultural values dividing the Muslim world and the West?[46] The well-known 'clash' thesis developed by Samuel Huntington also emphasised the effects of the enduring legacy of religious cultures on democratic values and beliefs throughout the world, including historical divisions within Europe into Protestant, Catholic, Muslim and Orthodox states.[47] The role of predominant religious cultures is expected to leave a deep and enduring imprint on the democratic, economic and social values which are widespread in contemporary societies, even though faith and active religious practices have faded in affluent secular societies.[48] Thus, even today Protestant Sweden and Catholic Italy are expected to show divergent values on many basic moral tenants, such as the value of marriage and the family, the role of the state or willingness to obey the law and pay taxes voluntarily, even though regular church-going has been abandoned in the Nordic states and both societies share many similar characteristics as affluent post-industrial economies and EU member states.

Accordingly, Model 4 in Table 4.2 entered the predominant religious tradition of each state, where Protestantism is treated as the default category. Finally, the Middle East is also entered as a dummy variable, to see if there is any residual impact from Arab states after controlling for Muslim cultures and the distribution of natural resources. The results in Model 3 show that once wealth and natural resources are controlled for, linguistic and religious ethnic heterogeneity, contrary to expectations, play an insignificant role as predictors of the PEI Index. Societies can be relatively homogeneous or they can be divided into many communities, but the model suggests that this in itself, based on these admittedly imperfect estimates, does not predict when elections will fail. Nevertheless, the type of predominant faith does seem to leave a cultural imprint; states in Eastern Europe with an Orthodox religious heritage, and also predominately Muslim societies, perform significantly worse in the quality of their elections than Protestant societies even after controlling for natural resources and levels of economic development. Moreover, it appears that, contrary to the claims of Alfred Stepan and Graeme Robertson,[49] it is the predominantly Muslim heritage more than being located in the Middle East and North Africa which has this effect.

Colonial legacies

The historical imprint left from colonial legacies can also be expected to prove important for development and democratisation, and by extension for electoral integrity as well.[50] An association between past type of colonial rule and contemporary patterns of democracy has been noted by several observers; for example Christopher Clague *et al.* report that lasting democracies (characterised by contestation for government office) are most likely to emerge and persist among poor nation states in ex-British colonies, even after controlling for levels of economic development, ethnic diversity and size of population.[51] Under British rule, they suggest, colonies such as Canada, Australia and India gained experience with electoral, legislative and judicial institutions, in contrast with countries under French or Spanish rule. Arguing along similar lines, Lipset and

Lakin also suggest that what mattered in ex-colonial states was whether the previous occupying power was itself democratic.[52] Settlers in the British colonies, they argue, inherited a pluralist and individualist culture and legislative institutions of self-government, which would prove critical to the development of democracy, notably in the United States, Canada, India and New Zealand. By contrast, colonists in Latin America were strongly influenced by the Spanish and Portuguese culture, with a more centrally controlled, hierarchical and paternalistic form of rule, at a time when the Spanish monarchy had few institutionalised checks on its power.

To examine the path-dependent role of the type of colonial legacies on contemporary patterns of electoral integrity, countries are coded for whether or not they were ex-British colonies. The year of national independence is also examined, on the grounds that longer experience of sovereignty is likely to consolidate institutions such as electoral systems, political parties, parliaments and courts over successive decades, whereas countries which have experienced more recent decolonisation, such as Georgia and Ukraine's independence from the USSR, and Timor Leste's independence from Indonesia, are likely to have more fragile institutions. Thus, Model 4 in Table 4.2 adds colonial histories to the structural conditions already considered. Although there are many reasons to assume that these historical conditions should matter, the results in fact suggest that, contrary to expectations, neither a British colonial legacy nor the year of independence proved significant predictors of the quality of elections.

State-building and state fragility

Path-dependent accounts also emphasise that the history of a state will leave an enduring mark in other ways beyond colonial legacies. In particular, elections held in fragile states and deeply divided societies emerging from conflict are regarded as at particular risk of failure. Since the early-1990s, during the post-Cold War era, elections have become a standard part of the international community's peace-building blueprint.[53] It is widely hoped that elections will facilitate the emergence of democratic governments with popular legitimacy and encourage political parties to channel grievances through conventional political means rather than armed conflict, and thus bring durable stability to deeply divided societies with a long history of bloodshed. Hence, United Nations peace-building missions assisted with organising transitional elections in Cambodia, Timor-Leste, Burundi, Sri Lanka, Sierra Leone, the Democratic Republic of Congo, Nepal, Liberia and Sudan.[54] In the most positive cases, elections do appear to have contributed towards durable peace settlements and the establishment of legitimate and stable governments, such as in Mozambique, El Salvador and Croatia.[55] Elsewhere the attempts of the international community to hold elections have often proved less effective, however, and states have continued to struggle to contain violence.[56] This problem is exemplified by continuing unrest in the Central Africa Republic, the Democratic Republic of Congo and Afghanistan, the three most fragile states ranked worldwide in 2013 by the Centre for

Systemic Peace.[57] Renewed ethnic conflict which broke out in Iraq in 2014, despite national elections in 2005 and 2010, can also be added to this list.

Moreover, scholars warn that instead of building sustainable peace, elections attempted prematurely during regime transitions are likely to backfire.[58] Mansfield and Snyder argue that where party competition remains poorly institutionalised, elections provide incentives for leaders to use ethnic and nationalist appeals when attempting to mobilise supporters and thereby gain power, indirectly intensifying the risks of inter-communal conflict. Instead of rushing into early elections, the authors recommend that a sequential process should be followed by peace-building missions where the most urgent priorities are to establish rule of law and security, effective public sector services, and public administration reforms – before subsequently seeking to hold competitive and democratic elections.[59] For all these reasons, states which have experienced recent conflict are likely to have elections which are at highest risk of further bloodshed. By contrast, path-dependent accounts emphasise that states which have consolidated democratic institutions over an extended period of time will have accumulated a deep reservoir of democratic culture, including the values of trust and tolerance, which makes them more likely to overcome any specific problems which may arise in a particular contest through peaceful mechanisms, such as the courts, rather than resorting to violence.

Accordingly, as a final step, Model 5 in Table 4.2 includes a summary measure of each country's previous historical experience or 'stock' of democracy (the sum of the annual Freedom House annual scores for political rights and civil liberties from the 'Third Wave' era in the early 1970s to 2010) as well as each country's experience of civil conflict (the sum annual scores for internal conflict from UNDP-PRIO's dataset from 1972 to 2004). Here, the results of the analysis do differ from the earlier models; in particular, in Model 5 the historical stock of democracy proved to be a strong and significant predictor of contemporary levels of the PEI Index while the economic indicators dropped out of the explanatory factors. Thus, if a country had a strong record of political rights and civil liberties throughout the 'third wave' era, contemporary elections were more likely to meet international standards of integrity. The evidence suggests that a large part of any electoral success or failure comes not from the particular contest itself but from state institutions, cultural values and political behaviours which evolve and consolidate over many decades. This is a path-dependency explanation, although at the same time it does leave numerous puzzles – not least, why have democratic regimes succeeded in some places and not in others? I have discussed this issue in detail elsewhere and it cannot be addressed here, particularly because we lack consistent time-series data to explore historical trends using the PEI Index, which only started with elections held in mid-2012.[60] Moreover, and contrary to expectations from the case-study literature, the summary measure of historical conflict experienced by a country over recent decades was *not*, unlike the democratic record, a significant predictor of electoral integrity today. This somewhat weakens the path-dependency argument, suggesting that past conflicts will not inevitably dampen attempts to strengthen the quality of contemporary contests through the ballot box.

Conclusions on electoral transitions

In accordance with the classic modernisation thesis electoral transitions, and indeed the quality of any subsequent elections, can be expected to prove most problematic where structural conditions produce unfavourable contexts. This includes the world's poorest societies, where contests are held among illiterate populations without access to news media, with poor infrastructure for communications and transport for managing polling and campaigning, and states lacking extended historical experience of democratic contests. An extensive literature in developmental sociology and political economy has debated these claims over more than half a century. The idea that underlying structural conditions greatly heighten the risks of failed elections is also a pervasive assumption in much popular commentary. What does the empirical evidence suggest?

Three key findings emerged from the empirical analysis. First, *wealth matters for the quality of elections*. Not surprisingly, according to the PEI Index richer economies usually had better quality elections. However, this process was observed to function primarily through a stepped shift rather than a linear development. Once countries reached a minimal threshold of around US$15,000 per capita GDP, elections commonly tended to meet international standards. Among poorer countries falling below this threshold, however, elections are riskier operations and malpractices tend to become more common. The impact of wealth continued to prove a significant predictor of the quality of elections across successive models with a progressively wider range of structural controls. This finding is hardly surprising given the extensive research literature over the last half a century linking wealth and democracy. Exactly why there are these contrasts between rich and poor societies, however, remains to be determined.

On the one hand, a sociological explanation in line with the classic Lipset argument suggests that more affluent societies expand the moderate middle classes and generate civic associations, labour unions and professional organisational networks; these serve as a buffer between citizens and the state, strengthen access to information through literacy, schooling and mass media, encourage cultural values of trust and tolerance associated with democracy and reduce the extremes of rich and poor common in agrarian societies. On the other hand, an institutional account suggests that more affluent nations have resources – including human, financial and technical capital – which strengthen the capacity of electoral authorities to organise elections that meet international standards. It is possible that both propositions could be at work.

Second, *natural resources* (measured by per capita oil exports) *do usually appear to operate as a 'curse'* for the quality of elections, as with broader processes of democratisation. This pattern was found to persist despite controlling for many other related structural factors, notably countries with a predominately Muslim religion. Thus, for Arab states oil seems to trump the type of faith, although it remains to be seen whether this pattern persists once more elections have been evaluated from the region. Nevertheless, this remains a probabilistic statement, not an inevitable destiny, which helps to explain the quality of contests in Equatorial Guinea and Turkmenistan more than an obvious outlier such as Norway. Natural resources and oil-dependent economies can generate rentier states which are plagued by an affluent few and stark socio-economic inequalities, lack of investment in human capital and basic welfare services, migrant workers and expatriate visitors without any citizenship rights and the patronage politics of crony state capitalism. Yet the contrasts observed between contests held in Kuwait and Equatorial Guinea suggest that even oil-rich authoritarian states can improve the quality of their elections.

Finally, once studies control for wealth and oil *many of the structural conditions* which might be considered plausible candidates for explaining the quality of elections around the world, *including the physical size of countries, colonial legacies and ethnic fractionalisation, were not observed to be significant predictors of contemporary patterns of electoral integrity*. Contests in states closer to the equator, and elections in countries with a predominant Orthodox or Muslim culture, were also often riskier propositions. By contrast, the history of democracy and autocracy in a country during the 'Third Wave' era since the early to mid-1970s was important for the contemporary quality of elections – with democratic institutions and cultures consolidated over successive contests. Consolidation means than even where specific irregularities occur – e.g. the Florida case – the reservoir of trust and confidence which institutions gradually accumulate over time is sufficient to overcome these problems through regular democratic channels, including the courts and legal reforms, rather than through direct actions which destabilise the electoral process, such as violent protests or boycotts. Thus, initial elections after transitions from autocracy and in the early stages of democratisation are indeed risky enterprises – perhaps illustrated most vividly in recent years by the experience of Egypt post-Mubarak, with the rise of the Muslim Brotherhood during the transitional multi-party elections, only to be followed by post-revolutionary instability and a backlash producing the popular election of a brutal dictatorship without respect for human rights under General Abdelfattah al Sisi. Yet, from a policy-making perspective, as the cases of Slovenia, the Czech Republic and Lithuania also illustrate – in some favourable circumstances middle-income societies which have lived for decades under authoritarian one-party states can still develop effective electoral processes that meet international standards within the space of a relatively few years.

Notes

1 For a fascinating and detailed account, see Coburn and Larson, *Derailing Democracy in Afghanistan*. See also UNDP, *Human Development Report 2013*.
2 For a discussion, see Birch, *Electoral Malpractice*; Ham, 'Why do Elections Fail?'.
3 Lipset, 'Some Social Requisites of Democracy'. See also Lipset, *Political Man;* Lipset *et al.*, 'A Comparative Analysis of the Social Requisites of Democracy'; and Lipset and Lakin, *Democratic Century*.
4 Lipset, 'Some Social Requisites of Democracy'.
5 Ibid. The most recent statement of this relationship by Lipset and Lakin suggests that capitalist free-market economies produce multiple commodities which are critical for democracy by creating more heterogeneous and diverse centres of wealth and power.

They suggest this reduces the economic control of the state and provides the basis for opposition organisations and the economic foundation for an active civil society. See Lipset and Lakin, *Democratic Century*, Chapter 5.
6 Rustow, 'Transitions to Democracy'.
7 Krieckhaus, 'Regime Debate Revisited'.
8 Jackman, 'On the Relation of Economic Development and Democratic Performance'; Bollen, 'Political Democracy and the Timing of Development'; Bollen, 'World System Position, Dependency and Democracy'; Bollen and Jackman, 'Political Democracy and the Size Distribution of Income'; Brunk *et al.*, 'Capitalism, Socialism and Democracy'; Huber *et al.*, 'Impact of Economic Development on Democracy'; Burkhart and Lewis-Beck, 'Comparative Democracy'; Helliwell, 'Empirical Linkages between Democracy and Economic Growth'; Vanhanen, *Prospects for Democracy*; Barro, 'Determinants of Democracy'; Przeworski *et al.*, *Democracy and Development*; Lipset *et al.*, 'A Comparative Analysis of the Social Requisites of Democracy'; Lipset and Lakin, *Democratic Century*; and Acemoglu *et al.*, 'Income and Democracy'.
9 Adam Przeworski *et al.*, 'What Makes Democracies Endure?'; Przeworski and Limongi, 'Modernization: Theories and Facts'; Adam Przeworski *et al.*, *Democracy and Development*.
10 Norris, *Driving Democracy*, Chapter 4.
11 Barro, 'Determinants of Democracy'.
12 Norris, *Driving Democracy*, p. 88.
13 Norris, *Why Electoral Integrity Matters*, Chapter 4.
14 Davidson, *The Black Man's Burden*.
15 Dahl, *On Democracy*.
16 Birch, *Electoral Malpractice*.
17 See the Quality of Government Institute, www.qog.pol.gu.se.
18 Chandra, *Why Ethnic Parties Succeed*; Daniel Posner, *Institutions and Ethnic Politics in Africa*.
19 Norris and Inglehart, *Cosmopolitan Communications*.
20 Transparency International Corruption Perception Index, www.transparency.org/research/cpi/overview.
21 The Varieties of Democracy Project, https://v-dem.net/.
22 Steenbergen and Marks, 'Evaluating Expert Judgments'.
23 Meyer and Booker, *Eliciting and Analysing Expert Judgment*.
24 For further details see Pippa Norris *et al.*, 'Assessing the Quality of Elections'; Norris *et al.*, 'Measuring Electoral Integrity'. See also www.ElectoralIntegrityProject.com.
25 Birch, *Electoral Malpractice*, Table 3.1 and Table 3.2.
26 Ibid.
27 Chauvet and Collier, 'Elections and Economic Policy in Developing Countries'.
28 Przeworski *et al.*, *Democracy and Development*.
29 Sen, *Development as Freedom*. The UNDP's Human Development Index (HDI) is a composite index that measures a country's average achievements across three basic dimensions of human development: a long and healthy life, as measured by life expectancy at birth; knowledge, as measured by the adult literacy rate and the combined gross enrolment ratio for primary, secondary and tertiary schools; and a decent standard of living, as measured by GDP per capita in purchasing power parity (PPP) US dollars.
30 See, for example, UNDP, *Deepening Democracy in a Fragmented World*; also the 2014 UNDP data, http://hdr.undp.org/en/content/table-1-human-development-index-and-its-components.
31 See, for example, Ross, 'Does Oil Hinder Democracy?'; Jensen and Wantchekon, 'Resource Wealth and Political Regimes in Africa'; Boix, *Democracy and Redistribution*; Ross, 'How do Natural Resources Influence Civil War?'; Haber and Menaldo, 'Do Natural Resources Fuel Authoritarianism?'; and Ross, *The Oil Curse*.

32 Collier and Sambanis, *Understanding Civil War*; Humphreys, 'Natural Resources, Conflict, and Conflict Resolution'; and Snyder, 'Does Lootable Wealth Breed Disorder?'.
33 Birch, *Electoral Malpractice*, pp. 64–65.
34 Andersson and Heywood, 'The Politics of Perception'.
35 Prominent papers in this literature include Paulo Mauro, 'Corruption and Growth'; Knack and Keefer, 'Institutions and Economic Performance'; and LaPorta et al., 'The Quality of Government'. This literature is surveyed in detail in Rose-Ackerman, 'Governance and Corruption'.
36 Alternative indices of corruption were tested and found to suffer from similar problems, such as the Bribe Payers Index and the World Bank Group's Control of Corruption.
37 Easterly and Levine, 'Tropics, Germs, and Crops'; Alesina and Spolaore, *The Size of Nations*; and Teorell, *Determinants of Democratisation*.
38 The Electoral Commission of India, http://eci.nic.in/eci_main1/the_setup.aspx; *The Times of India*, 'Polls to Cost country Rs 3,500 crore this year', 8 February 2014.
39 See Acemoglu et al., 'Reversal of Fortune'; Rodrik et al., 'Institutions Rule'.
40 Easterly and Levine, 'Tropics, Germs, and Crops', pp. 3–39.
41 Alesina et al., 'Fractionalization'; Alesina and La Ferrara, 'Ethnic Diversity and Economic Performance'; Kaufman, *Modern Hatreds*; Collier and Sambanis, *Understanding Civil War*; and Doyle and Sambanis, *Making War and Building Peace*.
42 For an argument challenging the conventional wisdom that more ethnically- or religiously-diverse countries are more likely to experience significant civil violence, see Fearon and Laitin, 'Ethnicity, Insurgency and Civil War'.
43 Snyder, *From Voting to Violence*; and Mansfield and Snyder, *Electing to Fight*.
44 See, for example, Paris, *At War's End*; Collier and Sambanis, *Understanding Civil War*; Doyle and Sambanis, *Making War and Building Peace*; and Kaufmann, 'Possible and Impossible Solutions to Ethnic Civil Wars'.
45 Alesina et al., 'Fractionalization'.
46 Stepan and Robertson, 'An "Arab" More Than a "Muslim"'; Dunning, *Crude Democracy*.
47 Huntington, *Clash of Civilizations*.
48 Norris and Inglehart, *Sacred and Secular*.
49 Stepan and Robertson, 'An "Arab" More Than a "Muslim"'.
50 Acemoglu et al., 'The Colonial Origins of Comparative Development'; and Acemoglu and Robinson, *Economic Origins of Dictatorship and Democracy*.
51 Clague et al., 'Determinants of Lasting Democracy in Poor Countries'.
52 Lipset and Lakin, *Democratic Century*, Chapter 11. See also similar findings in Hadenius, 'The Duration of Democracy'.
53 The expansion in peace-keeping activities and the settlement of civil wars has attracted a substantial literature. See, for example, Paris, *At War's End*; Jeong, *Peacebuilding in Post-conflict Societies*; Collier and Sambanis, *Understanding Civil War*; Dobbins et al., *The UN's Role in Nation-building*; Doyle and Sambanis, *Making War and Building Peace*; Jarsad and Sisk, *From War to Democracy*; Howard, *UN Peacekeeping in Civil Wars*; and Toft, *Securing the Peace*.
54 Kumar, *Post-conflict Elections*; McFaul, *Advancing Democracy Abroad*; and Zurcher et al., *Costly Democracy*.
55 Doyle and Sambanis, *Making War and Building Peace*.
56 Marshall and Cole, *Global Report 2014*. See also Fortna and Howard, 'Pitfalls and Prospects in the Peacekeeping Future'; Fortna, 'Does Peacekeeping Keep Peace?'.
57 These three states scored highest on the State Fragility Index 2013; see Marshall and Cole, *State Fragility Index and Matrix 2013*.
58 Snyder, *From Voting to Violence*; and Mansfield and Snyder, *Electing to Fight*.
59 Brancati and Snyder, 'Rushing to the Polls'.
60 This is discussed in detail in Norris, *Driving Democracy*.

5 Democratisation in the Asia-Pacific
Two steps forward?

Benjamin Reilly

Comparative studies of democratisation have produced two types of generalisations: those having nearly universal application and those applying more particularly to a given region.[1] The relationship between economic development and democracy is perhaps the standout example of the first theme in the democratisation literature, with the successful transitions to democracy of Northeast Asian 'tigers' such as Korea and Taiwan following decades of rapid industrialisation and economic growth providing a good example of this linkage in action. However, Asia also provides some of the best counter-examples of the democracy–development link too. In particular, when we turn to Southeast Asia, the relationship between economic development and democratic transition is stood on its head, raising profound challenges for students of democratisation and democratic theory. Similarly, key findings from the scholarly literature on democratic transitions – such as the expectation of democratic support from middle classes, the role of elite pacts and the institutional architecture considered most supportive for democratisation – all face major challenges in Asia.

This disjuncture between comparative generalisations and regional experience make Asia an important case for students of democratic transition. However, while the extent and variation in regime type across the region should make for an important testing ground for democratic theory, Asian cases remain marginal to much scholarly work on democratisation. Popular conceptions of the region are dominated by the ever-increasing influence of China, the world's most powerful authoritarian state, and media reports have often depicted a region of resiliently non-democratic regimes, ranging from North Korea's family-based despotism to Burma's former military junta. In addition, those scholarly studies of democratisation that do focus on the Asia-Pacific region take the form of edited collections comprising chapter-length studies of a single country.[2] While this has produced many excellent edited volumes, their strength tends to lie in individual case studies rather than truly thematic comparisons.

Given this, it remains the case that the Asia-Pacific region, with a few important exceptions, continues to be relatively neglected in comparative studies of democratisation and democratic transitions. Many of the major scholarly studies of democratic transitions rely heavily on European and Latin American cases but largely ignore Asia.³ Only a few thematic studies of democratic transitions place the Asia-Pacific region centre stage.⁴

This relative neglect of Asia is surprising. Today, more Asians live in genuine democracies than ever before and Asian regimes are increasingly using their democratic status to lift their prominence in the international arena. Indonesia, with a keen eye on its global role as the world's largest Muslim democracy, has become an outspoken advocate of democracy beyond its shores. New or restored democracies ranging from Mongolia in the north to East Timor in the south have joined Korea, Taiwan, the Philippines and Indonesia as classic 'Third Wave' democracies in which governments are chosen and changed via the electoral process. As one widely-read report observed:

> Over the past five years, the Asia-Pacific region has been the only one to record steady gains in political rights and civil liberties as measured by Freedom House. Although it is home to China, where over half the world's Not Free population lives and North Korea, the least free country in the world, a number of Asia-Pacific countries have made impressive gains in the institutions of electoral democracy – elections, political parties, pluralism – and in freedom of association.⁵

Since these words were written, Asia has seen another key democratic opening. Burma (also known as Myanmar) is the latest and possibly most important example of a democratic transition in Asia. One of the poorest countries in the region with a long history of authoritarian rule under both military and quasi-civilian regimes, Burma began a rapid political transformation in 2010 which culminated in the country's first democratic transition in late 2015. Burma's unlikely transition was facilitated by an elite opening shepherded by former president Thein Sein and underpinned by successively freer elections under international and domestic pressure for greater openness in all aspects of Burmese politics. This unprecedented process of political liberalisation in what was, until recently, one of Asia's most repressive autocracies has seen the country move from an isolated military dictatorship to Asia's newest electoral democracy. The landslide election victory of Aung San Suu Kyi and her National League for Democracy in the November 2015 national elections was a landmark event in Asian democratisation and constitutes one of the more remarkable democratic transitions of recent years. Whether Burma can convert its historic election into more broadly based democratic governance, however, remains to be seen.

Asia: no easy patterns

In Asia, newer democracies have often struggled to deliver on their promise: at the same time as the scope of democracy across Asia has spread, its quality has arguably declined. Some former promising democracies, such as Thailand, have experienced repeated and debilitating democratic failures while others, including the crucial case of Indonesia, have seen an erosion of democratic capacity and commitment.[6] This is particularly important given the fact that only a few Asian transitions have so far led to clear consolidation. In Southeast Asia in particular, this is a second or sometimes a third attempt at getting democracy right for many new democracies.

Emerging from colonialism at the end of the Second World War, numerous Asian states tried, and mostly failed, to build competitive political systems. Success stories like India, Japan and the Philippines all acquired their democratic systems as a result of foreign occupation, colonial rule or decolonisation. Independent Burma, Malaysia and Indonesia also began life as democratic regimes, but quickly succumbed to a combination of political stalemate and ethnic rebellion in the 1950s and 1960s. Indonesia's brief incarnation as a fragile but genuine democracy in the mid-1950s was undone by an immobilised parliament, erratic presidential leadership and threats to the integrity of the state from an Islamic rebellion, all of which alarmed the military. The imposition of 'guided democracy' and then military rule after 1966 can be traced back directly to this anxiety about maintaining territorial unity in a situation of great social diversity. Similar issues were (and are) present in Burma and several other Southeast Asian states.

A second round of democratic transitions began in the late 1980s with the popular uprising against the flagrantly corrupt Marcos regime in the Philippines in 1986 and the negotiated transitions from military-backed governments which began in Korea and Taiwan in 1987 – importantly, all events that occurred before the end of the Cold War, in contrast to the democratic revolutions in Eastern Europe. Indeed, the end of communism prompted only one clear case of Asian democratisation: that of Mongolia in 1991. Subsequent years saw the resumption of civilian government in Thailand in 1992, the United Nations (UN) intervention which (temporarily) brought democracy to Cambodia in 1993, the fall of Indonesia's Suharto regime in 1998 and the international rehabilitation of East Timor which culminated in 2001. Burma's 2015 transition is the first in over a decade, and is at the time of writing on a promising but uncertain trajectory.

There are also significant intra-regional variations in the manner and scope of democratic transitions across the Asia-Pacific region. In Northeast Asia, Korea and Taiwan, along with the post-communist case of Mongolia, stand out as three of the world's most successful transitions from authoritarian rule. It is notable that Korea, for example, showed no sign of flirting with a return to authoritarianism during the severe economic difficulties it faced as a result of the Asian economic downturn of the late 1990s – and in fact elected a prominent democracy activist, Kim Dae Jung, to the presidency in 1997. The election of opposition leader Chen Shui-bian to Taiwan's presidency in March 2000, the island's first democratic transfer of executive power, was a similar watershed event for Taiwanese democracy. Mongolia, in the midst of a mining-led economic boom, is less consolidated but has the benefit of two decades of unbroken competitive elections and numerous peaceful changes of government.

In Southeast Asia, by contrast, democracy has spread more widely but remains fragile and liable to reversal. Indonesia, with a majority Muslim population of over 250 million, is today the region's standout democracy along with the Philippines and East Timor – a country born out of the crucible of a liberation struggle and the international intervention which followed its 1999 vote to separate from Indonesia. While the core components of democracy are present in each of these states – competitive elections, a free press and basic human rights – there are questions over whether any could be said to be as yet truly consolidated, in the sense of democracy being considered 'the only game in town' and any reversion from it unthinkable. Indonesia, for all its remarkable democratic progress in recent years, remains beset by crippling levels of corruption, growing religious intolerance and an often inert political system. Despite an underperforming administration, the election in July 2014 of Joko Widodo as Indonesian president marked a break from the country's history of insider, elite dominated politics which may give new impetus to democratic reformers.

Another key achievement for Indonesia has been the marginalisation of the once dominant military from political affairs, easing them out of their entrenched role in the parliament – in contrast to Egypt, for example, where the army aborted the democratic experiment after only two years, and also to Burma today where twenty-five per cent of seats in parliament are reserved for the military (the same as in Suharto-era Indonesia). As Marcus Meitzner notes:

> The story of Indonesia's democratisation after 1998 is primarily a narrative of comprehensive civilianisation, both in the centre and in the regions. At the end of Suharto's rule, forty per cent of Indonesia's governors were retired or active military; by 2013, a mere six per cent.[7]

Indonesia's institutionalisation of competitive electoral procedures is similarly striking. These include four national elections since 1999, three of which led to peaceful changes in government, and over 1,000 polls held at the provincial and district level.

Elsewhere, in Asia, semi-democracy, quasi-democracy and outright authoritarianism remains predominant, for the time being at least. The 'China model' of closed and nominally Communist political systems with open and mostly competitive market economies reigns supreme not just in the People's Republic of China but in neighbouring Vietnam and Laos as well. However, even in single party autocracies such as Vietnam, there are signs of political loosening – with a more active and critical legislature and the election of some independent candidates, for example. Studies have shown that elections in such cases are not meaningless: while they may not change governments they do provide important signals to the ruling regime about public attitudes.[8]

Cambodia is only slightly more democratic than the Communist regimes. Since its UN-sponsored elections of 1993, Cambodia has been essentially a one-party state under the dominance of long time Prime Minister Hun Sen and his Cambodian People's Party (CPP). Again, however, there are recent signs that this may be starting to change. The July 2013 election saw a steep decline in support for the CPP government, which lost many formerly safe seats, and significant gains for the opposition Sam Rainsy Party with a resulting parliament which looks closer to a competitive party system than at any time since 1993. An electoral system which had been designed to advantage the ruling party instead aided a newly united opposition.[9]

This range of experience makes it difficult to generalise about Asia's contributions to democratic theory and democratic transitions in particular. However, there are some themes which stand out when viewed from a comparative perspective and which I will examine in the remainder of this chapter. The first is *the mode of democratic transitions prevalent in much of Asia*, and the contrast between the 'pacted' regime transitions cited in much of the scholarly literature and the mostly 'people power' revolutions that have prevailed in Southeast Asia in particular. Second, *elections have become increasingly consequential*, both as a route to more substantive democratisation in cases like Burma ('electorally-led democratisation') but also in institutional terms, with a distinctive 'Asian model' of electoral democracy which privileges some dimensions of democracy (e.g. concentrated power and majority rule) over others (e.g. broader representation and minority rights). My third theme touches on geopolitics: *nearly all the region's genuine democratic transitions have occurred in maritime rather than mainland Asia* – in part due to the competing spheres of influence of the United States and China in the Asia-Pacific, which has historically and will likely continue to influence Asian regimes and transitions.

Democratic transitions: top down or bottom up?

The democratic transitions literature remains closely tied to the 'Third Wave' experience of liberalisation from authoritarian rule that began in Southern Europe in 1974 before spreading to Latin America and, post-1989, the Eastern bloc states and further afield. This decade long process generated a raft of hypotheses about how the transition process affects post-transition governance and consolidation. The 'pacted transitions' model – in which incumbent elites from erstwhile authoritarian regime themselves initiate steps towards democratic reform, maintain control over the course of the transition process and engage in multilateral negotiation and compromise both with civil society and a democratic opposition – is perhaps the best known of these.

Scholarly analyses of the 'pacted transitions' model developed inductively, from detailed examination of the processes of transition from authoritarian rule in Southern and Eastern Europe.[10] Elite pacts were seen as giving democratic transitions their best chance of success: according to Guillermo O'Donnell and Philippe Schmitter, 'pacts are ... not always likely or possible, but we are convinced that where they are a feature of the transition, they are desirable – that is, they enhance the probability that the process will lead to a viable political democracy'.[11] Similarly, Terry Lynn Karl and Schmitter conclude that 'transitions by pact' are the most likely to lead to political democracy'.[12]

In the best known pacted transitions from Europe and Latin America, a three-way interaction between civil society, opposition elites and at least some government representatives has typically led to step-by-step negotiations in the direction of greater political liberalisation. Splits between hard- and soft-liners in government have often been present, with at least some members of the incumbent regime making strategic choices to liberalise some aspects of politics when it has become clear that the status quo is no longer viable. In Asia, the 2010–2015 transition in Burma is perhaps the best example of this process of regime-initiated democratisation in action, although it was pushed along by elections at strategic junctures too. South Korea and Taiwan are other Asian examples of top-down liberalisation, although both also experienced mass demonstrations and other 'bottom-up' processes. International pressure was also a major factor in all three cases.

As this suggests, in Asia 'pacting' tells only half the story. Rather, democratic transitions have actually followed multiple paths. Historically, bottom-up 'people power' movements predominated in larger, poorer Southeast Asian cases while top-down, incumbent-initiated democratisation has been the rule in the more developed cases of Northeast Asia. Even in Burma, the recent transition needs to be seen in the context of mass action over many years, including the student protests of 1988 (following Burma's last competitive elections, the results of which were never honoured) and the 'Saffron Revolution' in which monks took to the streets in 2007. In general, the Asian experience of transitions has seen less pacting and more direct action than familiarity with the comparative literature would have one believe. However, this may simply be illustrative of a broader bias in the political science literature: one study found that almost seventy per cent of all articles in the major comparative politics journals are focused on just two regions, Europe and Latin America, with 'strikingly few articles on populous regions such as Southeast Asia and South Asia'.[13]

In another challenge to the scholarly orthodoxy, middle classes in Asia have shown themselves to be much less supportive of democracy than the classic expectations of Barrington Moore ('no middle class, no democracy') would assume. While transitions in the Philippines and Indonesia featured combinations of students and middle-class activists, these have been the exceptions rather than the rule. In the region's non-democracies, in particular, the middle classes have seldom been the champions of democratisation. Experts on Singapore and Malaysia have long decried the quiescent and apathetic attitude displayed by most of the middle class in the face of flagrant rigging of the democratic rule book by incumbents.[14] In Thailand, the Bangkok-based middle class have confounded democratic theory by showing themselves to be actively hostile to majority rule, demonstrating repeatedly against the idea of 'one person, one vote' democracy under Thaksin Shinawatra, whose Thai Rak Thai (TRT) party rewrote the rule book for winning elected office in Thailand by actively courting the electoral support of rural majorities.[15] In China too, there is little evidence that the middle class is an engine for democratisation, with the Communist Party successfully co-opting China's huge urban middle class as the guarantor of economic growth with stability.[16]

This is a long way from classic 'people power' revolutions, such as the overthrow of the Marcos regime in the Philippines which remains a touchstone event in Asian democratisation. First elected president in 1965, Marcos had assumed quasi-dictatorial powers in 1972 and indulged in a patrimonial, oligarchic and ultimately kleptocratic form of authoritarianism. In 1986, amid systematic political repression, institutional decay and mounting domestic and international pressure, Marcos sought to demonstrate the legitimacy of his regime by calling (and then attempting to steal) a snap election. The large-scale and well documented fraud inspired massive popular protests as well as a revolt by some elements of the military. Amid a mounting national civil disobedience campaign, the Marcos regime collapsed in February 1986. 'People power' returned as a decisive force in Philippine politics in 2001 when the ailing presidency of Joseph Estrada was overturned by a combination of middle-class street protests, congressional impeachment and judicial action.

Elsewhere, incumbent autocratic regimes handled their exit from power more skilfully. In Taiwan and Korea, the dominant parties of the authoritarian period played a crucial role in opening up the political system to competitors. In Taiwan, the incumbent Kuomintang (KMT) party, which had ruled unchallenged since Taiwan's liberation from Japanese forces in 1945, initiated the decisive steps towards political liberalisation in the late 1980s. Opposition parties such as the Democratic Progressive Party (DPP) were legalised, media restrictions lifted and constitutional reforms enacted, resulting in the direct election of the Taiwanese parliament for the first time in 1991. Voters rewarded the KMT's skilful handling of this transition by re-electing them to office – an unusual outcome for a transition from authoritarian rule. It was not until March 2000 that a clear transfer of power across party lines occurred, when the DPP scored a narrow victory in presidential elections, ending more than five decades of unbroken KMT rule.

In Korea, similarly, political liberalisation in the run-up to the Seoul Olympics in 1988 began a chain reaction that resulted in the collapse of the authoritarian regime. International pressure as well as massive street protests and civil action forced the resignation in 1987 of incumbent premier Chun Doo-Hwan of the Democratic Justice Party, who had been in power since the proclamation of Korea's Fifth Republic in 1980. Chun's successor, Roh Tae-woo, announced a sweeping programme of political liberalisation, including direct presidential elections, press freedoms and human rights reforms, beginning a phased transition to democracy which saw the introduction of a new constitution and Korea's first competitive presidential elections. The subsequent victories of democracy campaigners Kim Young Sam in 1992 and Kim Dae Jung in 1997 – both former dissidents who had been subject to arrest and, in the latter's case, assassination attempts – constituted further landmarks in the ongoing consolidation of Korean democracy.

Another wave of Asia-Pacific democratisation occurred in the late 1990s, precipitated to a significant degree by the Asian economic crisis that swept the region in 1997. While the impact of the crisis was economically devastating, particularly in the hardest hit states such as Indonesia and Thailand, it also proved to be politically liberating, stimulating fundamental political reform in both countries.[17] The crisis also dealt a grievous blow to proponents of the much-heralded 'Asian model' of restrictive one-party politics with open competitive markets. In an atmosphere of political crisis, street protests and mass rallies in Bangkok and Jakarta were the spark for major political changes which swept discredited leaders from power.

In Indonesia, where concerns about poor governance, high-level corruption and the problems of 'crony capitalism' were most pronounced, the crisis precipitated the end of the Suharto era, paving the way for long awaited leadership transition and the possibility of large-scale political reform. Again, student protests and mass public rallies were critical to the fall of the regime, which had monopolised power since 1966. Indonesia's *reformasi* movement was an unlikely and in many ways chaotic amalgam of opposition campaigners, non-government organisations and student activists. In 1998, with the Indonesian economy crippled (thus undermining the regime's main claim to legitimacy), Suharto's fate was sealed. A combination of popular discontent, military pressure and mass riots that left over 1,000 people dead and many commercial centres in Jakarta destroyed saw him step down on 21 May 1998, to be replaced by Vice-President B.J. Habibie whose interim government began the process of serious democratic reform.

In June 1999, Indonesia's first competitive elections since 1955 were held amid great excitement and not a little trepidation at the uncertain consequences that might attend the liberalisation of national politics. Those and subsequent elections in 2004, 2009 and 2014 have not only brought a series of new democratic leaders to power but also opened up the space for a remarkably ambitious redesign of Indonesia's democratic institutions. These include the introduction of direct presidential elections; a new upper house to represent the country's provinces; revised electoral arrangements; and a massive decentralisation of power to the regional level. The result of these changes has been a profound reorientation of the Indonesian political system: despite persistent problems of electoral administration, as well as localised corruption, vote-buying and violence, the overall trajectory of Indonesian democracy has clearly been towards greater consolidation. Governments have changed, new elites recruited and older ones – particularly those associated with the military – discarded through the electoral process.

After Indonesia, it was Thailand that was most affected by Asia's economic emergency. The 1997 crisis exposed deep structural weaknesses in Thailand's governance architecture, prompting Thai politicians to embrace demands for a new 'people's constitution'. The resulting institutional reforms aimed to build a stronger, more stable political system, which helped Thaksin Shinawatra and his TRT party assume unprecedented power through successive election victories in 2000 and 2004. However, these contained the seeds of his downfall too: Thaksin assumed unheralded powers for a Thai prime minister, leading the first single party government in Thai history. Increasingly seen as a threat to both the

Bangkok elite and the monarchy, while travelling abroad in 2006 Thaksin was overthrown by the military in a bloodless coup. An extended period of military rule, and a further round of political reforms and elections in 2011 (won by Thaksin's sister Yingluck), was followed by a further coup in 2014 that appears to have set back Thai democracy for years to come.

Unsurprisingly, the Thai reforms have been characterised as a case of 'be careful what you wish for'[18]: so many incentives for cohesive parties and strong government were put in place by Thai reformers that they unbalanced the political landscape. Following the 2006 coup, many of these incentives for strong parties and stable government were revoked in direct response to the Thaksin years, which continue to echo through Thailand's contemporary politics. Given the ongoing strength of rural support for TRT's successor parties, particularly in the northwest, the military regime may well be tempted to try to further dilute the regions' vote share in future electoral reforms, considering the generals' determination to maintain the dominance of the Bangkok elite in Thai politics. Following a period of promising development towards democracy, Thai politics is now deeply dysfunctional. This is witnessed in the manner in which class, regional and societal divisions are exposed in the context of the unresolved succession of the Thaksin family.

The one transition to democracy in the region that did not share these characteristics was the case of East Timor. There, democratisation came about as a result of a number of factors: a prolonged independence struggle against Indonesian military forces which had invaded in 1975; the transition from Suharto to Habibie in Jakarta that opened the door for a referendum on the disputed jurisdiction's future; and mounting pressure from the international community. However, it was facilitated primarily by a 1999 UN-sponsored vote rejecting autonomy within Indonesia which unleashed a wave of violence, destruction and looting by pro-Indonesian militias across the half-island. Frantic international negotiations resulted in an Australian-led military intervention which restored basic security and placed East Timor under the control of the UN. Two years later, in its final act before handing back power to the East Timorese people, the UN organised East Timor's first free elections – to a constituent assembly which then drafted a constitution for the new state, renamed Timor-Leste.

The case of Burma, discussed in more detail below, is another example in which international pressure and economic decline have helped stimulate democratic transition. According to basic modernisation theory, however, it is the wealthy 'semi-democracies' of Singapore and Malaysia that should be the most likely contenders for a transition in the near future. In most of the world, economic development and democratisation have tended to go hand in hand – a basic tenet of modernisation theory which we see played out in Asia via the democratic transitions in middle-income Korea and Taiwan described above. Along with the long-standing democracy of Japan, these are among the richest and most developed countries in Asia. Singapore and Malaysia constitute long-running exceptions in the other direction – countries which according to modernisation theory should be more democratic than they actually are. Singapore, with a higher per capita income than the United States, is on some measures the richest country in human history not to have become a democracy.[19]

To be sure, some political loosening has occurred in both countries: Singapore's 2011 elections saw the best results for the opposition parties in decades, while in Malaysia, where demands for *reformasi* have ebbed and flowed since the late 1990s, a more fundamental political realignment appears to be underway. At the 2008 general elections, the long-ruling Barisan Nasional coalition first lost the two-thirds parliamentary majority it needed to freely amend the constitution, and also lost power to opposition parties in a number of key states. In 2013, it lost the popular vote as well, but was saved from electoral defeat by rural gerrymandering that opposition groups have long decried. In both cases, the declining popularity of long-ruling hegemonic parties has been offset by a highly unequal electoral, media and judicial playing field. As is the case in Burma, then, there is something to be said for the idea that repeated elections may help undermine authoritarian rule – a subject to which I now turn.

Democratisation by elections?

As Pippa Norris has evaluated in Chapter 4, some scholars argue that the process of 'electorally-led' democratisation represents a distinctive and viable means of transition from authoritarian rule. Proponents of this schema argue that the holding of repeated elections over time, even in a less than open political environment, can itself positively affect democratic rights and prospects.[20] While this idea of 'democratisation by elections' as a distinctive mode of transition has not been much applied to Asia, cases such as Burma provide some support. The process of reform which culminated in the 2015 transitional elections in Burma can be seen as being strongly connected to two prior (and less than competitive) elections in 2010 and 2012, which while hardly free and fair did contribute to meaningful democratic progress. The tightly controlled November 2010 elections, the first in Burma for twenty years, followed an incumbent-led process of constitutional change which ensured, among other things, a permanent role for the armed forces in Burma's legislature and government.

The political openings that have occurred since then may provide an example of the way in which flawed but partially competitive elections can themselves lead to greater democratisation. The 2010 elections were only marginally competitive, with the opposition National League for Democracy (NLD) barred from competing and Aung San Suu Kyi still under house arrest. The ruling junta's Union Solidarity and Development Party (USDP) won a tainted victory, but these elections also brought new ethnic and minority parties into parliament for the first time and kept up the momentum for further progress. The subsequent unbanning of the NLD saw them dominate by-elections in 2012, and Aung San Suu Kyi elected to parliament for the first time. This made credible the USPD's commitment to hold genuinely open elections in 2015, and witnessed opposition movements commit to the electoral process rather than pursue extra-constitutional avenues.

When they came the November 2015 elections proved to be a watershed. Amid intense international interest the NLD won an overwhelming victory, catapulting a party of ex-political prisoners and protesters into government. As Burma's first genuinely open elections in over fifty years, these elections have been one of the most dramatic shifts from autocratic to democratic rule seen anywhere in East Asia. However, even with its overwhelming victory, the NLD still has to cope with numerous constitutional impediments bequeathed by the former incumbents – including the military's ongoing grip on a quarter of legislative seats, contrived citizenship restrictions on the presidency (aimed directly at Suu Kyi) and a cumbersome mixed semi-presidential/military governance structure.

For political scientists who believe in rational actor models of politics, the Myanmar case also offers an unexplained puzzle: why did the incumbent USDP regime agree to free elections which they surely knew they would likely lose? Moreover, why has the military also acquiesced in their diminution of power inherent in the change of government? After all, we assume that politicians are rational office seekers, not turkeys voting for Christmas, but the direct result of the USDP's willingness to hold free elections is that their leadership is now out of office. Even taking into account pressure from the West, this appears to be a rare case of self-abnegating leadership from a departing autocratic regime. As for the military, it remains to be seen whether they will prove to be supportive of democratic change, as was the case in Indonesia and the Philippines, or reprise their former role as upholders of autocratic rule. Terrence Lee's comparative analysis of military responses to Asian democratisation movements suggests that the extent of popular support for the new government makes it more likely that the military will remain a behind-the-scenes player rather than attempt to resurrect the *ancien régime*.[21]

By contrast, other Southeast Asian examples such as Malaysia provide a cautionary note to hopes that elections in and of themselves can engender democratisation. Despite several decades of regular elections, Malaysian electoral politics has been characterised by limited competition and a playing field tilted markedly in favour of the government. Demands for greater openness and political liberalisation rising in step with the country's socio-economic development, and increasing frustration with the dominant Barisan Nasional coalition government, have seen growing popular disenchantment with the 'Malaysian model'. The reliance on heavy handed social management via a range of internal security laws, media restrictions, pro-government judiciaries and a distorted electoral process has provoked growing middle-class protests in recent years, particularly in urban areas. Elections have never resulted in a change of government, and decades of gerrymandering and malapportionment, suppression of basic freedoms and intimidation of political opposition, all aimed at ensuring the government's continuation in power, have only accentuated popular discontent. It would be hard to argue that this façade has strengthened democracy in Malaysia.

The issue of electoral system manipulation highlights another area where Asia's transitions have been relatively unusual compared to international practice – the choice of political institutions, not just constitutional but electoral too.

In Northeast Asia, for instance, all three of the successful transitions (Mongolia, Taiwan and South Korea) have included variants of semi-presidentialism in their constitutional formulas, despite well-known problems with this model.[22] In Southeast Asia, the 'perils of presidentialism' that Juan Linz and others warned about has apparently been discounted with all competitive democracies – Indonesia, the Philippines, East Timor and now Burma – being presidential or quasi-presidential systems. Moreover, Indonesia and East Timor combine this model with elections through proportional representation (PR) for the legislature, along Latin American lines, despite scholars identifying this as a particularly 'difficult combination' which can undermine the development of strong parties.[23] While hardly problem free, all three Southeast Asian democracies have experienced some combination of proportionality, multipartism and presidentialism for over a decade, or in the case of the Philippines, several decades. Such anomalies highlight once again Southeast Asia's divergence from the expectations of the political science literature.[24]

In the region's semi-democracies and autocracies, by contrast, majority rule parliamentary systems prevail. In particular, Malaysia and Singapore are in some ways the purest expression of Westminster left in East Asia, combining as they do parliamentary supremacy, plurality elections and enduring one-party dominance. Other cases such as Thailand (and even more so, Brunei) have sought, not always successfully, to combine parliamentary government with a strong monarchical system. Burma has reshaped its former parliamentary model into a complicated form of quasi-presidential and quasi-federal government. In sum, in sharp contrast to most other world regions where parliamentary models have a superior track record of democracy, democratic transitions in East Asia have been strongly associated with presidential and semi-presidential forms of government.[25]

Asia's electoral institutions have also become the subject of sustained (if not always successful) political engineering.[26] Thailand's 1997 constitution, for instance, aimed to promote stronger parties and more stable governments, with a new parliamentary model comprising a lower house of 400 members elected from single member districts and another 100 chosen by PR from a national list. Election rules included a 5 per cent list threshold (to weed out splinter parties), a strengthened prime minister's office and mandatory party membership for all MPs (to reduce pre-election party hopping). As discussed above, these reforms helped facilitate the breakthrough election victory and single party rule of Thaksin and his political movements and successors, with the law of unintended consequences on full display. Following Thailand's latest coup in May 2014, it is unclear when or if future elections will be held at all.

Other electoral innovations have had more positive impacts on democracy. Singapore's Group Representation Constituency (GRC) system, originally designed to assist the government by ensuring the delivery of all seats to the plurality winner, is one example. First introduced in 1988 with the ostensible aim of promoting greater diversity of representation, GRCs are multi-member constituencies in which electors cast a vote for predetermined party lists rather than for candidates, with the party that wins a simple plurality of votes in a district winning *every* seat. This makes Singapore's national electoral system one of the most 'mega-majoritarian' anywhere in the world. While providing a nominal diversity of representation via a requirement for ethnically mixed lists, the real aim of the GRCs has been to extend the already considerable over-representation of the governing People's Action Party, which regularly wins over ninety per cent of seats in parliament. However, these same majority enhancing rules had the effect of aiding the opposition Workers Party at the 2011 general election, enabling them to take all six seats in a GRC and become Singapore's first meaningful parliamentary opposition for many years.

A common aim in reform trends in Southeast Asia has been to strengthen ruling political parties and party systems, with institutionalised political parties seen as 'a crucial pillar in the functioning and consolidation of emerging democracies' and the 'missing link' in the quest for democratic consolidation across the region.[27] Efforts to restrict separatism and reward nationally focused parties have been present in Indonesia, the world's most populous and probably most diverse emerging democracy. Indonesian law requires all parties to establish an organisational network across the archipelago, no easy task in a nation of 17,000 islands. By effectively banning local parties, this has created putatively national parties with a cross-regional organisational basis by fiat, as parties must satisfy these branch structure requirements before they can compete in elections.[28]

Another form of electoral engineering has been the turn towards mixed-member majoritarian (MMM) electoral models in much of Asia. A range of East Asian states including Japan, Korea, Taiwan, Thailand, the Philippines and most recently Mongolia have introduced MMM systems over the past two decades, often with the hope of encouraging more stable and aggregative party systems to develop.[29] Unlike mixed-member systems in other world regions, the structural majoritarianism of Asian models advantages large parties with a national reach, making it difficult for smaller parties to gain election. In Northeast Asia, this majoritarian bias in the rules of the game has directly impacted political outcomes, with larger parties predominating and, in Japan and Taiwan (and to some degree in Korea and Mongolia), nascent two-party systems starting to take root. If Burma also adopts a mixed-member system as part of its democratic reforms, as some experts have proposed,[30] then this system will be entrenched as the dominant electoral system model across East Asia.[31]

In summary, strategic choices about institutions have been integral to Asia's democratic transitions. Incumbent regimes and opposition movements face different incentives over institutional choices depending on their electoral prospects. Established major parties or those who think they will be able to secure a clear plurality of the vote have an incentive to choose majoritarian models such as first-past-the-post plurality to maximise the seat bonuses that such systems typically provide to the largest party. Hence the support for such systems by parties such as Golkar in Indonesia in 1999 or the NLD in Burma in 2015. By contrast, declining governing parties or challengers less sure of their vote totals are better off choosing PR, to protect themselves from an electoral wipeout and to guarantee a fair share of seats (hence the late push for a shift to PR by the USDP in Burma). Mixed systems provide a good each-way bet in situations of even greater electoral uncertainty. In short, rational calculations of future electoral support are important strategic considerations for system choice.

Geopolitics: implications of democratisation in the broader Asia region

Democratic transitions are not just domestic events but also have international implications. As noted earlier, more Asian states today feature participatory elections, competitive politics and basic freedoms of speech and association than ever before. From what a little over a decade ago was a region dominated by authoritarian rule, there is now a clear trend towards democracy being the accepted means for choosing and changing a country's political leadership in Indonesia, Korea and the Philippines as well as the established democracy of Japan – four of East Asia's eight largest countries. With the addition of Burma, with its fifty-five million population, this marks a truly historic shift in Asian affairs. It is also likely to affect the balance of power across the region between China and the United States.

To understand why this is so, consider the map of Asian electoral democracy in Figure 5.1, which shows a striking geographic pattern: all the maritime states (bar Brunei) are democratic, while all the mainland states (bar Mongolia) are autocratic. Freedom House's division between 'electoral democracies' and non-democracies makes this pattern even clearer: most of mainland East Asia is non-democratic, almost all of maritime Asia is democratic and the semi-democracies are geographically in-between.[32] When it comes to Southeast Asia specifically, this mainland–maritime democratic divide has been stable now for over a decade. Within this period, only Thailand has changed its regime type, although Burma should jump straight from 'Not free' to 'Free' status in 2016 barring any unexpected mishaps.

How can we explain this clear geographic demarcation of regime type? One potential explanation that I have explored elsewhere is that the depth and intensity of a given country's relationship with China may offer a better explanation than more conventional analyses of what could be called Asia's distinctive 'geography of democracy'.[33] Under this interpretation, proximity to China – historically, geographically and ideationally – becomes a key causal factor in explaining the distribution of democracy in Asia.

This geopolitical perspective also helps to explain a puzzling anomaly: in Southeast Asia the classic 'Lipset thesis' linking democracy and development has been turned on its head, with democracy weak or absent in the region's wealthiest states – Singapore, Brunei and Malaysia – but present, to varying degrees, in three of its poorest, Indonesia, Timor-Leste and the Philippines. Democracy also appears to be unrelated to human development such as educational levels, literacy, maternal health and other public goods, given the standout performance of quasi-authoritarian Singapore and Malaysia. All of this

Figure 5.1 Freedom House 'electoral democracies' 2015 (source: Freedom House, 2015).
Note
Countries in black are electoral democracies.

challenges the key tenets of democratic theory, and indeed modernisation theory more generally.

Bringing in the China factor helps explain why this may be so. Historically, China's influence on its 'near abroad', particularly its southern border, has been profound. Southern border kingdoms which fell under China's tributary influence in the Ming dynasty (such as present-day Vietnam, Laos and Cambodia), or culturally Sinitic offshoots like Singapore, have been much more influenced by China than more distant maritime states such as Indonesia and the Philippines, which never experienced direct tributary relations. Similarly, in the contemporary era, Chinese support for communist revolutions and Leninist political structures in Laos and Vietnam, its nervousness about the possibility of transitions in traditional client border states such as Burma and North Korea, and the rapid economic integration of southern China with mainland Southeast Asian borderland states, have all impacted on the spread of democracy in countries which fall within China's sphere of influence.

The fact that most of Asia's genuine democracies are strategic allies of the United States may also help to explain this picture. For instance, it is often claimed that one reason China continues to support North Korea is its fear of a unified pro-United States Korea on its northern border. While none of the United States' treaty allies in Asia share any contiguous borders with China, those countries that do border China are inevitably influenced by the power of what is now the world's largest economy and see their political and economic futures tied to China's rise.[34]

As Southeast Asia has been increasingly divided along the mainland–maritime fault line over the last decade, democratisation has become a wedge issue for Asian geopolitics. For example, with the ascension of first India, Australia and New Zealand and now the United States and Russia into the East Asia Summit, the composition of Asia's peak geostrategic gathering is divided evenly between democracies and non-democracies. The confluence of reinforcing economic, political and strategic interests in East Asia's two spheres – a mostly non-democratic mainland in China's sphere of influence on the one hand and a mostly democratic and United States-aligned maritime Asia on the other – has underlined this division. Yet this process also highlights new challenges for democracy. In particular, it heightens the importance of the 'swing states' in the mid-zone between mainland and maritime Asia, such as Malaysia and Singapore, while making democracy much difficult for those within China's sphere of influence, such as Thailand.[35] Conversely, a genuine transition to democracy in Burma, sharing as it does a long land border with China, would be a radical change in the regime context of Chinese borderlands.

Conclusions

This chapter has highlighted a number of ways in which the experience of democratic transitions in the Asia-Pacific region both conforms to but also challenges some of the basic assumptions of political science scholarship. We see evidence in the Asia-Pacific of the main scholarly models of democratic transition including 'electorally-led' democratisation, 'pacted' regime transitions and 'people power' revolutions. While pacts play more of a role in Northeast Asia than in Southeast Asia, it is not clear that any one model has prevailed. Some cases, such as Burma, have seen combinations of each model, with earlier mass protests paving the way for a pacted and ultimately electorally-led transition to democracy. Even in Korea and Taiwan, nationwide street protests preceded pacting and continued unabated until the departure of the incumbent government. In short,

Asia's experience appears to be quite different to that of Latin America and Europe.

The East Asian experience also suggests that institutional reforms can play an important part in democratic evolution – but again, not in the way that much of the scholarly literature would predict. Most of Asia's newer democracies have adopted much more majoritarian institutional models than those in other regions, with a preference for presidential or quasi-presidential models of government and plurality or mixed-member electoral systems prevail over PR in most new cases. The emergence of Burma as Asia's newest democracy under a combined quasi-presidential and plurality system is a case in point: this is very different to the parliamentary-PR models typically advocated for new democracies in the scholarly literature.

Finally, as discussed above, democratisation in East Asia has an important geopolitical dimension with the region's genuine democracies today concentrated in maritime rather than mainland Asia – reflecting to some extent the competing influences of China and the United States. Again, Burma's transition may overturn this neat symmetry of geography and regime type, presenting the unusual prospect of a genuine democracy located on China's southern border. This is not the least of the challenges for Burma's transition, which will have to continue to defy expectations if it is to consolidate as Asia's newest democracy.

Notes

1. Bunce, 'Comparative Democratization'.
2. These include Diamond et al., *Democracy in Developing Countries*; Hewison et al., *Southeast Asia in the 1990s*; Friedman, *The Politics of Democratization*; Rodan, *Political Oppositions*; Taylor, *The Politics of Elections*; Laothamatas, *Democratization in Southeast and East Asia*; Diamond and Plattner, *Democracy in East Asia*; Marsh et al., *Democracy, Governance and Economic Performance*; Morley, *Driven by Growth*; Fuh-sheng Hsieh and Newman, *How Asia Votes*; Diamond et al., *Democracy in East Asia*; Case, *Routledge Handbook*.
3. These include Rustow, 'Transitions to Democracy'; Linz and Stepan, *The Breakdown of Democratic Regimes*; O'Donnell et al., *Transitions from Authoritarian Rule*; Linz and Stepan, *Problems of Democratic Transition and Consolidation*.
4. Important theoretically driven contributions are Haggard and Kaufman, *The Political Economy of Democratic Transitions*; Slater and Wong, 'The Strength to Concede'; Gilley, *The Nature of Asian Politics*.
5. www.freedomhouse.org.
6. See Case, 'Low-quality Democracy and Varied Authoritarianism'.
7. Meitzner, 'Political Evolution'.
8. Malesky and Schuler, 'The Single-Party Dictator's Dilemma'.
9. 'Electoral System Worked in Favour of United Opposition', *The Cambodia Daily*, 30 July 2013.
10. Linz and Stepan, *Problems of Democratic Transition and Consolidation*.
11. O'Donnell et al., *Transitions from Authoritarian Rule, Vol 4*, p. 39.
12. Karl and Schmitter, 'Modes of Transition'.
13. Munck and Snyder, 'Debating the Direction of Comparative Politics'.
14. Case, *Politics in Southeast Asia*.
15. Jones, 'Democratization, Civil Society and Illiberal Middle Class Culture'.

16 Chen, *A Middle Class Without Democracy*.
17 MacIntyre, *The Power of Institutions*.
18 Kuhonta, 'The Paradox of Thailand's 1997 "People's Constitution"'.
19 Diamond, 'Introduction', in Larry Diamond *et al.*, *Democracy in East Asia*, p. xiii.
20 Lindberg, *Democratization by Elections*.
21 Lee, *Defect or Defend*.
22 See Reilly, 'Semi-Presidentialism and Democratic Development'.
23 Mainwaring, 'Presidentialism, Multipartism and Democracy'.
24 A subject I cover in more detail in my chapter 'Parties, Electoral Systems and Governance' in Diamond *et al.*, *Democracy in East Asia*.
25 See Lijphart, *Democracies*; Lijphart, *Patterns of Democracy*; Gerring *et al.*, 'Centripetal Democratic Governance'.
26 Reilly, *Democracy and Diversity*.
27 Kuhonta *et al.*, 'Shadows from the Past'.
28 An exception to this rule applies in Aceh and was a key part of the 2005 peace agreement there. See Hillman, 'The Policy-Making Dimension of Post-Conflict Governance'.
29 However, the genesis of most Southeast Asian reforms differs from that of Northeast Asia, where reformists replaced semi-proportional single non-transferable vote models in the hope of encouraging more centrist two-party politics. In Southeast Asia, by contrast, mixed systems were introduced as a supplement to plurality or plurality-like systems such as the block vote, as used in pre-reform Thailand and the Philippines, or as an extension of it, as in Singapore.
30 Diamond, 'The Need for a Political Pact'.
31 Reilly, 'Democratisation and Electoral Reform in the Asia-Pacific Region'.
32 Freedom House's term 'electoral democracy' differs from 'liberal democracy' in that the latter also implies the presence of a substantial array of civil liberties. In the survey, all 'Free' countries qualify as liberal – i.e. both electoral and liberal democracies. By contrast, some 'Partly Free' countries qualify as electoral, but not liberal, democracies.
33 See Reilly, 'Southeast Asia'.
34 Ba, 'A New History?'.
35 Pongsudhirak, 'Thailand's Foreign Policy in a Regional Great Game'.

6 The transition in East-Central Europe

André Liebich

In the course of autumn 1989, the existing regimes in East-Central Europe collapsed. In August, Poland secured the first government in the region for some forty years to be headed by a non-Communist and containing a majority of non-Communist ministers. In September, Hungary allowed thousands of East Germans to leave for West Germany and, in October, it dropped its designation as a People's Republic, effectively ending over forty years of Communist monopoly power. The most dramatic event in the month of November 1989, and indeed in the course of that year, was the fall of the Berlin Wall, heralding the demise of the East German state, the German Democratic Republic (GDR). In November, Czechoslovakia's Communist leader resigned following increasingly huge anti-governmental demonstrations, as did Bulgaria's long-time Communist party chief – in the latter case as a result of an internal party coup. By the end of December, a leading dissident had been elected president of Czechoslovakia and the Romanian dictator had been summarily executed in the wake of the only mass bloodshed experienced in the region during those momentous months. Every one of these countries scheduled free legislative elections for 1990, with the exception of Poland where elections were to be held in 1991 – it was the partially free elections of June 1989 that had ushered in the Polish changes that year.

The suddenness, the speed, the encompassing nature and the definitiveness of the transformation were bewildering to outside observers and inside participants alike, so much so that commentators have likened the process to the breaking of a dam.[1] It is important to note that these events occurred well before the existence of Twitter and social media that have so often been invoked to explain the rapid succession of 'Arab Spring' revolutions. There was no social media, indeed there was no Internet in 1989. Western radio stations, notably the British Broadcasting Company (BBC) and Radio Free Europe, transmitted news of events from one country to another but their audience was limited. In the absence of media contagion, the rapid succession and similar outcomes of events in East-Central Europe suggest a common cause, though the modalities of change in each of the countries differed.

The most significant cause of the changes was external to the region. It lay in the reconfiguration of the international system which was largely due to the initiatives of the recently-elected Soviet leader, Mikhail Gorbachev. After attempting timid (and unsuccessful) internal reforms immediately after he came to power in 1985, Gorbachev embarked upon a campaign that shook the very foundations of the bipolar international order that had existed since World War II. There is much discussion about Gorbachev's intentions in launching these initiatives – whether they were a self-interested effort to compensate for Soviet military weakness and internal problems or a more generous attempt to break down years of hostility in order to promote the common interests of humanity.[2]

Whatever the motivations, Gorbachev inspired rapturous enthusiasm among Western, and particularly some parts of Western European, public opinion though not among East-Central Europeans who were to be the principal beneficiaries of his initiatives. These populations may not have been impressed by such shows of 'new thinking' as Gorbachev's United Nations speech in December 1988 where he promised to withdraw much of the Soviet military presence in East-Central Europe. However, Communist leaders in the region could not fail to note warnings from Moscow that they should not rely on Soviet force to maintain them in power, as it had in Berlin in 1953, in Hungary in 1956 and as it had threatened to do in Poland in 1981 (in Czechoslovakia in 1968 Soviet armed might actually overturned a reformist Communist government, a sort of Gorbachevism *avant la lettre*, to restore a traditional Communist regime). The proof of Soviet intentions in 1989 only came when Moscow gave its blessing to the composition of a non-Communist cabinet in Poland and even more emphatically so when it restrained its own as well as East German forces from quelling the demonstrations that culminated in the fall of the Berlin Wall.

The 'Gorbachev factor' as it has been aptly named[3] is too diffuse a process to be termed a 'triggering event'.[4] Moreover, its weight and even its relevance is hotly contested by East-Central Europeans who are loath to attribute the role of liberator to a leader who they are more likely to see as a prison warden. Even the metaphor of decolonisation, though seductive, does not fit the East-Central European case as these countries were more than nominally sovereign states, not colonies, and the withdrawal of the Soviet presence came about in a tempered manner that does not sufficiently explain the transformation that occurred. The Gorbachev factor may more accurately be considered a necessary but not sufficient framework for the changes that took place in East-Central Europe where the international system dictated the limits of each country's degree of autonomy but did not provide the agency for the actions that each country undertook. These actions differed significantly from one case to another, certainly more so than the apparently seamless sequence and similar outcomes of the events of 1989 would suggest. It is surely an exaggeration to say that there were no revolutions in 1989 only different reactions to the Soviet decision to pull out[5] but the weight of the external factor is undeniable.

Poland: a crucial and initial case

Poland occupies first place in any account of the transition away from Communism and not only in terms of chronology or because of its regional size – Poland's population, comparable to that of Spain, is twice that of the next country of concern here, Romania, and at least four times that of most other countries in the region – or its strategic position between Germany and the Soviet Union. In 1989, it was Poland that acted as a trailblazer challenging Soviet authority and testing Soviet commitment to non-intervention. Here, Poland's primacy built on the role it had played throughout the Communist period. The country had long enjoyed a record of openness: a recognised public profile for the Catholic Church, a non-collectivised agriculture, a degree of intellectual freedom unknown in the other 'people's democracies' of the region. It is for these reasons that Juan Linz and Alfred Stepan describe Poland as 'the only country in Eastern Europe that was always closer to an authoritarian than to a totalitarian regime'.[6] Moreover, Poland was the site of the region's largest and most protracted opposition to the Communist regime with the rise of Solidarity in 1980–1981, a trade union that became a movement which succeeded in mobilising millions of Poles around a national and democratic agenda.

In 1980–1981 Solidarity represented a powerful example of what can accurately be described as 'collective action in social movements'.[7] The twist here is that it was not this action that brought about regime change. In the decade that followed the rise of Solidarity, the movement was driven underground by a Pinochet-like assertion of military power. Even more significantly, Solidarity lost its dynamism as well its cohesion.[8] At the same time, the Communist state found itself paralysed, increasingly incapable of coping with the challenges brought about by a declining and heavily indebted economy and a restive society. It was therefore two weakened parties, still adversaries, that came together early in 1989 in round table negotiations. These were bitterly criticised – by hard core Communists, known in Poland as 'beton', by radicals from the Solidarity camp and by the populist right-wing that has since come to power in 2015 – for incarnating what scholars have called 'elite pact-making' (see Chapter 1). The result was the legislative elections of June 1989 with elections to the newly-created Senate entirely free as were thirty-five per cent of seats in the lower chamber. To the surprise of all sides, not least Solidarity campaigning under the banner of a 'Citizens' Committee', Solidarity swept all available seats in both the *Sejm* (the lower chamber) and the Senate, with the exception of a single senate seat. As the Solidarity leader and later president, Lech Walesa, put it, 'by a stroke of bad luck, we won the elections'.[9] This stunning victory alone was not sufficient to assure Solidarity of a majority in the *Sejm*, as the limit on seats freely contested had been set precisely to avert such an outcome. What tipped the situation in favour of a Solidarity-led government was the defection of two minor 'bloc' parties, the Peasant Party and the Democratic Party, to Solidarity.

Here, a brief excursion on the peculiarities of politics in the 'peoples' democracies' is in order. Contrary to the Soviet pattern where, within months, the

Bolshevik party had eliminated its only coalition partner, the Left Social Revolutionaries, in East-Central Europe the coalitions or national fronts established in the immediate aftermath of World War II persevered in a profoundly debilitated and essentially formal guise. There was no doubt about the 'leading role' of the Communist Party or the vigilance of the state security apparatus with regard to these non-Communist elements. Nevertheless, in Poland, Czechoslovakia and East Germany in particular, non-Communist parties continued to exist, servile and phantom-like. To the surprise of those, both Communists and non-Communists, who held them in contempt, these ghosts came alive in 1989. They provided a breakthrough in the impasse that arose out of the Polish elections of June 1989 and played an ancillary role in the transition from Communism in Czechoslovakia and in East Germany.[10]

The Polish experience was so striking and epoch-making that it has been invoked as a paradigm for the other transitions that were to follow. In fact, it has been argued that the Polish case,[11] and notably the presence of a numerous and mobilised civil society, represents an exception in the East-Central European region. Outside Poland, pre-existing civil society was too anaemic to serve as the spearhead of change. As a result, other modes of transition came into play; these have led scholars to refer to the Polish model as one of transaction, like Brazil, in contrast to Hungary, which experienced reform through extrication.[12]

Yet it is Hungary whose transition experience most closely resembles that of Poland, as it also experienced a 'pacted' transition negotiated at a round table. The difference is that in Hungary the opposition had to be induced by the government, one might say with forceps, to provide an opposite side at the government-sponsored round table. In 1987, reformist Communists and opposition intellectuals came together at a meeting discretely promoted by the government. This meeting engendered several contemporary Hungarian political parties, including today's governing Fidesz or Hungarian Civic Alliance, originally the Alliance of Young Democrats, whose ethos has changed significantly since its foundation. Nevertheless, in June 1988 there were still only a few hundred people at the commemorative ceremony for Imre Nagy, the emblematic figure of the 1956 Hungarian Insurrection. The following year the crowd had swelled to a quarter of a million.

The haste with which Hungary shed its Communist persona is astonishing. The Hungarian Socialist Workers' Party dissolved in October 1989 to re-emerge immediately as the Hungarian Socialist Party, the name under which it is still known today, albeit with a neo-liberal ideology that bears little resemblance to that of its Marxist predecessor. Other East-Central European Communist Parties, the most significant exception being the Communist Party of Bohemia and Moravia in the Czech Republic, followed the Hungarian example of discarding their previous names and identities and attempting to place themselves at various points on a non-Marxist spectrum, often claiming a vaguely social democratic inspiration. In Poland, the United Workers' Party disappeared in January 1990 to give way to Social Democracy of the Republic of Poland. In Bulgaria, the same process occurred in April 1990 as the Bulgarian Communist Party became the

Bulgarian Socialist Party. In East Germany, the Socialist Unity Party became the Party of Democratic Socialism in February 1990, whereas in Romania the Communist Party disappeared so comprehensively that it was only several years later that the Party of Social Democracy of Romania emerged as an unacknowledged though powerful successor.

Hungarian alacrity in abandoning communism has been explained in various ways. The weight of the Hungarian external debt was, undoubtedly, a factor. With a debt of US$20 billion – half of Poland's although in a country with a quarter of Poland's population[13] – as well as a relatively open economy but one that was in free fall and marked by commercial dependence on the West, Hungary was keen to shed the few remaining constraints preventing it from enticing Western capital. One of the side effects of Gorbachev's new approach to his East-Central European allies was that whereas previously lenders to those states had assumed that their loans were guaranteed by the Soviet Union, it became clear that this was no longer a valid assumption. A more penetrating analysis has been provided by one of Hungary's leading sociologists who asked the question directly: why did the Hungarian Communist Party retreat so quickly? The answer he provides points, as in conventional explanations, to economic decline, increasing dependence on Western capital and goodwill and competition for Western resources. Above all, however, the outcome of the analysis is that the process of abandoning communism was, in fact, a conversion of anachronistic bureaucratic power into market assets and real political power. Bureaucrats were eager to transform themselves into entrepreneurs and managers, thus enabling a much more substantial expropriation of wealth than their status as functionaries of state owned firms had allowed.[14] Others have applied the same reasoning to the process that occurred in Poland: 'the nomenklatura [i.e. the communist elite] ... set fire to their own houses.'[15]

Before 1989, Poland and Hungary were the most advanced reformist states of East-Central Europe, leaders in the march away from conformity to Soviet models.[16] Not surprisingly, therefore, it is these states that led the way in initiating the revolutions of 1989. What is more surprising is that apparently more stable, orthodox Communist regimes followed in the same path almost immediately. Czechoslovakia is the most striking case in point. Since the failure of the reform experiment in 1968 that had ended in a Soviet invasion, the Czechoslovak leadership had pursued an especially cautious policy averse to political and even economic reform. Both in Hungary and in Czechoslovakia the memory of Soviet invasion, in 1956 and 1968 respectively, loomed large; however, the leadership's reaction was quite different. Hungarian Communists, mindful of the danger of a new bloodbath, offered little resistance to the unleashing of social forces that moved in the direction of privatisation and other manifestations of capitalism. In contrast, the Czech leadership sought to provide consumer satisfaction, in the face of economic difficulties, while introducing as few structural changes as possible in the economic sphere and none in the political sphere. The result was a quiescent society where private car ownership, a key marker of consumerism, more than doubled between 1971 and 1989, and where the opposition consisted of only a few dissidents, the most prominent of which was Vaclav Havel better known abroad than at home.[17]

Muted rumblings in the late 1980s, notably in the religious sphere in a largely areligious society (this is true of the Czech lands but cannot be said of Slovakia), gave way to more robust demonstrations, notably by Prague and Bratislava students, in the course of November 1989. Police repression and reports of the death of a student (that later proved false and, in fact, a government provocation) had a snowball effect provoking massive mobilisation to which the government responded with panic. As the demonstrations grew in size and encompassed ever broader sections of the population, including the working class of whose loyalty the government had been confident, the Communist Party leadership resigned and the Party soon afterwards gave up its monopoly, giving way to a completely new configuration of power.

The Czech revolution can hardly be explained by the economic situation, stagnant and even deteriorating though it may have been. Czechoslovakia had been negatively affected by the rise in energy prices, dictated by recent Soviet policy, but it still had virtually no foreign debt. Gorbachev's warnings about the conservatism of the Czech leadership and his obvious sympathy for the Prague Spring of 1968 (against which the Czech leadership defined itself) played an important role. Most significant of all, however, was the example set by ongoing events in neighbouring countries, most notably in Germany.

The shadow of Germany has always loomed large over East-Central Europe, in both positive and negative ways. In this context, the GDR occupied a particular position within the Communist bloc. To a large extent, the existence of a Communist bloc in East-Central Europe was the Soviet response to the 'German Question' – the prospect of a resurgent German power made all the more ominous as the Federal Republic of Germany (GFR or West Germany), which had never come to terms with the division of Germany or formally accepted (until 1990) German territorial losses in the East, became a stalwart North Atlantic Treaty Organization (NATO) outpost. As the former epicentre of fascism in a Communist camp that defined itself in anti-fascist terms, the GDR never enjoyed the degree of sovereignty granted by Moscow to its other allies. In time, however, it became an ideologically orthodox pillar of the Soviet security system, held in awe by the other East-Central European states.

Rapid changes in the GDR thus sent tremors throughout its Eastern neighbours. In the summer of 1989, thousands of East Germans on vacation in Hungary passed through the newly opened Hungarian border with Austria to be immediately repatriated to West Germany, which had always considered them its own citizens. Protests from East Berlin that this laxness violated a Hungarian–GDR treaty remained unheeded in Budapest as well as in Moscow. Soon afterwards, a significant number of East Germans crowded into the West German embassy in Prague demanding, and obtaining, repatriation to the GFR. The effect of this mass movement was as demoralising as the regular anti-government demonstrations that were soon to take place throughout East Germany. Then, on 7 November, through a misunderstanding or even an accident by a flustered East

German official, the Berlin Wall was opened in what is considered by many to be the act that ended the Cold War.[18] In fact, the Cold War preceded the erection of the Berlin Wall in 1961 by over a decade, just as the Warsaw Treaty Organization, the Communist bloc's response to NATO, was still in existence when the Wall fell, and the Soviet Union survived for another two years. However, with the fall of the Wall, the process of German reunification got under way and it was to be finalised quickly, putting an end to the basic assumption upon which the Soviet bloc had been founded.

One of the premises of politics and culture in the East-Central Europe region, was that 'Central Europe', meaning Catholic countries with a Habsburg heritage (though often including Protestant and Wilhelminian East Germany), was fundamentally different from the 'Balkans' – countries of predominantly Orthodox religion with an Ottoman past. This thesis had been reinforced during the Communist period as neither of the principal Balkan countries, Romania and Bulgaria, unlike their northern counterparts, had ever initiated a revolt against Soviet power. To be sure, Bulgarian and Romanian policies were quite distinct: the former accepted Soviet hegemony quiescently; the latter pursued virulently nationalist policies with an anti-Soviet edge, though it remained nominally a member of the Soviet camp.

The 'Central Europeans' versus 'Balkan' distinction seemed to be confirmed in 1989 as Bulgaria, Romania (and, within a few months, fiercely independent but Stalinist Albania) followed their northern counterparts in shedding Soviet hegemony but, in contrast to the Central Europeans, retaining Communist power, overtly or in barely disguised form. In the course of November 1989, the Bulgarian Communist Party replaced its long-time leader, the longest serving party chief in the Communist bloc, with its foreign minister who took full charge of the country. The following month witnessed a bloody overthrow, some would say a staged overthrow, in Romania that brought to power a *soi-disant* National Salvation Front led by a sometime Communist formerly at odds with the country's deposed dictator. Significantly, and in sharp contrast to the Central European pattern, the first free elections in Bulgaria and Romania (as in Albania) resulted in the triumph of the revamped and renamed Communist establishments.

A close observer of the region has remarked that the story of 1989 is as much one of unintended consequences as of deliberate actions.[19] He was thinking of the accidental opening of the Berlin Wall and the faked but bungled death of a Czech police informer who was pretending to be a student, but his remark applies more broadly. Just one year before the momentous events of autumn 1989, the same observer had predicted a gradual 'Ottomanisation' of Communist Europe, a slow change measured in decades.[20] In fact, the change took place in a few months and turned out to be more radical than anyone had anticipated.

The early 1990s: uncertain prospects for democracy

With the end of the *annus mirabilis* of 1989, the first phase of the East-Central European transition ended and the second phase, arguably still ongoing, began.

As a leading figure in the Polish opposition, later foreign minister, put it early in 1990: 'the prospects for freedom are secured, but those for democracy remain uncertain'.[21] Transitologists have pointed out that the transition (meaning its first phase) had taken place in Romania and Bulgaria, but also in Czechoslovakia, before any significant domestic change occurred.[22] Moreover, East-Central European events, with the exception of those in Poland, appear to have refuted the suggestion that it is not the lack of legitimacy that threatens dictatorship but the presence of an opposition, inasmuch as the opposition was woefully weak in almost all of the countries in the area.[23] Weak though it may have been, the opposition to the old order had triumphed. With victory over the *ancien régime*, the question of what direction the East-Central states would now take came to the fore.

In contrast to the media and popular enthusiasm stirred by the events of autumn 1989, academic observers took a critical stance.[24] Leading scholars, often those who had previously shown no interest in the area, decreed, as one of their most eminent representatives put it, that 'a peculiar characteristic of this revolution [is] its total lack of ideas that are either innovative or orientated towards the future'.[25] The same illustrious philosopher commented complacently, and with an astonishing assumption of linear historical development, that this was a 'rectifying revolution that had simply put part of Europe back on the path of liberal democracy from which it had accidentally deviated'. A leading German political scientist agreed that this was an 'upheaval without a historical model and revolution without a revolutionary theory'.[26] He cautioned too against 'the suggestive temptation' of analysing East-Central European events with the instruments of transition theory. Lest this view, also expressed by such a notable scholar as Ralf Dahrendorf, be considered a peculiarly German academic obsession with theory, it should be noted that it was shared, in patronising form, by François Furet, the French historian of 1789. Furet also believed the revolutions of 1989 had unearthed no new ideas but he paid them the tribute of stating that they had endowed 'the famous principles of 1789 with a certain freshness and with renewed universality'.[27]

It is certainly true that if one could summarise in a single word the situation in the former Communist bloc at the turn of 1990 it would be in terms of a 'vacuum'. The disappearance of battered regimes, held in contempt by many and, as it turned out, far more brittle than anyone suspected, produced a void, most noticeable in the area of ideas and institutions. This void was rapidly filled by new ideologies that soon held uncontested sway and these ideologies were not invented but borrowed. The events of 1989 only confirmed that Marxism–Leninism, the ideology of 'really existing socialism' (a term which was soon to be used in an ironical way) had long been dead and it was now officially buried. Revisionist Marxism, the belief that socialism could reform itself from within, had finally met its definitive rebuttal in the failure of the 'Prague Spring' of 1968, an event which showed that 'socialism with a human face' could be crushed by Soviet tanks. Thereafter, Marxism–Leninism elicited only opportunistic lip service from some, even as it suffered widespread desertion by intellectuals – a movement long considered a first step towards revolution.[28]

With the abandonment of socialism, there was no longer any need to pretend allegiance to a discredited doctrine. The first successor ideals that came forward were disarmingly vague. They had, in fact, been in circulation, in an undercover way so to speak, even before 1989. The new ideologues in East-Central Europe, often emerging from the ranks of dissidents, demanded that their country, whether it be Poland, Hungary or Czechoslovakia, become a 'normal' country or that it 'rejoin Europe'.[29] A few intellectuals found such slogans, when echoed in the West, patronising,[30] but these individuals were very much a minority. In fact, both demands were self-delusionary inasmuch as 'normal' and 'European' meant attaining political and, above all, material standards attributed to the most prosperous members of the European Community, soon to become the European Union (EU). Historically, East-Central Europe (with the possible exception of Czech Bohemia) had long been a backward European periphery, lagging behind Western Europe in terms of political development and national income.[31] Such demands, 'wish-lists' in fact, readily found hard policy expression in the neo-liberal programmes first adopted in Poland and later endorsed – or at least lip service paid to them – in the rest of the ex-Soviet bloc.

The first non-Communist Polish premier declared that he was looking for his Ludwig Erhard, the architect of West Germany's social market economy. Instead, as one critic puts its acidly, he went to Chicago and Washington, both temples of strict market capitalism.[32] As the former planned economies sought to distance themselves from the Soviet pattern, they found their model, the only available alternative, in the capitalist economies of the West that had just completed the most anti-social decade in their history.[33] True, observers had already noted the earlier turn towards neo-liberalism, in theory for the moment, among Solidarity activists.[34] It should also be said that the socialist model had been totally discredited by the time it was discarded, both reforming and non-reforming economies having suffered the same fate in the Soviet 'co-stagnation sphere'.[35]

It was no use pointing out that the standard of living was still some thirty per cent higher in the East-Central European bloc than in the USSR, and that these economies had enjoyed an implicit Soviet subsidy in the form of energy provision amounting to as much as US$100 billion, offsetting early Soviet exploitation. More noticeable was the fact that Czechoslovakia's per capita income, close to or higher than Austria's in the interwar period, had dwindled to about half of the latter. All East-Central European countries had experienced rapid economic development in the first decades of socialist rule. Official figures, exaggerated though they certainly are, registered growth rates of as much as twelve per cent and fourteen per cent (for Bulgaria and Romania respectively) at the beginning of the 1950s, though this may be due to their early stage of development in the transition phase and to post-war reconstruction.[36] All the countries had positive, if diminishing, growth rates until the mid-1980s (with the exception of Poland where the economy stopped growing after 1980).

However, the gap with West European economies widened. In 1950, Poland's per capita GDP was some ten per cent higher than that of Spain. By 1973, it was forty per cent lower and by 1990 Spain's per capita GDP was two and a half times that of Poland.[37] In the face of such failures of centrally-planned economies and the successes of free market capitalism, a radical faith in the salvationary properties of a market economy, unhindered by any institutional, social or even economic constraints, took hold of the new decision-makers and, briefly, captured the imagination of broader sections of the population.

Market utopianism thus replaced socialist utopianism as a hegemonic trope, with disastrous immediate results. Most dramatically affected was Poland's economy where, following the introduction of 'shock therapy' in September 1989, industrial output fell by thirty per cent, inflation rose to 630 per cent, and unemployment climbed to close at twenty per cent. It was only in 1992 that the downward spiral in GDP was reversed and inflation was brought down to a mere (!) forty-four per cent – although unemployment continued to hover around fifteen per cent. In other countries where changes were more gradual, the figures were less dramatic. In Hungary, for instance, inflation reached a high of thirty-three per cent in 1991 and unemployment went up to thirteen per cent in 1993. Only in Bulgaria and Romania did inflation exceed 200 per cent (in 1991). As Poland was the first country to undergo deep reforms, it was also the first to recover. GDP started growing again, timidly, in Poland in 1992 whereas Hungary had to wait until 1994. The unemployment rate in Poland never fell much below fourteen per cent.[38]

The social tremors produced by the radical economic changes soon found expression in the political sphere. The belief that 'one could continue to work as under socialism but earn as if one were in America'[39] gave way to profound disillusion. Within a few years, all the East-Central European states had voted out their first post-Communist governments and exchanged them for their ideological opponents. In some countries, such as Poland and Hungary, voters replaced the winners of 1989 (in 1993 and 1994 respectively) with the now relabelled Communist parties. In the Balkans, the Communists or ex-Communists who had managed to retain power (or, in the case of Romania, seize power) were obliged to give way to their newly organised opponents, though Romania had to wait until 1996 for this to occur.

The first presidents, who had emerged from the ranks of dissidents in Poland, Hungary, Czechoslovakia (as of 1992, the Czech Republic) and Bulgaria, were also victims of the general disillusionment with the outcomes of the revolution that they had prompted. Their defeat was also the end of an idealist strand in politics as potent symbols such as Lech Walesa, the leader of Polish Solidarity, or Vaclav Havel, the charismatic playwright dissident famous in the West, bungled their presidencies and were repudiated by the electorate and outmanoeuvred by their political rivals. To be sure, radically anti-Communist political formations persisted in denouncing anyone who had ties to the previous Soviet regime. All the former peoples' democracies adopted 'lustration' laws, although with varying zeal. These laws often involved 'vetting' of candidates for political office but they were distinct from the vetting applied in Latin America and elsewhere as the main purpose of the lustration laws was to 'name and shame'. The

Czech Republic was the most ardent in applying this policy; Romania and Bulgaria practiced it least. Hungary introduced early but limited lustration and Poland's lustration practices quickly became politicised.[40]

In other respects, anti-Communist and post-Communist parties often pursued the same policies: alignment with the West in all respects, including policies of scaling back the welfare gains of the socialist period. It is perhaps the realisation that both camps, post-Communist and anti-Communist, followed the same line in most regards that explains the quiescence of the East-Central European working class. Workers, whether those who had risen up against Communist power, as in Poland in 1980, or those who had assented to it, passively or actively, fretted over the threats to their jobs but they accepted the harsher conditions of capitalism without resorting to revolt in the hope of avoiding what they feared.[41]

'The transition is over'

More than a quarter of a century after the momentous events of 1989, is the transition still ongoing? Experts appear to be stumped by this question.[42] Vaclav Klaus, Havel's nemesis and successor as Czech president, reportedly declared transition to be over in 1995. Five years was also the timeframe projected by American aid specialists[43] but most observers would agree that US expectations of a speedy transition were excessively optimistic and premature declarations were based on a very limited set of criteria. As the literature stresses, transitions take time,[44] so today the question of transition may still be posed but one must ask whether it is only East-Central Europe that is undergoing a transition towards a fixed point or whether all parts of Europe are interacting and transitioning – towards an unknown destination.

In international terms, the East-Central European countries are presently all firmly enmeshed in a dense network of regional and international organisations. The Council of Europe, a somewhat toothless organisation devoted to human rights, democracy and the rule of law (not to be confused with the EU's European Council), was the first to welcome new members between 1990 (Hungary) and 1993 (Romania). The Organisation for Economic Cooperation and Development (OECD), a successor of the Marshall Plan and now an elite group of advanced market economies, has admitted the four Central European countries and considers Romania and Bulgaria candidates. The real prizes, however, have been NATO and EU membership. Admission to both organisations has taken place in two steps: in 1999 the Czech Republic, Hungary, and Poland joined NATO; they, plus Slovakia, joined the EU in 2004. Bulgaria and Romania (and Slovakia) joined NATO in 2004 and the EU in 2007. Slovakia's different schedule was dictated by concerns about Slovak authoritarianism until 2002.[45]

It may seem paradoxical that countries which had so recently wrested their freedom from a hegemonic power would hasten to abandon part of their newfound and highly cherished sovereignty. Some have explained this eagerness in terms of a long-standing dependency symptom. One dissident, later Czech ambassador to Washington, suggested that her compatriots 'imagined the United

States to be a kind of rich Soviet Union',[46] within whose fold the East-Central Europeans would rest more comfortably than they had in that of their previous overlord. Others have been more caustic, claiming that inhabitants of ex-Communist countries view the world as a 'milk cow', childishly seeing themselves as eternal victims entitled to the largesse of others.[47] The more prosaic explanations for East-Central European eagerness to join NATO probably lie, first, in the fear provoked by the security vacuum engendered by the disappearance of the Warsaw Treaty Organization in 1991. The security challenges faced at that time involved mostly regional issues, such as tense Hungarian–Romanian relations.

It was the prevalence of these challenges that also prevented the East-Central European countries from cooperating effectively with one other, notwithstanding efforts such as those of the Visegrad group, comprising Poland, the Czech Republic, Hungary and Slovakia, which has steadily reduced its ambitions and (to a large extent) its rivalries since its creation in 1991. The second reason for hastening to join NATO was the sentiment, confirmed by later events, that NATO membership was an obligatory way station to EU admittance. Some members of the EU are not NATO members but no ex-Communist state has joined the EU without first being admitted to NATO. Finally, the demonisation of NATO in Communist times may have actually rendered NATO more attractive: what a delicious *frisson* one experiences in joining a club that has long been portrayed as forbidding and all-powerful.

Nevertheless, support for NATO membership varied across the area. The Polish president claimed in 1997 that ninety per cent of his people were in favour of membership.[48] In fact, the figure hovered around eighty per cent.[49] Be that as it may, both in Hungary and in the Czech Republic support at the time fell below one-third of the population; support was stronger in Slovakia, Bulgaria and, especially, in Romania, countries that were further from joining NATO. The painful realisation that membership entailed obligations – such as agreement for or participation in the war on Serbia over Kosovo or the war in Afghanistan – cooled enthusiasm. Early in the Kosovo War support for NATO membership in Poland fell to sixty-five per cent.[50] Within a decade of their admittance, however, the new members of NATO were pushing their own security agenda, with the connivance of some powerful older members, notably the US, but against the wishes of others, such as Germany. This more assertive position of some of the Alliance's new members found expression in support for further enlargement eastwards, towards Georgia and Ukraine. In the Ukrainian crisis since the end of 2013, it is Poland which has staked out the most radical position vis-à-vis Russia though it has not been followed by Hungary, the Czech Republic or Slovakia. Regardless of such disagreement and the common front presented by NATO as a whole, one commentator is surely correct in maintaining that 'the countries of the region are all chafing, to one degree or another at the 'adult supervision' provided by these multinational entities [NATO and the EU]'.[51] He might add that these entities or, at least, their older and dominant members, are also chafing at the demands of their new members.

The EU has long been a more popular goal for the ex-Communist countries than NATO. Even here, however, populations have shown apprehension. The number of respondents in favour of EU adhesion generally rose somewhat across these countries from 1993 to 2001; in Slovakia, in particular, it rose from a low of thirty-five per cent to fifty-one per cent. Elsewhere, numbers hovered just below or just above fifty per cent. However, as enlargement approached the number of those opposed grew, reaching twenty per cent in the Czech Republic in 2001 whereas it had stood at only three per cent in 1993, while virtually the same number (forty-five percent in 1993 and forty-six per cent in 2001) supported accession.[52] The fear of foreigners obtaining property rights, specifically, the fear of Germans returning to claim 'their' property, was particularly salient in Poland and the Czech Republic; it was partially alleviated by transitional measures conceded by the EU. Perhaps the decline of Euro-enthusiasm in the East was due in part to the 'grudging, timid and hypocritical' attitudes of Western Europe that had delayed admission for over a decade.[53] In large part, however, this decline was due to the rise of a powerful new ideology that filled the void left by the discrediting of earlier ideologies, hopes and illusions.

The new ideology that came to the fore was nationalism, understood as a belief in the superior rights of one's own country and ethnic group. Never completely submerged in Communist times, nationalism had been resuscitated selectively as the Communist regimes lost their appeal. After 1989, as a Czech sociologist has argued under the evocative heading of 'The Solidarity of the Culpable', identification with a nationality both bound people together on a non-class basis and excused people for their inevitable complicity with the Communist regimes.[54] As long as the ex-Communist states remained candidates for admission to the EU they respected its anti-nationalist ethos and adhered to European norms of minority protection – part of the Copenhagen Criteria for admission. Accordingly, they signed up to such Council of Europe instruments as the 1995 Framework Convention for the Protection of National Minorities and the 1992 European Charter for Regional or Minority Languages.

Since EU admission, however, under the impact of frustrated hopes and the ongoing economic crisis, the new member states have seen the rise of ultra-nationalist, populist parties, such as Jobbik in Hungary and Atak in Bulgaria, that have garnered, respectively, sixteen per cent and seven percent of the vote in recent elections.[55] In Poland, the newly-elected government party, Law and Justice, is very much nationalist, having absorbed smaller nationalist formations through coalition politics and popular appeal. In Hungary, the presence of a nationalist governing party, Fidesz, has not precluded the success of an even more nationalist party (Jobbik). Instead, one may argue that Jobbik has pushed Fidesz even further to the right. Whereas their ideological forefathers would have been anti-Semitic, in Hungary and the Czech Republic in particular, right-wing populist parties aim their exclusionary tactics primarily at the Roma minority. As the only significantly numerous ethnic minority throughout the area and one that also represents a social and economic underclass, the Roma Question is one of the most intractable problems to trouble the new members of the EU and, indeed, spill over into the rest of the Union because of widespread Roma migration.[56]

These developments in the new EU member states – a rise in nationalism, not to say xenophobia, vis-à-vis vulnerable minorities such as Roma as well as the electoral success of populist parties – parallel developments in the old EU. It is difficult to say whether the new EU states have significantly influenced the older members but there is a growing convergence across Europe whereby trends in the East reinforce those in the West regarding the nature of the Union. Whereas the first post-war generation that constructed the European Common Market in the West saw it as a means to prevent war and idealists envisioned the EU as a vast and emerging democratic community, today's EU is based on mutual interest.

The post-Communist states entered the EU not to surrender their sovereignty but to fortify it. It is this understanding that explains why Hungary, Poland and Romania occupy the first three positions regarding the proposition, 'the EU should become a federation of nation-states'.[57] Whatever the intentions of the survey designers and the understanding of other respondents to a 2014 European Commission survey on 'Public Opinion in the European Union', these countries put the emphasis on the perpetuation of 'nation-states'. All the post-Communist states, which are poorer than the average EU member state, have profited immensely from the Union's structural and cohesion funds which transfer vast amounts from its wealthier to its poorer parts. This explains why most East- Central Europeans are more likely than the average EU member to agree that the EU makes quality of life better in Europe; only in Slovakia and Hungary, the least inclined to agree, does forty-five per cent agreement just meet the EU average.[58]

Throughout the EU, economic issues are the most pressing concerns of Europeans.[59] Inasmuch as the economy occupies a central place in transition[60] this is particularly true for East-Central Europeans who learned soon after 1989 that 'the value of freedom could not be turned into cash'[61] and that the affluence they were dreaming of remained elusive. In the intervening twenty-five years or so, East-Central Europe has become thoroughly integrated into the world economy though observers may well ask whether the region is developing into a 'new prosperity zone or a new periphery'.[62] On the one hand, it is the area with the fastest growing wages in the world, outpacing even Asia; on the other hand, the steep rise reflects the low level of wages under Communism rather than increases in labour productivity which, in any case, have not kept pace with wage rises. Even today, wage levels in the Czech Republic and Poland are only one-third of those in Germany and Bulgarian wages are less than half of those in Poland, though they are higher than wage levels in Asia.

Western firms have taken advantage of low wages and a friendly business environment – what one critic has called a 'race to the bottom'[63] – to shift manufacturing to East-Central Europe, conveniently close to Western markets. To take a prime example, the automobile industry has moved into the region on a large scale. Western firms bought out local car producers, Volkswagen purchasing Skoda in the Czech Republic and Renault buying Dacia in Romania. Fiat built on its Communist-era investment in Poland to produce 600,000 cars annually and Suzuki made the automobile industry the pillar of the Hungarian manufacturing sector. Such developments created much needed jobs and helped the countries' commercial balances. They did little, however, to promote research and innovation and they proved alarmingly fragile. With the start of the economic crisis in 2008, the automobile market in the West shrivelled and foreign investment shrank. As in the 1930s, the countries of East-Central Europe, once again a capitalist periphery, bore the brunt of recession in the developed West. The pessimistic verdict that the story of Central and Eastern Europe in the twentieth century was one of trying to catch up by following several models and failing in each[64] appeared to have been projected into the twenty-first century.

Initially, it was Hungary that was the poster child of the transition. For many years, Hungary attracted the lion's share of all direct foreign investment in Central and Eastern Europe – as much as the Russian Federation although its population was barely 7 per cent of Russia's.[65] The Hungarian success story came to an end, however, in 2009, when investment flowed out of the country at an alarming rate; since then Hungary has been trying to scale down its outlays and repay the International Monetary Fund (IMF) loan that it was forced to take out. The present economic miracle is Poland which boasts of being 'Europe's most dynamic economy'.[66] In 2009, when the EU economy as a whole contracted by 4.5 per cent, the Polish economy grew by 1.6 per cent, not much in absolute terms but the only country in Europe to register positive growth. However, when examined more closely, the 'Polish miracle' too is fragile.[67] Though Poland is a fairly homogeneous country, the distribution of per capita GDP between the poorest and the richest regions of the country stands at a ratio of one to six. The unemployment rate, though down from its record of almost twenty-one per cent in 2003, was in the range of just above eleven per cent to nearly fourteen per cent during 2014. These figures were above the average EU unemployment rate (10.1 per cent in 2014). In comparison to West European countries (though in line with Bulgaria and Romania), Poland's emigration figures are extraordinarily high and continue to rise. Some 2.2 million Poles now live abroad, mostly beneficiaries of open borders with other EU member states.[68]

Although the 'Polish miracle' thus does have strong limitations, it has given Poland substantial influence within the EU. Further evidence of the reciprocal transformation that is ongoing within the EU as the new members acquire a stronger voice in Brussels is the appointment of the former Polish Prime Minister, Donald Tusk, as President of the European Council. Tusk, who spoke neither French nor English and only some German, gave his first press conference in Polish.

Political changes are, necessarily, concomitant with economic changes.[69] As Poland's star rose economically and politically, that of Hungary fell. The present Hungarian government is decried abroad for its 'authoritarian descent',[70] an assessment that overrides acknowledgement of its 'virtuous' adoption of austerity measures. Within the country, the government's campaign against foreign ownership of the economy enjoys significant popularity. What may be the most pressing issue today in East-Central European corruption is seen as both a political and an economic problem in Hungary. In its first ever report on corruption, issued in 2014, the EU pointed the finger at Bulgaria and Romania, 77th and 69th respectively on Transparency International's index of corruption perception by country (the EU also criticised Croatia, the Czech Republic, Lithuania and Greece). Indeed, corruption has become the way 'the post-communist public talks about politics and the economy, past and future'.[71] Denouncing corruption has become a discourse on the rise of inequality and a way of criticising the government without needing to submit alternatives to its policies; it has been suggested that the level of corruption is the most important determinant of attitudes to undemocratic alternatives. Intriguingly, a study has shown that although nine of the thirteen most corrupt countries in the EU are from among its new members, ten of the twelve EU states where corruption declined between 2004 and 2009 are also new members, whereas corruption increased in twelve old member states.[72]

Even as the costs of transition continued to weigh on post-Communist society, East-Central Europe appeared to have settled into a low-grade democratic routine. In the first free elections, at the start of the 1990s, forty-five parties competed in Hungary, sixty-seven in Poland and seventy-four in Romania.[73] Since then, electoral politics have crystallised around two, rarely more, large blocs, often of post-Communist or anti-Communist inspiration, as well as some minor parties, ethnically defined in the case of Romania and Bulgaria; these parties are sometimes able to acquire importance as 'balancers' between the blocs. A specificity of the region is that the question of completing the 'unfinished revolution' of 1989, that is, of dealing punitively with the Communist past, has again come to the fore.[74] This trend has recently been confirmed in Poland with the staggering victory in October 2015 of the populist party, Law and Justice, which repudiates '1989' entirely. It claims that the events of that year were a 'fraud', that Communists (if not Communism in its recognisable form) continued to hold power and that the Third Polish Republic would only now be able to emerge from the ashes of the 'Smolensk coup', the crash, attributed to Russian perfidy, of a Polish airplane in 2010 which caused the death of the sitting president and much of the country's elite.[75]

Such trends may spell the beginning of a post-transition period which confirms that movement towards liberal democracy is not foreordained. Until now, however, party formations have regularly alternated in government, perhaps disturbingly so as alternation suggests that governments fail to live up to their promises or to popular expectations. The idea of public service is held in low esteem and trust in government is low, as it is throughout the EU. Curiously, East-Central Europeans are more satisfied than the EU average with the workings of democracy in the EU, often considered a notoriously undemocratic institution, and they are more satisfied with democracy in the EU than in their own countries. This does not induce them to vote more readily in EU elections as participation of new members falls well below the EU average. Participation in national parliamentary elections stands much higher, hovering around fifty per cent, which is comparable to France though lower than that of the United Kingdom or Germany.[76]

The refugee crisis of 2015–2016 may prove to be a critical point in the transition process as this was the moment when post-Communist states first openly defied the EU. When asked to take a share of the incoming refugees, according to a quota system elaborated in Brussels, the four new EU members in East-Central Europe declined.[77] Romania and Bulgaria were not involved as they are not part of the Schengen system and therefore cannot act as passageways towards the heart of Europe; in any case, the refugees have not shown any interest in going there. Poland wavered for a brief moment, breaking ranks with its Visegrad allies in agreeing to take in a modest 9,000 refugees. The Prime Minister at the time returned home with the alluring announcement that Poland would receive up to €10,000 for each refugee.[78] With the change of government Poland withdrew its offer, vaguely referring to the Paris terrorist attacks in November 2015 but, in fact, confirming an anti-refugee stance that it had taken during the parliamentary election campaign in October, with the leader of the victorious party suggesting that the refugees carried diseases.[79] Presumably, the disease was not Islam though the Poles and other East-Central Europeans treated Islam as if it were such.

The attitude of the East-Central European countries has brought to the fore several characteristics which had been dormant as they sought to adapt to Western expectations of a smooth transition towards liberal democratic norms.[80] First, these countries have confirmed their tenacious attachment to national sovereignty. This may not be so surprising in new states, such as the Czech Republic and Slovakia, which are enjoying sovereignty for the first time or, indeed, in the states of the area which had chafed under the 'limited sovereignty' of the Soviet period. It has now become even more apparent that these new members of the EU joined the Union not to give up their sovereignty but to re-enforce it. Quotas imposed by Brussels were seen as a clear infringement of their hard won and very precious national sovereignty.

Second, the East-Central European countries do not share the bad conscience of the West and therefore they do not see themselves as owing a debt to humanity. Whereas in the West, many experience guilt over the colonial experience, exploitation of the Global South and the Holocaust (particularly among political and intellectual elites and especially in Germany which has been most receptive to refugees), East-Central Europeans see themselves, not others, as victims. The prevalent attitude in East-Central Europe is that people there have been victims of Communism as well as of neglect and abandonment by the West. Since 1989, the West has proven to be overbearing in its demands upon ex-Communist candidate countries and reluctant to admit them to the European 'club' to which these countries believe they naturally belong, delaying their admission for some fifteen years.

Finally, the East-Central Europeans have little experience of the 'Other' and do not consider diversity a value, as it has become among the older members of the EU. The East-Central Europeans are rather proud of their homogeneity, even exaggerating its degree by overlooking the presence of Roma and other minorities. The historical periods when these countries were indeed very diverse, the age of empires and the pre-World War II period, are not seen as positive references. Today, those who do not belong to the majority population are viewed with suspicion. Whereas West European countries are marked by very significant immigration from former colonial areas and elsewhere that has taken place since World War II, immigration to East-Central Europe, particularly from outside Europe, has been insignificant. During the Communist period this area was impenetrable to immigrants and, since then, has proved unattractive. The result is that whereas in Amsterdam or London seeing a veiled woman or hearing an African speak the local language is an everyday occurrence, this is not the case in East-Central Europe.

Conclusions

In many ways, East-Central Europe has been undergoing a successful, though fragile, transition to a liberal democratic order which is only now being called into question. After a breathtaking start in 1989, transition proceeded slowly, overcoming obstacles but encountering new ones. Hopes of catching up economically with Western Europe faded, even as the number of 'losers' in the transition process among the population declined without disappearing altogether. The pitfalls of integration into the world economy came into sharp focus with the recession of 2008 and the long-awaited goal of joining the EU coincided with widespread disenchantment with the Union within its ranks leading to outright rejection of EU norms in 2015. The danger of authoritarian backtracking has grown, as evidenced by the present course in Hungary and Poland and by the broadening appeal of populist discourse. In his first address as Czechoslovakia's president, Vaclav Havel lamented the country's 'polluted moral environment.'[81] He may have been referring to traits such as cynicism, mutual suspicion or distrust of the public sphere which persist in East-Central Europe; the transition will not be complete until they have been overcome.

Notes

1 Przeworski, *Democracy and the Market*, p. 3.
2 Savranskaya, *Masterpieces of History*.
3 Brown, *The Gorbachev Factor*.
4 See Chapter 2.
5 Hobsbawm, 'Eric Hobsbawm remembers Tony Judt', p. 14.
6 Linz and Stepan, *Problems of Democratic Transition and Consolidation*, p. 255.
7 See Chapter 2.
8 Ost, *The Defeat of Solidarity*.
9 Przeworski, *Democracy and the Market*, p. 79.
10 In Poland, the bloc parties were the United People's Party (or Peasant Party) and the Democratic Party, a repository for the intelligentsia. In the GDR, there was the Christian Democratic Union, the Liberal Democratic Party, the National Democratic Party and the Democratic Farmers' Party. The last Prime Minister of the GDR, Lothar de Mazière, came from the East German Christian Democratic Union, both facilitating and symbolising the transition in that country. In Czechoslovakia, the bloc parties

were the Czechoslovak People's Party, the Slovak Freedom Party and the Party of Slovak Revival. Most of these parties continued after 1989, sometimes under different names.
11 Kotkin, *Uncivil Society*.
12 Munck and Skalnik Leff, 'Modes of Transition and Democratization'.
13 Gati, *The Bloc That Failed*.
14 Hankiss, 'Reforms and the Conversion of Power'.
15 Kowalik, *From Solidarity to Sellout*.
16 Liebich, 'East Europe Today'.
17 Brown, *Surge to Freedom*.
18 Sarotte, *The Collapse*.
19 Ash, '1989!'.
20 Ash, 'The Empire in Decay'.
21 Jedlicki, 'The Revolution of 1989'.
22 Linz and Stepan, *Problems of Democratic Transition and Consolidation*, p. 239.
23 Przeworski, *Democracy and the Market*, p. 54.
24 Stefan Auer, 'The Revolutions of 1989 Revisited', *Eurozine*, 14 June 2004.
25 Habermas, 'What Does Socialism Mean Today?'.
26 Offe and Adler, 'Capitalism by Democratic Design'.
27 Furet, 'From 1789 to 1917 and 1989'.
28 Brinton, *Anatomy of Revolution*.
29 Reszler, *Rejoindre l'Europe*.
30 Heller, 'Twenty Years After 1989'.
31 Janos, 'Continuity and Change in Eastern Europe'.
32 Kowalik, *From Solidarity to Sellout*, p. 12.
33 Anderson, *The New Old World*.
34 Kowalik, *From Solidarity to Sellout*.
35 Gati, *The Bloc That Failed*.
36 Lavigne, *The Economies of Transition*.
37 Maddison, *The World Economy*.
38 European Bank for Reconstruction and Development (EBRD) cited in Hoen, *The Transformation of Economic Systems in Central Europe*.
39 Kowalik, *From Solidarity to Sellout*.
40 Horne, 'The Impact of Lustration on Democratization in Postcommunist Countries'.
41 Kowalik, *From Solidarity to Sellout*.
42 Lavigne, *The Economies of Transition*.
43 Wedel, *Collision and Collusion*.
44 See Chapter 2.
45 Krause, 'Slovakia's Second Transition'.
46 Cited in Wedel, *Collision and Collusion*, p. 23.
47 Slavenka Drakulic, 'Die Welt als Milchkuh', *Der Standard* [supplement] November 2007.
48 Kwasniewski, 'Poland in NATO'.
49 Bebler, *The Challenge of NATO Enlargement*, p. 103.
50 Simon, *Poland and NATO*.
51 John Feffer, 'NATO: Rebellion in the Ranks?', *Foreign Policy in Focus*, 29 October 2014.
52 Guerra, *Central and Eastern Attitudes in the Face of Union*.
53 'A Swamp of Paranoid Nostalgia', *The Economist*, 5 July 2007.
54 Siklova and Polackova Henley, 'The Solidarity of the Culpable'.
55 www.electionresources.org/eastern.europe.html.
56 www.erionet.eu/.
57 European Commission, 'Public Opinion in the European Union: First Results', *Standard Eurobarometer* 81, Spring 2014.

58 Ibid.
59 Ibid.
60 See Chapter 2.
61 Heller, 'Twenty Years After 1989', p. 56.
62 Apostolov, 'The End of the Post-Cold War World'.
63 Anderson, *The New Old World*, p. 55.
64 Hobsbawm, 'The New Threat to History'.
65 http://data.worldbank.org.
66 Stephen Faris, 'How Poland Became Europe's Most Dynamic Economy', *Bloomberg Businessweek*, 27 November 2013.
67 Kolodko, 'The Lessons to be Learned from the Great Post-Communist Change'.
68 www.indexmundi.com.
69 See Chapter 2.
70 Marton, 'Hungary's Authoritarian Descent'.
71 Krastev, 'A Moral Economy of Anti-Corruption Sentiments in Eastern Europe', in Elkana *et al.*, *Unraveling Ties*, pp. 99–116.
72 Pierre Verluise, 'UE-27: La Corruption reste un Défi', www.diploweb.com, 18 April 2010.
73 Suleiman, 'Bureaucracy and Democratic Consolidation: Lessons from Eastern Europe', in Anderson, *Transitions to Democracy*, pp. 141–159.
74 Mark, *The Unfinished Revolution*.
75 See Pyzik, *Poor But Sexy*.
76 www.idea.int.
77 'Eastern EU States Fight Migrant "Diktat"', *Financial Times*, 23 September 2015.
78 'EU to Pay Poland EUR 6,000–10,000 for Refugees?', *Radio Poland*, 2 October 2015.
79 'Poland Won't Relocate Migrants after Paris Attacks', www.euractiv.com, 14 November 2015.
80 The following argument is presented in greater detail in André Liebich, 'Central Europe and the Refugees', Tr@nsit Online, www.iwm.at/read-listen-watch/transit-online/central-europe-refugees, 2 November 2015.
81 Brown, *Surge to Freedom*, p. 179.

7 Successes and breakdowns
Democratisation in Sub-Saharan Africa

Julien Morency-Laflamme

In 1989, as Namibia held its first multi-party election since the country's independence, a wave of democratisation was ignited all over Sub-Saharan Africa (SSA). Until then, the sub-continent's regimes had, for the most part, been authoritarian.[1] After 1989, the evolution of SSA's regimes took a variety of directions: electoral democracies flourished in a number of cases, hegemonic authoritarian regimes remained in power and, in a majority of cases, hybrid regimes, also called anocracies, took shape. While the initial period of regime changes in the early 1990s eventually came to an end, SSA's regimes continued to change, sometimes quite drastically, over the following twenty years. Autocrats who had managed to hold on to power at the end of the twentieth century lost their power monopoly and had to leave office. Inversely, in certain states, democratic processes were derailed.

According to Polity IV, there were two periods of democratic rise: from 1988 to 1995 and then from 2000 to 2010.[2] These two sub-waves are at the core of this chapter's analysis of common trends among SSA's regime transitions. While the multiple regime trajectories of SSA states highlight that regime transitions do not have fixed outcomes, they also point to the importance of actors in transition stories.[3] In their key work on the 1989–1994 African democratic wave, Michael Bratton and Nicolas van de Walle claim that popular protests were the main igniter of regime change in Africa.[4] They also draw attention to the critical role played by the armed forces, which often 'determined' the fate of democratisation processes.[5] Other works examining the same period also highlight the critical role played by actors in African democratisation processes, indicating that the outcome of regime crisis was anything but fixed and that the decisions of domestic and international actors could be seen as the strongest explanatory factors.[6]

This chapter assesses the actions of four critical actors: the incumbent regime, opposition forces, armed forces and the international community. It then outlines the transitional paths that can be identified in Africa. Finally, it assesses the modes of transition taken by SSA states in order to find common characteristics among successful transition cases. While the transition processes varied greatly, from transition through ruptures to foreign-backed transitions, all successful transitions established political limitations on the actions of the various political forces; in a large number of successful democratisation cases, this political

Table 7.1 Regime status in Sub-Saharan Africa[7]

Democracies		Anocracies		Autocracies
Benin	Lesotho	Angola	Guinea-Bissau	Eritrea
Botswana	Liberia	Burkina Faso*	Ivory Coast	Swaziland
Burundi*	Namibia	Cameroon	Madagascar	
Cape Verde	Senegal	Congo	Mozambique	
Comoros	Sierra Leone	Democratic Republic	Rwanda	
Ghana	South Africa	of Congo	Sudan	
Kenya	Zambia	Djibouti	Tanzania	
		Equatorial Guinea	Togo	
		Ethiopia	Uganda	
		Gabon	Zimbabwe	
		Guinea		

Note
* The political situation in these states has evolved dramatically and they are still in flux today.

limitation was put in place through formal or informal agreements among the main actors. These constraints also came from other factors, namely the weakness of incumbent elites, demands by foreign actors or even fear that political alternatives could result in major civil strife and/or coups. Furthermore, with a few exceptions, successful democratisation was accompanied by the creation of relatively strong opposition parties to prevent the incumbent from monopolising power.

Incumbent regimes

In O'Donnell et al.'s *Transitions from Authoritarian Rule* (1986), the split of the ruling elite is what ignites the transition processes.[8] No political transition could be initiated without a division between those members of the ruling clique who favour, and those who oppose, the opening of the political space. Research on democratisation that came afterwards has been overly critical of this point of view, arguing that civil society and not ruling elites provided the impetus for transition from authoritarianism to democracy.[9] In the African context, Bratton and van de Walle state in their seminal work, *Democratic Experiments in Africa – Regime Transitions in Comparative Perspective*, that the neopatrimonial nature of Africa's authoritarian states precluded any fracture among the ruling coalition.[10] Political transitions are rather initiated as insiders – those who benefit from the autocrats' favours and patronage – are overpowered by those who do not benefit from it, the outsiders. In fact, the fear among insiders of losing their revenue source is so important that it would prevent any regime defection. Bratton and van de Walle argue that:

> Insiders typically have risen through the ranks of political service and, apart from top leaders who may have invested in private capital holdings, derive their livelihood principally from state or party offices. Because they

face the prospect of losing all visible means of support in a political transition, they have little option but to cling to the regime, to sink or swim with it.[11]

After more than twenty years of democratic experiments in SSA, we can provide a more nuanced view of the role played both by the ruling elite and civil society groups and the importance of elite division in transition processes in SSA. While in most countries unified ruling coalition precluded regime change, in a few notable exceptions cohesive ruling elites initiated political liberalisation processes that led to the creation of democratic regimes. In Tanzania, the ruling Chama Cha Mapinduzi (CCM) initiated political reforms and opened up to multi-party elections with only minimal pressure from foreign donors and civil society.[12] After independence, Botswana's ruling elite, the Botswana Democratic Party (BDP) had allowed multi-party elections despite its political hegemony.[13] In other cases, groups within the ruling autocratic regimes recommended political liberalisation as a way of overcoming the regime's challenges.[14] For the most part, however, the incumbent regime resisted early demands for political opening and was pushed to accept liberalisation by continuing civic resistance and international pressure. These unified ruling coalitions more often than not stopped short of creating democratic regimes; rather, they installed new reformed liberalised autocratic regimes where minimal democratic institutions failed to bring any real political change as the ruling party was still favoured through an uneven playing field.

Between 1989 and 1994, political protests preceded political liberalisation in no fewer than twenty-eight cases, meaning that these protests were the *source*, and not the *result*, of political liberalisation.[15] Two episodes best exemplify the role played by incumbent forces in this process: the experiences of Togo (1990–1993) and Guinea (2008–2010). Despite being nearly two decades apart, both cases demonstrate certain similarities that are shared with many other African states as their respective governments used minimal reform promises which did not level the political playing field, as well as heavy repression, in efforts to end the popular protests. It was only the refusal of protesters to end their civic resistance campaigns that led both of these states to initiate processes of political liberalisation.[16]

This does not mean that incumbent regimes played a secondary role in the African democratisation stories. They were in fact key players whose actions could derail many processes. The resistance of incumbent forces has, in fact, delayed or even impeded the entire process in some instances. Many autocrats' efforts have pushed back transitional processes in SSA over long periods of time. In Kenya, the Kenya African National Union (KANU) remained in power and prevented any political change in the country for over a decade. The then President Daniel Arap Moi managed to use state resources to co-opt members of the opposition and to force local militias to harass his main opponents. In Ivory Coast, Henry Konan Bédié and his allies modified the constitution to prevent his main opponent, former Prime Minister Alassane Ouattara (who subsequently became President in 2011 and was re-elected in 2015), from taking part in the 1995 elections. Robert Mugabe's constant use of youth militias to harass opponents reflects similar dynamics in Zimbabwe, namely the denial of the possibility of political change.

These strategies for holding onto power have long-term repercussions for the likelihood of peaceful transitions in SSA states; politicisation of ethnicity launched the Ivory Coast in a civil war while Kenya's main political forces employed ethnic militias against their opponents in strategic regions well into the twenty-first century.[17] In other states, ethnic alliances maintained the incumbent regime's hold on power and denied the political change demanded by other groups. In Togo, the political and military elite, mostly composed of northerners, held onto power despite continuous political opposition from the more populous southern regions. Similarly, in Burundi, a Tutsi-dominated officer corps staged a coup and ended the political transition in 1993. In other cases, former autocrats managed to regain power, either through electoral or violent means, after initially being defeated; while members of the former autocratic elites may not have ultimately derailed the transition process, like Mathieu Kérékou in Benin or John Atta Mills in Ghana, in most cases returning autocrats ended the democratic experiments in their country.[18]

The main explanation for the authoritarian ability to resist regime transition is, in fact, the lack of regime defections.[19] Incumbent elites who remained united generally maintained their power over long periods. Tanzania's CCM did implement political liberalisation, partly because the party knew that electoral defeat was virtually impossible as, outside of Zanzibar, there were no major member defections.[20] Cameroon's People's Democratic Movement (CPDM) and Zimbabwe's African National Union (ZANU) were also remarkably cohesive, as members of the ruling parties remained united in the face of electoral challenges.[21]

SSA cases of protracted and precluded transition demonstrate that, if anything, cohesive ruling circles can easily prevent regime change.[22] Regimes that managed to effectively prevent internal fractures – either through effective conflict-management mechanisms, usage of ethnicity or the provision of perks to its members – could use their full political strength to weaken opposition forces.[23] In some cases, as Barkan demonstrated, ruling elites could use their financial resources to create incentives for opposition leaders to defect to their side. For instance, Moi in Kenya bought members of the opposition throughout the 1990s in order to secure his own rule.[24] Other unified ruling coalitions could more easily use their security apparatus to repress opposition movements and prevent them from posing any real challenge to their rule. Gnassingbé Eyadéma, and his son Faure Eyadéma, relied on loyal armed forces throughout the 1990s and 2000s to neutralise any potential gains by the opposition parties. Cohesive ruling circles remained in power and generally prevented regime change.

Inversely, in cases of rapid transition regime members quickly abandoned the incumbent ruler to join the opposition forces, remained neutral or even founded their own political parties. In Mali, most members of Moussa Traoré's government had abandoned him by March 1991 and joined the democratic movement.[25]

In the early 1990s, many autocrats were abandoned by members of their ruling coalition, who either joined existing opposition movements, as was the case in Zambia, or set up new political parties, as in Malawi. In other cases, weakened ruling parties could not withstand popular and international demands and ultimately had to give in. During the 2002 election in Kenya and the 2012 election in Senegal, key regime opponents were defectors who managed to rally the opposition to their cause.[26] Regime defection weakened the relative capacity of incumbents to hold on to power and prevent regime change, as they increased the relative power of anti-incumbent coalitions by bringing their own political networks and financial resources. It is telling that these defector parties, such as Malawi's United Democratic Front (UDF), who later transformed into the Democratic Progressive party (DPP), or the Liberal Democratic Party (LDP) in Kenya, went on to become prominent political players in their respective countries. Similarly, in Nigeria, the first president in the post-military junta era was General Olusegun Obasanjo, a military opponent of the former military dictator, General Abacha.[27] In 2007, the defection of many members of the ruling Sierra Leone People's Party (SLPP), who then went on to create the People's Movement for Democratic Change (PMDC), greatly reduced the strength of the incumbent party in the incoming elections, which it ultimately lost.[28]

Elite defectors are usually members of the ruling coalition who gain fewer benefits from the status quo than other members of the ruling group.[29] They leave as opposition movements gain momentum and they begin to realise that they can obtain more benefits by joining the other camp. For instance, the senior members of the ruling KANU party in Kenya who left and formed the LDP had been embittered by the selection of Uhuru Kenyatta as the presidential candidate and the disregard for their own faction's preference for Raila Odinga.

The ability of authoritarian regimes to prevent elite defection is often the key to their survival in periods of regime crisis. The CCM in Tanzania, for instance, has managed to create a unifying ideology, Ujamaa, which has been modified over the years when there was a chance of defections from certain factions, alongside a well-oiled clientelist network that rewards loyal groups throughout the country.[30] Kenya's KANU maintained its power between 1989 and 2002 as only a few regime members defected to the opposition; only in 2002, as Raila Odinga and many other party members joined the National Alliance Rainbow Coalition, did KANU finally lose an election. As mentioned above, conflict-management and patronage networks are effective means of preventing regime defection. Another means is the use of ethnicity. This can prevent defection because ethnic identification forces an association between the regime and favoured groups in the eyes of other societal groups.[31] For instance, van de Walle concluded that Paul Biya in Cameroon could count on the army officers that he selected from the ethnic groups he deemed more loyal – mostly Beti and southerners – and that any change of power would 'result in the probable loss of a number of advantages from which they benefit'.[32]

While it is true that members of the ruling elite have not been the impetus behind democratisation processes in SSA, it does seem that regime defection, or the lack thereof, has been critical to the success of such processes. Autocrats who managed to prevent the defection of their allies were able to limit political liberalisation, at the very least, while those who failed to do so sometimes managed to hold on to power for a while, although their regime almost inevitably fell as defectors evened out the playing field.

Security forces

While the armed forces have often been treated, among others, as one of the ruling groups, it deserves special attention for the role it has played in regime transition processes in SSA. Since 1990, there have been sixty coups and coup attempts in SSA.[33] In the last twenty-five years, there have been more coups in Africa, and particularly in West Africa, than in any other region in the world. While there has been a reduction in the number of coup attempts – and their success rate – after 2000, SSA remains the most coup prone region in the world. Military coups have been one of the major forms of leadership change on the African continent into the independence period. In the 1970s, close to two-thirds of SSA regimes were military or military-backed. Today, there are only a few military rulers left on the African continent, but the military's actions must be taken into consideration in order to understand the successes and failures of Africa's democratisation processes.

Despite its importance, the military has been largely overlooked by general transition theories. O'Donnell and Schmitter did integrate the near veto power of the military into their theory through what they called the 'Military Moment', which acknowledges the need for would-be democratisers to accommodate military interests.[34] Similarly, Bratton and van de Walle acknowledged that, in SSA, 'as went the army, so went the transition'.[35] Other research followed and acknowledged the critical role played by the army in SSA transitions.[36] While much research assumes the would-be spoiler role of the army – an opponent of democratisation processes that needs to be accommodated – it has played a far more ambivalent role: sometimes an ally to would-be democratisers, and sometimes an ally to anti-democratic forces.

In some cases, military coups have marked the beginning of the transition process. In 1992, the officer coup led by colonel Amadou Toumani Touré marked the end of Moussa Traoré's rule and the beginning of the transition period in Mali; the unreliability of the armed forces in Benin in 1989 and the decision of Malawi's armed forces to protect protesters from the police who were still loyal to President Hastings Kamuzu Banda were also turning points in these countries' transition processes.[37] In Madagascar, as the military command declared its neutrality, elements of the armed forces acted in support of protesters to force the resignation of President Didier Ratsiraka in 2002 and President Marc Ravalomanana in 2009. In Niger in 2010, elements of the army ended months of protest against former President Mamadou Tanja's economic policies and attempts to consolidate his hold on power.[38] In Burkina Faso, the military stepped in to back popular demands for the removal of Blaise Compaoré in 2014 and then launched a counter-coup when the presidential guard tried to end the transition in 2015. While the military coup in Niger did bring about the reclamation of individual liberties, the same cannot be said for all the military coups. In Mali, the 2012 coup brought the country's democratic experiment to a halt,[39] while military coups in Togo (1991), Burundi (1993), Nigeria (1993) and Mauritania (2008) ended these countries' transitions.

Naturally, not all military coups are successful. In fact, only half of all *coups d'état* are successful in SSA.[40] However, even failed coup attempts have an important influence on the incumbent regime. The May 2015 coup attempt headed by General Godefroy Niyombare against the Burundian president Pierre Nkurunziza shook the confidence of the ruling National Council for the Defense of Democracy–Forces for the Defense of Democracy (CNDD–FDD) in the armed forces and was followed throughout the country by sporadic fighting and the dismissal of senior officers and ministers feared to be linked to the coup's ringleaders. Failed coups can signal to sitting autocrats that they are not in full control of their security forces, which could turn against them if the regime is challenged. President Mathieu Kérékou in Benin had been facing multiple failed coup attempts in 1988 and 1989 and thus could foresee that a significant number of officers and soldiers would side with the opposition forces during the national conference in 1990. President Kenneth Kaunda of Zambia also faced a similar situation as there was a coup plot against him in 1988 and a coup attempt in 1990, only a few years prior to the major protests that toppled him.[41]

Nonetheless, long-standing autocrats in SSA often had to rely on their armed forces to prevent the democratic opposition from seriously challenging their rule; Faure Eyadéma, the son of Gnassingbé Eyadéma, had to rely on the armed forces in order to rise to power after his father's death.[42] Similarly, Robert Mugabe and ZANU can still rely on a largely loyal army and security forces to crush the mobilisation of the opposition.[43] There are two situations in which the armed forces seem to be largely opposed to any regime transition: in loyalist armies and in liberation armies. As a result of decades of neo-patrimonial rule, many appointments and promotions within African armies – such as for senior officers and members of special units and paramilitary forces like presidential guards – are largely due to the goodwill of the autocratic leader; for these officers and soldiers, regime change means the loss of their privileges.[44] Liberation armies are held together by the memory of anti-colonial or civil war struggles. In Eastern and Southern Africa especially, armies and the political leadership are tied together by their past struggles. While some of these liberation armies are very inclusive, as in Mozambique, other armies have taken largely ethnic overtones – for example, the Zimbabwean army, which is almost exclusively composed of Shonas.[45] Loyalist armies are largely oblivious to demands for regime change, which they almost automatically see as a threat to their very survival. In Burundi, even though President Pierre Buyoya spearheaded the move towards greater integration of the Hutu-dominated opposition and tried to reassure his own followers, Tutsi officers still used repression to prevent any regime change.[46] While democratisation in countries where loyalist armies are present is not impossible, it represents one of the most difficult challenges to would-be democratisers.

In Niger, military coups followed increased popular mobilisation by factions from various social groups in 2010.[47] The same was true of similar cases of democratic transition in the first wave of democratisation in Africa between 1989–1994. For instance, Traoré's regime in Mali was abandoned by the armed forces after an increase in the level of protest following the killing of nearly 150 protesters.[48] In other cases, however, such as Cameroon during operation Ghost Town in 1991 and in Togo during the general strike in 1992, the armed forces remained loyal to the government.[49] What was missing in these two cases, yet found in cases of 'pro-democratic' coups, was the presence of officer cliques with sustained grievances against the regime. In Mali, for example, the armed forces resented the failure of government strategy against the rebels in the north in 1992.[50] Thus, popular pressure cannot by itself explain the circumstances under which the military favours regime change and democratisation as there are cases where the army resisted popular pressure over long periods.[51] More than any other group, the armed forces can maintain rulers in power even when faced with mounting popular and international pressure.

If this is so, then what are the circumstances under which the armed forces choose to oppose incumbents? Part of the answer lies in the factional nature of armies in authoritarian states.[52] Deeply divided armies tend to favour return to civilian rule and multi-party politics as a way of avoiding intra-military fighting, as they fear that military factions will use their arms in favour of their favourite candidates. In many cases, military factions have acted in favour of a transition to democracy when rival factions had been overly favoured in promotion procedures, the distribution of military assets and overall perks.[53] In Malawi in 1993, the armed forces acted against President Banda's government, which favoured paramilitary organisations and the police over the military.[54] Out of favour military cliques are more likely than any other group to act on their grievances. They either stay neutral, as the high command in Madagascar did in 2002 and 2009, or come out in favour of democracy, such as in Mali in 1992 and in Malawi.

The internal composition of the armed forces, and consequently its actions during regime transitions, is determined by years of recruitment policy, military training programmes and the general civil–military relations of a given state. In many cases, military recruitment has been linked with ethnic identity and/or party membership as long-standing autocratic leaders wanted to neutralise potential military rivals and insure that the armed forces obey their demands, including repressing domestic opponents.[55]

In SSA, ethnic tensions within the armed forces led to coup cycles; the losers of these cycles were officers from non-ruling ethnic groups. The 1982 coup in Kenya, for instance, was spearheaded by non-Kalenjin officers, angry at the swelling of the security forces with Kalenjin officers attached to Moi.[56] Similarly, in 1988, Fon officers were behind assassination attempts against President Kérékou, a Somba.[57] In Ivory Coast, the leaders behind the 2002 mutiny were northern officers who were threatened by the anti-northerner policy implemented during the 1990s.[58] Inversely, in Togo, the armed forces and the political leadership of the country are in the hands of the Kabyès; Kabyès officers came to the regime's defence whenever the opposition challenged its political monopoly.[59] In Cameroon, the officer corps is composed predominantly of Beti and southerners, groups loyal to long-standing President Paul Biya.[60]

How regimes retain control of the armed forces, and the demands for security sector reforms, are a key part of SSA transitions. While there was a reduction in military intervention in the late 1990s and early 2000s, recent military coups on the continent are a crucial reminder that African armies still hold considerable political power. Even where the army was at first an ally to the pro-democracy movements, it can still launch coups and end the democratic process in later years. Military power must be taken into account by would-be democratisers as well as by general theories on democratic transitions in SSA. While African leaders have launched security sector reform in order to diminish the military's influence in the political sphere, these reforms remain incomplete at best.[61] As long as these reforms are not achieved, military officers in Africa will remain in a position to virtually veto the continent's democratisation process.

Opposition forces[62]

Guillermo O'Donnell argued in a 2010 article that civil society and mass mobilisation were the driving forces behind the passage from mere political liberalisation to democratic transition.[63] The role of civil society, in contrast to the role of elites, has been the subject of a very heated debate among transitologists ever since O'Donnell *et al.*'s *Transitions from Authoritarian Rule* was published in 1986. The first theories on regime change that gave only a limited role to mass mobilisation in the process of democratic transition – largely as a tool to be controlled by more moderate pro-democracy elites – were challenged by additional research that concluded that regime divisions, including the decision by some elite groups to take a pro-reform stance, were driven by the desire to alleviate the political and economic consequences of mass mobilisation.[64] In the SSA context, however, democracy is clearly pushed not by elites (from above) but by civil society (from below). As Bratton and van de Walle observe, democracy has occurred most frequently in countries where popular protests pushed the incumbent regime to make political concessions.[65]

In most cases, it is popular mobilisation that marks the beginning of political liberalisation and/or regime change processes. In Guinea, protesters took to the streets in 2007 and again in 2008 against President Lansana Conte's autocratic rule; after his death, the leader of a successful coup, Captain Moussa Dadis Camara, also attempted to consolidate his power. Again, opposition forces took to the streets, but violence ensued as the security forces shot 150 protesters.[66] Continuing protests convinced members of Camara's close guard to intervene and after a failed opposition attempt Prime Minister General Sekouba Konaté negotiated a power-sharing agreement with the opposition forces; a new constitution was written and the new prime minister was from the opposition. In the 2010 presidential elections, the opposition candidate, Alpha Conde, won in the second round. In a somewhat similar story, two large waves of protests swept through Madagascar in 2001 when Marc Ravalomanana called his supporters to take to the streets of the capital when it became clear that Didier Ratsiraka was attempting to steal the election.[67] Ravalomanana was successful and his followers were able to take control of government buildings; Ratsiraka had to flee the country. Ravalomanana's own nepotism would bring his regime to an end in 2008 as Andry Rajoelina, the mayor of Antananarivo, led a series of massive protests which forced Ravalomanana into exile.

Similar events took place in other SSA states, where opposition forces continued to push authoritarian governments towards political openings and multi-party elections. In Benin, protests and a strike by civil servants in 1989 pushed the Mathieu Kérékou government to end Marxist-Leninism, legalise opposition parties, provide an amnesty for all political opponents and hold a national conference. In Zambia, Kaunda faced similar challenges and had to give in to the opposition's demands for multi-party elections and political reforms. In South Africa, the National Party was pushed to negotiate as the continuing mobilisation of anti-apartheid forces convinced an increasing number of its members and supporters that the regime could not continue in the long run.[68] Not all mobilisation processes were a success, however; the Nigerian pro-democracy mobilisation between 1990 and 1995 did bring together around 300,000 participants and a lobby for an election in 1993, but the election results were declared flawed and another military junta took control of the state.[69]

While opposition forces have often managed to push regime liberalisation through, the processes frequently stopped short of a full transition to democracy. A key reason for the ineffectiveness of opposition forces was their inability to join together in the face of the incumbent regime. Divided opposition forces are far less likely to either effectively pressurise autocratic regimes to implement political reforms or to topple incumbents in anocracies through electoral means.[70]

The opposition forces that appeared in the 1980s and 1990s in nearly all African states were deeply fragmented and how they dealt with their political differences largely determined their success. In Kenya, deep divisions within the opposition forces allowed Moi to hold onto power until his retirement in 2002. In Zambia, opposition forces rapidly united around key leaders, Kenneth Kaunda especially, and won the 1991 elections. While in Zambia opposition forces formed a single party called the Movement for Multi-party Democracy (MMD), in Benin there was still a constellation of political parties which did not formally unify; Benin's opposition forces agreed instead to support Nicéphore Soglo's candidacy during the second round of the presidential election.

Opposition unity, or at the very least a temporary agreement between opposition groups, levels the playing field with autocratic forces by increasing the relative strength of the opponents and preventing the incumbents from using opposition divisions to their advantage. In Gabon, between the end of the 1990s and today, most of the opposition parties have been integrated into the presidential coalition. In Senegal, appointments to the senate have been used by President Abdou Diouf and President Abdoulaye Wade as a reward for opponents who joined the ruling circle.[71]

The strength of opposition forces is not only a factor behind rapid regime transition, but also slow and incremental change. Through their electoral and political participation, strong opposition movements can gradually demand reforms that level the playing field by establishing more open policy-making processes, demanding greater division between the ruling regime and the state and putting in place checks and balance.[72] In Ghana, even though Rawling's National Democratic Congress (NDC) won all the elections between 1992 and 2000, new institutions were slowly put in place which gave the main opposition party, the New Patriotic Party (NPP), a chance to come out on top during an election.[73] In many countries, the quality of elections has improved over time thanks to the pressure and demands of opposition forces.[74] In Benin, during Soglo and Kérékou's presidencies, opposition parties used their control of the national assembly to put in place effective measures to counterbalance presidential power – such as an independent electoral commission – and with the help of the courts have resisted the presidents' attempts to centralise power.

Inciting defection within the incumbent party is a key mechanism through which opposition forces can push regime transitions forward. The opposition's growing strength becomes an indicator for recalcitrant members of the ruling circle that their regime's chance of survival is slim and that defection becomes more 'profitable'.[75] In Senegal, the growing strength of the Senegalese Democratic Party (PDS) during the 1990s convinced barons of the Socialist Party (SP) that their party's political monopoly was coming to an end; two of the SP's barons, Djibo Ka and Moustapha Niasse, formed their own party and took with them SP's political majority, enabling Abdoulaye Wade's victory in 2000.[76] In 2012, history repeated itself in Senegal as two of Wade's former ministers, Idrissa Seck and Macky Sall, came to the forefront of the anti-Wade coalition. After the first round of the 2012 election, in which Wade failed to obtain the necessary majority, all opposition forces, as well as some of Wade's supporters, rallied behind Sall.[77]

The massive mobilisation of the first SSA democratic wave was also accompanied, in most cases of regime change, by regime defections. In Benin, Niger, Mali, Madagascar, Malawi and Zambia, to name but a few cases, the huge protests of the early 1990s were accompanied by regime defections as pressure mounted against standing autocrats. These massive defections greatly reduced the regimes' relative capacity to withhold domestic and foreign pressure. In the absence of effective opposition forces, incumbent leaders rarely put in place reforms that truly deepened democratic principles. In Uganda, Yoweri Museveni (who became president in 1986 and was re-elected in 2016) remains unchallenged outside his own party and opposition forces face an increased number of barriers against their full participation in the electoral process.[78] The democratisation process has also stalled in Ethiopia, Rwanda and Tanzania and in all three cases opposition forces are too weak to challenge the incumbents. In Zambia, the

MMD, which came out as the main opponent to the United National Independence Party (UNIP) dictatorship, monopolised power and subverted state institutions throughout the 1990s and the early 2000s before the political party was divided into two, the Patriotic Front (PF) and the MMD, putting an end to its political monopoly.

There are, of course, exceptions where ruling political parties have respected democratic norms: the ruling parties in Botswana, Namibia and South Africa have all received large majorities in their respective states' multi-party elections but they remain among Africa's most shining examples of functioning democratic states. In most cases, however, unchallenged rule is a poor soil for democracy. In almost all African countries that democratised, or at the very least liberalised, popular protests and rising opposition movements marked the end of the incumbent's political monopoly. The increasingly plural societies that arose from this process demanded an opening of the political space and, in many cases, a change of the guard. Regime change was only possible, however, where opposition forces managed to unify, even temporarily, and incite the less fervent government partisans to defect to their ranks.

International actors

Since 1989, democratisation has increasingly been put forward as a major element of Western states' foreign policy, though political stability and economic interests remain the priority of many state's foreign policies.[79] The political conditionality attached to development aid and relief funds rarely created a level playing field where opposition forces stood a real chance of winning elections. As Stephen Brown notes, sitting leaders in Africa quickly learned how to implement reforms that satisfied the needs of foreign donors, yet still insured their political dominance.[80] In Tanzania, the CCM embraced multi-party elections to appease foreign donors, but changed the electoral rules to its advantage once the opposition parties began to organise.[81] Once minimal requirements have been met – such as multi-party elections, tolerance of the opposition and some degree of press freedom – foreign donors rarely pay close attention to electoral processes and the potential use of state resources to the incumbent's advantage. Furthermore, incumbent governments can take steps to limit foreign organisations' access to civil society and opposition forces in an effort to thwart their attempts to strengthen the opposition. As Thomas Carothers has pointed out, between 2004 and 2006, Ethiopia, Eritrea and Zimbabwe closed their doors to non-governmental organisations and foundations working on electoral transparency and/or the promotion of democracy.[82]

Nonetheless, there are clear cases where international actors did have an important role to play in SSA countries' transition to democracy. In Namibia, the presence of peacekeepers during the founding elections in 1989 and the mediation of a group of countries working towards Namibia independence were critical for the country's transition to democracy.[83] Foreign actors also played a key role in Liberia and Sierra Leone.[84] Both states fell into prolonged civil wars during the 1990s and conflict resolution was, in part, due to intervention by peacekeepers. Founding and subsequent elections were judged free and fair by most observers and a relatively even playing field now exists between the main political forces in the two states.[85] Neither state is free from its underlying problems, including the lack of trust among former belligerents and a culture of political violence. However, in Liberia the post-war agreement ensured equal access to state resources among political parties and the large peacekeeping forces assured a peaceful electoral environment.[86] In Sierra Leone, foreign pressure considerably limited the ability of the ruling SLPP to consolidate the state in its hands, levelling the playing field and enabling the All People's Congress (APP) and the PMDC to win the elections in 2007.[87]

In the three cases mentioned above, foreign actors pushed the domestic actors to respect democratic norms of governance for free and fair electoral processes. There are, however, cases of the international community's failure. The international community's presence in Rwanda failed to assure a pluralistic political landscape.[88] In the Central African Republic (CAR), successive peacekeeping missions since 1997 have not been able to bring peace and stabilise the political system, to the point where CAR is now considered an almost failed state.[89] Foreign-backed elections in Ivory Coast also failed to bring together the main protagonists of the civil war as Ouattara-backed militias attacked pro-Laurent Gbagbo troops and captured the south of the country in March 2011. International peace and democracy building efforts in Burundi were also thwarted as United Nations negotiations between 1994 and 1996 fell through. Still, in certain cases, foreign actors did help to level the playing field and provide incentives to potential spoilers.

While I will go into further detail in the following section, it suffices to say here that it seems that although foreign actors have little influence in most transition processes, they can still influence the fate of democratisation processes in post-civil war countries. When they enforce fair electoral rules and help to foster trust among former belligerents, mediators and peacekeepers can in fact help war-torn countries to transition into peaceful and democratic states.

Reflections on transitology

As Mohamedou and Sisk note in Chapter 2, transitions take different paths composed of various stages, all of which are reversible. The first section of this chapter on SSA sought to give examples of reversed transitions, such as those in Mali and Madagascar, or transitions that stalled at the liberalisation process, as in Tanzania and Togo. Transition dynamics, called 'modes of transition', are a good indicator of the relative strength of various actors and the presence or absence of particular inter-elite agreements. In this section, I will analyse SSA's transition modes and look more closely at which characteristics explain their ultimate outcomes.[90]

Transition through agreements

The 1989–1994 democratic wave in Africa began with a significant number of national conferences and other official negotiation processes. In 1990, Benin held the *Conférence nationale des forces vives* where government representatives, civil society members, formerly banned opposition political parties and members of the security forces gathered and negotiated their country's political and economic reforms. Between 1990 and 1994, South Africa was also the scene of various rounds of official negotiations.[91] Other states attempted to follow Benin's path of transition to democracy as there were national conferences in ten other states and the call for such meetings became the rallying cry of opposition forces in many others. In most cases, however, national conferences did not bring regime transition; only in Benin, Cape Verde, Congo-Brazzaville, Mali, Niger and Sao Tomé and Principe did the national conference lead to a *process* of democratic deepening, though in the case of Congo-Brazzaville it was short-lived.[92] There were other pact stories in this period: incumbent governments accepted negotiations on the holding of elections and/or transitional processes, as in Madagascar, or post-civil war negotiations brought together the various belligerents, such as in Angola and Namibia. While there were some successes, however, there were also many failures and stalled processes.

Pacts and accords between political forces were still an important part of Africa's transitions in the 2000–2010 wave. In 2006, Togo's ruling Rally of the Togolese People (RPT), renamed Union of the Republic (UNIR), and opposition parties signed the Global Political Accord (GPA), which provided for the installation of a unity government headed by Faure Eyadema as President and Yaowi Agboyibo as Prime Minister. In 2008, two other pacts were signed in Kenya and Zimbabwe, where the main political contenders agreed to unity governments and constitutional reforms.[93] Some post-civil war treaties also have pact-like characteristics, namely agreements on electoral rules and some forms of power-sharing. In Liberia, the warring parties, political parties and civil society groups agreed through the Accra Comprehensive Peace Agreement to create a unity government where all political parties would have ministerial positions. In Burundi, the main belligerents used the 2001 Arusha accords to negotiate major political reforms.[94] Guinea's post-2008 agreement between the ruling military junta and opposition forces and Niger's 2010–2011 reform process were similarly attempts to integrate all major social forces into the transitional process.

Agreements between rivals do not guarantee political stability or regime change. Togo's GPA and Zimbabwe's coalition government and subsequent political reforms failed to bring any real change to either country's political landscape while in Ivory Coast the 2007 peace agreement did not persuade Laurent Gbagbo to accept Ouattara's 2010 electoral victory. In the countries where pacts worked, the main political actors were pushed towards acceptance of the new 'democratic' rules over a long period. Benin's national conference, unlike most of its subsequent emulations, created a political environment where no single force could claim a monopoly; opposition parties could create institutional checks and balance and use the national assembly as the main counterbalance to the presidency.[95] Most national conferences failed to recreate the same cooperative and consensual political environment that had been created in Benin.[96] Similarly, the 'pacts' in Togo (2005) and Zimbabwe (2008) failed to level their respective states playing fields as the main source of political power, the presidency, remained unconstrained.[97]

In Niger, repeated failures to come to a political agreement that did not marginalise the political forces outside of Niamey largely explain the recurring breakdowns in the country's democratic experiment.[98] The success of pact-like transition processes hinges on the process's ability to bring together the various political actors and ensure respect of new rules of governance. Namibia and South Africa are examples of how, importantly, democratisation depends on the actors' respect for the new rules of the game. In both cases one political party, the South West Africa People's Organization (SWAPO) and the African National Congress (ANC) respectively, won an absolute majority in every post-transition election; however, despite their electoral hegemony, the dominant political parties have respected the transitional agreements which limit their own power.

This does not always mean that all political actors willingly agree to accept political compromise; attempts at electoral manipulation are common even in the most stable democratic SSA states. For pact-like transition to lead to democracy, certain mechanisms need to be in place to prevent potential spoilers from derailing the democratic process. For instance, Sierra Leone's SLPP could not use state resources to its advantage thanks to international donors, who acted as guarantors of the integrity of the electoral process.

Transition through reforms

Not all SSA states went through a negotiated transition. In some cases, initial reforms were decided unilaterally by the dominant political force, which was often only trying to legitimise its own rule. In most cases, such as in Tanzania or Uganda, this has led to stalled transitions as reforms were often only meant to satisfy international donors and boost the government's legitimacy. In other cases, however, controlled reforms did lead to a slow process of incremental change. Ghana, between 1989 and 2000, is a prime example of democratisation through reforms; in 1989, Jerry Rawlings and his party, the NDC, implemented a series of reforms to improve the country's international image.[99] The institutional changes implemented by the incumbent regime, however, planted the seed for the slow reinforcement of opposition parties and the continuation of the democratisation process.[100] By 2000, when Rawlings retired from the presidency, the playing field was even enough for the NPP to win the election.

Other countries experienced similar transformations, through sometimes different processes. In Senegal, the 1976–1981 legalisation of opposition forces and the 1991 reforms opened the path to multi-party elections; as the Socialist Party (PS) was still in control of state resources, however, the political landscape did not change throughout the 1990s. Still, the reforms opened the way for a slow reinforcement of opposition parties, which could then push for political reforms to limit the PS's hold on power.[101] The defection of key PS members ended its domination and led to Wade's victory in 2000. Similarly, Wade's attempts to reconsolidate rule opened the way for the strengthening of the opposition forces and defections within the incumbent party.[102] Kenya underwent a process similar to Senegal's, with KANU's control over the country gradually challenged by an increasingly powerful opposition coalition throughout the 1990s.

As mentioned earlier, not all planned transition processes lead to incremental change. In Burkina Faso, Blaise Compaoré and his Congress for Democracy and Progress (CDP) unilaterally set the terms of the 1991 political reforms and modified them to ensure they retained control. In Uganda, Yoweri Museveni similarly changed the constitution to increase the term limit on the presidency. In most of these cases, the opposition forces were either too weak or the incumbent forces prevented them from organising into a real electoral challenge. In the case of Burkina Faso, a civil society movement, *le Balai Citoyen*, ultimately removed Compaoré from power in 2014.

For planned transition to become an incremental democratisation process, the key variable seems to be the strengthening of opposition forces. The opposition parties in Ghana, Kenya and Senegal gained momentum in the 1990s, and this propelled them to victory early in the twenty-first century. In other states – namely Uganda and Tanzania – the opposition forces failed to challenge the incumbent's political domination. In other cases of planned transition, e.g. in Togo after 1993 and in Nigeria between 1993 and 1998, the armed forces prevented a relatively powerful opposition coalition from gaining power and have therefore stalled the transition process. In most cases, planned transitions are in fact more akin to political liberalisation than to regime transition. To be really effective modes of regime change, guided transitions must involve the strengthening of opposition forces and the reinforcement of institutions in order to level the playing field.

Foreign-backed transitions

In the section discussing foreign actors, I noted their importance, in certain contexts, to the transition process. In civil-war to democracy transitions, foreign actors can compensate for the weakness of state institutions and attempt to restore trust among belligerents.[103] As there has been a relatively high number of post-civil war states in SSA, these dynamics are critical. Five states highlight the relative success of this mode of transition: Comoros, Liberia, Mozambique, Namibia and Sierra Leone.[104] There are, however, a number of failed foreign-backed transitions, namely in Angola, Central African Republic, Ivory Coast, Rwanda and South Sudan.

In successful cases, the international community managed to bring the belligerents together and persuade potential spoilers to respect the new political rules. In Sierra Leone, the international community managed not only to end the conflict through the presence of a large peacekeeping force of over 17,000 soldiers, but also to organise the new rounds of elections that were deemed free and fair by most observers.[105] Furthermore, foreign pressure ensured that no political party was overly advantaged once it took power.[106] Similarly, foreign mediation brought nearly all warring parties in Burundi together around the negotiating table after 2001; the peace agreement that the parties signed allowed for military and constitutional reforms as well as the holding of free elections in 2005.

In cases of failed transition, however, spoilers derailed the peace process, either before or after the end of the transitional process. In Rwanda, radical Hutu factions led the country into the 1993 genocide to forestall a power-sharing agreement with the Tutsi-led Rwandan Patriotic Front (RPF). In Angola, once the Angolan Union for Total Independence (UNITA) leaders realised that they had lost the 1992 presidential election that was deemed unfair, war broke out once again; UNITA and the Popular Movement for the Liberation of Angola (MPLA) launched a series of offensives and counter-offensives. Despite the active mediation of the international community, sanctions on UNITA and the presence of a peacekeeping force, it took another ten years for the conflict to end. In both the Angolan and the Rwandan cases, the international community did not have enough resources in the field and/or the will to prevent the actions of spoilers.

Foreign intervention depends to a large extent on the willingness of belligerents to respect peace accords as well as the presence of strong pro-democratic forces. The case of Burundi is quite telling in this respect as it shows the limits of the concept of foreign-led democracy. According to Peterson, between 1996 and 2005 the main change was not in foreign attitudes towards the conflict but in the relationship between the different contenders in Burundi itself.[107] The 2010 election exhibited flaws, as the ruling CNDD-FDD victory was not recognised by opposition parties who refused to participate in the parliamentary and presidential elections. A major disagreement in the interpretation of the Arusha accords led to violent confrontations between the ruling CNDD-FDD partisans and those of opposition parties. The disagreement seriously comprised the democratic future of the country as all but one opposition candidate – Agathon Rwasa – refused to participate in the election. Violence continued and the army split between those opposed and those who favoured President Nkurunziza's third term of office. As long as the crisis remains unresolved, the fate of Burundi's democratic regimes will continue to be nebulous at best. Thus, the key to the effectiveness of foreign pressure towards democratisation seems to be the presence of domestic actors who also favour it. When such actors choose not to respect the new 'rules of the game' there is very little foreign actors can do to force their hands.

Transition through ruptures

A final mode of transition in SSA is through ruptures with the *ancien régime*, usually either through large social upheaval and/or coups d'état. The regime transitions in Mali (1991) and Guinea (2008–2010) followed similar processes of rupture, namely large popular protests and a subsequent military coup. In Mali, after months of continuing protests and the killing of nearly 250 protesters in March 1991, elements of the armed forces headed by Amadou Toumani Touré staged a coup against sitting president Moussa Traoré. In the months that followed, a new unity government, the *Comité de Transition pour le Salut du Peuple* (Transitional Committee for the Salvation of the People, CTSP), composed of military officers and representatives of the opposition coalition prepared the country's transition to democracy. In Guinea, the 2008 coup by Captain Moussa Dadis Camara came after nearly a year of mobilisation by opposition forces. While the new military government promised to head the country towards free elections in 2010, rumours of Camara's desire to remain in power reinvigorated the country's protest movement; in September 2009, 150 protesters were killed in clashes with the security forces. After a failed assassination attempt on Camara, his acting deputy, General Sekouba Konaté, agreed to form a unity government with the opposition forces. The new transitional government, the *Conseil National de Transition* (National Council of Transition, CNT), was spearheaded by long-time democratic activist Jean-Marie Doré and paved the way for the 2010 election.

There are also cases where coups resulted in a return to authoritarianism. The 2008 Mauritania coup ended the country's first democratic experiment as President Sidi Ould Cheikh Abdallahi was deposed by General Mohamed Ould Abdelaziz, who then went on to become the new president of Mauritania. Similarly, in 1996, Niger's Third Republic, which had been established by the 1991 national conference, was dissolved by a military coup. The coup planner, Colonel Ibrahim Baré Mainassara, led a new government and won elections deemed unfair by the international community. In both cases, this entailed a return to military rule. The refusal of most civil elites and of the general population to accept the legitimacy of Mainassara's government led to another coup in 1999 and the establishment of the Fifth Republic in Niger. The 2012 coup in Mali, in part caused by military grievances over the armed forces' anti-insurgent strategy in the north, ended the country's democratic experiment.[108]

Transitions through ruptures are marked by a lack of unity among the ruling elites, which gives cliques in the security forces an opportunity to intervene.[109] In the case of Guinea, Niger and Mali (1991), the military had to deal with organised and unified opposition forces. When the various social forces are integrated into the transitional process, transition through rupture takes the form of pacts.[110] The negotiation of political reforms in the Guinean and Malian cases came about because of the consensual nature of the transition government, as well its inclusiveness. Under these circumstances, military coups can thus open the way for a transition to democracy; in most cases, however, military coups initiate processes of authoritarian reversal or executive shuffling without regime change.

Conclusions

This chapter has examined the core dynamics behind successful and failed democratic transitions in Sub-Saharan Africa. Africa's democratisation stories highlight the importance of both the strength of opposition groups and their ability to initiate incumbent elite defections. Both civilian defectors, e.g. Macky Sall in Senegal or the members of the UDF in Malawi, and military defectors such as Touré in Mali, played a crucial role in paving the way for regime transitions in their respective states. The ability of opposition forces to encourage elite defections is equally related to the characteristics of opposition forces, namely their relative size, and the character of the incumbent regime. Civilian elites, as well as military officers, tend to defect when the political structures fail to provide them with sufficient incentives. While KANU failed to keep the party barons within its structure after 2000, the CCM in Tanzania has, for now, prevented major party defections.

Africa's democratic transitions seem to highlight a particular context through which the international community can play a more preponderant role: out-of-civil war processes. In this context, foreign actors can create the conditions through which major political forces agree on new rules of governance and comply with those rules. While most of these success stories are quite recent – for instance, Liberia and Sierra Leone – the stability of Namibia's democratic regime seems to indicate that foreign-backed transitions can create a steady political environment when domestic forces accept democratic norms in the long run.

Still, the persistence of some authoritarian and anocratic regimes in Africa also proves that incumbent powers do have the ability to prevent regime transitions, even when opposition movements are highly mobilised. Even after opposition forces have pushed through political liberalisation, reform processes have been derailed by former autocrats who regularly use the security forces' loyalty and the opposition forces' inherent divisions to their advantage. In Togo, the ruling RPT/UNIR has contained the opposition parties, partly by playing on their divisions and, when this strategy failed, through the use of its loyal security forces.

Successful democratic transitions do share a number of characteristics, namely the presence of strong opposition movements fit to challenge the ruling party in the polls – with the exception of Botswana, Namibia and South Africa – and either a configuration of actors or a form of agreement among actors to restrain the actions of political parties. The diversity of democratisation stories in Sub-Saharan Africa highlights the *uncertain* nature of regime transitions and, as exemplified by the case of Mali, even regimes once deemed 'shining examples of democracy' can break down.

Notes

1. Botswana, Senegal and Zimbabwe were already holding multi-party elections and had universal suffrage in 1989.
2. Gabrielle Lynch and Gordon Crawford argue that the latest wave of democratic reversal started earlier, namely in 2006; see their 'Democratisation in Africa 1990–2010'.
3. This is a key theme in transitology. See O'Donnell and Schmitter, 'Tentative Conclusions about Uncertain Democracies' in O'Donnell et al., *Transitions from Authoritarian Rule*.
4. Bratton and van de Walle, *Democratic Experiments in Africa*, pp. 200–203.
5. Ibid., p. 211.
6. See for instance Villalón and VonDoepp, *The Fate of Africa's Democratic Experiments*; Gazibo, *Les Paradoxes de La Démocratisation en Afrique*.
7. The Polity IV database does not include Sao Tome and Principe and the Seychelles. The results are for the year 2014; the political situation in some states, for instance Burundi and Burkina Faso, subsequently changed dramatically.
8. O'Donnell and Schmitter, 'Tentative Conclusions about Uncertain Democracies', pp. 15–16.
9. See for instance Nancy Bermeo, 'Myths of Moderation', p. 315; Bunce, 'Rethinking Recent Democratization'.
10. Bratton and van de Walle, *Democratic Experiments in Africa*, pp. 198–200.
11. Ibid., p. 197.
12. Hoffman and Robinson, 'Tanzania's Missing Opposition', p. 123.
13. Levitsky and Way, *Competitive Authoritarianism*, pp. 255–256.
14. On 'civil service' as political reform in Benin, see Richard Banegas, *La Démocratie à Pas de Caméléon*, p. 87.
15. Bratton and van de Walle, *Democratic Experiments in Africa*, p. 117.
16. Seely, 'The Legacies of Transition Governments', p. 363; Engeler, 'Guinea in 2008'.
17. Kagwanja and Southall, 'Introduction: Kenya – A Democracy in Retreat?'.
18. Didier Ratsiraka in Madagascar and Denis Sassou-Nguesso in the Republic of Congo are prime examples of authoritarian derailing of transition processes.
19. When members of the incumbent elites decide to either set up their own party or join opposition parties.
20. Hoffman and Robinson, 'Tanzania's Missing Opposition', p. 125.
21. Levitsky and Way, *Competitive Authoritarianism*, p. 60.
22. This is somewhat similar to the point made by Schmitter and O'Donnell when anti-transition forces (hardliners) dominate the ruling coalition.
23. On 'authoritarian resilience', see Brownlee, *Authoritarianism in an Age of Democratization*; Slovik, *The Politics of Authoritarian Rule*.
24. Barkan, 'Protracted Transitions among Africa's New Democracies'.
25. Clark, 'From Military Dictatorship to Democracy', p. 212.
26. Kelly, 'Senegal: What Will Turnover Bring?', p. 125; Brown, 'Theorising Kenya's Protracted Transition to Democracy', p. 331.
27. Lewis, 'Nigeria: An End to the Permanent Transition?', p. 152.
28. Kandeh, 'Rogue Incumbents', p. 605.
29. Van de Walle, 'Tipping Games', pp. 86–87.
30. Morse, 'Party Matters', p. 8.
31. See McLauchlin, 'Loyalty Strategies and Military Defection in Rebellion'.
32. Van de Walle, 'Tipping Games', p. 83.
33. Powell and Thyne, 'Global Instances of Coups'.
34. O'Donnell and Schmitter, 'Tentative Conclusions about Uncertain Democracies', pp. 36–40.

35 Bratton and van de Walle, *Democratic Experiments in Africa*, p. 217.
36 See for instance, Brownlee, '...And Yet They Persist'; Snyder, 'Explaining Transitions from Neopatrimonial Dictatorships'.
37 On Benin, see Dickovick, 'Legacies of Leftism', p. 1129. In a somewhat similar story, President Abdoulaye Wade in Senegal would have been persuaded partly by the Senegalese military command to accept electoral defeat; see Kelly, 'Senegal: What Will Turnover Bring?', p. 122.
38 Mueller, 'Democratic Revolutionaries or Pocketbook Protesters?'.
39 For an analysis of the societal problems in Mali leading up to the coup, see Whitehouse, 'What Went Wrong in Mali?'.
40 There has, however, been a marked increased since 2000 in the success rate of such operations. See Powell and Thyne, 'Global Instances of Coups' and Singh, *Seizing Power*, p. 53.
41 Thyne and Powell, 'Coup de'État or Coup d'Autocracy?', p. 8.
42 Seely, 'The Unexpected Presidential Election', p. 615.
43 Noyes, 'Securing Reform?', p. 33.
44 Bratton and van de Walle, *Democratic Experiments in Africa*, p. 216; Thiriot, 'La Place des Militaires dans les Régimes Post-transition d'Afrique Subsaharienne', p. 21.
45 Young, 'Chefs and Worried Soldiers'.
46 Uvin, 'Ethnicity and Power in Burundi and Rwanda'.
47 Mueller, 'Democratic Revolutionaries or Pocketbook Protesters?'.
48 Clark, 'From Military Dictatorship to Democracy', p. 210.
49 The strikes were important enough in both cases to plunge the respective states into economic recessions.
50 Similar grievances led to the 2012 coup. On the 1992 military grievances, see Lode, 'The Peace Process in Mali', p. 413.
51 Welch, *No Farewell to Arms?*, p. 196.
52 Geddes, 'What Do We Know About Democratization after Twenty Years?'; Welch, *No Farewell to Arms?*, pp. 196–197.
53 Bratton and van de Walle, *Democratic Experiments in Africa*, p. 216.
54 Levitsky and Way, *Competitive Authoritarianism*, p. 282.
55 On the use of ethnicity as a proxy for loyalty, see McLauchlin, 'Loyalty Strategies and Military Defection in Rebellion'.
56 N'Diaye, 'How Not to Institutionalize Civilian Control', p. 629.
57 Decalo, *Coups and Army Rule in Africa*, p.122, p.129.
58 Ousmane Dembele, 'Côte d'Ivoire: La Fracture Communautaire', *Politique Africaine*, 89, 2003, p. 21.
59 Comi M. Toulabor, 'Togo: Les Forces Armées Togolaises et le Dispositif Sécuritaire de Contrôle (1 and 2)', *CEAN & Sciences-Po*, 7, 10, 2005.
60 van de Walle, 'Tipping Games', p. 83.
61 N'Diaye, 'Francophone Africa and Security Sector Transformation'.
62 In this chapter, 'opposition forces' refers to political forces that are not part of the ruling regime.
63 O'Donnell, 'Schmitter's Retrospective', p. 30.
64 See, for instance, Wood, *Forging Democracy from Below*.
65 Bratton and van de Walle, *Democratic Experiments in Africa*, p. 119.
66 Bah, 'The Military and Politics in Guinea'.
67 Marcus, 'The Fate of Madagascar's Democracy', p. 161.
68 Wood, 'An Insurgent Path to Democracy', p. 882.
69 Chenoweth and Stephan, *Why Civil Resistance Works*, p. 33.
70 Bratton and van de Walle, *Democratic Experiments in Africa*, pp. 200–203.
71 Mozaffar and Vengroff, 'A "Whole System" Approach', p. 610; Kelly, 'Senegal: What Will Turnover Bring?', p. 123.

72 On the implementation of electoral commissions and its implication for democratisation processes, see Gazibo, 'The Forging of Institutional Autonomy'.
73 Which they ultimately did in 2000 against Rawling's successor, John Atta Mills.
74 See Lindberg, 'The Surprising Significance of African Elections', p. 141.
75 Van de Walle, 'Tipping Games', p. 85.
76 Mozaffar and Vengroff, 'A 'Whole System' Approach', p. 611.
77 Kelly, 'Senegal: What Will Turnover Bring?', p. 129.
78 Tripp, 'The Changing Face of Authoritarianism in Africa'.
79 See Brown, 'Foreign Aid and Democracy Promotion', p. 181.
80 Ibid., p. 184.
81 Hoffman and Robinson, 'Tanzania's Missing Opposition', p. 125 and p.128.
82 Carothers, 'The Backlash against Democracy Promotion', pp. 58–59.
83 Hartmann, 'Democracy as a Fortuitous By-product'.
84 Signé, 'The Tortuous Trajectories of Democracy', p. 4.
85 Both states are democracies according to the Polity IV database.
86 Harris and Lewis, 'Liberia in 2011', pp. 82–83.
87 Kandeh, 'Rogue Incumbents', p. 605.
88 Zuercher et al., 'External Democracy Promotion in Post-Conflict Zones', p. 243.
89 Villalón and VonDoepp, *The Fate of Africa's Democratic Experiments*, pp. 137–148.
90 This typology builds on those proposed in Bratton and van de Walle, *Democratic Experiments in Africa*, pp. 169–179 and Gazibo, *Introduction à la Politique Africaine*, pp. 176–80.
91 Hatchard and Slinn, 'The Path Towards a New Order in South Africa', pp. 6–9.
92 In Democratic Republic of Congo/ex-Zaïre and Togo, opposition forces held power for a few weeks before the autocrats took it back by force.
93 See Cheeseman and Tendi, 'Power-Sharing in Comparative Perspective'.
94 Peterson, 'A Beacon for Central Africa', p. 127.
95 See Seely, 'The Legacies of Transition Governments', p. 366.
96 Bratton and van de Walle, *Democratic Experiments in Africa*, p. 175.
97 See Seely, 'Togo's Presidential Election 2010', p. 373; Cheeseman and Tendi, 'Power-Sharing in Comparative Perspective', pp. 220–223.
98 Villalón and Idrissa, 'Repetitive Breakdowns and a Decade of Experimentations'.
99 Levitsky and Way, *Competitive Authoritarianism*, p. 301.
100 Dickovick, 'Legacies of Leftism', p. 1130.
101 Mozaffar and Vengroff, 'A "Whole System" Approach', p. 610.
102 Kelly, 'Senegal: What Will Turnover Bring?', pp. 125–126.
103 Hartmann, 'Democracy as a Fortuitous By-product', p. 27; Gurses and Mason, 'Democracy Out of Anarchy', p. 316.
104 Mozambique is a relative success as the country is an anocracy and there has been use of state resources by the Liberation Front, FRELIMO.
105 Signé, 'The Tortuous Trajectories of Democracy', pp. 34–35.
106 Kandeh, 'Rogue Incumbents'.
107 Peterson, 'A Beacon for Central Africa', pp. 128–129.
108 Mali was coded as democratic in the Polity IV database prior to the 2012 coup and subsequently regressed to an anocracy.
109 On military opportunity to stage coups, see Finer, *The Man on Horseback*, p. 98 and Clark, 'Armed Arbiters'.
110 Gazibo, *Introduction à la Politique Africaine*, p. 178.

8 Thirty years past
Transitology in the Southern Cone

Diego Abente-Brun and
Ignacio González-Bozzolasco

In the 1980s and 1990s, transitology, as a theoretical and analytical tool, triggered considerable interest in Latin American affairs and in the literature about Latin America more generally. This was the result of the special conjuncture the region had gone through, as well as the fact that most of the scholars addressing the issues were Latin Americans or Latin Americanists. The seminal work that sparked this rich literature was the four-volume work edited by Guillermo O'Donnell, Philippe Schmitter and Laurence Whitehead, *Transitions from Authoritarian Rule*, and, in particular, the final volume *Tentative Conclusions about Uncertain Democracies* written by O'Donnell and Schmitter. In this concluding volume, O'Donnell and Schmitter offer a theoretical, analytical and normative synthesis that draws upon the contributions in the previous volumes. Perhaps more importantly they offer a roadmap for the transitions in Latin America, both as reflection based upon historical experiences and as a sort of inventory of 'good practices' that democratic political forces could ignore only at their peril.

For these authors, transitions, aptly defined as 'uncertain', are characterised as an *interval* between two regime types – an authoritarian regime and a new one that may not necessarily be democratic. In fact, a 'transition' in this sense could lead to a revolutionary outcome, a mere liberalising opening or even a regression to a new authoritarian system.[1] O'Donnell and Schmitter characterise the period of transition as unpredictable. Far from prefiguring the emergence of democratic regimes, they see transitions as highly dependent upon the strategies chosen by the main political actors which redefine the political game, its rules and in the end the entire political system.

Processes and stages in democratisation

O'Donnell and Schmitter identify three stages in the transition process: liberalisation, democratisation and deepening. The process of *liberalisation* is marked by the redefinition and widening of the sphere of political rights. During this stage governments guarantee individuals and political groups a space for contestation free from the arbitrary threats of retaliation and repression that characterise authoritarian regimes. Political actors can thus enter the political game, though they do so under restrictive rules (de facto or *de jure*) concerning the nature and scope of such participation. The second stage of *democratisation* involves the adoption of a set of procedures for accessing power, such as free, unrestricted and competitive elections and freedom of the press and of association – as well as the means to exercise it, such as accountability. Third, comes the process of *deepening*. This involves the expansion of democratic procedures throughout society and meaningful equality not only in political terms but also in terms of social and economic rights. In a way, this stage resembles what Thomas Humphrey Marshall called the 'third stage' of democracy.[2]

O'Donnell and Schmitter stress that between the process of liberalisation and that of democratisation several outcomes are possible. The transition from liberalisation to democratisation may seem logically obvious, as without the former the latter cannot exist. However, the process can get stuck in the 'grey' territory of a *dictablanda* or a *democradura*. The former, a soft version of a dictatorship, is a form of liberalised authoritarianism where civil and political rights are generally respected but the essential question of who has access to power (and how they access it) remains off limits. Social and political pressures are thus eased and powerholders retain control. *Democraduras* or limited democracies, on the other hand, exhibit just the opposite traits. The process of democratisation displays a truncated profile, either because certain policy issues are excluded from the political agenda or because some actors are barred from participation.

From this point on, the work of O'Donnell and Schmitter focuses its attention on the paths and landmarks of transition. These can be summarised in four dimensions: democratic opening; political negotiations and pact-making; civil society mobilisation; and elections. All four areas are crucial as their nature determines the outcome of the transition process. The starting point of a transition is obviously the initial opening. What triggers it? It could be the collapse of a regime due to military defeat, as in Argentina after the Falklands/Malvinas War of 1982. More often, though, it is in response to the perceived need by a ruling elite to strengthen the legitimacy of its regime and improve its long-term sustainability. This, in turn, may be a response to increasing levels of civil society mobilisation.

Thus, as O'Donnell and Schmitter point out, two elements are common to all transitions. The first is the need to address specific grievances of the social and political forces that slowly emerge as an alternative to the status quo. The second is that as a legitimacy crisis develops and grows, the regime experiences a split between hard- and soft-liners, or *duros* and *blandos*. This, besides weakening the regime, opens the door to alliances between regime and opposition groups, be they open or hidden, strategic or tactical. Transitions tend to be triggered in some cases – or greatly facilitated in others – by a heightened conflict between *duros* and *blandos*, or hawks and doves. Such heuristic categorisation is developed to capture the behaviour of key political actors at crucial stages of the transition process. It does not necessarily constitute permanent attributes of political and social actors, but rather the strategic choices developed to deal with specific challenges posed by changing political conjunctures and power conflicts.

Duros are the groups that aim to maintain indefinitely an authoritarian regime, seeing it as necessary and indeed desirable. They may resort to disguising it behind different facades so long as they do not risk losing its essential core. Among the *duros*, one may find opportunists and fundamentalists. The former look at the situation from the point of view of their immediate standpoint, be it power positions or privileges, but they tend to neglect the long- or even medium-term viability and consequences of the regime. The latter, on the contrary, constitute the hard core of the *duros* and oppose any democratic opening as the prelude for chaos, anarchy and eventually a radicalist takeover.

Blandos, on the other hand, are the factions that began to modify their positions as they see the need to grant certain political freedoms and promote a degree of electoral legitimacy. These groups occupy key positions in the regime and are particularly concerned with the long-term stability and survival of the system as well as their own political fortunes. Among the *blandos*, we can distinguish three groups. First, there are those who have already attained their goals and are ready to leave the political system. A second group is made up of those willing to tolerate only a very limited opening that does not threaten their power position. Finally, there are those who believe in the viability of their ruling position and are prepared to enter a competitive contest convinced that they will do well.

The second landmark of transition is pact negotiation. Although not necessarily inevitable, the success of most transitions has been based on either explicit or tacit pacts. In the former case, this essentially consists of democrats refraining from exercising their newly-gained power to the detriment of the interests of certain key former regime actors. Those interests most often include preserving a degree of autonomy for the military, some sort of amnesty or *punto final* (end point) for those responsible for human rights violations and economic policies that do not threaten the interests of elite groups.

Building on the lines of inquiry notably developed by Antonio Gramsci on the dynamics of authoritarianism, O'Donnell and Schmitter speak of conceptualising the transition as a sequence of military, political and economic 'moments', each of which requires a specific set of pacts. Beyond this characteristic, pacts have the benefit of greatly reducing the uncertainty that accompanies regime change. In his contribution to the O'Donnell and Schmitter volume, Adam Przeworski defines democracy as a system that institutionalises the certainty of the rules and the uncertainty of the results. Similarly, pacts can be seen as institutionalising the uncertainty of the results but the certainty of a key range of policies. There are also cases where pacts are not part of the formula, mainly when the authoritarian regime has fallen into complete disrepute, such as in Argentina circa 1980, and has neither time nor sufficient internal cohesion to develop a successful negotiated exit. Likewise, these scenarios also emerge in 'transitions from above', e.g. in Paraguay, when authoritarian rulers retain sufficient resources and internal cohesion to implement their own agendas and their own timing.

A third landmark in transitions is the mobilisation of civil society and the restructuring of public space. The dynamics of transitions are not exclusively guided by the will and calculus of the elites. There are moments of great social mobilisation, in part possible due to newly acquired individual and collective freedoms that allow civil society to occupy previously restricted spaces and help shape the transition. With regard to Latin America, the case of Brazil's 1984 *Diretas ja* (Direct Elections Now) civil unrest movement is particularly relevant in this respect.

The fourth landmark, in a way the end point or even the endgame, is the call to elections. Around this central question of the transfer of power, a great deal of negotiation takes place and many pacts are made, as they establish the parameters of the new political and institutional order. Hardliners and softliners negotiate key questions, including procedures, deadlines, inclusion and/or exclusion of certain political actors and the rules of representation in parliament.

Three fundamental lessons

Based on the rich analytical framework of which the previous section is but a brief and sketchy sample, this discussion focuses on the distinguishing characteristics of the Southern Cone cases (Argentina, Brazil, Chile, Paraguay and Uruguay). The cases will be analysed in terms of the sequence of three historically relevant moments. These are:

1 *transitions from what*, i.e. the nature of the authoritarian regimes;
2 *transitions how*, i.e. their nature and main traits, including triggering factors, and their evolution; and
3 *transitions to what*, i.e. the nature of the regimes that resulted from the transition process and the challenges they pose.

First, understanding the nature of the authoritarian regimes in the Southern Cone is indispensable for evaluating the economic and social structures and the transformations of the 1960s and 1970s. Authoritarian regimes were not just authoritarian by capricious will of the military, or because of the ambition of a dictator; they were authoritarian in order to impose a set of exclusionary economic and social policies. Thus, transitions are not only political processes but also broader processes of gradual change from an exclusionary economic and social model to a more inclusionary one.

There are a number of cross-country similarities related to the end of the so-called 'easy' phase of the import substitution industrialisation (ISI) model. In fact, with the exception of the case of Paraguay, the political consequences of the crisis of this economic model underlie the emergence of bureaucratic–authoritarian regimes in the other three cases. In short, the emergence of these regimes can be seen as the political outcome of a deep systemic crisis, not just a political crisis or stalemate as in previous cases of the rise of authoritarian regimes. In the 1960s, the ISI was in crisis as an economic model but also, more importantly, as the material basis of political consent. The implementation of the 'deepening' phase of the model and the need to move to a greater opening of their economies implied a significant reformulation of the cost–benefit equation for critical actors, especially the urban working class and the elites, with far-reaching consequences. As María Conceicao Tavares has pointed out:

> Since 1968, clear trends in the 'transnationalisation model' emerged, both at the local and international levels. Not independent one from the other, they rather converged to generate a process of destabilisation. The main source of tension revolved around the difficulty of reorganising the model of development in such a way as to produce greater political cohesion among the main agents of the new 'associated dependent development' model and also a greater political exclusion of the popular sectors.[3]

Unlike the earlier state-supported ISI model that had facilitated a greater participation of the popular sectors in its benefits, the new economic policies reduced the benefits they obtained and generated greater inequality; hence, the new policies could not rely on the same basis of political support. Unable to alter this status quo by political means – i.e. by consent – the objective was attained by coercion, and especially through the repressive role played by the armed forces. As Tavares adds:

> [T]here are certain South American countries where [this contradiction] has been aggravated by extreme repressive forms of domination by military or civilian cliques unable to represent the 'national interest' even when this interest is only tantamount to that of the 'good capitalist' sector of the economy. For these countries, the length, depth and breadth of the 'solution' to the crisis could have far reaching consequences for their future as societies and nations.[4]

In an enlightening interpretation of these processes, O'Donnell develops a detailed explanation of this critical juncture in *Modernización y Autoritarismo*, first published in 1979.[5] He demonstrates conclusively that the possibilities of the emergence of bureaucratic–authoritarian regimes are greater where the ruling coalition of economic elites has lost control of economic policies and sees mass mobilisation and popular demands as the principal obstacle to overcoming the stalemate. O'Donnell makes it clear, however, that the cause of the crisis is not the demands or mobilisation of the popular sector, but rather the exhaustion of the 'easy' phase of the ISI model of development. He also highlights regime variations related to the timing of its inception. Thus, if the military coup that promotes the bureaucratic–authoritarian regime takes place prematurely, the possibilities of failure are greater. This is because the level of social and political polarisation is not wide enough while the possibilities of fragmentation are still considerable. Conversely, if the coup takes place at a moment of heightened tensions, deep economic crisis and high social mobilisation, the chances of the regime enduring are far greater.

A perusal of the Latin American cases reveals a sequential order: Paraguay (1954), Brazil (1964), Argentina (1966), Uruguay (1973), Chile (1973) and

Argentina again (1976). In all these cases, again with the exception of Paraguay, the bureaucratic–authoritarian regimes emerged in the context of a deep economic crisis due to the exhaustion of the 'easy' phase of the ISI model, high inflation and growing social mobilisation and political demands. In the case of Paraguay, as O'Donnell himself notes,[6] traditional authoritarian forms persist: a small and homogeneous political elite dominates a highly undifferentiated social structure with low levels of political participation. Economically, the traditional export-oriented bourgeoisie remain the leading sector and there has been no attempt to subordinate it to an expansion of domestic demand or a process of industrialisation. Yet, as in the other cases, the regime emerged in the context of a profound economic crisis and high inflation[7] and in the midst of high levels of instability and division and conflict within the ruling elites.

Once the regimes had been installed, the consequential decision about how to deal with the existing political parties arose. In the majority of cases, parties were suspended outright or banned (even though some of them would resurge later on, in one way or another). In other cases, limited space for electoral participation and action was tolerated but under highly restrictive norms. In the Argentinian case, the instability of the party system can be traced back as far as the first quarter of the twentieth century. The succession of coups since the 1930s has contributed to configuring a highly conflictive and unstable political landscape. Even though the two main parties, the Peronists and the radicals, reached a peace of sorts by the mid-1970s, the death of President Juan Perón in July 1974 and the ensuing crisis reopened the wounds. Besides, the chaotic coexistence of popular mobilisations in the streets, an active leftist guerrilla movement and right-wing paramilitary bands operating under the shadows of the government generated a crisis of unseen proportions. The intervention of the military thus became a foregone conclusion. As Silvia Dutrenit Bielous remarked: 'The democratic experience restarted in 1973 was abruptly challenged by a leftist Peronist guerrilla, in opposition to the ruling Peronist government, and by right-wing para-military bands that ended in a new military coup'.[8]

The Brazilian experience exhibits significant differences from the case of Argentina throughout the 1964–1985 period. Through the authoritarian structure the regime kept in place a highly supervised system of political parties with restricted electoral rules. Two factors emerged as putative causes of such dynamics: the existence of a strong and centralised state apparatus and the pre-existence of a highly fragmented party system. As Liliana De Riz notes:

> While in Argentina the weakness of political actors led to the direct politicisation of interest groups, in Brazil [did not] emerge movements able to consolidate institutions and identities strong enough to challenge the supremacy of the state and transform it into an arena to settle political conflict as in Argentina.[9]

In the case of Chile, two different stages can be identified. The first spans from the coup of 1973 until the timid opening after the 1982 economic crisis and the emergence of a process of growing popular mobilisation. The second extends from that point until the plebiscite of 1988. During the first phase, the regime dissolved the parties of the Unidad Popular and decreed the 'recess' of the others. In that context, and as a signal that it did not intend to compete with the military, the right-wing Partido Nacional decided to dissolve itself, while the Christian Democratic Party challenged the decision and resolved to remain as active as it possibly could. A new decree from 1977 dissolved all political parties but failed to impede the activism of the left and of the Christian democrats.[10]

During the second stage, which started after the economic crisis of 1982, the dictatorship approved a limited and restricted role for all parties except the Communists, which remained outlawed. The majority of the opposition parties, including the Christian democrats, the socialists and other smaller parties, agreed to play by these restrictive rules and eventually participated in the plebiscite of 1988. Their objective was to defeat the military regime electorally and hence open up a new political game to trigger a transition process.

In the case of Paraguay, the Alfredo Stroessner regime began a limited and tightly controlled process of liberalisation in the early 1960s. This gave some political space to the opposition while retaining the government's effective control of the ruling coalition. Thus, a transition from a one-party (1954–1963) to a restricted multi-party system slowly took place.[11] With this opening and under rules that established a limited relationship between political parties and civil society, a number of electoral practices emerged, although as mere formalities rather than effective methods of decision-making. The regime was then able to use this as a facade to try to deflect international criticism and as a mechanism to keep the opposition divided, weak and precariously organised.

> Every time the possibility of a broad opposition front has emerged, as in the early 1960s and most notably in 1977, the regime has managed to invent a new 'opposition' leadership willing to play by rigged rules, sabotage the real opposition, and reproduce the dual arena, in exchange for some spoils. Given the overwhelming control of the press, the judiciary and the repressive apparatus, this is hardly a difficult task. The government strategy has been facilitated by the fact that the Liberal Party, the largest opposition party, has a history of divisions and conflicts, and because its social base of support is wide, loose and has a significant degree of bossism or political machine built into it.[12]

The Paraguayan case (1989) constitutes the best example of a transition from above triggered by the impending succession crisis of the regime. Having been settled in favour of the *blandos*, a new scenario emerged and through a protracted process of demands and concessions the transition finally ended with competitive elections in 1998. Finally, in the case of Uruguay, one can observe a scenario that combines elements of both the Chilean and the Argentine cases. At the beginning of the process, there was a complete suspension of the activities of political parties and a tight delimitation of a 'permitted' political arena. Later, the dissolution of congress (1973) completed the military takeover of government and leftist political parties were outlawed and repressed. The traditional Colorado and National parties, which at the beginning of the process had supported the military takeover as a way of stopping the leftist insurgency of the Tupamaros, remained paralysed thereafter.[13]

Conclusions

In all five Latin American cases examines above it is important to note the *strategic* behaviour of the main political actors, namely the democratising forces. This was highlighted by Diamond *et al.* who noted that 'the development and maintenance of democracy is greatly facilitated by values and behavioural dispositions (particularly at the elite level) of compromise, flexibility, tolerance, conciliation, moderation and restraint'.[14] Understanding the nature of the transitions or *transitions how* (pacted, cautious, socially 'minimalist', economically prudent) is key to understanding why they were successful. Yet if that path ensured the endurance of the new regimes, the process also contains clues to understanding the challenges of democracies today. Those democracies which in their first stage placed a heavy emphasis on the protection of political and civil rights must now tackle a new set of problems, chiefly the challenges of poverty, inequality and social exclusion. In the Southern Cone, the common denominator has been to dismantle the extreme neo-liberal policies put in place in the early stages of democratic transition.

Without abandoning macroeconomic stability, achieved through prudent fiscal and monetary policies, most regimes have addressed the heavy social debt of poverty not through an attempt to re-enact the revolutionary agenda of past decades or the well intentioned but ill-conceived economic formulas of the past, but through the pragmatic construction of a welfare state of sorts. So far, this has worked far better than any other past method, in terms of growth, presence in the new globalised world and social inclusion. In short, *democratic transitions have not only been an exercise in redefining political rules but also in reframing the economic and social bases upon which they rest*. These transitions would not have been successful had they been reduced to the mere craftsmanship of a new political formula, important as this may be. The success lay, ultimately, in *simultaneously* articulating a new political and a new socio-economic pact which, as time has shown, has served as the springboard for successful social and economic reform in the framework of democracy.

Notes

1 Thomas Carothers developed a critique of what he called the 'transition paradigm' arguing that: 'Five core assumptions define the transition paradigm. The first, which is an umbrella for all the others, is that any country moving away from dictatorial rule can be considered a country in transition toward democracy'. See Carothers, 'The End of the Transition Paradigm'. O'Donnell responded that from the beginning his work and that of his colleagues stressed quite explicitly the uncertainty of the outcomes

of the transition process. See O'Donnell, 'In Partial Defence of an Evanescent "Paradigm"'.
2 Marshall, *Class, Citizenship and Social Development*.
3 Tavares, 'El Desarrollo Industrial Latinoamericano y la Presente Crisis del Transnacionalismo'.
4 Ibid.
5 O'Donnell, *Modernización y Autoritarismo*.
6 Ibid., p. 140.
7 Birch, 'Estabilidad Política y Rezago Económico', p. 169.
8 Bielous, 'Dictaduras y Partidos Políticos en Argentina, Brasil y Uruguay'.
9 de Riz, 'Political Parties and Democratic Consolidation', p. 72.
10 Garreton, *The Chilean Political Process*, p. 407.
11 Arditi, *La Reconstrucción de la Política en el Paraguay*.
12 Abente-Brun, 'Stronismo, Post-stronismo and the Prospects for Democratisation in Paraguay'.
13 Rial, 'Los Partidos Politicos Uruguayos *en el Proceso de Transición hacia la Democracia*'.
14 Diamond et al., *Democracy in Developing Countries – Latin America, Volume Four*.

9 Transitology *à l'Arabe*
Confirmation and challenge

Bahgat Korany

If a short definition could be given of the 2011 Arab Spring, it would be the decline of people's fear and the expansion of political public space, which in turn has had significant implications for constitutional empowerment and institutional change over time.[1] This is why places such as Tahrir Square in Cairo or Avenue Bourguiba in Tunis have become household names both inside and outside the Arab world, implying a 'new Middle East'.[2] A French addition to the flood of literature on the Arab Spring compares it to the '1989 revolutions in the East'.[3] This claim may be an exaggeration – the latter revolutions led to the fall of the Berlin Wall, the end of the bipolar Cold War and ultimately the collapse of the Soviet Union itself, while the Arab Spring had no such immediate strategic *global* consequences. It did, however, share a key feature with the 1989 revolutions: a surprising onset of popular protest that revealed the vulnerability of authoritarian rule. Given the raging controversy about authoritarian durability and resilience in the conceptual literature, this point is indeed crucial.

The linkages between the opening of public spaces and the question of the durability of authoritarian rule touches on a little understood issue: a more conceptual and comparative orientation of the Arab Spring events in the light of the emerging transition paradigm or transitology. Consequently, this chapter evaluates such linkages between the Arab transformative moments in these very public demonstrations, their relationship to the revolutionary process and the concepts and issues of transitology. The chapter teases out some propositions of this emerging transition paradigm to see how they fare in the face of the events of the Arab Spring, and vice versa, to assist a fruitful cross-fertilisation between emerging conceptualisation and data on the ground. This encounter between available conceptualisation and events is overdue, especially as the belief in 'Arab exceptionalism' is refuted and even discredited and the Arab world is increasingly viewed through the lenses of transitology as a conceptual newcomer.

The Arab Spring raises another important question beyond its assumed exceptionalism and the implications for the resilience of authoritarianism. Given the region's geo-cultural location and the power of its Islamist organisations, the Arab Spring addresses a second critical issue in the democratisation literature: the relationship between secularism and democracy. Though the Arab Spring, as its adjective indicates, involves only a maximum of 400 million (mostly Muslim) people (among the 1.6 billion Muslims globally – approximately twenty-five per cent) they are in a region that is at the core of the Muslim world. Not only is this region the birthplace of Islam (and other monotheistic religions), but the region also harbours the city of Mecca to which pious Muslims turn in their prayers five times a day and hope to visit for pilgrimage and salvation at least once in their lifetime. Consequently, the Arab Spring's response to the basic question of how to combine Islam and democracy resonates throughout the Islamic world and beyond. Its transitional experiences provide insights into the general debate about secularism and democracy in the light of similar analyses and findings about the role of the Catholic Church in Poland and of liberation theology in Latin America.

This chapter first explores the initial patterns of protests and in particular the varieties and challenges of the Arab Spring five years after the start of mass protests in 2011. Four major indices (processing forty-three indicators) for the years 2009–2014 (and 2015 when data are available) are presented for five countries identified with the Arab Spring: Egypt, Libya, Syria, Tunisia and Yemen (see the respective endnotes for each table's index definition and data). Second, the chapter explores the idea that there is indeed a transition paradigm, and critically assesses some of its contributions as well as its challenges in relation to particular details of the Arab Spring. Third, the analysis addresses what characterises any major transition, including the Arab Spring: the transformative process and the entry of new political actors – in this case the entry of Islamists into legal and formal political life. These are important components of what is dubbed here 'the three Ms': the Masses, especially their liberal-leftist youth segment, the Mosque (or Islamists) and the Military. Youth constitute the majority in all Arab societies and they pioneered the mass protests. The detailed analysis focuses here, however, on the Mosque or Islamists. Their legalisation and legitimisation constitutes an important characteristic of the ongoing process of transition. We know for instance that the military's impact – the 'deep state'– is primarily due to its coercive capacities. The Mosque or Islamists – even their armed groups – do not constitute an equal counterpower. The cases of Al Qaeda in Yemen and the Islamic State/Da'esh in Syria apart, both Tunisia's Al Nahda and Egypt's Muslim Brotherhood were admitted as regular political groups. They constituted their own political parties, ran for elections and won a majority – a first in the Arab world. Even when they were no longer in government, this still begs the question: Why do they constitute such a formidable counterpart? Is it because they represent 'deep society'? Hence, the chapter investigates in greater detail the patterns of organisation and recruitment as manifested in Egypt's Muslim Brotherhood (MB), the mother organisation of Islamist political action across most of the Arab and Muslim worlds.

The rise and subsequent demise of the Mosque as an explicit political actor should equally shed light on the (under-researched) role of religion in transitology. In the fourth section of the chapter, I evaluate the Mosque's ideological appeal and approaches to mobilisation, especially the characteristics of the Islamists' membership and organisational power. Though in many countries the

'Brothers' (Al Ikhwan) are *old organisations*, they are in the recent transition process *new political actors* assuming novel governance roles in the Arab world and beyond. Hence attention needs also to be devoted to the concept of political learning. The fifth section details challenges to Islamist-oriented governance that offset its huge assets and finally brought about its decline. A sixth section returns to the implications of the Arab Spring experience for the transitology paradigm: transition is an inherently conflictual process that arises during, and as a response to, a crisis of the state and of society. In conclusion, the chapter puts forward general propositions based on some of the principal patterns from the Arab Spring case to advance the conceptual debate on transitology and its implications for democratisation in the region.

What was the 'Arab Spring'?

The Arab Spring was not a unitary whole. In terms of principal actors and transition processes, these are multiple rather than a single or monolithic pattern of change. Though street protests have been widespread in Arab streets since the mid- to late-1980s, the 'Arab Spring' started in the small town of Sidi Bouzid in Tunisia's southern countryside on 17 December 2010, with the self-immolation of a street-side fruit vendor, Mohamed Bouazizi. Bouazizi was more than a regular street peddler. He was a university graduate who failed to find a job and had to resort to the informal economy to survive. A policewoman arrested and humiliated him in public, and the humiliation continued in the police station. The interesting question is that many street peddlers are arrested on a daily basis on Arab streets: Why did Bouazizi's case become the spark for a collective protest movement throughout much of the Arab world?

Equally intriguing is the speed of the collapse of the regime in Tunisia: President Ben Ali fled to Saudi Arabia on 14 January 2011, less than a month after Bouazizi's self-immolation and the start of the protests. A regional demonstration effect, a contagion, followed. Egypt's mass protests erupted on 'Police Day', 25 January, and forced Mubarak to resign on 11 February, a mere seventeen days after they started. Mass protests continued to dislodge presidents (Ali Abdallah Saleh in Yemen in February 2012), or kill them (Muammar Qaddafi in Libya in October 2011) or force those who persisted to go through a bloody civil war (e.g. Bashar al Assad's Syria since March 2011).

Though protests reached some monarchies – notably Bahrain, Jordan and Morocco – protesters in these countries did not demand a change of regime or continually repeat the street slogan of the republics: *irhal* (get out). Monarchs in these countries immediately turned to rewards (or bribes) and concessions to placate popular discontent. For instance, the king of Saudi Arabia promised a package of US$140 billion to meet accumulated housing problems and social needs. The monarchs of Jordan and Morocco embarked on processes of constitutional reform, as they had done in the past, to appear responsive to citizen demands for change. However, an underlying reason why the republics were particularly under attack was the extreme longevity of their presidents. Libya's

Qaddafi ruled for forty-two years, Yemen's Saleh for thirty-four years, Egypt's Mubarak for almost thirty years and Tunisia's Ben Ali for twenty-four years. As some Arab sociologists rightly remarked, the Arab street used the neologism *gumluka* ('Republican monarchies') to distinguish them from the usual connotation of a republican regime. *Gumluka* was even more justified when many of these presidents were grooming their sons to succeed them. Indeed, in Syria Bashar Al-Assad did succeed his father, Hafez Al-Assad and the constitution was hastily modified in June 2000 to allow it.

Comparing Arab Spring countries: from spark to fire

The tables below indicate that transition is indeed a time of crisis, and to reflect this situation faithfully the transitology paradigm itself needs a basic reorientation, a shift. Rather than implying a smooth process of democratisation, transitology needs to be linked more to the 'post-conflict society' paradigm. Such a shift should not only be in labelling, but also in conceptualisation and even epistemology. This implies different conceptual components and data collection. We should look for standard indicators of inter-group conflicts rather than primarily peaceful evolution issues of negotiation and group rehabilitation. I follow up more on the centrality of this conflictual dimension below.

Despite differences, standard indicators for the Arab Spring countries are all in the red, even for the *relative* successes of Egypt and Tunisia. Over the five years, they all deteriorated in terms of the United Nations Development Programme (UNDP) Human Development Index, the Fragile/Failed State Index, the Global Peace Index and the World Bank's Governance Index. All indices start one or two years before 2011 to compare 'before' and 'after'. In the five Arab Spring countries, the four indices with their multiple indicators do demonstrate that the period 2011–2015 was costly. As if to emphasise these tables and the data they contain, the 7th Arab Strategy Forum held in Dubai in December 2015 went further in specifying a catastrophic cumulative cost of the Arab Spring. The overall cost was estimated at US$833.7 billion; the cost of rebuilding destroyed infrastructure amounted to US$461 billion; there were US$289 billion in GDP losses; the refugee crisis that followed cost US$48.7 billion; securities markets and investment losses amounted to US$35 billion; Arab countries lost more than 103 million tourists in those five years; fourteen million Arabs were displaced; and 1.34 million people were killed or injured. The future is at stake, with Syria a case in point. For instance, as many as 2.7 million school children have dropped their schooling. Therefore, a large number of the next generation could already be disempowered. Another depressing estimate is that, as of 2016, Syria would need about thirty-eight years to reach its 2010 human development level. Even success at this level would not bring back the hundreds of thousands who died or heal the many more who will be scarred and traumatised for life.

Does this mean that the Arab Spring failed? Was it a chimera? This is the question hotly debated both inside and outside the Arab world, and the issue is highly relevant to transitology itself. Indeed, the conflict is intense and the crisis

Table 9.1 The Human Development Index[4]

Country	Rank in 2010	Rank in 2011	Rank in 2012	Rank in 2013	Rank in 2014
Egypt	101	113	112	112	108
Libya	53	64	64	64	94
Syria	111	119	116	118	134
Tunisia	81	94	94	94	96
Yemen	133	154	160	160	160

Table 9.2 The Fragile/Failed State Index[5]

Country	Rank in 2009	Rank in 2010	Rank in 2011	Rank in 2012	Rank in 2013	Rank in 2014	Rank in 2015
Egypt	43	49	45	31	34	31	38
Libya	112	111	111	50	54	41	25
Syria	39	48	48	23	21	15	9
Tunisia	121	118	108	94	83	78	86
Yemen	18	15	13	8	6	8	7

Table 9.3 The Global Peace Index[6]

Country	Rank in 2009	Rank in 2010	Rank in 2011	Rank in 2012	Rank in 2013	Rank in 2014	Rank in 2015
Egypt	68	52	64	111	112	143	137
Libya	54	50	138	148	147	133	149
Syria	109	115	118	152	160	162	162
Tunisia	37	35	41	73	75	79	76
Yemen	121	133	141	145	152	147	147

is raging. However, for this book and political analysis generally, the question of the consequences of the Arab Spring raises the basic issue of indicators and their substantive inferences. While they are valid in the sense of measuring what they purport to measure, they are correlations rather than causality. In other words, the existing governance crisis and the socio-economic problems identified had started long before the Arab Spring. This chapter's argument is that, rather than the Arab Spring causing these problems, it is in fact a *response* to them. This is why Bouazizi's self-immolation became such a general spark across all state borders unifying, in a way, around a protesting Arab street.

The transition paradigm: transformative process and new actors

Controversial as it is, the existing literature on, for example, post-communist regimes as well as on the Arab Spring demonstrates the existence of a transitology paradigm in the sense of a research programme.[7] This paradigm is now providing a conceptual map and a research agenda to decode the accelerating events of the Arab Spring. Equally important, the tenets of the paradigm help experts – especially area specialists – to frame research questions and findings in comparative perspective.

Such a perspective enriches both Arab Spring analysis and transitology analyses more generally. However, for these assets to materialise fruitfully, the paradigm has to be looked at critically. Indeed, the presence of such a democratisation paradigm does not mean that its tenets are accepted. In the case of the region that interests us here, the Arab world, the paradigm's deficiencies start with the quasi-neglect of the region in considering it 'exceptional'[8] – that all regions change and democratise except the Arab Middle East – a remnant of Orientalist thinking.[9] However once the Arab Spring emerged, transitologists began serious evaluation of the region in terms of the paradigm. To their credit, some started re-evaluating their earlier conceptualisation as a result of direct contact with the situation on the ground, with the possibility of redefining/reformulating some aspects of the transitology paradigm.[10] This is an important indicator of transitology's conceptual flexibility. Its most important asset in relation to the Arab Spring is its emphasis on the transformative process and its potential focus on new political actors. Indeed, one of the main reasons for this non-linearity is the influx of new political actors, from the (liberal-leftist) youth to the legalised Islamists.

New political actors: the youth

Youth, or those below twenty-nine years of age, now constitute more than sixty per cent of the population of the Arab world. However, the Arab Spring showed that they are not a quantum only; they are also a political driving force. Bouazizi was a young unemployed graduate whose self-immolation acted – literally and metaphorically – as the spark that spread the Arab Spring from the Tunisian countryside to the rest of the region. Youth actions and perspectives became the standard to the extent that others' are defined in relation to them.[11] They are above all the prime users and promoters of the new social media, the basic mobilisation tool that fuelled – but did not cause – the Arab Spring.

In both the *ancien régime* and during the Arab Spring, the media had a huge impact. According to Lina Khatib:

> Private satellite channels have become Arab countries' primary media outlets, rising from one hundred in January 2004, to 450 in January 2009, to 1,100 in 2012, at least six hundred of which are available to the public free of charge. Satellite channels reach ninety-five percent of homes in Arab countries, where some 250 million viewers tune in. Technology for viewing programs on mobile devices is rapidly boosting satellite channel penetration. The number of independent Arab newspapers has also grown substantially. Although several newspapers have been shut down, new ones have emerged bringing the total from 144 in 2003 to 189 in 2009.[12]

Table 9.4 The Governance Index[13]

	Rank in 2009	Rank in 2010	Rank in 2011	Rank in 2012	Rank in 2013	Rank in 2014
Egypt						
Voice and accountability	14.69	13.74	14.55	26.54	17.54	14.78
Political stability and absence of terrorism	25.59	19.34	6.60	7.58	7.11	7.77
Government effectiveness	47.37	43.06	35.55	23.44	21.05	20.19
Regulatory quality	46.89	46.89	41.71	33.01	27.75	25.00
Rule of law	54.03	51.18	42.72	39.81	33.65	31.25
Control of corruption	41.15	34.29	27.96	33.49	32.06	32.21
Libya						
Voice and accountability	2.84	2.84	6.10	20.85	19.91	16.26
Political stability and absence of terrorism	74.88	45.28	11.79	6.64	4.74	4.37
Government effectiveness	12.92	12.92	7.11	5.26	5.74	2.88
Regulatory quality	11.96	9.57	4.74	2.87	1.91	0.48
Rule of law	20.85	18.96	12.68	12.80	6.16	2.88
Control of corruption	8.13	5.24	5.21	2.39	0.96	1.44
Syria						
Voice and accountability	6.16	4.74	4.23	3.32	3.79	2.96
Political stability and absence of terrorism	28.44	21.70	2.83	0.47	0.47	0.00
Government effectiveness	34.45	32.54	38.39	10.05	8.13	6.73
Regulatory quality	18.18	20.57	20.85	4.31	4.31	3.85
Rule of law	37.91	36.49	30.05	14.22	3.32	6.73
Control of corruption	12.92	12.86	15.64	10.53	7.66	2.40

Tunisia						
Voice and accountability	9.95	9.95	35.68	42.18	44.08	49.75
Political stability and absence of terrorism	47.39	44.34	34.43	22.27	18.48	15.05
Government effectiveness	65.55	63.16	55.92	53.59	52.63	48.56
Regulatory quality	53.11	53.11	46.45	44.98	39.71	40.87
Rule of law	60.66	59.72	51.17	50.71	48.82	53.37
Control of corruption	56.46	54.76	55.92	53.59	54.07	55.77
Yemen						
Voice and accountability	11.85	10.90	8.92	9.95	11.37	10.34
Political stability and absence of terrorism	1.90	1.89	1.89	1.42	1.90	1.46
Government effectiveness	12.44	14.35	12.32	9.09	11.96	7.21
Regulatory quality	27.75	30.14	22.27	26.79	24.40	21.63
Rule of law	14.22	13.27	8.45	8.06	12.32	8.17
Control of corruption	15.79	10.00	8.53	8.13	9.09	1.92

The 'new social media' was civil society's means of coping with this softer form of the regime's repression, its subtler way of controlling the mind. As Khatib's data shows:

> over the last decade, the Arab region has also witnessed a large rise in the use of new media, especially among young people. Between 2000 and 2011, Internet use grew 3.458 percent, and the region now has an estimated 107 million Internet users. In 2007, regional broadband penetration stood at five percent; by 2010 it had risen to seventeen percent and was expected to reach twenty-two percent by the end of 2011. The popular revolutions in Arab countries have demonstrated just how vital social media have become to Arab Internet users. Facebook saw its users skyrocket. An Arabic version of Twitter, launched in October 2009, played a prominent part in the popular movements of 2011.[14]

The new social media is primarily the work of the youth, 'the children of the dot. com era'. Wael Ghoneim, Google's Middle East executive is the embodiment of both new social media and especially its political impact.[15] However, the 'youth studies' literature is rather thin on the actual political socialisation of youth: a basic actor in the present transition stage and its challenges.[16] The tracing of such patterns of political socialisation indicates youth frustration with, and avoidance of, existing political institutions – both governmental and opposition. Fieldwork and interviews show that after initial enthusiasm at launching the Arab Spring mass protests, disillusionment settled in. Youth, the great demographic majority, ended up fragmented and losing power – they became the lonely crowd, with very few political tools and little effectiveness. Many of them continue to oscillate or associate with Islamist groups.[17]

New political actors: the Islamists

It is now accepted that the Islamists,[18] like any other group, are actually composed of sub-groups. They range from the Sufis – usually uninterested in political participation and more concerned with spiritual matters – to the Salafis; the very orthodox Al Qaeda and Da'esh-type, by way of the Muslim Brotherhood (MB) in the Mashreq and Al Nahda in Tunisia. The specific mosque's power is partly a function of the history of the Middle East. In a region which has witnessed the birth of three main religions, any organisation that uses religious symbols is able to master an impressive mobilisational power. These symbols became associated with daily life issues, identity and bonding in a convenient combination of *din* (religion) and *dunya* (daily life). Though not all shades of Islamists aimed to govern (e.g. Sufis and some Salafists), their core group, known as political Islam and represented by the Egypt-based Muslim Brotherhood, had waited more than eighty years since its inception in 1928 to take power. This long awaited moment finally came with the Arab Spring in 2011. Such graduation into political power was evident in countries such as Egypt (and

Tunisia) which managed to dismiss their presidents relatively easily and essentially peacefully.

In fact, in Egypt's case, the ease with which Islamists achieved power represents a minor puzzle. The Muslim Brotherhood hesitated to join the demonstrations against the Mubarak regime. The persistence of most of its rank and file pushed the Brotherhood to allow its young members to join Tahrir but only as individuals. It made sure it was on record as abstaining as an organisation. However, it finally joined the revolt on 28 January 2011, when the tide was changing in favour of the demonstrators and security forces were overpowered, indeed already on the run on the evening of 27 January. However, despite this wavering and procrastination, Islamist forces soon after became the revolution's trump card. Why? There are multiple reasons which can be categorised into two groups: societal/contextual and organisational.

Since the Middle East is the birthplace of three principal religions, religious appeal is central in society. Religious groups are usually *primus inter pares*. Their slogans are easily digested and quickly become appealing. For instance, the simple (and simplistic) 'Islam is the solution' has strong mobilisation power. Contrary to the mass perception of the official opposition and its politicians as opportunistic power seekers and hypocritical paper tigers, Islamists are perceived as pious people, disinterested in the mundane and caring only for their relationship with God. As the popular public image puts it, they are 'God's people' (*bito' rabina*). Their documented harassment, repression and torture by the regimes reinforce this positive image. They become martyrs for the sake of their religious belief and 'love of God'. When governing regimes are manifestly Westernised and dependent on foreign powers, Islamists thus appear as the real defenders of the people and national interests against those of 'alien' ideology and 'agents of the world of unbelief'. Islamists usually capitalise on this positive perception and draw analogies between their suffering and that of early converts to Islam in the seventh century, *al muhajireen wal Ansar*.

Islamists can demonstrate this godly association practically, in the field. Empirical research now shows that they are the most heavily involved in making up for state deficiencies in providing basic social services. In poor areas, in slums or informal housing neighbourhoods in towns (*'ashwiyaat*, informal housing) and especially in the countryside, Islamists worked to establish health clinics, student tutoring and many social solidarity projects, e.g. informal credit/savings groups known as *gam'iyya* or rotation loans. They became trustworthy social workers and helpers in poverty alleviation efforts.[19] These are important elements of social capital that can easily be translated into political capital – and at short notice. This is precisely what happened following the dismissal of Mubarak and of Ben Ali and his discredited socio-political elite. The Mosque itself was at hand to use this social capital for the political recruitment of a mass of potential sympathisers.

The organisational assets of the Brotherhood is still one of the most under-researched aspects of Islamist organisations in general. Apart from one classic work (Richard Mitchell's 1969 *The Society of the Muslim Brothers*), we do not have very much information that is trustworthy about such basic features of the organisation as membership numbers, financing and the process of policy-making. Some memoirs exist[20] but they do not answer many of the basic questions and are sometimes apologetic or justificatory. These sources do, however, agree on some general aspects. All the texts by former members of the organisation reveal that the Muslim Brotherhood is a close-knit organisation, almost like an iron container. It usually recruits people from a very young age and members share bonds beyond mere membership of the organisation. Members usually have close friendships or kin relationships and connect with each through business. They also intermarry with the help and active participation of the organisation's representatives. All these factors help to increase membership and create a highly organic cohesion.

Members are actively encouraged to recruit other members. To maintain the internal iron uniformity, members are subjected to a rigorous process of internal promotion that lasts for five to eight years, during which a rising Muslim Brother ascends through four membership ranks before finally becoming a fully-fledged 'active brother'. At each level, brothers are tested on their completion of a standardised Brotherhood curriculum, which emphasises rote memorisation of the Quran as well as the teachings of Brotherhood founder Hassan Al Banna and radical Brotherhood theorist Sayyid Qutb. Rising Muslim Brothers are also vetted for their willingness to follow the leadership's orders, and Muslim Brothers ultimately take an oath to 'listen to and obey' the organisation's edicts. Members are thus well indoctrinated foot-soldiers obeying orders from the twenty-member executive Guidance Office at the top of the pyramid-shaped hierarchy. They are integrated into thousands of 'families' – cells that range from five to twenty members. If they ever disobey orders, they are simply banished. This is what happened to Abdel Moneim Abu El Fetouh, head of the political party Strong Egypt and top presidential candidate. He suffered banishment because he declared his presidential candidacy in mid-2011 when the movement's strategy at the time was against such a policy. Even though the organisation eventually changed course, Abu El Fetouh's excommunication persisted.

The hierarchical structure of the Muslim Brotherhood includes the composition and functioning of militias. The Egyptian sociologist Saad Eddin Ibrahim, who encountered many in the Muslim Brotherhood leadership while in prison, estimates that the militias number between 200,000 and 300,000 men. In 2007, photographs were leaked showing Muslim Brotherhood masked militias training within Al Azhar University. Because many in the leadership were pursued and had to live and work in exile, they were able to send money back to finance many of the organisation's activities and bolster its social capital. Strong man Khairat Al Shater – the Vice-Supreme Guide – is usually characterised as a model successful businessman who financed many of the organisation's activities. These financial resources may include petromoney, *zakat* or other charitable activities, or even illicit sources – e.g. hold-ups of non-Muslim goldsmiths.

As finance comes to fix yet more multiple bonds – early friendships, neighbourhood proximity, local 'cultural traits', family and/or marriage relationships – there is little distinction between public and private space. The organisation increasingly invades members' private space and takes it over, willingly or not. As many individual members bring their families into the organisation, the distinction between 'household' and 'organisation' activities is blurred. Contrary to conventional views, women are increasingly integrated into the organisation. Quranic study groups or *nadwas* propagate 'the faith' and provide religious guidance. These *nadwas* create a life outside the home for women and constitute a place to seek advice and find solace for the alleviation of problems. *Nadwas* are not only an occasion for 'guidance' or indoctrination but also provide an emotional outlet for 'excluded' women. *Nadwas* take place in private homes and/or in the mosque.

Repressive regimes in the Middle East and North African region have usually attacked and even destroyed any opposition's headquarters. However, they failed to control mosques. When sermons were controlled in many of the 'official' mosques, non-official ones (or *zawya*) mushroomed. Many of these were established by those who were not members of the Muslim Brotherhood and who wanted to meet the needs of their people, especially in isolated areas of the countryside or even near the rich, gated communities outside big cities. Yet by offering a place for meeting and coming together around the common religious denomination, mosques and their attendees were capitalised upon politically by the Muslim Brotherhood. The result – as mentioned above – is that the organisation ended up having, even in the most repressive regimes, the possibility of five meetings per day (corresponding to prayer times) and a big general assembly every Friday (corresponding to Friday noon prayer). Very few political parties or social organisations, even in developed countries, could achive this scale of mobilisation and socialisation. As a result of these significant societal–contextual and organisational assets, Mosque organisation became deeply rooted in society. In fact, it represented deep society *par excellence*. It became what is known in social movement theory as an effective 'network of shared meaning', a well-knit organisation identified with society at large. It was thus able – contrary to other political forces – to inherit political power once the *ancien régime* and its governing political elite were dismissed.

An important indicator of these assets is that Islamists won almost all the battles necessary to inherit the post-*ancien régime* era. Thus, in Egypt, they campaigned for the Constitutional Declaration in March 2011 and won seventy-eight per cent of the popular vote. In the first parliamentary elections in late 2011, when the Supreme Council of Armed Forces (SCAF) was running the country, they won about seventy per cent of the seats. Though the People's Assembly was later dissolved and the results of the parliamentary elections were annulled, the Islamists continued their rise. In June 2012, they captured the highest political post: the presidency. In fact, the head of the newly-constituted political wing of the Muslim Brotherhood (the Freedom and Justice Party), Mohamed Morsi, was the first civilian ever to hold this post. Why then were these impressive societal and organisational assets not maintained? Why did the Mosque in power not have the plain sailing that was expected? Why did the organisation become increasingly contested and why was the legitimacy of its power eroded?

The indicators of governance under strain are varied and multiplying. The Islamist-dominated Constituent Assembly in Egypt, nominated to draft a constitution, lost as much as a third of its membership in protest, including members representing the church and even Al Azhar. Though the referendum on the post-revolution constitutional draft was to be the occasion for celebration, it became instead a cause of great controversy and even calls for a boycott. Contrary to the 2011 Constitutional Declaration, which passed with seventy-eight per cent of the popular vote, this constitution won the approval of less than sixty-four per cent of those who voted. Tahrir square itself, the revolution's icon, became associated with occasions of chaos, vandalism and bloody clashes. Insecurity spread and in late January 2013, the president had to decree a state of emergency and curfew on the three Canal cities of Port-Said, Ismaillia and Suez, though with very little effect. In fact, a wave of civil disobedience was spreading that could endanger the Suez Canal as an international passageway. Economic indicators – with an overall decline in tourism and foreign investment and rising deadlocks – are too obvious to detail. Suffice it to say that the Egyptian pound lost as much as nine per cent of its value in relation to the dollar in less than a month and domestic debt reached the dangerous threshold of almost eighty per cent of Gross National Product (GNP) – an increase of about eight per cent in less than two years. With as many as 5,500 factories reducing their activities or closing down over a two-year period (2014–2016), unemployment was on the rise and poverty levels increased. And with a growing number of stolen cars and hold-ups, police reports depicted a Hobbesian 'state of nature' and 'war of all against all'.

At the top political level, the strain of governance was also spreading. Decisions were improvised, then contested in public even by members of the governing team and finally cancelled or halted. Cabinet reshuffles were frequent. Suitable ministerial candidates were sometimes difficult to find – a surprising phenomenon in a country where long queues existed of people ready to accept any post and at almost any price. In November 2012, on the occasion of a presidential decree adding to the president's powers, as many as seven of the president's assistants and advisors resigned. On 18 February 2013, the Presidential Advisor for Environmental Affairs held a press conference to explain his departure amid accusations and counter-accusations of misuse of public funds – a clear indicator of both governing elite fragmentation and legitimacy erosion. The government did not attempt to refute these indicators of governance strain. It affirmed, however, that the problems were the making of the 'counter-revolution' and the *felool* – the remnants of Mubarak's regime. Indeed, there might have been some infiltrators who were exploiting the chaotic situation. However, most of the protests were mobilised by youth groups, many of whom were allies of the Muslim Brotherhood and had in fact campaigned for the election of Morsi against his rival, General Ahmed Shafiq. Public political divisions were also reaching the very top of the regime. The question, then, has to be reiterated: Why did the Muslim Brotherhood elite fail to maintain its initial capital and legitimacy impetus? The reasons can again be classified in the two categories of contextual–societal and organisational factors.

Challenges for transitology: mass pressure cookers, societal stress and inexperienced leadership

The Arab Spring presents three important challenges for transitology, particularly its ability to explain transition *from* authoritarian rule.[21] The first challenge is part of what I conceptualise as the 'pressure-cooker' effect of the Arab Spring. Put simply, the pressure cooker effect means that since people have been suppressed for so long under authoritarian rule, they tend to associate such rule with all their problems, whatever these may be. Consequently, once they have removed the political ruler and the government, they assume that *all* their needs will be met and problems will be solved almost *immediately*. According to these expectations, not only will democracy be achieved overnight, but such nagging problems as unemployment, corruption, poverty or traffic jams will come to an end with the removal of the *ancien régime*. Given such high and unrealistic expectations, disappointment is bound to follow. Disillusionment sets in and is translated into frustration and even extremist behaviour towards whatever new authority is in power.

While the Muslim Brotherhood has had to cope with this special context, it particularly suffered from this 'pressure cooker' effect for two reasons: presidential candidate Morsi inflated his electoral promises to about sixty-four, such promises describing paradise on earth; and the resources to meet demands, even the most pressing ones, were insufficient. Resources dwindled because of protests, sit-ins, work stoppages, factory closures and a general decline in taxes and national income. The result of this demand/resource gap was stagflation and mistrust towards the governing authority. Another handicap emanating from the context of transition is more focused on elite politics and its dynamics. Political forces were released and found themselves in uncharted terrain. Since they had not learned the political skills required to work together, the political arena became a conflict arena. Political polarisation and zero-sum relationships characterise such a situation. The political arena was reminiscent of Frank Sinatra's classic song *Strangers in the Night*. Albeit, these strangers were not exchanging glances but blows, often below the belt. Political skills were deficient and the political learning curve low and slow.

This general contextual challenge characteristic of the transition phase worsened with the Mosque in power. Islamists had previously been excluded from open political action and the Muslim Brotherhood had been officially named *Al Mahdhoura* (the banned or illegal). As a result, most Islamists spent most of their life working underground, in cells. Such conditions impose rules of secrecy, primacy of short-term manoeuvrability and a tendency towards opportunism. In the face of imminent and constant threats, any means of guaranteeing political and even physical survival are acceptable. Insecure and having been waiting for so long underground, the militants of the Brotherhood became impatient and eager for the maximum power grab. This past insecurity and subsequent haste to take power rendered many of them crude in their political dealings. 'They make a deal, then manipulate to break it, then swear to God that you are the one in the wrong'.[22] These contextual elements, at the core of the Mosque's inability to contribute to an inclusionary and smooth political process, are compounded by their own organisational structure.

At the crossroads between the contextual–societal and the organisational stands the Muslim Brotherhood's 'Al Nahda' programme. In essence, this programme is too general to be operational and still reflects such slogans as 'Islam is the solution' (*al Islam houa al hal*) rather than a blueprint for action. It represents a failure to move from politics to policies. Consequently, once it attained governance the organisation's top brass was busy, as was the case during its few months in power, elaborating the necessary blueprint. However, this attempt to adapt to the new governance situation engendered new problems. Specifically, the elaboration of a new programme of action had to deal with the lingering tension between ideological–religious appeal and the effective management of day-to-day issues – i.e. the practical issues of governance and problem-solving. Though manifestly economic problems such as rising unemployment, petrol shortages or inflation are easy to identify, the core challenge is political: how to gain the confidence of the electorate and control of the streets. There is a necessity for confidence-building measures between the top state authority and the forces of mobilisation, expanding in the face of the regime's policies. If such confidence is not re-established, state–society partnership can become deficient, if not absent. Society and state representatives could go on undermining each other rather than working together. Any scheme of governance would then be ineffective.

Because the organisational decision-making structure is tight, centralised and extremely hierarchical around the Supreme Guide and his council (many members still kiss the Supreme Guide's hand), the Muslim Brotherhood lacks flexibility and is indeed handicapped when dealing with day-to-day problems. Problem-solving requires practical flexibility. This organisational rigidity is compounded by a nativist mindset where solutions to present day problems are sought in seventh century issues around the birth of Islam or the relationship between the Prophet and his companions in the face of non-believers (*kuffar*). It is a continuous tangle between the principled function of the preacher and the pragmatic policy maker. While the confusion of functions plagues policy-making bodies and traps them in heated generic polemics, daily problems pile up, become aggravated and turn into crises and serious bottlenecks that threaten to bring the country to a standstill. As a result, Egypt moved into a complex situation between 2012–2014 where problems in various sectors – economic, social and political – intermingled and reinforced each other and almost led to a national breakdown. For instance, in less than two months, two high profile train accidents resulted in more than seventy deaths and hundreds of injured amid repeated promises to deal with 'railway problems'. To deal with shortages of spare parts, the solution was to resort to recycled parts – an indicator of the fragility of basic national infrastructure linking the country together both economically and socially. Both electricity and water cuts became frequent, with different ministries accusing each other of being responsible. Given the increasing energy problems, national transport was in danger. Stagflation problems, black market dealings and continuing daily insecurity were on the rise. Facebook interactions revealed the increasing frequency of terms such as 'grief', 'disappointment', 'sad transition', 'mourning' and the 'need to get out'.

Strong leadership seemed to be lacking with the Mosque in power, even at the very top: the presidency. To start with, Mohamed Morsi was the Muslim Brotherhood's second choice as presidential candidate – or, as some segments of the Egyptian street termed it, he was a 'spare part'. Even though he was the head of the newly-established Freedom and Justice Party, the Brotherhood's first choice was engineer Khairat El Shater, an influential businessman and a strong man of the Guidance Council. However, El Shater was disqualified because of his criminal record (a court case and imprisonment). Morsi was a professor of engineering at Zaqazeeq University. Although he had a degree earned abroad from the University of Southern California, he was considered 'Mr Average' in the corridors of the Brotherhood – a nice, humanitarian man but not at all a figure known for his influence in the organisation's decision-making. In fact, many rather considered him in his new post as simply overseeing the presidential duties for the Supreme Guide and the Guidance Council. His assistant for 'Democratic Transition', the Copt Samir Morcos, resigned because he had not been consulted on various matters. Many top officials followed suit for the same reason. The Vice-President, Justice Ahmed Mekki, disclosed that he had not been consulted either. The crucial questions, then, were: Who exactly was the main decision-maker and where was the locus of crucial decisions? Because of inexperienced, weak leadership and eroding legitimacy, Morsi had no choice but to count on the organisation which had brought him to power. His street base was weak. In the presidential elections, he received only 51.7 per cent of the popular vote. Moreover, many seemed to vote *against* his rival General Ahmed Shafiq, Mubarak's last Prime Minister, rather than for Morsi himself.

Morsi's legitimacy as president went on declining because he was perceived less as the president of all Egyptians and more as the spokesman of the Muslim Brotherhood and its representative for a power grab. Claims multiplied about his collusion in the 'Brotherhoodisation' of top state positions. There were accusations of gerrymandering or adding to the number of parliamentary seats allocated to some constituencies in order to favour countryside constituencies where the Brotherhood was popular. This perception of mistrust added to economic and social problems further eroded the leader's legitimacy. Towards the end of the Muslim Brotherhood's rule in July 2013, a public opinion survey showed that President Morsi's popularity was eroding, with his strongest support in the countryside and among those of modest education – the usual constituency of the Muslim Brotherhood. Massive street protests, estimated to amount to thirty million people, preordained the president's demise and the decline of the Mosque in Power.

Conclusions: revisting transitology in the Arab Spring

The main argument of this chapter is that there is a transition paradigm, a research programme identified as transitology. Though this paradigm has limitations, it also shapes our thinking about 'waves' of political elite/regime change in an increasing number of countries. Transitology is thus bound to influence our research on these dominant phenomena of the twenty-first century. It has also provided some conceptual and empirical assets. For instance, we have already accumulated data on various – and potentially comparable – aspects of transition in different regions of the world, from Latin America to Southern and Eastern Europe and to an emerging 'New Middle East'. Such 'mini data-banks' are bound to help trans-region comparisons. Moreover, and thanks to transitology as a transformative process, we are now going beyond the simplistic dichotomies of authoritarianism versus democratic regimes to more refined classification criteria and especially of typology-building in each category, from 'upgraded authoritarianism' to 'democracy with adjectives' to 'hybrid regimes'.[23] Related to this is the decline of fetishism about elections as being synonymous with democracy. There is indeed some rethinking about what democracy itself is and how it is to be measured, given its travel to exotic lands far away from the places where it originated and has been practiced for centuries.[24]

However, our analysis of the Arab Spring shows that transitional politics look much less like smooth democratisation and much more like zero-sum interaction and mutual undermining, which impedes a serious search for the common ground. It is no longer the pattern of balance of power, but rather the balance of weakness. This increase in negative energy derailed the basic transition process from the coalition-building required for its successful continuation. Economic and social problems not only remained without solution but they even increased. For instance with prevalent instability, tourists – who represent a substantive ten per cent and more of Egypt's and Tunisia's national income – changed destinations, as did foreign investors. For the proverbial man in the street, the transition was costly, even discredited. This is why it is suggested that transitology should be less focused on 'democratisation' with its positive aspects and implications of plain sailing. Rather, the transitology paradigm should be related to 'post-conflict society' literature and concepts[25] in order to make an important point about transition's serious challenges and regression possibilities rather than its teleology and linearity. Other general propositions based on this analysis of the Arab Spring follow from the primacy of this conflictual process.

Transition is a time of multilayered conflict

Such conflict intensity and the chances of transition to overcome the challenges are a function of societal characteristics as well as the manner in which the former autocratic regime collapsed. In the case of the Arab Spring, four heads of state have been arrested, killed or had to resign: Tunisia's Zein El Abdine Ben Ali, Egypt's Hosni Mubarak, Libya's Muammar Qaddafi and Yemen's Ali

Abdullah Saleh. Each of these leaders has been eliminated in a different way. The two extreme cases were Libya and Yemen. Though both witnessed 'foreign intervention', such intervention also played out in different ways. The cases of Tunisia and Egypt look more similar, as both leaders were forced to give up power with the military playing an effective and explicit role in this outcome. However, again even in these seemingly similar cases, the transition process was substantially different. In Tunisia, the military returned to their barracks. In Egypt, on the contrary, the Military Council of Armed Forces became the guardian of the transition and was in power for more than a year until both parliamentary and presidential elections took place and a new (Mosque) president took office in June 2012. However, as noted, the latter's governance was synonymous with crisis and he was eventually deposed by the military on 30 June 2013.

The tables in this chapter present data on economic decline, failure of governance and the rise of failed state phenomena. Even the relative success of Tunisia featured the assassination of prominent political actors and several terrorist attacks which negatively affected the required coalition-building. This also led to the exclusion or at least marginalisation of the Islamists as political actors. Tunisia's Al Nahda came second in the 2014 parliamentary elections and opted for voluntary political retreat. Egypt's post-Morsi polarisation of the 'two Ms', Military versus Mosque, also directs attention to this lack of focus on the conflictual dimension. Though economic issues occupy a central place, the transition process brings in existential or identity issues. More generalised conflict patterns dominate in Libya and Yemen: the increasing decline of state authority and the rise of tribal militias and warlordism, indeed bloody civil wars. Though the numbers of refugees and internally displaced persons are not as great as in the Syrian case, transition in Libya and Yemen became associated more with violent street wars than with democracy-building. A common characteristic of transition in the Arab world is thus the outpouring of rapidly multiplying and long-simmering demands and the desire that these should be met immediately. These demands range from basic material needs to issues of identity or the role of religion in society, the status of minorities and the characteristics of a civil state – hard nuts to crack for any mode of governance, and obviously worse for those groping to find a functioning formula.

Even in the pioneers of the Arab Spring, Egypt and Tunisia, which are not plagued any tribal/civil wars, conflict is predominant. The transition is marked by disillusionment, due to a widening gap between initial expectations and actual achievements. It is true that these initial expectations were highly exaggerated due to the legacy of the *ancien régime*. They became like a pressure cooker that could not keep the lid on any longer. But then the new regimes worsened this discontent by failing to deal effectively with this unfulfilled expectations–achievements gap and contributed to the derailing of the transition process. In the end, occasional proliferation of promises, political fragmentation and general lack of political skills acted like oil on the fire. In addition to this intense conflictual dimension, whose centrality cannot be overemphasised, what else does the Arab Spring tell transitology? Apart from following up on a 'newsworthy' region, why should we invest in knowing about the Arab Spring's occurrence, evolution and possibilities? Is it because this is the most recent case of 'democratisation' and announced the fourth wave in a region that was deemed 'exceptional' and usually cited as substantiating 'authoritarian durability'? The end of assumed exceptionalism – Arab or otherwise – is certainly a valid reason empirically and conceptually. Data from the Arab Spring could, however, illuminate and refine the transition paradigm in other respects so as to make it as universal as possible.

Political authoritarianism is fragile

Much more important than the collapse of so-called 'Arab exceptionalism' is the fragility of authoritarian rule itself. The Arab Spring showed that the robustness of such political rule seems to be much more perceptual than real. It took twenty-three days to force Ben Ali to flee Tunisia and a mere seventeen days to convince Mubarak to give up his presidency. The Arab Spring indicates that assertions about 'authoritarian resilience/durability' need to be reconsidered and refined. Such authoritarian fragility and the initial speedy success of street protests created serious problems for the delicate issue of transition *to* rather than *from*, i.e. the shape and opportunities of the 'day after'. Moreover, the supposed authoritarian durability might be then a function of the weakness/fragmentation of the other political forces rather than authoritarianism's inherent strength – what I have called the balance of weakness rather than of power. As demonstrated above, such fragmentation/balance of weakness explains why a 'messy' transition process caused mass frustration and mistrust, facilitating the return of some actors of the *ancien régime*, even in the relatively successful cases of Egypt and Tunisia.

Disenchantment derails transition

This 'messy' transition process contrasted with the speedy and easy success of the initial process of dislodging *gumluka*. In the context of (over-)optimism that followed, expectations soared high with the belief that *all* problems – from misgovernance, unemployment, corruption and the vagaries of daily life – would be fully resolved and, especially, immediately. When such speedy solutions did not materialise, accumulated expectations turned into rising frustrations. Negative energy prevailed, detracting from serious efforts to keep the transition on track and establish its credibility, e.g. through coalition-building.

Transitions' success rests on the new actors' political learning

Mismanagement of the rising expectation/frustration gap was aggravated by the flood of new actors, principally youth and Islamists, who by definition lacked political experience. Neither of them were monolithic, and consequently they became fragmented and fell prey to infighting, as witnessed in the case of

Tunisia's Al Nahda or Egypt's Muslim Brotherhood both versus the Salafists. Not only were these new actors inexperienced, but they were also taken by surprise by their victory and the immediacy to participate in governance. They did not have a programme of governance and hence improvised on the way, with a multitude of trial and error sequences amidst fragmentation and controversy. For the masses and even some of the elites, the transition process lacked credibility.

Transition is neither linear nor irreversible

With the rise of socio-economic problems and a political vacuum, it was easy for old traditional forces to jump in. Tunisia elected as president eighty-nine-year-old Beji Caid Essebsi, an old hand politician not only with Zeine El-Abidin Ben Ali, but with the country's first president, Habib Bourguiba, immediately after Tunisia gained independence in the 1950s. As for Egypt, former Minister of Defence General Sisi deposed the Muslim Brotherhood president and subsequently won elections in June 2014. He thus continued the tradition of Egypt's military presidents going back to 1952.

Because of the lack of emphasis on the primacy of this conflictual dimension, the transitology paradigm's 'pathways to transition' is the most problematic; some transitologists have wisely emphasised transition from rather than to. In their early formulations, such pathways assumed linearity and teleology: the final destination is liberal Western-type democracy. However, empirical cases up until now do not codify a single transition path to democracy and, in fact, indicate reversibility. Moreover, the 'Arab Spring' data and experiences indicate that intense conflict and reversibility – even occasional nostalgia for 'authoritarian stability'– are as probable as progress on the road towards democratisation.

Rather than ushering in democratic consolidation, transition is not only time-consuming but, especially, open-ended. Even if Tunisia's and Egypt's new 'regimes' are declaring their intention to become 'new democratic' regimes, at present they are at best hybrid and dominated by an *authoritarian bargain*. An 'authoritarian bargain' regime is similar to what is taking place in many Gulf States. Most people have as a first item on their agenda the satisfaction of basic socio-economic needs, with core democratic values (e.g. freedom of speech, of association, even of assembly) coming next. In fact, this agenda debate is a basic difference and element of contention between elites and masses. Most of the latter focus at present on day-to-day issues such as finding a job, guaranteeing personal security and obtaining energy supplies and/or basic commodities at reasonable prices. This is why the demand for so-called 'technocratic' governments is increasingly repeated. Ultimately, the prevalence of the 'authoritarian bargain' brings in a new type of legitimacy, besides Max Weber's three well-known types – tribal, charismatic and rational–legal. It is rather the legitimacy of achievement, of delivering the goods – all goods, immediate and less immediate. Though the less immediate benefits (such as education, inequality and human rights) look less urgent than basic day-to-day goods, they are still kept on the agenda and could indeed launch the next stage of the Arab Spring if first order priorities are not satisfied.

Notes

1 Though increasingly contested, the term 'Arab Spring' is used here. It describes the major transformative moment that started in Tunisia in late December 2010 and led to the flight of its president on 17 January 2011, followed by mass demonstrations in Egypt and the dismissal of former President Hosni Mubarak on 11 February 2011, followed by Libya (October 2011) and Yemen (2012). Though, in retrospect, and given the serious troubles of the republics' transition, the term 'Arab Spring' still applies, it denotes here the effective culmination of mobilisation and protest movements in a revolutionary process and the enlargement of the political space. After all, Europe's 1848 revolutions took time to mature, and the Hungarian 1956 'revolution' and the 1968 Prague Spring took a generation to succeed. The Arab Spring is thus the beginning of a changing Middle East, a new Middle East that has made an impact across the world. Moreover, to counter scepticism about misleading associations with the 'real spring', we should remember that *meteorologically* the spring in most Arab lands is not associated with budding flowers but with sand storms, known as *Khamaseen* – the days of dust that stifle and force people to stay inside behind closed doors and windows. With setbacks in the Arab transition process, meteorological handicaps now have their political equivalents.
2 Danahar, *The New Middle East*; Gerges, *The New Middle East*.
3 Camau and Vairel, *Soulèvements et Recompositions Politiques dans le Monde Arabe*.
4 The Human Development Index was developed by the United Nations Development Programme. The criteria for assessing the development of nations acknowledge that the goal is the assessment of the people and their capabilities. This is done through a summary of yearly average achievements in key dimensions of human development. These dimensions set indicators in the following areas: long and healthy life, being knowledgeable and having a decent standard of living. The index uses these three key dimensions to assess the ranking of every country based on the available data. The report produced each year is based on data gathered from the previous year. The index includes 197 countries; however only a range of 169–187 countries are within the ranking as there are incomplete data for the rest of the countries. It should be noted that since 1990 the report has been published on an annual basis except in 2012. Consequently, the ranking for 2011 and 2012 is taken from the 2013 index. The nearer to the top spot a country climbs, the more developed it is supposed to be. For instance, while oil-rich Libya deteriorated by forty-one ranking points in the last five years, Yemen continues its race to the bottom.
5 The Failed State Index was published in 2005 to highlight the risks that people faced as a result of their 'failed states'. The main purpose behind using the term 'failed' was not to label a state that has already failed but to focus attention on the degree of the state's failure. However, the term attracted much controversy that detracted from the aim of the index, so in 2014 it was changed to the Fragile State Index. The aim is to help states with services provided by the state and to enhance protection of human security. Contrary to many indexes, the higher a country is in the ranking, the more seriously in trouble it is: it is actually deteriorating, as it is 'advancing' in becoming more fragile/failed. Somalia has the dubious distinction of being ranked number one in recent years. Yemen is not very much below. There are twelve indicators that set the ranking in the index as follows: *four social indicators* (demographic pressures, refugees or internally-displaced persons, group grievance and human flight); *two economic indicators* (uneven economic development and economic decline); and *six political and military indicators* (legitimacy of the state, public service, human rights and the rule of law, security apparatus, factualised elite and external intervention). Until 2012, the index included 177 countries; it currently includes 178 countries after the integration of South Sudan in 2013.

6 The Global Peace Index aims to measure national peacefulness. It uses twenty-two quantitative and qualitative indicators to achieve the global ranking. Such indicators include but are not limited to: criminality in the society, security officers and the police, homicide, percentage of those jailed from the population, access to weapons, violent crimes, political instability, terrorist activity, displaced people, UN peacekeeping funding, military expenditure and death resulting from conflict. The countries ranked at the top have a lower score and are the most peaceful. The indicator currently includes 162 countries within its ranking, however in 2009 only 143 countries were included and the number has been increasing each year.
7 For the details of actual transition experiences from Africa to Asia and Latin America told by its prime actors and political leaders, see the statements in the June Cairo meeting organised by the UNDP and its synthetic analysis in Korany, ed., *Arab Human Development*, pp. 337–340. For a general conceptual overview, see Geddes 'What Do We Know about Democratization'; Geddes 'What Causes Democratization?'; Dobry, 'Les Transitions Démocratiques'; Shin, 'On The Third Wave of Democratization'; and Coppedge, *Democratization and Research Methods*.
8 For an early attempt at dealing with this assumed exceptionalism, see Korany *et al.*, *Liberalization and Democratization in the Arab World*. For a conceptually oriented analysis of the Egyptian case, see Korany and El-Mahdy, *The Arab Spring in Egypt*.
9 The literature on Orientalism is vast, but the classic study is Said, *Orientalism*. See also Curtis, *Orientalism and Islam*.
10 This is the case in respect of both Alfred Stepan and Philippe Schmitter. Schmitter especially has visited the region more than three times in the period 2011–2013.
11 'Youth in Mediterranean Countries' concept paper, CIDOB, Barcelona, September 2014. See also the Special issue of *Mediterranean Politics*, 17, 1, March 2012 and in particular Murthy's article, 'Problematizing Arab Youth'.
12 Khatib, 'Transforming the Media'.
13 The Worldwide Governance Indicators (WGI) developed by the World Bank measures indicators of governance across countries. The research project has been active since 1996 and is conducted in 200 countries. The governance indicators are measured across six areas: voice and accountability, political stability and absence of violence/terrorism, government effectiveness, regulatory quality, rule of law and control of corruption. Measurements are provided in percentile rank in comparison to all the other countries. Zero corresponds to the lowest rank and 100 corresponds to the highest rank relative to the others.
14 Khatib, 'Transforming the Media', pp. 68–69.
15 Ghoneim, *Revolution 2.0*.
16 For further details, see Korany, 'Microsm of Revolution'.
17 Dina Shehata, 'Youth Movements and the 25 January Revolution' in Korany and El-Mahdi, *The Arab Spring in Egypt*, pp. 105–124; Hosny, 'The Moslem Brotherhood Youth'. For details, see Korany, 'From Prison to Authority and Back'. See also Kandil, *Inside the Brotherhood*; Wickham, *The Muslim Brotherhood*.
18 El-Suwaidy and El-Safty, *Political Islam*; El-Suwaidy and El-Safty, *Islamists and the Democratic System*; and Amghar, *Le Salafisme d'Aujourd'hui*.
19 Clark, 'Democratisation and Social Islam'.
20 Abdel-Hadi, *My Journey with the Muslim Brotherhood Sisters*; El Fetouh and Tamam, *A Witness of the History of the Islamist Movement*; Habib, *Memoirs*; El Kharabawy, *Secret of the Temple*; Nada, *Inside the Muslim Brotherhood*; and Kandil, *Inside the Brotherhood*.
21 For details, see Korany, 'The Birth Pangs of Transitioning from Authoritarianism: The Long Spring of Empowerment', in Korany, *Arab Human Development*, pp. 327–351; Brynen *et al.*, *After the Arab Spring*.

22 El-Rashidi, 'Egypt'.
23 Levitsky and Way, *Competitive Authoritarianism*.
24 Korany, 'Arab Democracy'.
25 For an introduction, see Berdal and Zoum, *Political Economy of State-Building* and Zoum, 'Beyond the Liberal Peace?'.

10 From transitology to consolidology

Philippe C. Schmitter

At the first conference I attended in Eastern Europe on democratisation, a distinguished Hungarian sociologist, Elémer Hankis, introduced me to the audience as 'that well-known transitologist ...'. I felt just like Monsieur Jourdan in Molière's *Le Bourgeois Gentilhomme* – enormously pleased to learn that I had been speaking prose all along without knowing it! Here I was, a supposedly renowned expert in a scientific discipline whose very existence I ignored.

The neo- and, perhaps, pseudo-science of transitology was expected to explain and, hopefully, guide the way from an autocratic to a democratic regime. Its founder and patron saint, if it has to have one, should be Niccoló Machiavelli. For the 'wily Florentine' was the first great political theorist, not only to treat political outcomes as the artefactual and contingent product of human action, but also to recognise the specific problematics and dynamics of regime change. He, of course, was preoccupied with change in the inverse direction – from republican to 'princely' regimes – but his basic insights remain all too valid.[1]

Machiavelli gave to transitology its fundamental principle, uncertainty, and, its first and most important maxim:

> There is nothing more difficult to execute, nor more dubious of success, nor more dangerous to administer than to introduce a new system of things. For the innovator has for enemies all those who have done well under the old condition, and lukewarm defenders in those who may do well under the new.[2]

Furthermore, he warned us that the potential contribution of the discipline would always be modest. According to his estimate, 'in female times', i.e. during periods when actors behaved capriciously, immorally and without benefit of shared rules, only fifty per cent of political events were understandable. The other half was due to unpredictable events of *fortuna*. Hence, transitology was born (and promptly forgotten) with limited scientific pretensions and marked practical concerns. At best, it was doomed to become a complex mixture of rules of invariant political behaviour and maxims for prudential political choice – when it was revived almost 500 years later.

The more prosaic origins of consolidology

Consolidology has no such obvious patron saint. It reflects a much more consistent preoccupation among students of politics with the conditions underlying regime stability. At least since Plato and Aristotle, theorists have sought to explain why – under the kaleidoscopic surface of events – stable patterns of authority and privilege manage to survive. While they have rarely devoted much explicit attention to the choices and processes that brought about such institutions in the first place – this would be, strictly speaking, the substantive domain of transitology – they and their empirical acolytes have amassed veritable libraries on the subject of how polities succeed in reproducing themselves over extended periods of time. It does not seem excessive (to me) to claim that American political science since the Second World War has been obsessed with the issue of 'democratic stability' in the face of class conflict, ideological polarisation, the threat of Communist aggression, tensions between developed, developing and underdeveloped nations, the cyclical crises of capitalism and so forth.

The consolidologist, therefore, has a lot of 'orthodox' theoretical assumptions and 'well-established' empirical material to draw upon. However, if he or she has previously been practicing transitology, it will be necessary to make some major personal, as well as professional, adjustments. The consolidation of democracy (CoD) poses distinctive problems for political actors and hence to those who seek to understand (usually retrospectively) what they are doing. It is not just a prolongation of the transition from authoritarian rule. CoD engages different actors, behaviours, processes, values and resources. This is not to say that everything changes when a polity 'shifts' towards it. Many of the persons and collectivities will be the same, but they will be facing different problems, making different calculations and (hopefully) behaving in different ways.

This suggests possible contradictions between stages of the regime change process and the pseudo-sciences seeking to explain them. The 'enabling conditions' that were most conducive to reducing and mastering the uncertainty of the transition may turn into 'confining conditions' that can make consolidation more difficult. The shift in the substance of politics tends to *reduce* the significance of actors who previously played a central role and *enhance* the role of others who by prudence or impotence were marginal to the demise of autocracy or the earlier phases of transition.

The transitologist who becomes a consolidologist must personally make an epistemological shift in order to follow the behavioural changes that the actors themselves are undergoing. During the early stage of regime transformation, an exaggerated form of voluntaristic 'political causality' tends to predominate in a situation of rapid change, high risk, shifting interests and indeterminate strategic reactions. Actors believe that they are engaged in a 'war of movement' where dramatic options are available and the outcome depends critically on their choices. They find it difficult to specify *ex ante* which classes, sectors, institutions or groups will support their efforts – indeed, most of these collectivities are likely to be divided or hesitant about what to do. Once this heady and dangerous moment has passed, some of the actors begin to 'settle into the trenches'. Hopefully, they will be compelled to organise their internal structures more predictably, consult their constituencies more regularly, mobilise their resource bases more reliably and consider the long-term consequences of their actions more seriously. In so doing, they will inevitably experience the constraints imposed by deeply rooted material deficiencies and normative habits – most of which will not have changed with the fall of the *ancien régime*.

The consolidologist must shift from thinking in terms of a particularly exciting form of 'political causality' in which unpredictable and often courageous individuals take singular and even unprecedented choices and adjust to analysing a much more settled form of 'bounded rationality'. This is both conditioned by capitalist class relations, long-standing cultural and ethnic cleavages, persistent status conflicts and international antagonisms, and staffed by increasingly professional politicians who fill more predictable and less risky roles. From the heady excitement and under-determination of the transition from autocracy, he or she must adjust to the prosaic routine and over-determination of well-consolidated democracy.

The likelihood that practitioners of this embryonic and possible pseudo-science can draw more confidently from previous scholarly work should be comforting – even if there remains a great deal of work still to do before we understand how the behaviour of actors can become more predictable, how the rules of democracy can be made more mutually acceptable and how the interactions of power and influence can settle into more stable patterns. Apprentice consolidologists in the contemporary world also have two additional problems. First, they must sift through the experience of established 'real-existing democracies' (REDs) in order to separate the idiosyncratic and contingent properties from the eventual outcomes; and second, they must decide to what extent lessons taken from these past experiences can be applied to the present dilemmas of 'newly-existing democracies' (NEDs). The fallacies of 'retrospective determinism' – assuming that what did happen is what had to happen – and of 'presentism' – assuming that the motives and perceptions of the past are the same as those of the present are all too tempting and could quite easily defeat the credibility of their efforts.[3]

Let us, however, suspend our incredulity for a moment, and imagine that transitology and consolidology could become innovative and significant sub-disciplines within the broader scope of political science. What might the fundamental assumptions of these two pseudo-sciences be? What general maxims would be most useful in orienting future research – and in guiding the practice of politicians?

In my previous work as a transitologist and, then, consolidologist, I have collected and articulated a substantial number of fundamental assumptions, maxims of prudence or just plain working hypotheses about the shift from one to the other. Most of the transitological ones focus on the implications of *uncertainty* and *unexpectedness*, and can be found in the book I co-wrote with Guillermo O'Donnell. They will not be repeated here.[4] Below, I have extracted and will briefly discuss some 'generic reflections' about consolidology, leaving to the reader the task of determining whether they constitute a promising foundation for this new pseudo-science.

Reflection one: non-inevitability

Democracy is not inevitable and it is revocable. Democracy is not a necessity. Neither does it fulfil a functional requisite for capitalism, nor does it respond to some ethical imperative of social evolution. Hence, its consolidation requires a concerted and extraordinary effort. Only after a lengthy period of 'habituation', can politicians and citizens look forward to the routinised (and usually boring) perpetuation of stable democracy. Even then, there is always the prospect of a subsequent 'deconsolidation' if and when its institutions fail to adapt to changing external parameters or pervasive internal contradictions.

Reflection two: diversity of outcomes

Transitions from autocratic or authoritarian regimes can lead to diverse outcomes – four of which seem generically possible, although their probability varies considerably from case to case. The first is a regression to autocracy. Based solely on the historical experiences of the three previous waves of democratisation, this would seem to be the most probable outcome. Few countries have reached democracy on their first attempt or by strictly linear and incremental means. Most had to revert to some version of the *status quo ante* or to pass through periods of rule by sheer coercion.

Nevertheless, each previous wave did leave in its wake some cases of consolidated democracy. While there are several reasons to suspect that the present post-1974 wave may leave behind more cases of successful consolidation more widely distributed around the world than ever before – if only because so many of the countries involved have already tried and failed several times in the past – it is sobering to recall that in purely statistical and static terms, regression to some form of autocracy probably remains the most likely end product.

The second possible outcome is the formation of a hybrid regime which does not satisfy the full procedural criteria for political democracy, but which does not regress to the *status quo ante*. These *dictablandas* and *democraduras* probably do not constitute a stable and enduring solution to the generic problems of government. Either of them can, however, offer a very useful improvisation in order to gain time – either for an eventual regression to autocracy (as seems most likely in the case in Africa) or for an eventual progression to some form of (still imperfect) democracy (as has been the case in El Salvador, Guatemala, the Philippines and Peru).

The third logical outcome may be the most insidious – and the most probable under contemporary circumstances. Rarely has it been identified by political theorists who prefer to work with more clearly defined and juxtaposed categories which makes it especially difficult to identify and analyse it. I have called it 'unconsolidated democracy'. Regimes trapped in this category are, in a sense, condemned to democracy without enjoying the consequences and advantages that it offers. They are stuck in a situation in which all the minimal procedural criteria for democracy are respected, but without the mutually acceptable rules of the game to regulate the competition between political forces. Actors do not manage to agree on the basic principles of cooperation and competition in the formation of governments and policies. Each party considers itself uniquely qualified to govern the country and does what it can to perpetuate itself in power. Each group acts only in the furtherance of its own immediate interests and without taking into consideration its impact upon the polity as a whole. Whatever formal rules are enunciated in the constitution or basic statutes are treated as contingent arrangements to be bent or dismissed when the opportunity presents itself.

The fourth possible outcome is the most desirable one, namely, a democracy consolidated by mutually acceptable rules and valued institutions of fairness, tolerance, cooperation and competition among its major actors. Defining the precise moment when this occurs or measuring accurately the extent to which this has been accomplished is not an easy task. Indeed, insisting too much upon it could lead to a contradiction in terms since democracies are never completely consolidated. They are unique among regime types in their presumed capability for self-transformation and in the degree to which they incorporate uncertainty into their normal functioning. Nevertheless, behind the changes in personnel, party and policy that are intrinsic to this form of domination, there are limits to the range of tolerable variation in a consolidated democracy. These may be difficult to specify and measure in advance – and some polities tolerate much greater 'normal instability' than others[5] – but when they have been exceeded contingent consent breaks down and the process of deconsolidation becomes increasingly manifest.

Reflection three: diversity of democracies

It is not democracy that is being consolidated, but one or another type of democracy. There is no single democracy; there are only democracies. Many different rules and organisational forms can ensure the accountability of rulers to citizens, as well as satisfy the criteria of contingent consent among politicians and gain the eventual assent of the people. The central problem remains the same, i.e. how to come up with rules of competition and cooperation that the former will actively respect and the latter will passively (and belatedly) accept, but the possible solutions are varied. They are not, however, infinite since they must ultimately respect the citizenship principle if the polity is to become and remain democratic. At any given moment in time, it is likely that some 'foreign model' may well appear preferable to all others, although efforts simply to imitate it are bound to fail – unless substantial modifications are made to accommodate it to the national historical experience, social and ethnic composition, economic structure and international context.

Reflection four: what determines selection among types?

If so much diversity in rules and institutions is possible, what determines the selection of the type of democracy that actors will attempt to consolidate? Terry Karl has advanced the hypothesis that the type of democracy will depend significantly (but not exclusively) on the mode of transition from autocracy.[6] This very uncertain period sets the context within which actors choose the arrangements that are going to govern their future cooperation and competition. Most importantly, the mode of transition influences the identity and power relations of actors. Also, depending on the mode, they may be compelled to make choices in a great hurry, with imperfect information about the available alternatives and without much reflection upon longer-term consequences. Their fleeting arrangements, temporary pacts and improvised accommodations to crises tend to accumulate and to set precedents. Some may find their way into more formal, even constitutional, norms. It is, therefore, useful to consider the possibility of 'birth defects' in the democratisation process that are due, not just to structural features long present in the society, but also to conjunctural circumstances that surround the moment of regime change itself. Each generic mode of transition seems to 'push' towards a different outcome.

Reflection five: pathways to consolidation

Each type of democracy has its own distinctive way of consolidating itself – especially its own rhythm and sequence. No single path to consolidation is necessarily a guarantee for the future stability or viability of RED. All types of democracy, in other words, have their own problems and their own vulnerabilities. In the end, the success of CoD will depend on cleavages within the social structure, the rates and extent of economic change and the cultural processes of political socialisation and ethical evaluation. These, however, lie in the distant and unforeseeable future. What counts in the here and now are differences in the point of departure.

NEDs in Latin America face an especially acute problem since, in terms of status inequalities, income distribution, access to property and economic marginalisation, their initial situation is much worse than in the NEDs of Southern and Eastern Europe, Asia and Africa – and rapidly growing even worse. So great are these disparities that a number of well-informed observers (among them, Guillermo O'Donnell) have questioned whether it is conceivable that actors with such different material and cultural resources will be able to come up with mutually acceptable rules.[7] Will they even be able to identify each other as 'fellow citizens' deserving of political equality – much less agree upon the defining line between public and private realms, the appropriate scope for property rights, the mix of decision rules involving the counting of numbers and the weighing of intensities and so forth? Past experience suggests not, but as we have seen above, there are sufficient new elements in the present equation – especially coming from the international context – that an eventually favourable outcome in Latin America cannot be ruled out.

The NEDs of Eastern Europe and the former Soviet Union faced the inverse challenge. Their respective points of departure were characterised by greater equality in class, status and income. The ineluctable coincidence of democratisation coupled with the transformation from a planned to a market economy ensures that the first stages of regime change will be associated with radical increases in all forms of social, economic and cultural inequality. This raises three questions:

1   Is it possible to consolidate some type of 'Western-capitalist' democracy without the prior formation of stable and predictable cleavages based on class, sector or profession?
2   Can this be accomplished while these cleavages are emerging in erratic and unpredictable ways?
3   And can this be accomplished when these cleavages are likely to be accompanied by dramatic increases in material and social inequality?

Given the unprecedented nature of the situation, no one can answer these questions with any assurance, although hindsight has clearly demonstrated that such 'simultaneity' can be overcome – especially when conditioned by the prospects of membership of the European Union (EU).

Reflection six: democracy as legitimating

In this historical moment – almost without exception – democracy (or, better, one or another type of democracy) is the only legitimate form of political domination. Only it can offer a stable consensual basis for the exercise of public authority. In the past, there were always alternative state regimes that seemed to be viable –and that were even perceived as more efficacious or desirable by certain social classes or groups. Today, the only competing suppliers in the market at the international level are 'Iranian theocracy', 'Chinese meritocracy', 'Islamic monarchy' or 'Russian neo-Czarism' – which have a culturally and geographically restricted potential clientele.

As we have seen, this convergence in aspirations does not imply a convergence in trajectories and outcomes. The NEDs of the present wave will attempt to adopt and adapt the current practices of REDs and, hence, they will not follow (and, especially, they will not be able to repeat) the paths to democracy already trodden by established regimes in Western Europe and North America. They will be plagued, whether they like it or not, by the prospect of acquiring the most advanced institutions of present-day democracy, but without having passed through the same processes of gradualism, apprenticeship and experimentation as the democracies that preceded them. In other words, these latecomers are going to collect all the 'flora and fauna' – including the most exotic species – of post-modern democracy at almost the same time. This has its relative advantages and disadvantages, but the main implication is that they will have to 'catch up' in much less time and without being able to rely on pre-established strategies and rules.

This primary 'unrepeatability' of the democratisation process has incalculable secondary consequences for the NEDs, all connected with profound changes both in domestic and international contexts and in the nature of already established democracies. Unfortunately, most of these changes have been ignored by contemporary democratic theorists; consequently it is very risky to extract valid 'lessons from the experience of their predecessors'.[8] The embryonic sciences of 'transitology' and 'consolidology' are going to have to reflect on these ensuing changes, and cannot presume that the NEDs of this wave are going to simply repeat the patterns established by the previous three waves. There are a number of points that need to be considered.

First, the rhythm of change in NEDs will be much faster and more compressed in time (but not in space where it has become much more extensive). There will be much less time for hesitation, for allowing processes to mature, for making gradual concessions or for being able to wait for a more propitious moment of economic growth or international circumstance. Second, the political actors will not be the same as before. The effective citizens of well-established democracies are organisations, not individuals. They are vastly better endowed, informed and aware than were their forerunners. They can act in multiple sites, over a wider span of issues and for more protracted periods. They can draw upon a greater variety of resources, domestic and foreign. Few NEDs will begin with a full set of such 'organisational citizens', but if and when their consolidation proceeds they will acquire them.

Analysts of the 'Third Wave' of democratisation after the Second World War – particularly those studying the 'new nations' produced by the decolonisation of Africa and Asia – made the erroneous assumption that individual leaders in general, and gifted, 'charismatic' ones in particular, would play the most significant role in guiding regime change to a successful conclusion. When and where those leaders emerged, they failed miserably – not just at democratisation but at the creation of any kind of lasting institutions of governance. It is highly significant that the concept of charisma has almost never appeared in the contemporary discourse about democratisation and that the few recent experiments with highly personalistic leadership that have occurred have not succeeded in consolidating democratic institutions – quite the contrary![9]

Third, most of the politicians who participate – through their respective organisations – in the process of regime change are not amateurs, but professionals. They may start out, of course, with little or no experience in the job, but they rather quickly learn to depend upon it. In short, politicians in modern democracies – new and old – tend to live more and more *from* politics and not *for* politics. Frequently, they have no social status or economic base other than that provided by their elected or appointed position. They enter into politics with the intention of working at it full-time and, if possible, for their entire professional life. This has profound implications for the formation of a distinctive political stratum and, most particularly, for the way that the rotation of parties in power is organised – if at all.

Fourth, domestic structures and international contexts have changed so much since the Third Wave that contemporary democratisers cannot rely on the same strategies of consolidation. There is so much more diversity in class and sectoral and professional structures that the grand ideological formulas and partisan confrontations of the past are no longer convincing. The end of the Cold War and the collapse of Soviet power have also contributed more recently to a further fragmentation of symbolic identities and interest conceptions. The tacit assumption that modern democracy would lead inexorably to 'Leftist' policies and, hence, to an expansion of the role of the state as competing parties offered public compensation and subsidisation to broader constituencies has given way to neo-liberal expectations of the inverse: privatisation, deregulation, monetary orthodoxy, balanced budgets, tax cuts and the overriding importance of protecting property rights and the international competitiveness of producers. The initial 'success' of neo-liberalism may well be dispersed once its longer-term effects, especially on the CoD, have been revealed and registered, but in the short- to medium-term it has meant that the NEDs of Latin America, Eastern Europe, Asia and Africa have emerged in an international, ideological and programmatic context that is much more hostile to political solutions and capable of placing barriers in the way of institutional experimentation.

Reflection seven: changing political intermediaries

The bottom line formed by these four 'unrepeatable changes' is that the role played by different intermediary institutions – political parties, interest groups and social movements – has changed irrevocably. All types of modern political democracy are based on representation. Citizens hold rulers accountable indirectly, i.e. through the competition and cooperation of their representatives. Moreover, these channels of representation have developed, multiplied, specialised, professionalised, internationalised and become increasingly autonomous over time. The NEDs may not yet have acquired the full gamut of intermediaries that REDs already have (and they vary considerably among themselves in this regard), but the NEDs cannot avoid benefitting and suffering from these major changes in their respective roles.

The most important of these changes is the decline in the historic role previously played by political parties. Their ideologies are no longer so convincing; their symbols are less present in everyday life; their patronage is less capable of providing welfare; their organisations cannot even replace the activists who die or desert their ranks; their leaders are less capable of mobilising the public to attain collective goals – indeed, they are less and less successful at controlling the voting behaviour of their members or even at inspiring them to vote at all. Parties rarely provide individual citizens with their principal element of political self-identification and they are much less significant in the process of political socialisation. They cannot demand the same discipline of their followers or even of their parliamentary deputies. They have lost (if they ever had) their monopoly on the process of government formation and can no longer prevent other intermediaries from directly exercising influence over public policy. In summary, one can say that political parties remain indispensable for the formal organisation of electoral competition at all levels of government, but that they have lost a great deal in terms of activists, supporters, internal participation, programmatic coherence and credibility with the general public.

The next change concerns the role played by social movements. NEDs benefit (and suffer) from the coincidence that they emerged almost at the same time that an enormous variety of 'new social movements' were appearing in REDs and penetrating their political processes. Some of these generic 'causes' – e.g. feminism, pacifism, anti-racism, regionalism, municipalism, environmentalism and consumer protection – combined with demands that were more intrinsic to the problems of regime change itself: human rights, political amnesty, compensation for victims, protection of ethnic minorities, civilian control over the military and police forces and so on. The net effect has been to widen considerably the policy agenda during democratisation. The tactics of protest of these movements, their extra-parliamentary orientation, their mass mobilisations and their concentration on single causes or themes spread across the polity and, in some cases, made a major contribution to bringing down the *ancien régime*. Mostly, however, they contributed collectively – through the resurrection of civil society – to propelling timid and hesitant efforts at political liberalisation into a more profound process of democratisation.

However, once fair elections of uncertain outcome have been convened and the first popularly elected government installed, the activities and importance of these social movements tends to diminish – in large part, because some of their major demands have been met and they have trouble focusing on subsequent issues. My hunch is that, with few exceptions, such movements have not significantly altered the outcome, that is to say, they have not determined either the degree of consolidation or the type of democracy. Nevertheless, there is no doubt that their presence has broadened and complicated the policy agenda of most NEDs.

This leaves us with the third generic category of organised intermediaries: associations that represent the interests of classes, sectors and professions. No one questions that the importance of these associations has increased in REDs or that NEDs will have to confront and accommodate a wider range of better organised interests than their predecessors at a comparable stage of development. To a degree, the rise in associability is responsible for the decline in the significance of political parties. The social classes that formed the historic bases for parties have fragmented into specialised sectoral and professional clienteles, created novel forms of collective expression and demanded new channels of access to policy-making.

Two generic alternatives are available, both of which are compatible with modern political democracy – even if they lead to quite different outcomes in terms of public policy, economic performance and governability.[10] On the one hand, pluralism could emerge if the previous system of organised interests degenerates into a set of autonomous, competitive and overlapping organisations with strictly voluntary memberships and without any subsidisation or control over their activities by the state. On the other hand, the state corporatism or party monism of the previous regime could be replaced by societal corporatism. This could occur if the previous system retains its basic structure of representational monopoly, official recognition and hierarchic coordination, and the new democratic government only indirectly supports existing associations through favourable financial and legal privileges and delegates to them major responsibilities for the making and implementing of public policies – but does not directly attempt to control their activities.

Reflection eight: processing simultaneous demands

Transitions to democracy rarely happen in isolation – i.e. without the simultaneous presence of other demands and other processes of profound change in socioeconomic structures and cultural values. The circumstances that lead to the demise of autocracies are varied, but they invariably involve crises and deficiencies in several institutions and spheres of society. It would be difficult to restrict the agenda of regime change only to political transformation, i.e. only to changes in the rules of the game, in the access of citizens to participation and in the accountability of rulers. In favourable (but rare) cases, the *ancien régime* may have already accomplished some of the necessary tasks – for example, it may have established national identity and boundaries, imposed civilian control over the military, increased the efficiency of the fiscal system, privatised inefficient state enterprises and/or stabilised the value of national currency. Normally, however, the inverse is the case and neo-democrats inherit an accumulation of problems across social, economic and cultural domains, along with the inevitable difficulties of political structure and practice.

The first implication of this unenviable situation is that the eventual outcome of democratisation depends in large measure on the sequence with which actors tackle the inevitable multiple transformations that are necessary. This, in turn, hinges on their collective capacity to control the political agenda sufficiently so that pressing and consequential choices do not have to be made simultaneously. When the agenda gets saturated and deals with many differing objectives at the same time, unwanted consequences and unusual combinations tend to emerge at unexpected times.

Up to a point, these dysrhythmic and asynchronic happenings are normal. Even well-established liberal democracies occasionally suffer from 'unfortunate coincidences' – despite the efforts of their incumbent politicians to manipulate the political business cycle in their favour.[11] The processes of economic, social, cultural and political change have their own distinctive rhythms in terms of the time it takes to formulate issues, mobilise their beneficiaries or victims, decide on a course of action, implement the policies chosen and to register and absorb their effects.

Democracies, especially presidential ones, impose upon themselves a rhythm fixed by the periodicity of the electoral cycle – which may or may not coincide with the trends, cycles or events generated by other domains. In retrospect, it appears relatively easy to introduce some political reforms: to convene elections, revise the electoral roll, choose an electoral law, recognise multiple parties, concede civic freedoms and so forth. Moreover, these reforms almost immediately affect elite and mass behaviours – even if the results are not always what was predicted or preferred. One of the reasons for this is that they combine or clash with other patterns of change that are slower, more diffuse or less predictable. Any type of regime will have to face unexpected and unwanted coincidences, but the NEDs are particularly susceptible to them simply because they are under pressure to accomplish so much more, in so much less time, and because actors are more likely to lose control over the agenda of sequential responses.

Yet even if 'consolidators' could control the order of the day and manipulate it to avoid simultaneity – admittedly, a utopian thought under present circumstances, especially in Eastern Europe and the former Soviet republics – what should they do first? Or second? Or third? So far, economists have dominated what little overt discussion of this issue has occurred. This has had two implications: that only such items as liberalisation of prices, sale of public holdings, currency stabilisation, product and service deregulation, budgetary balance, elimination of industrial subsidies and the establishment of favourable incentives for foreign investment have been taken into consideration; and that it has been widely presumed that these economic reforms should precede, not succeed, the consolidation of democracy.

Allegedly, unless one works fast to take advantage of initial enthusiasm and impose 'shock treatments' in large, comprehensive packages before the actors affected can get organised to defend their (changing but nonetheless vested) interests, the reforms will prove impossible to effect.[12] The fact that such actions – however initially popular and 'insulated' the elites are that take them – virtually guarantee that it will be more difficult to consolidate democracy in the longer run does not seem to have been taken into account.[13] As apprentice consolidologists, it is our responsibility to inform those in power of the eventual political consequences of their choices – and to remind them that democracy (even liberal democracy) is not just an arrangement for protecting property rights and ensuring the most efficient operation of a capitalist economy.

Reflection nine: imperatives of unity

There is, however, one rule that all consolidologists are likely to agree upon: it is preferable, if not essential, that national identity and territorial boundaries be established before introducing reforms in political (or economic) institutions.[14] Moreover, there is no democratic way of deciding what should be the effective political unit. This issue cannot be settled democratically either by normal or exceptional means. Self-determination of peoples or nations is an appealing phrase, but it tells us nothing about how this determination is to be made. The classical mechanism, used frequently after the First World War and occasionally after the Second, is the internationally supervised plebiscite. This, however, simply leaves in abeyance such crucial questions as who is eligible to participate and what is to be done about the rights of eventual minorities.

It is a sad fact that modern consolidated democracy depends on obscure and extremely complicated historical processes that were themselves not democratic. These acts of war, marriage, diplomacy and empire somehow produced physical boundaries and cultural identities that have come to be accepted by their respective populations as appropriate, even natural. Within their 'given' confines, these populations may eventually agree to practice democracy.

In some unfortunate cases, especially in Eastern Europe and the successor republics of the former Soviet Union, 'the national question' has far outweighed 'the social question' or 'the military question' in importance.[15] Their liberation from imperial tutelage and subsequent democratisation have jointly raised issues not only of external boundaries that do not correspond to national self-definitions, but also of internal barriers to full citizenship and legal equality.

About all consolidologists can offer are a few, not very compelling, suggestions about how to engineer party systems, civil societies and territorial units so as to maximise the opportunities for elite cooperation across ethno-religious lines and reiterate the pessimistic message that it is difficult to imagine any progress being made towards CoD until actors somehow agree upon a demarcation of their respective 'national' units. Worse yet, they would have to admit that there is no reliable democratic way of arriving at such a solution. Only military victory, protracted stalemate or mutual exhaustion, coupled with eventual diplomatic negotiation and treaty-making, seems to have worked in the past.[16] About the only encouraging novelty on the horizon is that the 'international community', as expressed through regional or global institutions, has shown some willingness to actively intervene to bring about peace settlements in such conflicts and to provide scarce resources to those parties which agree to solve their disputes peacefully and democratically.[17]

Reflection ten: waves in time and place

As noted, democracies tend to emerge 'in waves', i.e. they occur in different polities during a relatively short time period and within a relatively contiguous geographical area. Participants in the first cases, e.g. Portugal and Spain in the mid-1970s, could not possibly have been conscious that they would be instrumental in forming a wave that would eventually extend to cover almost the entire surface of the earth. Each subsequent case, however, is linked to the previous ones through processes of diffusion and imitation. Each success (or failure) in one country creates a 'model' to follow (or to avoid).

One major implication of the above is that the relevance of the international context tends to increase monotonically and to change in intensity with each successive demise of autocracy and attempt to establish democracy. Those that arrive later are destined to suffer more external influence than their predecessors. While it would be risky to assume that these latecomers will learn from the mistakes of others, it is nonetheless possible that there are certain advantages to 'delayed democratisation', analogous to those that some economists have claimed for 'late developers'.

From this growing internationalisation come two derived consequences. First, each successive case of democratisation contributes to the development of more formal organisations and informal networks for the promotion of human rights, the protection of ethnic minorities, the supervision of elections, the provision of political and economic advice and the creation of inter-professional contacts. Since 1974, an entirely new infrastructure has been created at the international level for the promotion and protection of democracy. This simply did not exist at the time of the first democratisations in Southern Europe, when outsiders had to improvise in order to bring their influence to bear. Now, there is not a country in the world that even as it begins experimenting with democracy is not literally invaded by foreign associations, movements, foundations, firms and even celebrities. This network of non-governmental organisations (NGOs) has certainly made some contribution to the fact that the contemporary wave has – so far – produced so few overt regressions to autocracy when compared to previous ones.

Moreover, the very existence of this embryonic 'transnational civil society' seems to have influenced the classic diplomatic behaviour of national governments. Those whose citizenries have most supported the efforts of these multitudinous NGOs find themselves obligated to support officially and resolutely efforts at democratisation in ways that go beyond normal calculations of 'national interest'. Traditional protestations of 'non-interference in domestic affairs' have become less and less compelling while the distinction between the realms of national and international politics has become more and more eroded.

Second, and even more significant in the long run, may be the increased reliance upon multilateral diplomacy and transnational organisations to bring pressure to bear on remaining autocracies or recidivist democracies. 'Political conditionality' has taken its place alongside the 'economic conditionality' practiced so long by the International Monetary Fund (IMF) and the International Bank for Reconstruction and Development (IBRD).[18] Global and regional organisations explicitly link the concession of credits, the negotiation of commercial agreements, entry into the ranks of their memberships and so forth to specific demands that receiving polities take measures to reform political institutions, hold honest elections, respect human rights and protect the physical safety and culture of ethnic or religious minorities. In extreme cases – and Eastern Europe seems to have been one of them – the different levels of bilateral and multilateral conditionality combine in such a fashion as to restrict considerably the margin for manoeuvre of new democratic leaders. Even more peculiar has been the spectacle of these leaders literally demanding to be subjected to international conditionality so that they can tell their respective populations that they had no choice but to take certain unpopular decisions!

The European Union, with its multiple levels and diverse incentives, has been of considerable importance in the successful consolidation of democracy in Southern Europe.[19] Its role was even more significant in Eastern Europe, despite the growing evidence of its members' unwillingness to make equivalent concessions and commitments to other countries in that area. The fiasco of the EU's inability to act collectively and decisively to prevent war between the former republics of Yugoslavia, however, is a sobering reminder of the limits of multilateralism, as are the present stalemates in Macedonia and Kosovo.

No other region of the world has an institutional infrastructure as complex and resourceful as Western Europe's. The Organisation of American States (OAS/OEA) and the Organisation of African Unity/African Union (OAU/AU) have both taken some steps towards providing collective security for NEDs and relaxing their traditional inhibitions against interfering in the domestic affairs of their members. The League of Arab States and the Association of Southeast Asian Nations have been conspicuously silent and ineffective on the issue. With or without the intervention of an international organisation, when a region such as Latin America becomes almost saturated with international pressure tensions will mount in the few autocracies that remain and recidivists to autocracy may find themselves cast out of the fold; however, neither seems to be sufficient to guarantee democratisation as demonstrated by the cases of Cuba and Haiti.

Reflection eleven: possibilities for progress

Based largely on the empirical cases of democratisation in Southern Europe and South America, the embryonic science of consolidology has taught us that it is possible (but not necessarily easy) to move from various types of autocracy to various types of democracy without necessarily fulfilling the preconditions or prerequisites that political science has long considered indispensable for a task of such magnitude and difficulty. These missing conditions are as follows:

1 *Without violence*, revolution or the physical elimination of the protagonists of the previous autocracy. Although most established liberal democracies did pass through a revolution or a civil war (or both in the case of the United States) before achieving political stability, the NEDs of the Fourth Wave have frequently managed to consolidate their respective democracies without such discontinuities, loss of life of destruction of property.
2 *Without a great deal of popular mobilisation* that brings about the fall of the *ancien régime* and determines the timing of the transition. Nevertheless, once the transition has begun (usually under other auspices), a veritable explosion of mass participation tends to resurrect a dormant or suppressed civil society which, in turn, pushes the change process further than intended by its initiators; this, in turn, affects the pace and extent of eventual consolidation.
3 *Without having attained a high level of economic development*. One could even affirm that democratisation tends to bring about at least a momentary fall in the rate of economic growth as the price that has to be paid for freedom of assembly and expression, both of which revive long suppressed popular demands. In the longer term, however, these freedoms of action and thought are indispensable for sustained growth.

4 *Without effecting a substantial redistribution of income or wealth.* Most citizens of neo-democracies seem to harbour no illusions about an alternative to capitalism based on radical equality and, therefore, have proven surprisingly tolerant of existing inequalities; that is not to say that subsequent political competition will not aim at regulating capitalism's accumulative effort and better distributing its benefits.

5 *Without the prior existence of a national bourgeoisie.* Not only has the existing bourgeoisie rarely been in the vanguard of the struggle for contemporary democracy, but it has frequently been contaminated by its close association with the previous autocracy. With the emergence of highly mobile international capital, technology and managerial skills, it is not even as clear as in the past that development is contingent upon a dynamic group of native entrepreneurs.

6 *Without a civic culture,* how individuals could expect to learn norms of mutual trust, tolerance, compromise and personal efficacy under autocratic rule has always been something of a mystery. However, what is becoming increasingly obvious is that democracy is compatible with a wide range of cultural dispositions – not just those that contributed to its emergence in the first place. The formation of a civic culture is not a prerequisite for, but a product of, democracy.

Finally, what seems to count for more than a normative commitment to democracy, or a personal predilection to act democratically, is a pattern of group interactions that encourages contingent consent and reduces the boundaries of uncertainty. Once politicians have agreed to compete under specified rules and prove willing to continue playing by these rules – even when they have been defeated – and once citizens assent to these rules and come to accept the intrinsic uncertainty of the outcomes they produce, the minimal basis for democracy has been established. Only subsequently is one likely to find more convinced democrats behaving in a culturally civic fashion.

No one, least of all among us consolidologists, would question that some or all of the above conditions – non-violence, popular mobilisation, a high level of economic development, greater equality of income, a dynamic and liberal business class, a civic culture and lots of democratically-minded individuals – are desirable. They may even be prerequisites for its long-term stability, since they are likely to be produced by its regular functioning. This is not to say, however, that they are necessary (and they are certainly not sufficient) for the initiation and immediate consolidation of democracy – which has been my concern in this chapter.

Conclusions

Democracy is not a necessity; it is a collective and contingent choice. It demands a continuous and extraordinary effort because it depends on a complex process of cooperation and competition involving a large number of independent citizens; *and* because the formal equality it establishes in a limited political role is put in question everyday by the informal equality of the socio-economic system into which it is inserted.

Eventually, the present Fourth Wave will crest and may even recede. I am convinced that it will leave behind more cases of consolidated democracy dispersed over a wider area than all previous waves, but some polities could well be dragged by the undertow back to autocracy. I am also certain that it will produce a profound sense of *desencanto* (or disenchantment and disillusionment) when people discover that modern liberal, constitutional, representative political democracy does not resolve many of the palpable inequalities and much of the unhappiness in this world. We are still very far from 'the end of history'.

To the contrary, I believe that once democracy has become the established norm within a given region and no longer faces a rival regime-type that is so markedly inferior, then and only then, are the disenchanted citizens going to demand that their leaders explain why their persistent practices are so far removed from the ideals of democracy. I suspect that democracy consecrated will become democracy contested – that the triumph of democracy in the last decade of this century will lead to renewed criticism of democracy well into the next.

Notes

1 Schmitter, 'Speculations about the Prospective Demise of Authoritarian Regimes (I)'; and 'Speculations about the Prospective Demise of Authoritarian Regimes and its Possible Consequences (II)'.
2 Machiavelli, *The Prince* (Chapter VI, 'Conquests by Virtue').
3 On presentism, see Fischer, *Historians' Fallacies*. On retrospective determinism, see Bendix, 'Social Stratification and Political Power'.
4 See the other chapters in this volume.
5 This implies that consolidation is not identical with stability. It is, therefore, quite possible for a democracy to be thoroughly consolidated and still quite unstable in such things as the composition of governments. Post-war Italy was an especially apposite case – at least until the recent deconsolidation of its long-standing partisan arrangements.
6 Karl, 'Dilemmas of Democratization in Latin America'.
7 O'Donnell, 'Poverty and Inequality in Latin America'.
8 Robert Dahl's work is a notable exception to this generalisation. Also Manin, 'Métamorphoses du Gouvernement Représentatif'.
9 On the concept and role of leadership, see Diamond and Jay, *Developing Democracy*, pp. 34–42. They do not discuss the prospects for charismatic leadership.
10 On governability, see Schmitter, 'Interest Intermediation and Regime Governability'.
11 See Nordhaus, 'The Political Business Cycle'.
12 On shock treatments, see Balcerowicz, 'Fallacies and Other Lessons'; Blanchard *et al.*, *Reform in Eastern Europe*; Frydman and Rapaczynski, *Privatisation in Eastern Europe*; Lipton and Sachs, 'Creating a Market Economy in Eastern Europe'; Sachs, 'The Transition at Mid-Decade'; Crawford and Lijphart, 'Explaining Political and Economic Change in Post-Communist Eastern Europe'.
13 Przeworski, *Sustainable Democracy*.
14 Rustow, 'Transitions to Democracy'.

15 This is not to say that democratisation might not eventually prove to be subversive of existing national units in Africa – if and when the process becomes sufficiently rooted. The abortive elections in Nigeria throughout the Third Republic showed that, despite a massive effort at 'political engineering' by the authoritarian rulers, the voting patterns still closely followed regional and ethnic lines. Inversely, the transitions from autocracy in Asian countries such as the Philippines and Taiwan seem (so far) to have made it relatively easier to resolve (or, better, to defuse) long-standing conflicts along ethnic–cultural–religious cleavages. Malaysia has long run a *democradura* based on a delicate balance of ethnically-based 'national' forces.

16 Even the 'Velvet Divorce' of the Czech and Slovak Republics was hardly a paradigm of democratic virtue. While the national elites involved were able to avoid violence, their solution was not subjected to a plebiscite by the citizenry of either country and seems to have depended on a rather momentary configuration of party strengths in the respective national assemblies.

17 For a case study of what may become a model for this multilateral intervention and coupling of peace-making with democratisation, see Karl, 'Imposing Consent?'.

18 Schmitter, 'The International Context, Political Conditionality and the Consolidation of Neo-democracies'.

19 Pridham, *Encouraging Democracy*.

References

Abente-Brun, Diego. 'Stronismo, Post-stronismo and the Prospects for Democratisation in Paraguay'. Working Paper 119, Kellogg Institute, University of Notre Dame, 1989.
Abdel-Hadi, Fatma. *My Journey with the Muslim Brotherhood Sisters*. Cairo: Dar El-Shorooq, 2012 (in Arabic).
Acemoglu, Daron and James A. Robinson. *Economic Origins of Dictatorship and Democracy*. New York: Cambridge University Press, 2006.
Acemoglu, Daron, Simon Johnson and James A. Robinson. 'The Colonial Origins of Comparative Development: An Empirical Investigation'. *The American Economic Review*, 91, 5, 2001, pp. 1369–1401.
Acemoglu, Daron, Simon Johnson and James A. Robinson. 'Reversal of Fortune: Geography and Institutions in the Making of the Modern Income Distribution'. *The Quarterly Journal of Econometrics*, 118, 2002, pp. 1231–1294.
Acemoglu, Daron, Simon Johnson and James A. Robinson. 'Income and Democracy'. *American Economic Review*, 98, 3, 2008, pp. 808–842.
Alesina, Alberto and Eliana La Ferrara. 'Ethnic Diversity and Economic Performance'. *Journal of Economic Literature* 43, 3, 2005, pp. 762–800.
Alesina, Alberto and Enrico Spolaore. *The Size of Nations*. Cambridge, MA: Massachusetts Press, 2003.
Alesina, Alberto, Arnaud Devleeschauwer, William Easterly, Sergio Kurlat and Romain Wacziarg. 'Fractionalization'. *The Journal of Economic Growth*, 8, 2003, pp. 155–194.
Alvarez, Michael, José Antonio Cheibub, Fernando Limongi and Adam Przeworski. *Democracy and Development: Political Institutions and Well-Being in the World, 1950–1990*. Cambridge: Cambridge University Press, 2000.
Aly, Abdel Monem Said and Karim Elkady. *The Good, the Bad and the Ugly of Egypt's Political Transition*. Crown Centre for Middle East Studies, 70, March 2013.
Amghar, Samir. *Le Salafisme d'Aujourd'hui: Mouvements Sectoriels en Occident*. Paris: Michelon, 2011.
Anderson, Lisa, ed. *Transitions to Democracy*. New York: Columbia University Press, 1999.
Anderson, Perry. *The New Old World*. London: Verso, 2009.
Andersson, Staffan and Paul M. Heywood. 'The Politics of Perception: Use and Abuse of Transparency International's Approach to Measuring Corruption'. *Political Studies*, 57, 4, 2009, pp. 746–767.
Apostolov, Mario. 'The End of the Post-Cold War World: Do We Have Now What We Expected Then?', in Jaci Eisenberg and Davide Rodogno, eds., *Ideas and Identities – A Festschrift for Andre Liebich*. Bern: Peter Lang, 2014, pp. 123–146.

References

Arditi, Benjamin. *La Reconstrucción de la Politica en el Paraguay*. Asuncion: RP Ediciones, 1992.
Armijo, Leslie Elliott, Thomas J. Biersteker and Abraham F. Lowenthal. 'The Problems of Simultaneous Transitions'. *The Journal of Democracy* 5, 4, 1994, pp.161–175.
Ash, Timothy Garton. 'The Empire in Decay'. *The New York Review of Books*, 35, 14, 29 September 1988, pp. 52–60.
Ash, Timothy Garton. '1989!'. *The New York Review of Books*, 56, 17, 5 November 2009, pp. 4–8.
Åslund, Anders. *How Ukraine Became a Market Economy and Democracy*. Washington, DC: Petersen Institute of International Economics, 2009.
Ba, Alice D. 'A New History? The Structure and Process of Southeast Asia's Relations with a Rising China', in Mark Beeson, ed., *Contemporary Southeast Asia*, 2nd edn. New York: Palgrave, 2008.
Bah, Mamadou Diouma. 'The Military and Politics in Guinea: An Instrumental Explanation of Political Stability'. *Armed Forces and Society*, 41, 1, 2015, pp. 69–95.
Balcerowicz, Leszek. 'Fallacies and Other Lessons'. *Economic Policy*, 9, 1994, pp. 18–50.
Baldez, Lisa. 'Women's Movements and Democratic Transitions in Chile, Brazil, East Germany and Poland'. *Comparative Politics* 35, 3, 2003, pp. 253–272.
Banegas, Richard. 'Les Transitions Démocratiques: Mobilisations Collectives et Fluidité Politique'. *Cultures & Conflits*, 12, Winter 1993, pp. 2–20.
Banegas, Richard. *La Démocratie à Pas De Caméléon – Transition et Imaginaires Politiques au Bénin*. Paris: Karthala, 2003.
Barkan, Joel D. 'Protracted Transitions among Africa's New Democracies'. *Democratization* 7, 3, 2000, pp. 227–243.
Barro, Robert J. 'Determinants of Democracy'. *Journal of Political Economy* 107, 6, pp. 158–183.
Bayat, Asef. *Life as Politics – How Ordinary People Change the Middle East*. Stanford, CA: Stanford University Press, 2009.
Bebler, Anton, ed. *The Challenge of NATO Enlargement*. Westport, CT: Praeger, 1999.
Beissinger, Mark R. *Nationalist Mobilisation and the Collapse of the Soviet State*. Cambridge: Cambridge University Press, 2002.
Bekoe, Dorina, ed. *Voting in Fear – Electoral Violence in Sub-Saharan Africa*. Washington, DC: United States Institute of Peace Press, 2013.
Bendix, Reinhard. 'Social Stratification and Political Power'. *American Political Science Review*, XLVI, June 1952, pp. 357–375.
Benkirane, Reda. 'The Alchemy of Revolution: The Role of Social Networks and New Media in the Arab Spring', *GCSP Policy Paper*, 7. Geneva: Geneva Centre for Security Policy, 2012.
Bennani-Chraïbi, Mounia and Olivier Fillieule. 'Pour Une Sociologie des Situations Révolutionnaires: Retour sur les Révoltes Arabes'. *Revue Française de Sciences Politiques* 62, 5–6, 2012, pp. 767–796.
Berdal, Mats and Dominik Zoum, eds. *Political Economy of State-Building*. London and New York: Routledge, 2013.
Bermeo, Nancy. 'Myths of Moderation: Confrontation and Conflict During Democratic Transitions'. *Comparative Politics* 29, 3, 1997, pp. 305–322.
Bielous, Silvia Dutrenit. 'Dictaduras y Partidos Políticos en Argentina, Brasil y Uruguay: Anotaciones para una Historia Comparativa'. *Revista Uruguaya de Ciência Política*, 7, 1994, pp. 51–63.

References

Birch, Melissa. 'Estabilidad Política y Rezago Económico: El Gobierno de Federico Chaves 1949–1954', in Fernando Masi and Dionisio Borda, eds., *Estado y Economía en Paraguay (1870–2010)*. Asunción: Centro de Análisis y Difusión de la Economía Paraguay (CADEP), 2011.

Birch, Sarah. *Electoral Malpractice*. Oxford: Oxford University Press, 2012.

Blanchard, Olivier, Rudiger Dornbusch, Paul Krugman, Richard Layard and Lawrence Summers. *Reform in Eastern Europe*. Cambridge, MA: MIT Press, 1992.

Boix, Carles. *Democracy and Redistribution*. Cambridge: Cambridge University Press, 2003.

Bollen, Kenneth A. 'Political Democracy and the Timing of Development'. *American Sociological Review*, 44, 4, 1979, pp. 572–587.

Bollen, Kenneth A. 'World System Position, Dependency and Democracy: A Cross-National Analysis'. *American Sociological Review*, 48, 4, 1983, pp. 468–479.

Bollen, Kenneth A. and Robert W. Jackman. 'Political Democracy and the Size Distribution of Income'. *American Sociological Review*, 50, 4, 1985, pp. 438–457.

Börzel, Tanja A., Thomas Risse and Assem Dandashly. 'Responses to the "Arabellions": The EU in Comparative Perspective'. *Journal of European Integration*, 37, 1, 2014, pp. 1–17.

Boudreau, Vincent. *Resisting Dictatorship – Repression and Protest in Southeast Asia*. Cambridge: Cambridge University Press, 2004.

Bracati, Dawn. 'Pocketbook Protests: Explaining the Emergence of Pro-Democracy Protests Worldwide'. *Comparative Political Studies* 47,11, 2014, pp. 1503–1530.

Bracati, Dawn and Jack L. Snyder. 'Rushing to the Polls: The Causes of Premature Post-conflict Elections'. *Journal of Conflict Resolution* 55, 3, 2011, pp. 469–492.

Bratton, Michael and Nicolas van de Walle. *Democratic Experiments in Africa – Regime Transitions in Comparative Perspective*. Cambridge: Cambridge University Press, 1997.

Brinton, Crane. *Anatomy of Revolution*. New York: Vintage, 1965 (revised and expanded edn.).

Brookings Doha Centre. 'The Beginnings of Transition – Politics and Polarisation in Egypt and Tunisia'. Doha, April 2012.

Brown, Archie. *The Gorbachev Factor*. New York: Oxford University Press, 1996.

Brown, J.F. *Surge to Freedom – The End of Communist Rule in Eastern Europe*. Durham, NC: Duke University Press, 1991.

Brown, Nathan. 'Egypt's Failed Transition', *Journal of Democracy* 24, 4, 2013, pp. 45–58.

Brown, Stephen. 'Theorising Kenya's Protracted Transition to Democracy'. *Journal of Contemporary African Studies* 22, 3, 2004, pp. 325–342.

Brown, Stephen. 'Foreign Aid and Democracy Promotion: Lessons from Africa'. *The European Journal of Development Research* 17, 2, 2005.

Brownlee, Jason. '…And Yet They Persist: Explaining Survival and Transition in Neopatrimonial Regimes'. *Studies in Comparative International Development* 37, 3, 2002, pp. 35–63.

Brownlee, Jason. *Authoritarianism in an Age of Democratization*. New York: Cambridge University Press, 2007.

Brumberg, Daniel. 'The Trap of Liberalised Autocracy'. *Journal of Democracy*, 13, 4, 2002, pp. 56–68.

Brunk, Gregory C., Gregory A. Caldeira and Michael S. Lewis-Beck. 'Capitalism, Socialism and Democracy: An Empirical Inquiry'. *European Journal of Political Research* 15, 4, 1987, pp. 459–70.

Brynen, Rex, Pete Moore, Basel Salloukh and Marie-Joelle Zahar. *After the Arab Spring*. Boulder, CO and London: Lynne Rienner, 2013.
Bunce, Valerie. 'Comparative Democratization: Big and Bounded Generalizations'. *Comparative Political Studies*, 2000, 33, 6/7, pp. 703–734.
Bunce, Valerie. 'Rethinking Recent Democratization'. *World Politics* 55, 2, 2003, pp. 167–192.
Burkhart, Ross E. and Michael S. Lewis-Beck. 'Comparative Democracy: The Economic Development Thesis'. *American Political Science Review*, 88, 4, 1994, pp. 903–910.
Camau, Michel and Frédéric Vairel, eds. *Soulèvements et Recompositions Politiques dans le Monde Arabe*. Montreal: Montreal University Press, 2014.
Carothers, Thomas. 'The End of the Transition Paradigm'. *The Journal of Democracy*, 13, 2, 2002, pp. 5–21.
Carothers, Thomas. 'The Backlash against Democracy Promotion'. *Foreign Affairs* 85, 2, 2006, pp. 55–68.
Carothers, Thomas. 'Stepping Back from Democratic Pessimism'. Carnegie Endowment for International Peace, Carnegie Paper No. 99, February 2009.
Carothers, Thomas and Nathan J. Brown. 'The Real Danger for Egyptian Democracy'. Carnegie Endowment for International Peace, Policy Brief, 2010.
Carothers, Thomas and Oren Samet-Marram. 'The New Global Marketplace of Political Change'. Carnegie Endowment for International Peace, April 2015.
Carothers, Thomas and Richard Youngs. 'The Complexities of Global Protest'. Carnegie Endowment for International Peace, October 2015.
Case, William. *Politics in Southeast Asia: Democracy or Less*. London: Routledge, 2002.
Case, William. 'Low-quality Democracy and Varied Authoritarianism: Elites and Regimes in Southeast Asia Today'. *The Pacific Review*, 22, 3, 2009, pp. 255–269.
Case, William, ed. *Routledge Handbook of Southeast Asian Democratization*. Abingdon, UK and New York: Routledge, 2015.
Chambers, Simone and Jeffrey Kopstein. 'Bad Civil Society'. *Political Theory* 29, 6, 2001, pp. 837–865.
Chandra, Kanchan. *Why Ethnic Parties Succeed – Patronage and Ethnic Headcounts in India*. Cambridge: Cambridge University Press, 2004.
Chauvet, Lisa and Paul Collier. 'Elections and Economic Policy in Developing Countries'. *Economic Policy*, 24, 59, 2009, pp. 509–550.
Cheeseman, Nic and Blessing-Miles Tendi. 'Power-Sharing in Comparative Perspective: The Dynamics of "Unity Government" in Kenya and Zimbabwe'. *The Journal of Modern African Studies* 48, 2, 2010, pp. 203–229.
Chen, Jie. *A Middle Class Without Democracy: Economic Growth and the Prospects for Democratization in China*. Oxford: Oxford University Press, 2014.
Chenoweth, Erica and Maria J. Stephan. *Why Civil Resistance Works – The Strategic Logic of Nonviolent Conflict*. New York: Columbia University Press, 2011.
Cichok, Mark. 'Transitionalism vs. Transnationalism: Conflicting Trends in Independent Latvia'. *East European Politics and Societies*, 16, 2, 2002, pp. 446–464.
Clague, Christopher, Suzanne Gleason and Stephen Knack. 'Determinants of Lasting Democracy in Poor Countries: Culture, Development and Institutions'. *Annals of the American Academy of Social Sciences*, 573, 2001, pp. 16–41.
Clark, Andrew F. 'From Military Dictatorship to Democracy: The Democratization Process in Mali'. *Journal of Third World Studies* 12, 1, 1995, pp. 201–222.

Clark, Janine. 'Democratisation and Social Islam: The Case of Health Clinics', in Rex Brynen, Bahgat Korany and Paul Noble, eds., *Political Liberalisation and Democratisation in the Arab World*. Boulder, CO, Lynne Rienner, 1995.

Clark, John F. 'Armed Arbiters: When Does the Military Step into the Electoral Arena?', in Andreas Schedler, ed., *Electoral Authoritarianism – The Dynamics of Unfree Competition*. Boulder, CO: Lynne Rienner, 2006, pp. 129–148.

Coburn, Noah and Anna Larson. *Derailing Democracy in Afghanistan – Elections in an Unstable Political Landscape*. New York: Columbia University Press, 2013.

Collier, Paul and Nicholas Sambanis, eds. *Understanding Civil War*. Washington DC: World Bank, 2005.

Coomaraswamy, Radhika, ed. 'Preventing Conflict, Transforming Justice, Securing the Peace: A Global Study on the Implementation of United Nations Security Council Resolution 1325'. UN Women, New York, 2015.

Coppedge, Michael. *Democratization and Research Methods*. Cambridge: Cambridge University Press, 2012.

Crawford, Beverly and Arend Lijphart. 'Explaining Political and Economic Change in Post-Communist Eastern Europe: Old Legacies, New Institutions, Hegemonic Norms, and International Pressures'. *Comparative Political Studies*, 28, 2, 1995, pp. 171–199.

Curtis, Michael. *Orientalism and Islam: European Theories on Oriental Despotism in the Middle East and India*. Cambridge and New York: Cambridge University Press, 2009.

Dahl, Robert A. *On Democracy*. New Haven, CT: Yale University Press, 1998.

Daloz, Jean-Pascal. *Transitions Démocratiques Africaines – Dynamiques et Contraintes (1990–1994)*. Paris: Karthala, 1994.

Danahar, Paul. *The New Middle East: The World after the Arab Spring*. London and New York: Bloomsbury, 2013.

Davidson, Basil. *The Black Man's Burden – Africa and the Curse of the Nation-State*. New York: Random House, 1992.

Dawisha, Karen and Bruce Parrott, eds. *The Consolidation of Democracy in East-Central Europe*. Cambridge: Cambridge University Press, 1997.

de Riz, Liliana. 'Political Parties and Democratic Consolidation: Argentina, Brazil and Uruguay', in *Latin America and Caribbean Records*, Volume VI. New York: Holmes & Meier, 1989.

Decalko, Samuel. *Coups and Army Rule in Africa – Studies in Military Style*. New Haven, CT: Yale University Press, 1990.

Della Porta, Donatella. *Mobilising for Democracy – Comparing 1989 and 2011*. Oxford: Oxford University Press, 2014.

Diamond, Larry. 'Elections Without Democracy: Thinking About Hybrid Regimes'. *The Journal of Democracy*, 13, 2, 2002, pp. 21–35.

Diamond, Larry. 'The Need for a Political Pact'. *The Journal of Democracy*, 23, 4, 2012, pp. 138–149.

Diamond, Larry. 'Facing Up to the Democratic Recession', in Larry Diamond and Marc F. Plattner eds., *Democracy in Decline?*. Baltimore, MD: John Hopkins University Press, 2015, pp. 98–118.

Diamond, Larry and Larry Jay. *Developing Democracy – Toward Consolidation*. Baltimore, MD: John Hopkins University Press, 1999.

Diamond, Larry and Leonardo Morlino. *Assessing the Quality of Democracy*. Baltimore, MD: John Hopkins University Press, 2005.

Diamond, Larry and Marc F. Plattner, eds. *Democracy in East Asia*. Baltimore, MD and London: Johns Hopkins University Press, 1998.

Diamond, Larry and Marc F. Plattner, eds. *Democracy in Decline?* Baltimore, MD: John Hopkins University Press, 2015.

Diamond, Larry, Juan Linz and Seymour Martin Lipset, eds. *Democracy in Developing Countries: Asia*. Boulder CO: Lynne Rienner, 1989.

Diamond, Larry, Juan Linz and Seymour Lipset, eds. *Democracy in Developing Countries – Latin America, Volume Four*. Boulder, CO: Lynne Rienner, 1989.

Diamond, Larry, Marc F. Plattner and Yun-han Chu, eds. *Democracy in East Asia: A New Century*. Baltimore, MD: John Hopkins University Press, 2013.

Diamond, Larry, Francis Fukuyama, Donald L. Horowitz and Marc F. Plattner. 'Reconsidering the "Transition Paradigm"'. *The Journal of Democracy*, 25, 1, 2014, pp. 86–100.

Dickovick, J. Tyler. 'Legacies of Leftism: Ideology, Ethnicity and Democracy in Benin, Ghana, and Mali'. *Third World Quarterly* 29, 6, 2008, pp. 1119–1137.

Dobbins, James, Seth G. Jones, Keith Crane, Andrew Rathmell, Brett Steele, Richard Teltschik and Anga Timilsina. *The UN's Role in Nation-building: From the Congo to Iraq*. Santa Monica, CA: Rand Corporation, 2005.

Dobry, Michael. 'Les Transitions Démocratiques: Regards sur l'État de la "Transitologie"'. *Revue Française de Sciences Politiques* 5, 5, 2000, pp. 579–584.

Doyle, Michael W. and Nicholas Sambanis, *Making War and Building Peace*. Princeton, NJ: Princeton University Press, 2006.

Dunning, Thad. *Crude Democracy, Natural Resource Wealth and Political Regimes*. New York: Cambridge University Press, 2008.

Easterly, William and Ross Levine. 'Tropics, Germs, and Crops: How Endowments Influence Economic Development'. *Journal of Monetary Economics*, 50, 1, 2003, pp. 3–39.

Ekiert, Grzegorz, Jan Kubik and Milada AnnaVachudova, 'Democracy in the Post-Communist World: An Unending Quest?'. *East European Politics and Societies*, 21, 7, 2007, pp. 7–30.

El-Fetouh, Abdel-Moneim Abou and Hossam Tamam. *A Witness of the History of the Islamist Movement in Egypt 1970–1984*. Cairo: Dar El-Shorooq, 2012.

El-Kharabawy, Tharwat. *Secret of the Temple*. Cairo: Al Nahda, 2012.

El-Rashidi, Yasmine. 'Egypt: The Victorious Islamists'. *New York Review of Books*, 7 February 2013.

El-Suwaidy, Jamal and Ahmed El-Safty. *Islamists and the Democratic System: Trends and Experiences*. Doha: Arab Center for Research and Policy Studies, 2013 (in Arabic).

El-Suwaidy, Jamal and Ahmed El-Safty, eds. *Political Islam: Rise and Demise*. Abu Dhabi: Center for Strategic Studies and Research, 2014 (in Arabic).

Elkana, Yehhuda, Ivan Krastev, Elisio Macamo and Shalini Randeria, eds. *Unraveling Ties: From Social Cohesion to New Practices of Connectedness*. Frankfurt: Campus Verlag, 2002.

Engeler, Michelle. 'Guinea in 2008: The Unfinished Revolution'. *Politique Africaine* 112, 2008, pp. 87–98.

Fearon, James D. and David D. Laitin. 'Ethnicity, Insurgency, and Civil War'. *American Political Science Review* 97, 1, 2003, pp. 75–90.

Finer, Samuel E. *The Man on Horseback – Military Intervention into Politics*. Harmondsworth, UK: Penguin, 1975.

Fischer, D.H. *Historians' Fallacies – Toward a Logic of Historical Thought*. London: Routledge, 1971.

Foran, John. 'Beyond Insurgency to Radical Social Change: The New Situation'. *Studies in Social Change*, 8, 1, 2014, pp. 5–25.
Fortna, Virginia Page. 'Does Peacekeeping Keep Peace? International Intervention and the Duration of Peace after Civil War'. *International Studies Quarterly* 48, 2, 2004, pp. 269–292.
Fortna, Virginia Page and Lise Morjé Howard. 'Pitfalls and Prospects in the Peacekeeping Future'. *Annual Review of Political Science*, 11, 2008, pp. 283–301.
Freedom House. *Freedom in the World 2016*. Freedom House, Washington DC, 2016.
Friedman, Edward, ed. *The Politics of Democratization – Generalizing East Asian Experiences*. Boulder, CO: Westview Press, 1994.
Frydman, Roman and Andrzej Rapaczynski. *Privatization in Eastern Europe – Is the State Withering Away?* London: Central European University Press, 1993.
Fuh-sheng Hsieh, John and David Newman, eds. *How Asia Votes*. New York: Chatham House Publishers, 2002.
Fukuyama, Francis. *Political Order and Political Decay – From the Industrial Revolution to the Globalization of Democracy*. New York: Farrar, Straus and Giroux, 2014.
Furet, François. 'From 1789 to 1917 and 1989: Looking Back at Revolutionary Traditions'. *Encounter*, 75, 2, 1990, pp. 3–7.
Gans-Morse, Jordan. 'Searching for Transitologists: Contemporary Theories of Post-Communist Transitions and the Myth of a Dominant Paradigm'. *Post-Soviet Affairs*, 20, 4, 2004, pp. 320–349.
Garreton, Manuel Antonio. *The Chilean Political Process*. Boston, MA: Unwin Hyman, 1989.
Gati, Charles. *The Bloc That Failed – Soviet East European Relations in Transition*. London: I. B. Tauris, 1990.
Gazibo, Mamoudou. *Les Paradoxes de La Démocratisation en Afrique – Analyse Institutionnelle et Stratégique*. Montreal: Presse de l'Université de Montréal, 2005.
Gazibo, Mamoudou. *Introduction à la Politique Africaine*. Montreal: Presse de l'Université de Montréal, 2006.
Gazibo, Mamadou. 'The Forging of Institutional Autonomy: A Comparative Study of Electoral Management Commissions in Africa'. *Canadian Journal of Political Science* 39, 3, 2006, pp. 611–633.
Geddes, Barbara. 'What Do We Know About Democratization after Twenty Years?'. *Annual Review of Political Science* 2, 1, 1999, pp. 115–144.
Geddes, Barbara. 'What Causes Democratization?', in Susan C. Stokes and Charles Boix, eds., *The Oxford Handbook of Comparative Politics*. Oxford: Oxford University Press, 2009, pp. 317–399.
Gerges, Fawaz Gerges, ed. *The New Middle East: Protest and Revolution in the Arab World*. New York and Cambridge: Cambridge University Press, 2014.
Gerring, John, Strom C. Thaker and Carola Moreno. 'Centripetal Democratic Governance: A Theory and Global Inquiry'. *American Political Science Review*, 99, 4, 2005, pp. 567–581.
Ghoneim, Wael. *Revolution 2.0: The Power of the People is Greater than the People in Power*. London: Fourth Estate/Harper Collins, 2012.
Gilley, Bruce. 'Democratic Triumph, Scholarly Pessimism'. *The Journal of Democracy*, 21, 1, 2010, pp. 160–167.
Gilley, Bruce. *The Nature of Asian Politics*. New York: Cambridge University Press, 2014.

Grugel, Jean and Matthew Louis Bishop. *Democratisation: A Critical Introduction*. London: Macmillan, 2013.

Guerra, Simona. *Central and Eastern Attitudes in the Face of Union – A Comparative Perspective*. New York: Palgrave Macmillan, 2013.

Gurses, Mehmet and T. David Mason. 'Democracy Out of Anarchy: The Prospects for Post-Civil-War Democracy'. *Social Science Quarterly* 89, 2, 2008, pp. 315–336.

Haber, Stephen and Victor Menaldo. 'Do Natural Resources Fuel Authoritarianism? A Reappraisal of the Resource Curse'. *American Political Science Review* 105, 1, 2011, pp. 1–26.

Habermas, Jürgen. 'What Does Socialism Mean Today? The Rectifying Revolution and the Need for New Thinking on the Left'. *New Left Review*, 183, 1, 1990, pp. 3–21.

Habib, Mohamed. *Memoirs*. Cairo: Dar El-Shorooq, 2012.

Hachemaoui, Mohammed. *La Tunisie à la Croisée des Chemins – Quelles Règles pour Quelle Transition*. German Institute for International and Security Affairs, August 2013.

Hadenius, Axel. 'The Duration of Democracy', in David Beetham, ed., *Defining and Measuring Democracy*. London: Sage, 1994.

Haggard, Stephan and Robert R. Kaufman. *The Political Economy of Democratic Transitions*. Princeton, NJ: Princeton University Press, 1995.

Hale, Henry E. *Patronal Politics – Eurasian Regime Dynamics in Comparative Perspective*. Cambridge: Cambridge University Press, 2014.

Ham, Caroline van. 'Why do Elections Fail? Explaining Election Integrity in Third and Fourth Wave Regimes'. Paper presented at the Annual Conference of the American Political Science Association, 28–31 August 2013, Chicago.

Hamid, Shadi. *The Temptations of Power – Islamists and Illiberal Democracy in a New Middle East*. New York: Oxford University Press, 2013.

Hankiss, Elemer. 'Reforms and the Conversion of Power', in Peter R. Weilemann, Georg Brunner and Rudolf L. Tökés, eds., *Upheaval against the Plan – Eastern Europe on the Eve of the Storm*. Oxford: Berg, 1991.

Harris, David and Tereza Lewis, 'Liberia in 2011: Still Ploughing Its Own Democratic Furrow?'. *Commonwealth and Comparative Politics* 51, 1, 2013, pp. 76–96.

Hartmann, C. 'Democracy as a Fortuitous By-product of Independence UN Intervention and Democratization in Namibia'. *Taiwan Journal of Democracy* 5, 1, 2009, pp. 27–50.

Hatchard, John and Peter Slinn. 'The Path Towards a New Order in South Africa'. *International Relations* 12, 4, 1995, pp. 1–26.

Heine, Jorge and Brigitte Weiffen. *21st Century Democracy Promotion in the Americas – Standing up for the Polity*. London: Routledge, 2015.

Heller, Agnes. 'Twenty Years After 1989', in Vladimir Tismaneau with Bogdan C. Jacob, ed., *The End and the Beginning – The Revolutions of 1989 and the Resurgence of History*. Budapest: Central European University Press, 2012.

Helliwell, John F. 'Empirical Linkages Between Democracy and Economic Growth'. *British Journal of Political Science*, 24, 2, 1994, pp. 225–248.

Hewison, Kevin, Richard Robison and Garry Rodan, eds. *Southeast Asia in the 1990s – Authoritarianism, Democracy and Capitalism*. Sydney: Allen and Unwin, 1993.

Heydemann, Steven. 'Upgrading Authoritarianism in the Arab World'. Centre for Middle East Policy Analysis Papers, The Brookings Institution, October 2007.

Higley, John and Michael G. Burton. 'The Elite Variable in Democratic Transitions and Breakdowns'. *American Sociological Review* 54, 1, 1989, pp. 17–32.

Hillman, Benjamin. 'The Policy-Making Dimension of Post-Conflict Governance: The Experience of Aceh, Indonesia'. *Conflict, Security and Development*, 11, 5, 2012, pp. 533–553.

Hippler, Jochen, ed. *The Democratisation of Disempowerment – The Problem of Democracy in the Third World*. London: Pluto, 1995.

Hobsbawm, Eric J. 'The New Threat to History'. *The New York Review of Books*, 40, 21, 16 December 1993.

Hobsbawm, Eric J. 'Eric Hobsbawm Remembers Tony Judt'. *London Review of Books*, 34, 8, 26 April 2012.

Hoen, Herman Willem. *The Transformation of Economic Systems in Central Europe*. Northampton, MA: Edward Elgar, 1998.

Hoffman, Barak and Lindsay Robinson. 'Tanzania's Missing Opposition'. *The Journal of Democracy* 20, 4, 2009, pp. 123–136.

Holzer, Jan. 'The End of the Transitological Paradigm? Debate on Non-Democratic Regimes and Post-Communist Experience'. Paper presented at the Twentieth International Political Science Association (IPSA) World Congress, Fukuoka, 9–13 July 2009.

Horne, Cynthia M. 'The Impact of Lustration on Democratization in Postcommunist Countries'. *The International Journal of Transitional Justice*, 8, 3, 2014, pp. 496–521.

Hosny, Dina. 'The Moslem Brotherhood Youth'. M.Sc thesis, American University in Cairo, 2013.

Howard, Lise Morjé. *UN Peacekeeping in Civil Wars*. New York: Cambridge University Press, 2009.

Huber, Evelyne, Dietrich Rueschemeyer and John D. Stephens. 'The Impact of Economic Development on Democracy'. *Journal of Economic Perspectives*, 7, 3, 1993, pp. 71–86.

Hughes, Barry, Devin Joshi, Jonathan Moyer and Timothy D. Sisk. *Strengthening Governance Globally*. Oxford: Oxford University Press, 2014.

Humphreys, M. 'Natural Resources, Conflict, and Conflict Resolution – Uncovering the Mechanisms.' *Journal of Conflict Resolution*, 49, 4, 2005, pp. 508–537.

Huntington, Samuel P. *Political Order in Changing Societies*. New Haven, CT: Yale University Press, 1968.

Huntington, Samuel P. *The Third Wave: Democratisation in the Late Twentieth Century*. Norman, OK: University of Oklahoma Press, 1991.

Huntington, Samuel P. *The Clash of Civilizations and the Remaking of World Order*. New York: Simon & Schuster, 1993.

Inglehart, Ronald and Christian Welzel. *Modernisation, Cultural Change and Democracy: The Human Development Sequence*. New York: Cambridge University Press, 2005.

Jackman, Robert. 'On the Relation of Economic Development and Democratic Performance'. *American Journal of Political Science* 17, 3, 1973, pp. 611–621.

Jankauskas, Algimantas and Liutauras Gudžinskas. 'Reconceptualizing Transitology: Lessons from Post-Communism'. *Lithuanian Annual Strategic Review 2007*, Military Academy of Lithuania, Vilnius, 2008, pp. 181–199.

Janos, Andrew C. 'Continuity and Change in Eastern Europe: Strategies of Post-Communist Politics'. *East European Politics and Society*, 8, 1, 1993, pp. 1–31.

Jarsad, Anna and Timothy D. Sisk, eds. *From War to Democracy*. New York: Cambridge University Press, 2008.

Jedlicki, Jerzy. 'The Revolution of 1989: The Unbearable Burden of History'. *CES Working Paper*, Harvard University, 1990.

References

Jennings, Ray Salvatore. 'Democratic Breakthroughs – The Ingredients of Successful Revolts'. United States Institute of Peace, 2012.
Jensen, Nathan and Leonard Wantchekon. 'Resource Wealth and Political Regimes in Africa'. *Comparative Political Studies* 37, 7, 2004, pp. 816–841.
Jeong, Ho-Won. *Peace-building in Post-conflict Societies*. Boulder, CO: Lynne Rienner, 2005.
Jones, David Martin. 'Democratization, Civil Society and Illiberal Middle Class Culture in Pacific Asia', in Howard J. Wiarda, ed., *Comparative Politics: Critical Concepts in Politics*. London: Routledge, 2005.
Jones, Mark P. 'Gender Quotas, Electoral Laws and the Election of Women: Evidence from the Latin American Vanguard'. *Comparative Political Studies* 42, 1, 2009, pp. 56–81.
Kagwanja, Peter and Roger Southall. 'Introduction: Kenya – A Democracy in Retreat?'. *Journal of Contemporary African Studies* 27, 3, 2009, pp. 259–277.
Kalandadze, Katya and Mitchell A. Orenstein. 'Electoral Protests and Democratisation: Beyond the Colour Revolutions'. *Comparative Political Studies* 42, 11, 2009, pp. 1403–1425.
Kaldor, Mary and Diego Muro-Ruiz. 'Religious and Nationalist Militant Groups', in Helmut Anheier, Mary Kaldor and Marlies Glasius, eds., *Global Civil Society*. Oxford: Oxford University Press, 2003.
Kamrava, Mehran and Frank O. Mora. 'Civil Society and Democratisation in Comparative Perspective: Latin America and the Middle East'. *Third World Quarterly*, 19, 5, 1998, pp. 893–915.
Kandeh, Jimmy D. 'Rogue Incumbents, Donor Assistance and Sierra Leone's Second Post-Conflict Elections of 2007'. *Journal of Modern African Studies* 46, 4, 2008, pp. 603–635.
Kandil, Hazem. *Inside the Brotherhood*. Cambridge: Polity Press 2014.
Kaplan, Robert. 'Was Democracy Just a Moment?'. *The Atlantic Monthly*, December 1997.
Karl, Terry. 'Imposing Consent? Electoralism versus Democratization in El Salvador', in Paul Drake and Eduardo Silva, eds., *Elections and Democratization in Latin America, 1980–1985*. Center for Iberian and Latin American Studies, Center for US/Mexican Studies, University of California, San Diego, 1986, pp. 9–36.
Karl, Terry Lynn. 'Dilemmas of Democratization in Latin America'. *Comparative Politics*, 23, 1, 1990, pp. 1–21.
Karl, Terry Lynn. 'From Democracy to Democratization and Back: Before Transitions from Authoritarian Rule'. CDDRL Working Paper 45, Centre on Democracy, Development and the Rule of Law, Stanford, CA, September 2005.
Karl, Terry Lynn and Philippe C. Schmitter. 'Modes of Transition in Latin America, Southern, and Eastern Europe'. *International Social Sciences Journal*, 128, May 1991, pp. 269–284.
Kaufmann, Chaim. 'Possible and Impossible Solutions to Ethnic Civil Wars'. *International Security* 20, 4, 1996, pp. 136–175.
Kaufman, Stuart J. *Modern Hatreds – The Symbolic Politics of Ethnic War*. Ithaca: Cornell University Press, 2001.
Keane, John, ed. *The Power of the Powerless – Citizens against the State in Central-Eastern Europe*. London: Hutchinson, 1985.
Keane, John, ed. *Civil Society and the State – New European Perspectives*. London, New York: Verso, 1988.

Kelly, Catherine Lena. 'Senegal: What Will Turnover Bring?'. *The Journal of Democracy* 23, 3, 2012, pp. 121–131.

Khatib, Lina. 'Transforming the Media: From Tools of the Ruler to Tool of Empowerment', in Bahgat Korany, ed., *Arab Human Development in the Twenty-First Century: The Primacy of Empowerment*. New York and Cairo: American University in Cairo Press, 2014, pp. 67–104.

King, Stephen J. *The New Authoritarianism in the Middle East and North Africa*. Bloomington, IN: Indiana University Press, 2009.

Knack, Stephen and Philip Keefer. 'Institutions and Economic Performance: Cross-country Tests Using Alternative Institutional Measures'. *Economics & Politics*, 7, 3, 1995, pp. 207–227.

Kolodko, Grzegorz. 'The Lessons to be Learned from the Great Post-Communist Change', in Joseph E. Peeters, ed., *Politics and Economics of Central and Eastern Europe*. New York: Nova Science, 2012, pp. 143–152.

Korany, Bahgat. 'Arab Democracy: A Poor Cousin?'. *Politics and Political Science*, 27, 3, 1994, pp. 511–513.

Korany, Bahgat. 'From Prison to Authority and Back: the Muslim Brotherhood's Experience of Governance in Egypt', in Jamal S. El-Suwaidi and A. R. El-Safty, eds., *Islamic Political Movements and Authority in the Arab World – The Rise and Fall*. Abu Dhabi: Emirates Centre for Strategic Studies and Research, 2013.

Korany, Bahgat, ed. *Arab Human Development in the 21st Century*. New York and Cairo: American University in Cairo Press, 2014.

Korany, Bahgat. 'Microcosm of Revolution: The Sociology of Tahrir', in Mehran Kamrava, ed., *The Ruling Bargain in the Middle East*. London: Taurus, 2014.

Korany, Bahgat and Rabab El-Mahdy, eds. *The Arab Spring in Egypt: Revolution and Beyond*. New York and Cairo: American University in Cairo Press, 2012.

Korany, Bahgat, Rex Brynen and Paul Noble, eds. *Liberalization and Democratization in the Arab World*. Boulder, CO and Oxford: Lynne Rienner, 1998.

Kotkin, Stephen. *Uncivil Society – 1989 and the Implosion of the Communist Establishment*. New York: The Modern Library, 2009.

Kowalik, Tadeusz. *From Solidarity to Sellout – The Restoration of Capitalism in Poland*. New York: Monthly Review Press, 2012.

Krause, Kevin D. 'Slovakia's Second Transition'. *The Journal of Democracy* 14, 2, 2003, pp. 65–79.

Krieckhaus, Jonathan. 'The Regime Debate Revisited: A Sensitivity Analysis of Democracy's Economic Effect'. *British Journal of Political Science*, 34, 4, 2004, pp. 635–655.

Kudelia, Serhiy. 'The Sources of Continuity and Change of Ukraine's Incomplete State'. *Communist and Post-Communist Studies*, 45, 3–4, 2012, pp. 417–428.

Kudelia, Serhiy. 'If Tomorrow Comes: Power Balance and Time Horizons in Ukraine's Constitutional Politics'. *Demokratizatsiya*, 21, 2, 2013, pp. 151–178.

Kudelia, Serhiy. 'The House that Yanukovych Built'. *The Journal of Democracy*, 25, 3, 2014, pp. 19–34.

Kuhn, Randall. 'On the Role of Human Development in the Arab Spring'. Working Paper, Institute for Behavioral Science, University of Colorado, September 2011.

Kuhonta, Erik. 'The Paradox of Thailand's 1997 "People's Constitution": Be Careful What You Wish For'. *Asian Survey*, 48, 3, 2008, pp. 373–392.

Kuhonta, Erik, Martinez Kuhonta and Allen Hicken. 'Shadows from the Past: Party System Institutionalization in Asia'. *Comparative Political Studies*, 44, 5, 2011, pp. 572–597.

Kumar, Krishna, ed. *Post-conflict Elections, Democratization and International Assistance*. Boulder, CO: Lynne Rienner, 1998.

Kwasniewski, Aleksander. 'Poland in NATO – Challenges and Opportunities'. *NATO Review* 45, 5, 1997, pp. 4–7.

Laothamatas, Anek, ed. *Democratization in Southeast and East Asia*. Singapore: Institute of Southeast Asian Studies, 1997.

LaPorta, Raphael, Florencio Lopez-de-Silanes, Andrei Shleifer and Robert Vishny. 'The Quality of Government'. *Journal of Law, Economics, and Organizations*, 15, 1, 1999, pp. 222–279.

Lavigne, Marie. *The Economies of Transition – From Socialist Economy to Market Economy*. Basingstoke, UK: Macmillan, 1999.

Lee, Terrence. *Defect or Defend: Military Responses to Popular Protests in Authoritarian Asia*. Baltimore, MD and Singapore: John Hopkins University Press and ISEAS, 2015.

Levitsky, Steven and Lucan A. Way. *Competitive Authoritarianism – International Linkage, Organizational Power and the Fate of Hybrid Regimes*. Cambridge: Cambridge University Press, 2010.

Lewis, Peter. 'Nigeria: An End to the Permanent Transition?'. *The Journal of Democracy* 10, 1, 1999, pp. 141–156.

Liebich, André. 'East Europe Today: Marching Out of Step'. *Behind the Headlines*, 18, 3, 1986.

Lijphart, Arend. *Democracies – Patterns of Majoritarian and Consensus Government in Twenty-One Countries*. New Haven: Yale University Press, 1984.

Lijphart, Arend. *Patterns of Democracy – Government Forms and Performance in Thirty-Six Countries*, New Haven, CT: Yale University Press, 1999.

Lindberg, Staffan I. 'The Surprising Significance of African Elections'. *The Journal of Democracy* 17, 1, 2006, pp. 139–151.

Lindberg, Staffan, ed. *Democratization by Elections: A New Mode of Transition?* Baltimore, MD: John Hopkins University Press, 2009.

Linz, Juan and Alfred Stepan, eds. *The Breakdown of Democratic Regimes* (three volumes). Baltimore, MD: John Hopkins University Press, 1978.

Linz, Juan and Alfred Stepan. *Problems of Democratic Transition and Consolidation – Southern Europe, South America, and Post-Communist Europe*. Baltimore, MD: John Hopkins University Press, 1996.

Lipset, Seymour Martin. 'Some Social Requisites of Democracy: Economic Development and Political Legitimacy'. *American Political Science Review*, 53, 1959, pp. 69–105.

Lipset, Seymour Martin. *Political Man – The Social Bases of Politics*. New York: Doubleday, 1960.

Lipset, Seymour Martin and Jason M. Lakin. *The Democratic Century*. Norman, OK: University of Oklahoma Press, 2004.

Lipset, Seymour Martin, Kyoung-Ryung Seong and John Charles Torres. 'A Comparative Analysis of the Social Requisites of Democracy'. *International Social Science Journal*, 45, 2, 1993, pp. 154–175.

Lipton, David and Jeffrey Sachs. 'Creating a Market Economy in Eastern Europe: The Case of Poland'. Brookings Paper on Economic Activity 1, The Brookings Institution, 1990, pp. 75–114.

Liu, Ted. 'Transition Challenges in the Arab World – Lessons from the Past'. Fride Policy Brief 144, January 2013.

Lode, Kåre. 'The Peace Process in Mali: Oiling the Works?'. *Security Dialogue* 28, 4, 1997, pp. 409–424.

Lowe, Keith. *Savage Continent – Europe in the Aftermath of World War I*. New York: St. Martin's Press, 2012.
Lowenthal, Abraham and Sergio Bitar. *Democratic Transitions: Conversations with World Leaders*. Baltimore, MD: John Hopkins University Press, 2015.
Lynch, Gabrielle and Gordon Crawford. 'Democratization in Africa 1990–2010: An Assesment'. *Democratization* 18, 2, 2011, pp. 275–310.
McAdam, Doug, Sidney Tarrow and Charles Tilly. *Dynamics of Contention*. Cambridge: Cambridge University Press, 2001.
McFaul, Michael. *Advancing Democracy Abroad*. New York: Rowman & Littlefield, 2010.
Machiavelli, Niccoló. *The Prince*. New York: Penguin, 2005 [1532].
MacIntyre, Andrew. *The Power of Institutions – Political Architecture and Governance*. Ithaca: Cornell University Press, 2003.
McLauchlin, Theodore. 'Loyalty Strategies and Military Defection in Rebellion'. *Comparative Politics* 42, 3, 2010, pp. 333–350.
Maddison, Angus. *The World Economy, Volume II – Historical Statistics*. Paris: OECD, 2006.
Mainwaring, Scott. 'Presidentialism, Multipartism, and Democracy: The Difficult Combination'. *Comparative Political Studies*, 26, 2, 1993, pp. 198–228.
Malesky, Edmund and Paul Schuler. 'The Single-Party Dictator's Dilemma: Information in Elections Without Opposition'. *Legislative Studies Quarterly*, 35, 4, 2011, pp. 491–530.
Manin, Bernard. 'Métamorphoses du Gouvernement Représentatif', in Daniel Pécaud and Bernardo Sorj, eds., *Les Métamorphoses de la Représentation au Brésil et en Europe*. Paris: Éditions du CNRS, 1991.
Mansfield, Edward D. and Jack Snyder. *Electing to Fight: Why Emerging Democracies go to War*. Cambridge, MA: MIT Press, 2007.
Marcus, Richard R. 'The Fate of Madagascar's Democracy: Following the Rule While Eroding the Substance', in Leonardo A. Villalón and Peter VonDoepp, eds., *The Fate of Africa's Democratic Experiments – Elites and Institutions*. Indianapolis, IN: Indiana University Press, 2005.
Mark, James. *The Unfinished Revolution – Making Sense of the Communist Past in Central-Eastern Europe*. New Haven, CT: Yale University Press, 2010.
Marsh, Ian, Jean Blondel and Takashi Inoguchi, eds. *Democracy, Governance, and Economic Performance – East and Southeast Asia*. Tokyo: United Nations University Press, 1999.
Marshall, Monty G. and Benjamin R. Cole. *State Fragility Index and Matrix 2013*. Center for Systemic Peace, University of Maryland, 2013. http://systemicpeace.org/inscr/SFImatrix2013c.pdf.
Marshall, Monty G. and Benjamin R. Cole. *Global Report 2014*. Center for Systemic Peace, University of Maryland, 2014.
Marshall, Thomas Humphrey. *Class, Citizenship and Social Development*. Chicago, IL: University of Chicago Press, 1963.
Marton, Kati. 'Hungary's Authoritarian Descent'. *International New York Times*, 4 November 2014.
Masoud, Tarek. 'Has the Door Closed on Arab Democracy?'. *The Journal of Democracy*, 26, 1, 2015, pp. 74–87.
Mauro, Paulo. 'Corruption and Growth'. *Quarterly Journal of Economics*, 110, 3, 1995, pp. 681–712.

Meitzner, Marcus. 'Political Evolution: Indonesia's Strong Base for Democratic Development'. *East Asia Forum Quarterly* 5, 4, 2013.

Mendelson, Sarah E. and John K. Glenn, eds. *The Power and Limits of NGOs – A Critical Look at Building Democracy in Eastern Europe*. New York: Columbia University Press, 2002.

Meyer, Mary and Jane Booker. *Eliciting and Analyzing Expert Judgment – A Practical Guide*. Society for Industrial and Applied Mathematics, 2001.

Mohamedou, Mohammad-Mahmoud Ould. *Understanding Al Qaeda – Changing War and Global Politics*. London: Pluto Press, 2011.

Mohamedou, Mohammad-Mahmoud Ould. 'Neo-Orientalism and the e-Revolutionary: Self-Representation and the Arab Spring'. *Middle East Law and Governance* 7, 2015, pp. 120–131.

Møller, Jørgen and Sven-Erik Skaaning. 'Regime Types and Democratic Sequencing'. *The Journal of Democracy*, 24, 1, 2013, pp. 142–155.

Moore, Barrington Jr. *Social Origins of Dictatorship and Democracy – Lord and Peasant in the Making of the Modern World*. Boston, MA: Beacon Press, 1966.

Morley, James W., ed. *Driven by Growth – Political Change in the Asia-Pacific Region*. Armonk, New York: M.E. Sharpe, 1999.

Morlino, Leonardo. *Changes for Democracy: Actors, Structures, and Processes*. New York: Oxford University Press, 2011.

Morse, Yonatan L. 'Party Matters: The Institutional Origins of Competitive Hegemony in Tanzania'. *Democratization* 21, 4, 2014, pp. 655–677.

Mozaffar, Shaheen and Richard Vengroff. 'A "Whole System" Approach to the Choice of Electoral Rules in Democratizing Countries: Senegal in Comparative Perspective'. *Electoral Studies* 21, 4, 2002, pp. 601–616.

Mueller, Lisa. 'Democratic Revolutionaries or Pocketbook Protesters? The Roots of the 2009–2010 Uprisings in Niger'. *African Affairs* 112, 448, 2013, pp. 398–420.

Müller, Klaus and Andreas Pickel. 'Transition, Transformation and the Social Sciences: Towards a New Paradigm'. TIPEC Working Paper 1/11, Trent International Political Economy Centre, Peterborough, Ontario, November 2001.

Munck, Gerardo L. and Carol Skalnik Leff. 'Modes of Transition and Democratization: South America and Eastern Europe in Comparative Perspective', in Lisa Anderson, ed., *Transitions to Democracy*. New York: Columbia University Press, 1999, pp. 193–216.

Munck, Gerardo L. and Richard Snyder. 'Debating the Direction of Comparative Politics: An Analysis of Leading Journals'. *Comparative Political Studies* 40, 1, 2007, pp. 5–31.

Murthy, Emma. 'Problematizing Arab Youth: Generational Narratives of Systemic Failure'. *Mediterranean Politics*, 17, 1, 2012, pp. 5–22.

Nada, Youssef (with Douglas Thompson). *Inside The Muslim Brotherhood*. Cairo: El-Shorooq, 2012.

Najŝlová, Lucia. 'Foreign Democracy Assistance in the Czech and Slovak Transitions – What Lessons for the Arab World?'. Fride Working Paper, 18 February 2013.

Nayed, Aref Ali. 'Beyond Fascism: New Libya Actualised'. Dubai: Kalam Research and Media, January 2013.

N'Diaye, Boubacar. 'How Not to Institutionalize Civilian Control: Kenya's Coup Prevention Strategies, 1964–1997'. *Armed Forces and Society* 28, 4, 2002, pp. 619–640.

N'Diaye, Boubacar. 'Francophone Africa and Security Sector Transformation: Plus Ça Change…'. *African Security* 2, 1, 2009, pp. 1–28.

Nordhaus, William D. 'The Political Business Cycle'. *Review of Economic Studies*, 42, 2, 1975, pp. 169–190.

Norris, Pippa. *Driving Democracy – Do Power-sharing Institutions Work?* New York: Cambridge University Press, 2008.
Norris, Pippa. *Why Electoral Integrity Matters.* New York: Cambridge University Press, 2014.
Norris, Pippa and Ronald Inglehart. *Cosmopolitan Communications.* New York: Cambridge University Press, 2009.
Norris, Pippa and Ronald Inglehart. *Sacred and Secular*, second edn. New York: Cambridge University Press, 2011.
Norris, Pippa, Richard W. Frank and Ferran Martinez i Coma. 'Measuring Electoral Integrity: A New Dataset'. *PS Politics and Political Science* 47, 4, 2014, pp. 789–798.
Norris, Pippa, Ferran Martinez i Coma and Richard W. Frank. 'Assessing the Quality of Elections'. *The Journal of Democracy*, 24, 4, 2014, pp. 124–135.
Noyes, Alexander. 'Securing Reform? Power Sharing and Civil-Security Relations in Kenya and Zimbabwe'. *African Studies Quarterly* 13, 4, 2012, pp. 27–52.
O'Donnell, Guillermo. 'Poverty and Inequality in Latin America: Some Political Reflections', in Victor E. Tokman and Guillermo O'Donnell, eds., *Poverty and Inequality in Latin America – Issues and New Challenges*. Notre Dame, IN: University of Notre Dame Press, 1998.
O'Donnell, Guillermo. 'In Partial Defence of an Evanescent "Paradigm"'. *The Journal of Democracy*, 13, 3, 2002, pp. 6–12.
O'Donnell, Guillermo. 'Schmitter's Retrospective: A Few Dissenting Notes'. *The Journal of Democracy* 21, 1, 2010, pp. 29–32.
O'Donnell, Guillermo. *Modernización y Autoritarismo.* Buenos Aires: Prometeo Libros, 2011.
O'Donnell, Guillermo, Philippe C. Schmitter and Laurence Whitehead. *Transitions from Authoritarian Rule – Comparative Perspectives.* Baltimore, MD: John Hopkins University Press, 1986.
Offe, Klaus and Pierre Adler. 'Capitalism by Democratic Design: Democratic Theory Facing the Transition in East Central Europe'. *Social Research* 58, 4, 1991, pp. 865–892.
Olson, David M. 'Democratisation and Political Participation: The Experience of the Czech Republic', in Karen Dawisha and Bruce Parrott, eds., *The Consolidation of Democracy in East-Central Europe*. Cambridge: Cambridge University Press, 1997, pp. 150–196.
O'Neil, Patrick H. 'The Deep State: An Emerging Concept in Comparative Politics'. Social Sciences Research Network, 20 August 2013.
Ost, David. *The Defeat of Solidarity – Anger and Politics in Postcommunist Europe.* Ithaca, New York: Cornell University Press, 2005.
Paris, Roland. *At War's End – Building Peace after Civil Conflict.* New York: Cambridge University Press, 2005.
Peterson, Dave. 'A Beacon for Central Africa'. *The Journal of Democracy* 17, 1, 2006, pp. 125–131.
Pishchikova, Kateryna. *Promoting Democracy in Postcommunist Ukraine – The Contradictory Outcomes of US Aid to Women's NGOs.* Boulder, CO: Lynne Rienner, 2011.
Pishchikova, Kateryna and Lesia Ogryzko. 'Civic Awakening: The Impact of Euromaidan on Ukraine's Politics'. Fride Working Paper 124, July 2014.
Plattner, Marc. 'Is Democracy in Decline?'. *The Journal of Democracy*, 26, 1, 2015, pp. 5-10.

200 References

Pongsudhirak, Thitinan. 'Thailand's Foreign Policy in a Regional Great Game'. IDEAS Report, *The New Geopolitics of Southeast Asia*, London, 2012.

Posner, Daniel. *Institutions and Ethnic Politics in Africa*. Cambridge: Cambridge University Press, 2005.

Powell, Jonathan M. and Clayton L. Thyne. 'Global Instances of Coups from 1950 to 2010: A New Dataset'. *Journal of Peace Research* 48, 2, 2011, pp. 249–259.

Pridham, Geoffrey. *Encouraging Democracy – The International Context of Regime Transition in Southern Europe*. New York: St. Martin's Press, 1991.

Przeworski, Adam. *Democracy and the Market: Political and Economic Reforms in Eastern Europe and Latin America*. Cambridge: Cambridge University Press, 1995.

Przeworski, Adam, ed. *Sustainable Democracy*. Cambridge: Cambridge University Press, 1995.

Przeworski, Adam and F. Limongi. 'Modernization: Theories and Fact'. *World Politics* 49, 2, 1997, pp. 155–183.

Przeworski, Adam, Michael E. Alvarez, José Antonio Cheibub and Fernando Limongi. 'What Makes Democracies Endure?'. *The Journal of Democracy* 7, 1, 1996, pp. 39–55.

Przeworski, Adam, Michael E. Alvarez, Jose Antonio Cheibub and Fernando Limongi. *Democracy and Development – Political Institutions and Well-Being in the World, 1950–1990*. New York: Cambridge University Press, 2000.

Putnam, Robert D., Robert Leonardi and Raffaella Y. Nonetti. *Making Democracy Work – Civic Traditions in Modern Italy*. Princeton, NJ: Princeton University Press, 1993.

Pyzik, Agata. *Poor But Sexy: Culture Clashes in Europe East and West*. Alresford, UK: Zero Books, 2012.

Razumkov Centre. *Ukraine 2015–2016 – The Reform Challenge (Assessment)*. Kiev: Razumkov Centre, 2016.

Reilly, Benjamin. *Democracy and Diversity: Political Engineering in the Asia-Pacific*. Oxford: Oxford University Press, 2006.

Reilly, Benjamin. 'Democratization and Electoral Reform in the Asia-Pacific Region: Is There an "Asian Model" of Democracy?'. *Comparative Political Studies*, 40, 11, 2007, pp. 1350–1371.

Reilly, Benjamin. 'Semi-Presidentialism and Democratic Development in East Asia', in Robert Elgie, Sophia Moestrup and Yu-shan Wu, eds., *Semi-Presidentialism and Democracy*. New York: Palgrave Macmillan, 2011.

Reilly, Benjamin. 'Parties, Electoral Systems and Governance', in Larry Diamond, Marc F. Plattner and Yun-han Chu, eds., *Democracy in East Asia – A New Century*. Baltimore, MD: John Hopkins University Press, 2013.

Reilly, Benjamin. 'Southeast Asia: In the Shadow of China'. *The Journal of Democracy*, 24, 1, 2013, pp. 156–164.

Reszler, André. *Rejoindre l'Europe*. Geneva: Georg, 1991.

Rial, Juan. 'Los Partidos Politicos Uruguayos en el Proceso de Transición hacia la Democracia'. Working Paper 145, Kellogg Institute, University of Notre Dame, 1990.

Rodan, Gary, ed. *Political Oppositions in Industrializing Asia*. London: Routledge, 1996.

Rodrik, Dani, Arvind Subramanian and Francesco Trebbi. 'Institutions Rule: The Primacy of Institutions over Geography and Integration in Economic Development'. *Journal of Economic Growth*, 9, 2, 2004, pp. 131–165.

Roeder, Philip and Donald Rothchild, eds. *Sustainable Peace – Power and Democracy after Civil War*. Ithaca, New York: Cornell University Press, 2005.

Rose-Ackerman, Susan. 'Governance and Corruption', in Bjørn Lomborg, ed., *Global Crises, Global Solutions – Costs and Benefits*. Cambridge: Cambridge University Press, 2004, pp. 301–344.

Ross, Michael L. 'Does Oil Hinder Democracy?'. *World Politics*, 53, 2001, pp. 325–361.

Ross, Michael L. 'How do Natural Resources Influence Civil War? Evidence from Thirteen Cases'. *International Organization* 58, 1, 2004, pp. 35–67.

Ross, Michael L. *The Oil Curse – How Petroleum Wealth Shapes the Development of Nations*. Princeton, NJ: Princeton University Press, 2013.

Rostow, W.W. *The Stages of Economic Growth – A Non-Communist Manifesto*. Cambridge: Cambridge University Press, 1960.

Roy, Olivier. 'There Will Be No Islamist Revolution'. *The Journal of Democracy*, 24, 1, 2013, pp. 14–19.

Rueschemeyer, Dietrich, Evelyne Huber Stephens and John D. Stephens. *Capitalist Development and Democracy*. Chicago, IL: University of Chicago Press, 1992.

Rustow, Dankwart A. 'Transitions to Democracy: Toward a Dynamic Model'. *Comparative Politics* 2, 3, 1970, pp. 337–363.

Sachs, Jeffrey. 'The Transition at Mid-Decade'. *American Economic Review*, 86, 2, 1996, pp. 128–33.

Said, Edward. *Orientalism*. New York: Pantheon, 1978.

Sarotte, Mary Elise. *The Collapse – The Accidental Opening of the Berlin Wall*. New York: Basic Books, 2014.

Savranskaya, Svetlana. *Masterpieces of History – The Peaceful End of the Cold War*. Budapest: Central European University Press, 2010.

Sayigh, Yazid. 'Above the State: The Officers' Republic in Egypt'. Working Paper, Carnegie Endowment for International Peace, August 2012.

Schedler, Andreas. 'What is Democratic Consolidation?'. *The Journal of Democracy* 9, 2, 1998, pp. 91–107.

Schedler, Andreas. 'Taking Uncertainty Seriously: The Blurred Boundaries of Democratic Transition and Consolidation'. *Democratization* 8, 4, 2001, pp. 1–22.

Schlumberger, Oliver, ed. *Debating Arab Authoritarianism – Dynamics and Durability in Nondemocratic Regimes*. Stanford, CA: Stanford University Press, 2007.

Schmitter, Philippe C. 'Interest Intermediation and Regime Governability in Contemporary Western Europe and North America', in Suzanne D. Berger, ed., *Organizing Interests in Western Europe – Pluralism, Corporatism, and the Transformation of Politics*. Cambridge: Cambridge University Press, 1981, pp. 285–327.

Schmitter, Philippe C. 'Speculations about the Prospective Demise of Authoritarian Regimes (I)'. *Revista de Ciência Politica*, 1, 1985, pp. 83–102

Schmitter, Philippe C. 'Speculations about the Prospective Demise of Authoritarian Regimes and its Possible Consequences (II)'. *Revista de Ciência Politica*, 2, 1985, pp. 125–144.

Schmitter, Philippe C. 'Some Propositions about Civil Society and the Consolidation of Democracy'. Reihe Politikwissenschaft, Institut für Höhere Studien, Vienna, September 1993.

Schmitter, Philippe C. 'The International Context, Political Conditionality, and the Consolidation of Neo-democracies', in Laurence Whitehead, ed., *The International Dimensions of Democratization – Europe and the Americas*. Oxford: Oxford University Press, 1996, pp. 27–57.

Seely, Jennifer C. 'The Legacies of Transition Governments: Post-Transition Dynamics in Benin and Togo'. *Democratization* 12, 3, 2005, pp. 357–377.

Seely, Jennifer C. 'The Unexpected Presidential Election in Togo, 2005'. *Electoral Studies* 25, 3, 2006, pp. 611–616.
Seely, Jennifer C. 'Togo's Presidential Election 2010'. *Electoral Studies* 30, 2, 2011, pp. 372–375.
Sen, Amartya. *Development as Freedom*. New York: Anchor Books, 1999.
Shin, Doh Chull. 'On The Third Wave of Democratization: A Synthesis and Evaluation of Recent Theory and research'. *World Politics* 47, 1, 1994, pp. 135–170.
Signé, Landry. 'The Tortuous Trajectories of Democracy and the Persistence of Authoritarianism in Africa'. CDDRL Working Paper, Center on Democracy, Development and the Rule of Law, Stanford University, 2013.
Siklova, Jirina and Kaca Polackova Henley. 'The Solidarity of the Culpable'. *Social Research* 58, 4, 1991, pp. 765–773.
Simon, Jeffrey. *Poland and NATO – A Study in Civil-Military Relations*. Lanham, MD: Rowman & Littlefield, 2003.
Singh. Naunihal. *Seizing Power: The Strategic Logic of Military Coups*. Baltimore, MD: John Hopkins University Press, 2014.
Sisk, Timothy D. *Democratization in South Africa – The Elusive Social Contract*. Princeton, NJ: Princeton University Press, 1995.
Slater, Dan. 'The Architecture of Authoritarianism: Southeast Asia and the Regeneration of Democratization Theory'. *Taiwan Journal of Democracy* 2, 2, 2006, pp. 1–22.
Slater, Dan and Joseph Wong. 'The Strength to Concede: Ruling Parties and Democratization in Developmental Asia'. *Perspectives on Politics*, 11, 3, 2013, pp. 717–733.
Slovik, M.W. *The Politics of Authoritarian Rule* New York: Cambridge University Press, 2013.
Snyder, Jack. *From Voting to Violence – Democratization and Nationalist Conflict*. New York: W.W. Norton, 2000.
Snyder, Richard. 'Explaining Transitions from Neopatrimonial Dictatorships'. *Comparative politics* 24, 4, 1992, pp. 379–399.
Snyder, Richard. 'Does Lootable Wealth Breed Disorder? A Political Economy of Extraction Framework'. *Comparative Political Studies*, 39, 8, 2006, pp. 943–968.
Spencer, Claire, Jane Kinninmont and Omar Sirri, eds. 'Iraq: Ten Years On'. Chatham House Programme Report, Royal Institute of International Affairs, London, May 2013.
Steenbergen, Marco R. and Gary Marks. 'Evaluating Expert Judgments'. *European Journal of Political Research*. 46, 3, 2007, pp. 347–366.
Stepan, Alfred and Juan J. Linz. 'Democratisation Theory and the "Arab Spring"'. *The Journal of Democracy* 24, 2, 2013, pp. 15–30.
Stepan, Alfred and Graeme B. Robertson. 'An "Arab" More Than a "Muslim" Electoral Gap'. *The Journal of Democracy*, 14, 3, 2003. pp. 30–44.
Stoner, Kathryn and Michael McFaul, eds. *Transitions to Democracy – A Comparative Perspective*. Baltimore, MD: John Hopkins University Press, 2013.
Tavares, María Conceicao. 'El Desarrollo Industrial Latinoamericano y la Presente Crisis del Transnacionalismo: Algunos Interrogantes'. *El Trimestre Económico* 42, 168, 1975, pp. 933–956.
Taylor, Robert H., ed. *The Politics of Elections in Southeast Asia*. Cambridge, UK and New York: Cambridge University Press and Woodrow Wilson Center, 1996.
Teorell, Jan. *Determinants of Democratization – Explaining Regime Change in the World, 1972–2006*. New York: Cambridge University Press, 2003.

Thiriot, Céline. 'La Place des Militaires dans Les Régimes Post-transition d'Afrique Subsaharienne: La Difficile Resectorisation'. *Revue Internationale de Politique Comparée* 15, 1, 2008, pp. 15–34.
Thyne, Clayton L. and Jonathan M. Powell. 'Coup d'Etat or Coup d'Autocracy?: How Coups Impact Democratization, 1950–2008'. *Foreign Policy Analysis* 0, 2014, pp. 1–22.
Tilly, Charles. *Social Movements – 1768–2004*. Boulder, CO: Paradigm Publishers, 2004.
Todorov, Tzvetan. *Les Ennemis Intimes de la Démocratie*. Paris: Robert Laffont, 2012.
Toft, Monica. *Securing the Peace – The Durable Settlement of Civil Wars*. Princeton, NJ: Princeton University Press, 2010.
Tripp, Aili Mari. 'The Changing Face of Authoritarianism in Africa: The Case of Uganda'. *Africa Today* 50, 3, 2004, pp. 3–26.
United Nations. 'Uniting our Strengths for Peace, Politics, Partnerships and People'. Report of the High-Level Independent Panel on United Nations Peace Operations, United Nations, New York, 16 June 2015. www.un.org/sg/pdf/HIPPO_Report_1_June_2015.pdf.
United Nations. 'The Challenge of Sustaining Peace'. Report of the Advisory Group of Experts on the 2015 Review of the United Nations Peacebuilding Architecture, United Nations, New York, 29 June 2015.
UNDP. 'Deepening Democracy in a Fragmented World'. Human Development Report 2002, United Nations Development Programme, New York, 2002.
UNDP. 'The Political Economy of Transitions – Analysis for Change'. Paper for discussion at UNDP-NOREF Conference, Oslo, 8–9 November 2012. www.undp.org/content/dam/undp/library/Democratic%20Governance/OGC/The-Political-Economy-of-Transitions-Analysis-for-Change.pdf.
UNDP. 'The Rise of the South: Human Progress in a Diverse World'. Human Development Report 2013, United Nations Development Programme, New York, 2013.
Uvin, Peter. 'Ethnicity and Power in Burundi and Rwanda: Different Paths to Mass Violence'. *Comparative Politics* 31, 3, 1999, pp. 253–271.
Vanhanen, Tatu. *Prospects for Democracy – A Study of 172 Countries*. New York: Routledge, 1997.
Villalón, Leonardo A. and Abdourahmane Idrissa. 'Repetitive Breakdowns and a Decade of Experimentations: Institutional Choices and Unstable Democracy in Niger', in Villalón and VonDoepp, eds., *The Fate of Africa's Democratic* Experiments, pp. 43–46.
Villalón, Leonardo A. and Peter VonDoepp, eds. *The Fate of Africa's Democratic Experiments – Elites and Institutions*. Indianapolis, IN: Indiana University Press, 2005.
Walle, Nicolas van de. 'Tipping Games: When Do Opposition Parties Coalesce?', in Andreas Schedler, ed., *Electoral Authoritarianism: The Dynamics of Unfree Competition*. London: Lynne Rienner, 2006, pp. 77–94.
Way, Lucan. *Pluralism by Default*. Baltimore, MD: John Hopkins University Press, 2015.
Wedel, Janine R. *Collision and Collusion – The Strange Case of Western Aid to Eastern Europe*. New York: St. Martin's Press, 1998.
Welch, Claude E. *No Farewell to Arms?: Military Disengagement from Politics in Africa and Latin America*. Boulder, CO: Westview Press, 1987.
Whitehouse, Bruce. 'What Went Wrong in Mali?'. *The London Review of Books* 34, 16, August 2012, pp. 17–18.
Wickham, Carrie R. *The Muslim Brotherhood*, Princeton, NJ: Princeton University Press, 2013.
Wigell, Mikael. 'Mapping "Hybrid Regimes": Regime Types and Concepts in Comparative Politics'. *Democratisation*, 15, 2, 2008, pp. 230–250.

Wood, Elisabeth Jean. *Forging Democracy from Below: Insurgent Transitions in South Africa and El Salvador*. New York: Cambridge University Press, 2000.

Wood, Elisabeth Jean. 'An Insurgent Path to Democracy: Popular Mobilisation, Economic Interests and Regime Transition in South Africa and El Salvador'. *Comparative Political Studies* 34, 8, 2001, pp. 862–888.

Young, Eric T. 'Chefs and Worried Soldiers: Authority and Power in the Zimbabwe National Army'. *Armed Forces & Society*, 24, 1, 1997, pp. 133–149.

Zakaria, Fareed. 'The Rise of Illiberal Democracy'. *Foreign Affairs*, 76, 6, 1997, pp. 22–43.

Zaum, Dominik. 'Beyond the "Liberal Peace"'. *Global Governance*, 18, 1, 2012, pp. 121–132.

Zuercher, Christoph, Nora Roehner and Sarah Riese. 'External Democracy Promotion in Post-Conflict Zones: A Comparative-Analytical Framework'. *Taiwan Journal of Democracy* 5, 1, 2009, pp. 241–259.

Zurcher, Christoph, Carrie Manning, Kristie D. Evenson, Rachel Hayman, Sarah Riese and Nora Roehner. *Costly Democracy – Peacebuilding and Democratization after War*. Stanford, CA: Stanford University Press, 2013.

Index

9/11 terrorist attacks 13, 18

Abacha, Sani 117
Abdullah, Abdullah 50
accountability 21, 32, 37, 40, 150–1, 165n13
Accra Comprehensive Peace Agreement 126
Aceh 92n28
advocacy xviii
Afghanistan 19, 49–50, 69, 104
Africa, African 7–8, 17–18, 20, 53, 110, 113–34, 165n7, 172, 174, 175, 184n15
African National Congress (South Africa) 127
African National Union (Zimbabwe) 116
African Union (AU) 181
Agboyibo, Yaowi 126
agency 45
aid 49
Al Azhar University 154, 156
Al Ikhwan 146
Al Mahdhoura 157
Al muhajireen wal Ansar 153
Al Nahda, party (Tunisia) 145, 163
Al Nahda, programme (Egypt) 157
Al Qaeda 152
Al Qaeda in Yemen 145
Al Shater, Khairat 154, 159
Albania 99
Alesina, Alberto 67
Algeria 16
All People's Congress (Sierra Leone) 125
Alliance of Young Democrats (Hungary) 96
Alvarez, Michael 51
America *see* United States
Americas 13, 25
amnesty, law 36, 122, 176

Amsterdam 110
anarchy 137
ancien régime 19, 21, 85, 100, 149, 155, 157, 161–2, 168, 176–7, 181
Anderson, Lisa 28n34
Angola 12, 59, 114, 126, 128–9
Angolan Union for Total Independence (UNITA) 129
anocracy 12–13, 113, 122, 134n104
Antananarivo 122
anti-racism 176
apartheid 14–15, 122
Arab Awakening 10n4
Arab Human Development Report 8, 14
Arab League *see* League of Arab States
Arab nationalism 8
Arab revolutions 10n4
Arab Spring 1–3, 6, 13–15, 17, 25, 39, 93, 144–66
Arab states 68, 71
Arab Strategy Forum 147
Arab street 146–8
Arab Uprisings 10n4
Arab world 16–17, 144–66
Arabellions 3
Arabists 17
Argentina, Argentine 13, 56, 136–40
Aristotle 9, 168
Army, armed forces *see* military
Arusha Accords 126, 129
'ashwiyaat 153
Asia, Asian 7, 25, 75–91, 106, 165n7; 172, 174–5, 184n15
Asia-Pacific 7, 75–91
Asian model 7, 79, 82
Asian Tigers 75
Assad, Bashar Al 146–7
Assad, Hafez Al 147
assistance 49

206 Index

Association Agreement with the European Union (Ukraine) 33, 36
Association of Southeast Asian Nations (ASEAN) 181
Atak (Bulgaria) 105
Australia 68, 90
Austria 56, 98, 101
authoritarianism: backtracking 110; bargain 163; bureaucratic 13, 138, 139–40; collapse 2, competitive 18; control 46; descent 107; durability 9, 116, 144, 162; dynamics 37, 137; electoral 31; fragility 9, 162; hegemonic 31, 113; hybrid 160; impact 17; kleptocratic 81; liberalised 44, 136; neo- 19; neo-patrimonial 2; nostalgia 163; oligarchic 81; outcome 30; patrimonial 81; quasi- 88; reconstitution 40; regime 79, 160, 170; regression to 8, 135; resilience 132n23, 144, 162; return 40, 77, 130; reversal 1, 130; robustness 67, 162; rule 49, 76, 144, 157; semi- 18; stability 163; strength 162; structure 140; upgraded, upgrading 37, 160
autocracy, autocrats 1–3, 5–7, 12, 18, 37, 41, 44, 46, 49–52, 72, 76, 85, 118, 120, 122, 160, 167–70, 177, 181–2, 184
Avenue Bourguiba 144
Azerbaijan 67

Ba'ath 17
Bahrain 2, 61, 146
Balai Citoyen (Burkina Faso) 28n49, 128
Balkans 102
Banda, Hastings Kamuzu 118, 120
Banegas, Richard 28n34
Bangkok 82–3
Bangladesh 54, 66
Banna, Hassan Al 154
Barisan Nasional coalition 84–5
Barkan, Joel D
Bastille, La 25
BBC (British Broadcasting Corporation) 93
Bédié, Henri Konan 115
Beijing 14
Ben Ali, Zine Abidine 146–7, 153, 160, 162–3
Benin 114, 116, 118–19, 122–3, 126–7, 133n37
Berlin 94
Berlin Wall 93–4, 99, 144
Berman, Sheri 28n34

Beti 121
beton (Poland) 95
Bhutan 57, 59
Bielous, Silvia Dutrenit 140
Birch, Sarah 53, 55, 59
Biya, Paul 117, 121
blandos 136–7, 141
Bohemia 101
Boix, Carles 28n34
Bolchevik Party (Soviet Union) 95
Bosnia-Herzegovina 67
Botswana 114–15, 124, 131, 132n1
Botswana Democratic Party 115
Bouazizi, Mohamed 17, 146, 148
Bourgeois Gentilhomme, le 167
Bourgeoisie 140, 182
Bourguiba, Habib 163
boycott 156
Bratislava 98
Bratton, Michael 114, 118, 121
Brazil, Brazilian 13, 96, 139–40
breakthrough paradigm 25
Britain, British 52, 68–9
British Isles 67
Brown, Stephen 124
Brunei 86, 88
Brussels 109
Budapest 98
Bulgaria 93, 96, 99–109
Bulgarian Communist Party 96, 99
Bulgarian Socialist Party 97
Bunce, Valerie 28n34
Burkina Faso 28n49, 114, 118, 128, 132n7
Burma 75–8, 80, 83–4, 86, 88, 90–1
Burton, Michael 21
Burundi 69, 114, 116, 119, 125–6, 129, 132n7
Bush, George W. 16
Buyoya, Pierre 119

ça suffit (Chad) 28n49
Cairo 38, 144, 165n7
Camara, Moussa Dadis 121, 130
Cambodia 56, 69, 77–8, 89
Cambodian's People Party 78–9
Cameroon 114, 117, 120–1
Canada 68–9
Cape Verde 114, 126
capital capitalism, capitalist production 7, 51, 72, 82, 97, 102–3, 107, 168, 170, 178, 182
Carothers, Thomas 28n34, 124, 142n1
Catholic Church 95, 145
Catholics 64, 67

Index 207

Central African Republic 69, 125, 128
Central Europe 7, 99, 107
Centre for Systemic Peace 70
Chad, Chadian 28n49
Chama Cha Mapinduzi (Tanzania) 115–17, 124, 131
Chauvet, Lisa 56
Chechnya 67
Cheibub, José Antonio 51
Chile, Chilean 13, 56, 138–41
China, Chinese 7, 14, 75–6, 78, 80, 88–91, 173
Christian Democratic Party (Chile) 141
Christian Democratic Union (GDR) 110n10
Christmas 85
civic activism 32, 37, 40–2, 45, 58
civic culture 182
civic organisation 37
civic resistance, disobedience 15, 81, 113, 115
civil liberties 7, 92n32
civil service 132n14
civil society 4, 15–16, 24, 28n49, 32, 34, 37, 72, 73n5, 79–80, 96, 114, 121, 124, 126, 136–8, 141, 152, 176, 179–81
civil war 1, 17–18, 125–6, 128, 161, 181
civil-military relations 120
citizens, citizenry 6, 8, 15, 31, 50
citizenship 39
Clague, Christopher 68
Clash of Civilisations 68
clientelism 61
coalition 5, 20, 33–4, 36, 115–17, 126, 130, 161–2
coercion 139, 170
Cold War 6–8, 13–14, 18, 31, 44, 69, 77, 99, 144, 175
Collier, Paul 56
Collier, Ruth Berins 28n34
Colorado Party (Paraguay) 142
colonialism, colonial legacy 13, 52, 54, 64–5, 68–9, 72, 77, 109, 119
Colour Revolutions (East Europe) 15
Comité de Transition pour le Salut du Peuple (Mali) 130
Communism/communist; post-communist/post-communism 7–8, 78, 80, 90, 93, 95–7, 99–110, 148, 168
Communist Party of Bohemia and Moravia 96
Communist Party (China) 14
Communist Party (Czech Republic)
Communist Party (Romania) 96

Comoros, Islands of 114, 128
Compaoré, Blaise 28n49, 118, 128
Comparative Politics 21
Conférence nationale des forces vives (Benin) 126
Conde, Alpha 121
conditionality, economic 124, 180
conflict 5, 16, 19, 23–4, 36, 43, 49–50, 70, 146, 168
conflict-management 3, 116
Congo, Republic of 114, 132n18
Congo, Democratic Republic of 56, 59, 69, 114, 134n92
Congo-Brazzaville 126
Congress for Democracy and Progress (Burkina Faso) 128
Conseil National de Transition (Mali) 130
consent 138–9, 171, 182
consolidation 1, 16, 45, 52, 72, 79
consolidologist 167–84
consolidology 9, 167–84
constituent assembly 22, 156
constitution 3, 5, 3, 17, 22, 29, 33, 38–9, 41, 82, 84, 121, 126, 128, 144, 156
Constitutional Declaration (Egypt) 155
Conte, Lansana 121
contestation 68, 135
Copenhagen criteria 105
corporatism 18, 176–7
corruption 31, 34–6, 50, 53–5, 59, 61–2, 78, 82, 108, 150–1, 157, 162, 165n13
Côte d'Ivoire 19
Council of Europe 103, 105
coup 38–9, 42, 44, 83, 116, 118–21, 129–31, 134n108, 139–40
court 49, 72
Crimea 53–4
Croatia 54, 69, 108
Cuba 181
Czech Bohemia
Czech Republic 2, 72, 96, 98–9, 102–8, 184n16
Czechoslovak People's Party 111n10
Czechoslovakia 1, 93–4, 96–8, 100–2, 110, 184n16

Dacia 106
Dae'sh 145, 152
Dahl, Robert 28n34; 53
Dahrendorf, Ralf 100
Déby, Idriss 28n49
decentralisation 82
decolonisation 13, 53, 69, 77, 94, 174
deep society 9

deep state 9, 25, 28n45, 38, 41–2, 145
dégage (Tunisia) 7
democracy, democratic: achievement 157; activism 44; aid; assistance; breakdown; breakthrough 6, 37, 44–5; building 161; challenge 90, 142; commitment 41, 182; competitive 86; components 78; compromise, concept 18; consecration 183; consolidation 1–2, 5, 31, 53, 87, 163, 168–70, 172–3, 178–9; constitutional 183; contestation 183; criticism, culture, deconsolidation 170; degree 46; delayed, demand 17; demise, development 69, 88, 142; diversity 171; economic development 75, 181; electoral 8, 55, 76, 88, 92n32, 113; emerging 87; erosion 77; façade 18; flourishing 53; foreign-led 129; fully-institutionalised 12; geography 88; guided 77; habituation 170; history 65, 72; hybrid 163; ideals 183; illiberal 18; inclusive 1, 3; instant 4; Islam and 145; legitimacy, legitimation 23, 173; liberal 31, 92n32, 100, 182; limited 136; maintenance 143; measurement 160; necessity, newly-existing 169, 172–6, 178, 181; non-inevitability 170; norms 47n37, 109; opening 13, 137; order, outcome 170; patterns 68; people's 95, 102; political 79, 175, 183; probability 52; process 2, 51, 67, 91, 121, 126; promotion 124, 180; prospects 100; quality 4; quasi- 78; real-existing 169, 172–6; realisation 20; reform 40, 79; regime 160, 163, 167; representative 45, 183; reversal 132n2; revocability 170; roadmap 26; routine 108; rule 9, 85, 169; secularism and 144–5; semi- 78, 83; stability 168; stages 136; stories 131; support 36, 47n35; sustainable 20; theory 79: transnational, triumph 183; type 172; uncertainty 137; unconsolidated 171; unstable, values 68, 163; wave 3, 15, 126, 179; wealth and 51;Western-capitalist 173; Western-style 163; worldwide 1
democradura 136, 170, 184n15
Democratic Farmers' Party (GDR) 110n10
Democratic Justice Party (Korea) 81
Democratic Party (Poland) 95, 110n10
Democratic Progressive Party (Taiwan) 81
Democratic Progressive party (Malawi) 117

democratisation: choice; commitment 23, 38; country-specific 1; culture 24, 70; delayed 179
demonstrators *see* protest, protestors
desencanto 182
developing nations 53
development 21, 51–3, 63, 66, 68, 139
developmental studies 50
Di Palma, Giuseppe 28n34
Diamond, Larry 28n34, 31, 142
dictablanda 136, 170
dictator, dictatorship 4, 100, 117, 136, 138, 141
din 152
Diouf, Abdou 123
diplomacy 180
Diretas ja 138
dirigisme 40
discontent 49, 146, 161
discourse 174; electoral/electorally-led 55, 79, 84, 90; failed 41; from authoritarian rule 1; geopolitical implications 146; incremental 36–7; indicators 51; literature 18, 30, 75, 144; middle class 80; misuse 16; outcome 136, 177; pacted 90; paradigm 149; probabilities 53; process 3, 5, 7, 20, 49–50, 63, 71, 113, 117–18, 121, 125, 134n72, 136, 147, 172; road map 26; roots 31; security 53; sequencing 32; smooth 160; stages 72, 135–8; steps 52; stock 70; studies 75; substantive 79; successful 8, 45, 114; template 29; theory 6, 15, 25, 32, 50; unrepeatability 174; wave 5, 8, 113, 120, 170
disempowerment 147
disenchantment 110, 162, 182
disillusionment 152, 157, 161, 182
disorder 17
Djibouti 56–7, 59, 114
Dnipropetrovsk 47n35
Donbas 30, 35–6, 44
donors 124
Doo-Hwan, Chun 81
Doré, Jean-Marie 130
Dubai 147
Dunya 152
duros 136–7

East Asia 7, 85–8
East Berlin 98
East Central Europe, East Central European 93–5, 97–110
East German Christian Democratic Union

East Germans 93, 96–8
East Germany *see* German Democratic Republic
East Timor, East-Timorese 76–8, 83, 86
Easterly, William 66
Eastern Europe 7, 17, 20, 68, 77, 79, 107, 160, 167, 172–3, 175, 178–80
Economic Intelligence Unit 56
education 14, 50, 55, 58, 163
égalité 23
Egypt 1–4, 6, 29–30, 32, 37–46, 47n37, 78, 145–65
El Salvador 14, 69, 170
El Shater, Kheirat
election, electoral; accountability 54, 62; administration 55; competitive 70, 78, 84, 136, 176; contentious 7, 15, 49; democratic 25; failed 50, 52–3; fair 129, 176; flawed 53, 84; foreign-backed 125; founding 14; fraud 19; fraudulent 49; free 31, 85, 93, 108, 130, 136; honest 180; institutionalisation 32; integrity 50, 53–4, 57, 66–7, 70, 72; legitimacy 137; legislative 93; malpractice 53, 55, 59; manipulation 127; models 54; moment 18; multi-party 49, 53, 113, 115, 122, 124, 132n1; parliamentary 19, 35, 40, 53, 155, 161; participation, participatory 88, 140; plurality 86; practices 141; premature 70; presidential 81–2, 161; process 3, 19, 51, 69, 78, 177–8; quality 7, 50, 55, 59, 61–3, 66, 70–2, 123; regular 85; repeated 84; rule 86, 125; semi-competitive 37; sequencing 7, 24, 67, 72; standards 55; successful 50, 52; supervision 180; system 79; transitional 49–50; transparency 124; uncertainty 88; uncontested 136; violence 25
electorate 158
El Fetouh, Abdel-Moneim Abu 154
electoral commission 123, 134n72
Electoral Integrity Project 55
elite; agency 32; agreement 125; civil, civilian 130–1; contingency 22; decision 25; defection 117, 131; domination 78; economic 139; fragmentation 156; group 137; incumbent 5, 22, 79, 114, 132n19; insulated 178; leadership 21, 41; motivation 19, 25; new 82; opening 76; opposition 80; pact 3, 32, 45, 75, 95; patronage 49; political 37, 116, 155, 160; popular 178; process 15; recruitment; role 121; ruling 50, 59, 114–17, 140; empowerment 23

end of history 183
Entelis, John 28n34
environmentalism 176
Equatorial Guinea 57–9, 72, 114
Erhard, Ludwig 101
Eritrea 114, 124
Essebsi, Beji Caid 163
Estado Novo (Portugal) 12
Estrada, Joseph 81
Ethiopia 114, 123–4
ethnicity 52, 63, 66–7, 72, 77, 116–17, 120, 133n55, 169, 176, 184n15
Euromaidan 25, 33–7, 43–4, 47n29
Europe, European 25, 39, 68, 75, 91, 100–3, 106
European Charter for Regional or Minority Languages 105
European Commission 106
European Common Market 106
European Community 101
European Council 107
European Neighbourhood Policy 47n37
European Parliament 53
European Union (EU) 8, 33, 36, 43, 47n37, 53–4, 68, 101, 104–10, 173, 180
Eyadéma, Faure 116, 119, 126
Eyadéma, Gnassingbé 116, 119

Facebook 152, 159
failed state *see* state
Falklands, War 136
fascism 98
Federal Republic of Germany *see* German Federal Republic
felool 156
feminism 176
feudalism 49
Fiat 87
Fidesz (Hungary) 96, 105
Fifth Republic (Korea)
First World War *see* World War I
Fish, Steven M. 28n34
Florida 72
fortuna 167
Fourth Wave 181–2
fractionalisation *64*, 67
Fragile/Failed State Index 147–8, 164n5
Framework Convention for the Protection of National Minorities 105
France, French 4, 68, 100, 108, 144
fraud 81
Freedom and Justice Party (Egypt) 38, 155, 159
Freedom House 56, 70, 76, 88, 92n32

FRELIMO (Mozambique) 134n104
Furet, François 100

Gabon 114, 122
Gaddafi, Muammar 16
gam'iyya 153
Gbagbo, Laurent 125–6
GDP, per capita 56–9, 62, 71, 73, 102, 107, 147
Geddes, Barbara 28n34
Gender Inequality Index 50
Georgia 15, 69, 104
German Federal Republic (GFR) 93, 98, 101
German Democratic Republic (GDR) 93, 98, 110n10
German Question 98
German reunification 99
Germany, Germans 13, 95, 98, 100, 104–9
gerrymandering 84, 85
Ghana 114, 116, 123, 127–8
Ghoneim, Wael 152
Global Peace Index 147–8, 165n6
Global Political Accord (Togo) 126
Global South 109
globalisation 6, 13–14
Golkar (Indonesia) 87
Google 152
Gorbachev, Mikhail 94, 97–8
Gorbachev Factor 94
Gorbachevism 94
governance, governability 10n1, 15, 17, 53, 76, 79, 82, 146, 148, 156, 158, 161–3, 174
Gramsci, Antonio 137
Greece 108
grievances 136, 164n5
Group Representation Constituency (Singapore) 86–7
Guatemala 54, 170
guerrilla 140
Guidance Council/Office (Muslim Brotherhood) 154, 159
Guinea 2, 114–15, 121, 126, 130
Guinea-Bissau 114
Guinea Equatorial 57, 114
gumluka 147, 162

Habibie, B.J. 82–3
Habsburg 99
Haggard, Steven 28n34
Haiti 181
Hankis, Elémer 167
Havel, Vaclav 98, 102, 110
Held, David 28n34

Helsinki Charter 14
Hermet, Guy 28n34
Higley, John 21
Hindu monarchy 22
Hollande, François 4
Holocaust 109
human development 52–3, 55, 164n4
human rights 40, 49, 72, 78, 103, 137, 163, 164n5, 176, 180
Hungarian Civic Alliance 96
Hungarian Communist Party 97
Hungarian Socialist Workers' Party 96
Hungary, Hungarian 93–4, 96–8, 101–5, 107, 110, 167
Huntington, Samuel P. 23, 28n34, 68
Hussein, Saddam 13, 17
Hutu 119, 129
hybridity 37, 42–3, 46

Ibrahim, Saad Eddin 154
identity 9, 32, 36, 40, 54, 140, 161
illiberalism 39, 42
Import Substitution Industrialisation (ISI) 138–9
impunity 34
incivility 43
inclusion, inclusivity, inclusiveness 14, 20, 130
Independent Election Commission (Afghanistan) 50
India 54, 66, 68, 77, 90
Indonesia, Indonesian 13, 54, 69, 76–8, 80, 82–3, 85–9
industrialisation 55
inequality 53, 142, 163
Institute for Good Government 55
institution/s 9, 17, 19, 37, 49, 51–3, 69, 72, 76, 85, 100, 115, 123, 128, 140, 152, 168, 172–4, 177, 180
internally-displaced persons (IDPs) 161, 164n5
international assistance 25
International Bank for Reconstruction and Development (IRBD) 180
international community 40, 42, 53, 69, 124–5, 128–30, 179
International Monetary Fund (IMF) 107, 180
International Political Science Association 55
Internet 93, 152
intervention: foreign 161; humanitarian 14; international 78; military 4, 95, 121
Iran, Iranian 173

Iraq 13, 16–17, 19, 58, 70
irhal 27, 146
Islam, Islamic 77, 109, 144–5, 157–8, 173
Islamic State (IS), organisation of the 19
Islamist/s 41, 44, 145–7, 149, 152–9, 162
Ismaillia 156
Israel 47n37
Issoufou, Mahamadou 11
Italy 68, 183n5
Ivory Coast 114–16, 120, 125–6, 128

Jakarta 82
Jamaica 54
Japan 13, 77, 87–8
Jennings, Ray Salvatore 25
jihadists 40
Jobbik (Hungary) 105
Jordan 146–7
Journal of Democracy 18
Jowitt, Ken 28n34
judiciary 141
Jung, Kim Dae 77

Ka, Djibo 123
Kabyès 121
Kagamé, Paul 19
Kalenji 120
karama 23
Karl, Terry Lynn 79, 172
Karzai, Hamid 19
Kaufman, Robert 28n34
Kaunda, Kenneth 119, 122
Kenya 114–17, 120, 122, 126, 128
Kenya African National Union 115, 117, 128
Kenyatta, Uhuru 117
Kérékou, Mathieu 116, 119–20, 122–3
Khamaseen 164n1
Khartoum 19
Khatib, Lina 149, 152
Klaus, Vaclav 103
kleptocracy 62
Konaté, Sekouba 121, 130
Korea 75–7, 81, 83, 87–8, 90
Kosovo 104, 181
Kosovo war 104
kuffar 158
Kuomintang 81
Kuwait, Kuwaiti 57–9, 72
Kyi, Suu 85
Kyiv 36
Kyrgyzstan 15
Kyrovohrad 47n35

Labour union 51, 71
Laos 78, 89–90
Latin America, Latin American 7, 8, 15, 17, 20, 30, 32, 75, 79–80, 86, 91, 135–43, 145, 160, 165n7, 172, 175, 181
Law and Justice Party (Poland) 105, 108
leadership 5, 36, 118, 154, 183
League of Arab States 181
Lee, Terrence 85
Left Social Revolutionaries (Soviet Union) 95
legitimacy 43, 51, 67, 81–2, 100, 127, 155–6
Leninism (Vladimir Lenin) 90, 100
Lesotho 114
Levant, the 25
Levine, Ross 66
Levitsky, Steven 28n34
liberal, liberalism 40, 42, 96, 149, 175
Liberal Democratic Party (GDR) 110n10
Liberal Democratic Party (Kenya) 117
Liberal Party (Paraguay) 141
liberalisation *see* political liberalisation
liberation theology 145
Liberia 69, 114, 124–6, 128, 131
Libya 1–3, 14, 16–17, 22, 24, 145–65
Lijphart, Arend 28n34
Limongi, Fernando 51
Linz, Juan J. 16, 28n34, 86, 95
Lipset, Seymour Martin 14, 28n34, 31, 50–1, 55, 57, 68, 71, 72n5, 88
literacy 50–1, 71, 88
Lithuania 56, 72, 108
London 110

Macedonia 181
McClintock, Cynthia 28n34
McFaul, Michael 28n34
Machiavelli, Niccoló 167
Madagascar 114, 118, 120, 122, 123, 126
Maghreb 25
Maidan *see* Euromaidan
Mainassara, Ibrahim Baré 130
malapportionment 85
Malawi 118, 120, 123, 131
Malaysia 51, 77, 80, 83–5, 88, 90, 184n15
Malaysian Model 85
Maldives 2
Mali 4, 57, 116–20, 123, 126, 129, 131, 133n39, 134n108
Malvinas, War 136
Marcos, Ferdinand 14, 77, 81
Marshall, Thomas Humphrey 136
Marshall Plan 103

Marxism, Marxist 96, 100
Marxism-Leninism 100
Mashreq 152
mass media 50, 55, 70, 75, 84, 100, 152
mass mobilisation 3, 32, 98, 130, 139, 146, 152, 176
Mauritania 119, 130
Mazière, Lothar de 110n10
Mecca 145
Mediator 125
Mekki, Ahmed 159
middle class 51
Middle East 2, 4–5, 9, 10n4, 14, 16–17, 20, 25, 52, 64, 67, 144–66
military 13, 22, 29, 38, 41, 43, 53, 77–8, 82–3, 85, 113, 116, 118–20, 129, 138–9, 145, 161, 176, 179
militia 154, 161
Mills, John Atta 116, 134n73
Ming dynasty 89
minority rights 7, 39, 79, 178
Mitchell, Richard 153
mobilisation 1, 18–19, 35, 45, 121, 123, 136–8, 140, 145, 149, 153, 155, 158, 164n1, 181
modernisation 14, 21, 50–2, 55, 57–8, 70, 83, 89
modernity 20
Moi, Daniel Arap 115–16, 120, 122
Molière 167
monarchy 86
Mongolia 76–7, 86–8
monism 176–7
Monsieur Jourdan 167
Montenegro 53
Moore, Barrington Jr. 27n14, 28n34, 80
Morcos, Samir 159
Morocco 3, 146–7
Morsi, Mohamed 38–9, 41–2, 155, 157, 159, 161
Moscow 94, 98
mosque 145, 153, 157, 159, 161
Movement for Multiparty Democracy (Zambia) 122
Mozambique 12, 69, 114, 119, 128, 134n104
Mubarak, Hosni 4, 29, 37–8, 42–3, 72, 146–7, 153, 159, 160, 162, 164
Mubarakism 38
Mueller, John 28n34
Mugabe, Robert 116, 119
Müller, Klaus 20
multipartism 86
municipalism 176

Museveni, Yoweri 123, 128
Muslim Brotherhood 29, 37–41, 43, 44, 145–6, 152–9, 163
Muslim religion, world 64, 68, 71, 76, 78, 144–66
Myanmar 1, 20, 76, 85
Mykolaiyv 47n35

nadwas 155
Nagy, Imre 96
Namibia 113–14, 124, 126–8, 131
National Alliance Rainbow Coalition (Kenya) 117
national conference 17, 126–7
National Congress Party (Sudan) 19
National Council for the Defence of Democracy (Burundi) 119
National Defence and Security Council (Ukraine) 34
National Democratic Congress (Ghana) 123, 127
National Democratic Party (GDR) 110n10
national identity 178
national interest 139, 180
National League for Democracy (Myanmar) 76, 84–5, 87
National Party (Chile) 142
National Party (South Africa)
national question 179
National Salvation Front (Bulgaria) 99
National Salvation Front (Egypt) 39
national unity 21–2
nationalism 8, 105–6
NATO (North Atlantic Treaty Organization) 16, 98–9, 103–5
natural resources 71–2
negotiated exit 137
neo-conservatives (United States) 16
neo-czarism 173
neo-democracies, neo-democrats 177, 182
neo-liberalism 101, 142
neo-Orientalism 17
neo-patrimonialism 114, 119
Nepal 2, 22, 57, 69
nepotism 122
Netherlands, the 56
New Patriotic Party (Ghana) 123, 127
New Order (Indonesia) 13
New Zealand 90
news media *see* mass media
Niamey 127
Niasse, Moustapha 123
Nicaragua 14
Niger 118–20, 123, 126–7, 130

Index

Nigeria 54, 117, 119, 122, 128, 184n15
Niyombare, Godefroy 119
Nkurunziza, Pierre 119, 129
Nobel Prize 4
nomenklatura 97
non-violence 182
Nordic states 68
North Africa 2, 4–5, 9, 10n4; 14, 16–17, 20, 25, 67, 144–66
North America 173
North Korea 75, 90
Northeast Asia 80, 86–8, 90, 92n29
Northern Ireland 67
Norway 56, 59, 72
Nour, al (Egypt) 38

O'Donnell, Guillermo 22, 28n34, 31, 79, 114, 118, 121, 132n22, 135–6, 137, 139, 142n1, 169, 172
Obama, Barack 4
Obasanjo, Olusegun 117
Odinga, Raila 117
Olympics 81
Oman 53
Operation Ghost Town (Cameroon) 120
opposition 5, 13, 33, 100, 114, 116–17, 119, 121, 123–4, 128, 130–1, 133n62, 141, 152–3
Orange Revolution 6, 34–5, 40, 43, 153
Organization of African Unity (OAU) 181
Organization of American States (OAS) 181
Organization for Economic Cooperation and Development (OECD) 103
Orientalism 149, 165n9
orthodox, state, society 64, 68, 72
Ottaway, Marina 28n34
Ottoman empire 99
Ouattara, Alassane 115–16, 125–6
Ould Abdelaziz, Mohamed 130
Ould Cheikh Abdallahi, Sidi 130

pacifism 176
pact, pact-making 13, 16–17, 34, 45, 75, 79, 90, 126–7, 136–7, 142
Pakistan 66
Paraguay 138–40
Paris 109
parliament 34, 47n29, 49, 69, 77–9, 87, 91
Partido Nacional (Chile) 140
Party of Democratic Socialism (GDR) 97
Party of Regions (Ukraine) 33–4, 47n35
Party of Slovak Revival 111n10
Party of Social Democracy of Romania 97
party system 45

path-dependent 69–70
Patriotic Front (Zambia) 124
patronage 61, 72
peace-building 7, 49, 70
peace-keeping, peacekeepers 74n53, 125, 128–9, 165n6
Pearl Square (Bahrain) 25
Peasant Party (Poland) 95
People power (Philippines) 7, 14, 79–81, 90
People's Action Party (Singapore) 87
People's Assembly (Egypt) 155
People's Democratic Movement (Cameroon) 116
People's Movement for Democratic Change (Sierra Leone) 117
People's Republic (Hungary) 93
People's Spring (1848) 2, 164n1
perestroika 27
Perón, Juan 140
Peronists 140
Peru 13, 170
Philippines, the 14, 76–8, 80–1, 85–9, 92n29, 170, 184n15
Pickel, Andreas 20
Plato 9, 168
Plaza de Mayo (Argentina) 25
plebiscite 184n16
pluralism 34, 46, 76, 176
Poland, Polish 14, 93–7, 100–10, 145
Police Day (Egypt) 146
Polish model 96
Polish miracle 107
political: behaviour 7; change 5; choice 167; communication 3; competition 41, 46, 182; conditionality 180; culture 8, 27n14, 32, 49, 52; development 53; domination 128; economy 50, 53, 71; fragmentation 161; instability 165n6; Islam 152; learning 146; liberalisation 1–3, 6, 20, 37, 76, 80, 85, 114, 121, 128, 131, 141; negotiations 136; participation 3, 140, 181; polarisation 157; rights 7, 136; science 90, 168–9, 181; socialisation 152, 155, 172; sociology 50, 55; stability 150–1, 165n1; transformation 76; violence 6, 15, 125
politics from above 9
politics from below 9
Polity project, database 12–13, 113, 132n7, 134n108
Popular Movement for the Liberation of Angola (MPLA) 129
Pora (Ukraine) 35

Poroshenko, Petro 34
Port Said 156
Port Sudan 19
Portugal, Portuguese 1, 13, 69, 179
poverty 50, 142, 156–7
power-sharing 41, 50, 121, 126, 129
Prague 98
Prague Spring 1, 2, 10, 100, 164n1
predatory politics 46
presentism 169, 183n3
presidentialism 86
press 124, 136, 141
pressure cooker effect 157, 161
Pridham, Geoffrey 28n34
privatisation 8, 97, 175
proportionality 86
Protestant 67–8, 99
Protestantism 68
protests, protestors 115, 118, 130, 145, 152, 159, 164n1
Przeworski, Adam 28n34, 51, 137
public administration 70
public opinion 55, 94, 106, 159
Puerta del Sol (Spain) 25
punto final 137
Putnam, Robert D. 28n34
Pye, Lucian W. 16, 28n34

Qaddafi, Muammar 146–7, 160
Qatar 53
Quality of Government Institute 73n17
Quran, Quranic 154–5
Qutb, Sayyid 154

Radio Free Europe 93
Rajoelina, Andry 122
Rally of the Togolese People (Togo) 126
Ratsiraka, Didier 118, 122, 132n18
Ravalomanana, Marc 118, 122
Rawlings, Jerry 127, 134n73
rebellion 2, 16, 59, 77
reconciliation 43
referendum 53
reform 115, 129, 131, 132n14, 146
reformasi (Indonesia) 82, 84
refugee, refugees 109, 147
regime: anocratic 131; authoritarian 44–5, 53, 81, 95, 113, 131, 138; autocratic 1, 25, 115; bureaucratic-authoritarian 138; challenge 119; change 116–17, 119, 121, 124, 126, 136, 160, 167–8, 173–4; collapse; communist 97; corrupt 1, 44; crisis 113; defection 117, 123; democratic 70, 114, 177; durability 37; grey-zone 15; hybrid 6–7, 31, 53, 113, 170; incumbent 80; legitimacy 136; liberalisation 122; military 1, 115; multiparty 86; princely 167; republican 147; semi-authoritarian 13; semi-democratic 13, 18; stability 168; totalitarian 95; transformation 3, 168; transition 128; transitional 53; type 3, 6, 135; uncertain 18; viability 137
regionalism 176
religion 5, 9, 40, 67, 78, 152–3, 161
Renault 106
rentier state 59, 61, 67, 72
representation 20
repression 40, 42, 152–3
resource curse 59
Responsibility to Protect 14
revolt 4, 15
revolution 4, 43, 100, 102, 108, 135, 144, 152, 156, 164n1
Revolution of the Carnations (Portugal) 1, 12
Right Sector (Ukraine) 36
Robertson, Graeme 68
Roma, the 105–6, 109
Romania, Romanians 54, 93, 95, 99–109
Rostow, W.W. 31
rule of law 31–2, 36–7, 66, 70, 103, 150–1, 164n5, 165n13
rupture 16, 21
rupture pactada 17
Russia, Russian 25, 43, 51, 90, 104, 173
Russian Federation 107
Rustow, Dankwart A. 28n34, 21, 51
Rwanda 19, 59, 67, 114, 123, 125, 128–9
Rwandan Patriotic Front 19, 129
Rwasa, Agathon 129

Saffron Revolution 80
Sahel 25
Salafis, Salafists 38–9, 152, 163
Salamé, Ghassan 28n34
Saleh, Ali Abdallah 146–7, 160–1
Sall, Macky 123, 131
Sam, Kim Young 81
Sam Raintsy Party 79
Sao Tomé and Principe 126, 132n7
Sassou-Nguesso, Denis 132n18
Saudi Arabia 39, 53, 59, 146–7
Schedler, Andreas 28n34
Schengen system 109
Scotland, Scottish 67
Seck, Idrissa 123
Second World War *see* World War II

sectarian violence 19
secular, secularism 68
security dilemma 19, 23
security sector reform 121
Sein, Thein 76
Sejm (Poland) 95
semi-presidentialism 86
Sen, Amartya 28n34; 58
Sen, Hun 78
Senegal, Senegalese 114, 117, 123, 127–8, 132n1, 133n37
Senegalese Democratic Party 123
Seoul 81
Separatism 87
Serbia 15, 104
Seychelles, the 132n7
Shafiq, Ahmad 159
Shinawatra, Thaksin 80, 82–3, 86
Shinawatra, Yingluck 83
Shonas 119
Shui-bian, Chen 77
Sidi Bouzid 146
Sierra Leone 59, 69, 114, 124, 128, 131
Sierra Leone People's Party 117, 125
Sinai 40
Sinatra, Frank 157
Singapore 80, 83–4, 87–90
Sisi, Abdelfattah Al 39–40, 43, 72, 163
sit-in 157
Skoda 106
Slovak Freedom Party 111n10
Slovakia 2, 98, 103–6
Slovenia 72
Smolensk coup 108
Snyder, Jack 19
social contract 1, 4, 15, 24
social media 25, 93, 149, 152
social mobilisation 1, 32, 46
social movements 5–6, 14–17, 32, 45, 51, 155, 176
social question 179
social violence 18
socialism 100–2
Socialist Party (Senegal) 123, 127–8
Socialist Unity Party (GDR) 97
society 67
Soglo, Nicéphore 122–3
Solidarity (Poland) 95, 101
Solidarność 27
Somalia 164n5
Somba 120
South Africa 1, 14–15, 114, 124, 126–7, 131
South America 181; *see also* Latin America
South Asia 80
South Korea 86
South Sudan 19, 53, 128, 164n5
South West Africa People's Organisation (SWAPO) 127
Southeast Asia 7, 75, 80, 90, 92n29, 181
Southern Africa 119
Southern Cone 8, 135–43
Southern Europe 20, 30, 32, 79, 160, 172, 180–1
sovereignty 109
Soviet Republics 178
Soviet Union 2, 18, 33–5, 41, 47n37, 94, 95, 97–101, 103, 144, 173, 175, 179
Spain, Spanish 68–9, 95, 179
spoilers 129
Sri Lanka 67, 69
state; authority 158, 161; colonial 69; divided 49; failed 67, 125, 161, 164n5; formation 17; fragile 49, 53, 69, 164n5; functioning 25; hegemonic 113; legitimacy 24, 164n5; mutation 27; nation- 54; power 19, 24; regime 173; relationship with citizen 1; rentier 59, 61; retreat 18; secession 53–4; sovereignty 14; supremacy 140; violence 35; weak 27n22
state-building 7, 49, 69
Stepan, Alfred 16, 68, 95, 28n34, 165n10
Stokes, Susan 28n34
Strangers in the Night 157
street politics, protests 41, 81
Stroessner, Alfredo 141
Sub-Saharan Africa 8, 17–18, 113–34
Sudan 19, 54, 67, 69, 114
Suez 156
Suez Canal 156
Sufis 152
Suharto 13, 77–8, 82
Supreme Council of the Armed Forces, SCAF (Egypt) 38, 161
Supreme Guide (Muslim Brotherhood) 158–9
Suu Kyi, Aung San 76, 84
Suzuki 106
Svoboda, party (Ukraine) 36
Swaziland 114
Sweden 54, 68
swing state 90
Sykes-Picot (Treaty) 17
Syria 2–3, 17, 145–65
Syrian civil war 25

Tae-woo, Roh 81

216 Index

Tahrir Square (Egypt) 25, 44, 144, 153, 156
Taiwan 75–7, 81, 83, 86–7, 90, 184n15
Tajikistan 57
Taksim Square (Turkey) 25
Tanja, Mamadou 118
Tanzania 114–16, 123–5, 128
Tavares, María Conceicao 139
technology xviii, 13, 26, 149, 182
terrorism, terrorist 40, 150–1, 165n6
Thai Rak Thai Party 80
Thailand 76–7, 80, 82–3, 86–8, 90, 92n29
theocracy 173
Third Wave 30, 70, 72, 76, 79, 174
Tiananmen Square 14
Timor Leste 69, 83
Togo 114–16, 119, 120, 125–8, 131, 134n92
torture 153
totalitarianism 7–8
Touré, Amadou Toumani 118, 130–1
transition: aborted 37; actors 113; agreement 126; authoritarian 157, 168; changeability 45; contemporary 1; context 157; controlled 23; cost 108; cycle 6; deepening 135; democratic 20–1, 75, 79, 122, 124, 131; derailing 132n18, 161; direction 46; dynamics 43; electoral 50; end 7; failed 8, 129, 131; foreign-backed 113, 128–9, 131; from authoritarian rule 1, 81; global; government 130; hijacked 5; ideal-type 25; inevitability 16; landmark 136; leadership 82; linearity 160, 163; management 6; messy 162; mode 52, 125, 172; models 90; moment 23, 30, 137; monolithic 9; movement 23; new 5; orderly 4; outcome 14, 31–2, 113, 125, 142n1, 172; pace 44; pact-like 127; pacted 5, 7, 96, 142; paradigm 15, 17, 20, 142n1, 144–6, 160, 162; partial 6; path 23, 125, 136; pathways 6, 14, 163; peaceful 10; phases 21, 100; planned 128; political 20, 116; post-globalisation 6; process 18, 109–10, 125, 161, 163; protracted 116; rapid 116; regime, regimes 49, 119; regime-to-regime 3; regime-type 5; religion; reversibility 23, 45, 125, 163; roadmap 135; sad 159; sequence 20, 24, 103, 138–42; setback 164n1; socio-economic 2; stages 4, 24, 125, 136; starting point 136; struggle; successful 50, 113, 131, 142, 162; teleology 160, 163; theory 7, 21, 29, 44, 100; through reform 127–9; through rupture 129–31; time 23; timing 181; to democracy 4, 51; transnational 6, 20, 25; uncertainty 131, 135, 137, 142n1; 167–9; unexpectedness 169; wave 5, 22, 45, 160
transitional justice 3, 13
transitologist 100, 121, 167, 169
transitology 1–5, 7, 9–10, 14–18, 20–1, 24–5, 45, 125, 132n3; 135, 144–9, 157, 160–3, 167–9, 174
transnational organisations 180
transnationalism, transnationalisation 3, 15, 25, 139, 180
transparency 40
Transparency International 55, 62
Transparency International Corruption Perception Index 61–2, 73n20, 108
Traoré, Moussa 116, 118, 120, 130
tribal, tribe 161, 163
trust 67, 72
truth and reconciliation commission 13
Tunis 144
Tunisia 1–4, 17, 22, 145–65
Tupamaros 142
Turchynov, Oleksandr 34
Turkmenistan 71
Tusk, Donald 107
Tutsi 116, 119, 129
Twitter 93, 152
tyranny 51

Uganda 114, 123
Ujamaa (Kenya) 117
Ukraine 6, 15, 29–30, 32–7, 40–6, 53, 69, 104
Umbrella Square (Hong Kong) 25
unemployment 102, 156–8, 162
Unidad Popular (Chile) 140
Union of the Republic (Togo) 126
Union Solidarity and Development Party (Myanmar) 84–5
United Democratic Front (Malawi) 117, 131
United Kingdom 108
United National Independence Party (Zambia) 124
United Nations 24, 77–8, 94, 125
United Nations Development Programme (UNDP) 8, 50, 55, 57, 70, 164
United Nations Development Programme Human Development Index (HDI) 50, 58, 62, 73n29, 147–8, 164n4
United People's Party (Poland) 110n10

United States 4, 7, 16, 25, 36, 39, 43, 47n37, 56, 69, 84, 88, 90, 102–4, 181
United States Institute of Peace (USIP) 25
United Workers' Party (Poland) 96
unity government 126, 130
Universal Declaration of Human Rights 14
University of Gothenburg 54
University of Southern California 159
uprising 16, 29
urbanisation 51, 53, 55
Uruguay 138–9, 141
USSR (Union of the Soviet Socialist Republics) 69
Utopianism 102
utumwa 23

Varieties of Democracy Project 55, 73n21
Velvet Divorce 184n16
Venezuela 51
Vietnam 78, 89–90
violence 36, 42–3, 50, 70, 74n42; 165n13, 181, 184n16
Visegrad group 104, 109
Volkswagen 106
vote-buying 62, 82

Wade, Abdoulaye 123, 128
Wales, Welch 67, 102
Walesa, Lech 95
Walle, Nicholas van de 114, 117–18, 121
war-torn country 125
warlordism 161
Warsaw Treaty Organization 99, 104
Washington 103
Way, Lucan A. 28n34
wealth 52–3, 58–9, 62–3, 66, 68, 71–2
Weber, Max 163
West, Western nations 53, 68, 85, 94, 97, 101, 103, 106–9, 124

West Africa 118
West Germany *see* German Federal Republic
Western Europe, Western European 17–18, 94, 101, 105, 110, 173, 181
Westminter 86
Whitehead, Laurence 22, 28n34
Wiarda, Howard 28n34
Widodo, Joko 78
Wolesi Jirga (Afghanistan) 49
World Bank 47n36, 56, 59
World Bank Governance Index 62, 147–8
World War I 13, 178
World War II 13, 94, 96, 110, 168, 174, 178
Worldwide Governance Indicators (WGI) 165n13

xenophobia 107

Yanukovych, Viktor 29, 33–6, 41–2, 45, 47n35
Yatsenyuk, Arseniy 34
Yemen 1–3, 146–8, 164n1
Young, Crawford 28n34
Young Sam, Kim 81
youth 145, 149, 152, 156, 162
Yugoslavia 17

Zaïre *see* Congo, Democratic Republic of
zakat 154
Zambia 114, 117, 119, 122–3
Zanzibar 116
Zaporizhzhya 47n35
Zaqazeeq University 159
zawya 155
Zimbabwe, Zimbabwean 2, 114, 116, 119, 124, 126–7, 132n1

Taylor & Francis eBooks

Helping you to choose the right eBooks for your Library

Add Routledge titles to your library's digital collection today. Taylor and Francis ebooks contains over 50,000 titles in the Humanities, Social Sciences, Behavioural Sciences, Built Environment and Law.

Choose from a range of subject packages or create your own!

Benefits for you
- Free MARC records
- COUNTER-compliant usage statistics
- Flexible purchase and pricing options
- All titles DRM-free.

Benefits for your user
- Off-site, anytime access via Athens or referring URL
- Print or copy pages or chapters
- Full content search
- Bookmark, highlight and annotate text
- Access to thousands of pages of quality research at the click of a button.

REQUEST YOUR FREE INSTITUTIONAL TRIAL TODAY — **Free Trials Available** We offer free trials to qualifying academic, corporate and government customers.

eCollections – Choose from over 30 subject eCollections, including:

Archaeology	Language Learning
Architecture	Law
Asian Studies	Literature
Business & Management	Media & Communication
Classical Studies	Middle East Studies
Construction	Music
Creative & Media Arts	Philosophy
Criminology & Criminal Justice	Planning
Economics	Politics
Education	Psychology & Mental Health
Energy	Religion
Engineering	Security
English Language & Linguistics	Social Work
Environment & Sustainability	Sociology
Geography	Sport
Health Studies	Theatre & Performance
History	Tourism, Hospitality & Events

For more information, pricing enquiries or to order a free trial, please contact your local sales team:
www.tandfebooks.com/page/sales

The home of Routledge books

www.tandfebooks.com